MW00770589

Figure C-5a and b. **The human figure as focal accent.** *[Wilcox Electric, Inc., Kansas City, Missouri. Photograph: © Paul S. Kivett]*

Light: The Shape of Space

Light: The Shape of Space

Designing with Space and Light

Lou Michel

Professor of Architecture and Urban Design
The University of Kansas

VAN NOSTRAND REINHOLD
I(T)P™ A Division of International Thomson Publishing Inc.

New York • Albany • Bonn • Boston • Detroit • London • Madrid • Melbourne
Mexico City • Paris • San Francisco • Singapore • Tokyo • Toronto

Cover photo courtesy of Balthazar Korab
Cover design: Mike Sun

Van Nostrand Reinhold Staff
Editor: John Griffin
Production Editor: Carla M. Nessler
Production Manager: Mary McCartney

Copyright © 1996 by Van Nostrand Reinhold
I(T)pTM A division of International Thomson Publishing Inc.
     The ITP logo is a trademark under license

Printed in the United States of America
For more information, contact:

Van Nostrand Reinhold
115 Fifth Avenue
New York, NY 10003

Chapman & Hall GmbH
Pappelallee 3
69469 Weinheim
Germany

Chapman & Hall
2-6 Boundary Row
London
SE1 8HN
United Kingdom

International Thomson Publishing Asia
221 Henderson Road #05-10
Henderson Building
Singapore 0315

Thomas Nelson Australia
102 Dodds Street
South Melbourne, 3205
Victoria, Australia

International Thomson Publishing Japan
Hirakawacho Kyowa Building, 3F
2-2-1 Hirakawacho
Chiyoda-ku, 102 Tokyo
Japan

Nelson Canada
1120 Birchmount Road
Scarborough, Ontario
Canada M1K 5G4

International Thomson Editores
Campos Eliseos 385, Piso 7
Col. Polanco
11560 Mexico D.F. Mexico

All rights reserved. No part of this work covered by the copyright hereon may be reproduced or used in any form or by any means—graphic, electronic, or mechanical, including photocopying, recording, taping, or information storage and retrieval systems—without the written permission of the publisher.

1 2 3 4 5 6 7 8 9 10 COU-WF 01 00 99 98 97 96

Library of Congress Cataloging-in-Publication Data

Michel, Lou.
    Light: the shape of space / author, Lou Michel,—1st ed.
        p. cm.
    Includes bibliographical references and index.
    ISBN 0-442-01804-5
    1. Space (Architecture) 2. Visual perception. 3. Light in architecture.   I. Title.
    NA2765.M53 1995
    729—dc20   94-23794
                                                       CIP

To
Diane Swanson Michel,
my wife and loyal companion,
whose love, faith, and spirit
are continual sources of support and inspiration.

Contents

Part 2: Analysis of Architectural Space

Part 3: Designing with Space and Light

Portia: *That light we see is burning in my hall.*
How far that little candle throws his beams!
So shines a good deed in a naughty world.

Nerissa: *When the moon shone, we did not see the candle.*

Portia: *So doth the greater glory dim the less . . .*

—Shakespeare
The Merchant of Venice

Preface

A beautifully designed and sensitively illuminated architectural environment is a gratifying sensory experience. During the process of design, each time a line is drawn to identify a room partition, floor, ceiling, concourse, portal, or ramp, it designates what eventually will be a light-reflecting surface that affects human feelings and communicates cultural identity. When those lines are organized into certain relationships, they shape space. Obviously, not all the surfaces around us are the results of formal design, nor do they stem from the hand of a single designer. The environments we encounter in our private and social lives come about by the composite actions of a number of individuals, both professional and nonprofessional. The "designer" can be an architect, interior designer, lighting designer, engineer, landscape architect, building contractor, owner, or renter. At one time or another, each places or replaces objects and surfaces that will receive light, and the work of one may modify or subvert the intent of another.

Considering the fact that most often the architectural world is produced by a mixture of professional activities and different personal tastes, this book attempts to bridge the specialized professions related to architecture by interrelating two key elements of the environments we inhabit: space and light. It is in illuminated spaces that people live, and that is where architecture is experienced most directly. That viewpoint provides a common focus for the diversified specialists, directing their thought to the realities of how people see and accordingly use architectural space. To establish that viewpoint, a perspective was constructed from the vantage ground of human *visual perception of space,* illuminated by natural or electric light or both, demonstrating how human vision responds to the stimulation of illuminated surfaces that surround the eye. By placing attention on how people perceive the lighted spaces in which they live, this book intentionally bypasses designing by style, fad, or fashion, and takes an *ergonomic* approach to design for the humanization of architecture.

Ergonomics is the study of the way people relate to their environment physiologically and psychologically.

Ergonomic design, therefore, involves the art and technology of constructing the human habitat in ways to promote the comfort and well-being of people in their architectural surroundings, avoiding excessive or unnecessary strain on the nervous system or any of the body's functions.

This book has put together a body of "space and light theory." In the context of architecture, *space* refers to the living environment bounded by colored architectural surfaces that are perceived by human vision for a person standing in or walking through a building or sector of a city. *Light* refers to the illumination that makes architectural space visible. Space and light influence one another in mutual interaction. The surfaces defining space respond to the quality and quantity of light they receive, and illumination changes once it strikes those surfaces. The interchange between the two is what the eye sees, but the blend is not always what was intended by the designer of space or the lighting engineer. For this reason, this book is not one that endorses a design philosophy that first arranges architectural spaces in composition, and then adds lighting as a later and independent step simply to make the spaces functional. The intent of this book is not to isolate lighting from architectural design, but to integrate the two to produce environments that are meaningful for the human experience. It was also intentional to avoid a line of thinking in terms of architectural, interior, and lighting design that is often referred to in terse references like "the craze of the 1970s" or what was "fashionable in the 80s."

This is not a book on the technology of architectural lighting. Given the prevailing winds of contemporary society, it is safe to say the flow of technical texts and journal articles will continue to appear, including the recent popularity of daylighting. In the United States and worldwide, many changes are coming into the architectural world through the lighting industry. In America those changes will be accelerated as a result of the passage of the long overdue National Energy Policy Act of 1992, directed toward energy-saving lighting design.

It is specifically the rapid and sweeping changes of

present-day technology that validate this kind of book. New surfacing materials and lighting fixtures and systems enter the global markets daily, while at the same time many fall into obsolescence. By centering attention on the interaction of light and surface reflectances as perceived by human vision, a practical position is taken by the designer for creating a human-centered environment while contending with the ebb and flow of product availability.

A primary goal of the book is to promote continuing education for the professional designer and contribute to the learning experience of students. A helpful feature found throughout the text is the distillation of design "principles," a teaching method I have found immensely advantageous in the university classroom. These principles are stated as convenient guidelines for design and provide some stability in face of the inevitable changes in technology and fashions. Some of those principles are new, specifically formulated for working with space and light theory; others took root in conventional design fundamentals. They are intended to influence the development of quality architectural design, and contribute to aesthetics and architectural criticism. Another goal was to formalize a working terminology for use in space and light analysis, such as the *spatial envelope, subspace, zone of transition,* and the like.

A major aspect of working with color relationships in spatial design is the brightness capabilities of architectural surfacing materials. To establish designer guidelines for the selection and placement of those materials, research in the Space and Light Laboratory (see Appendix) has created a scale for judging the comparative brightness of color values that appear as luminance (reflected light) on the surfaces of architecture. Chapter 5 introduces the Luminance Brightness Rating (LBR) System for evaluating the appearance of building materials in zones on a brightness scale. The system is part of an ongoing laboratory project, and has application to architectural and interior design, illuminating engineering, and the design of manufactured building materials. A beginning has been made by assigning an LBR to 42 wood species used for architectural interiors and furniture. Work continues on a wide range of building materials, but assignment of an LBR requires extensive laboratory testing, and producing a larger list of materials would have delayed publication of this book. So Chapter 5 was written to lay the groundwork for the LBR System, and to encourage industry and lighting research to engage in further development of the system.

A variety of spatial designs appears in the chapters to illustrate different aspects of architectural design and lighting, and to give examples of the different conditions encountered by designers and engineers in professional practice. Not all the photographs were selected for their merits of design, but were chosen for their value in illustrating specific principles of space and light theory. Images taken by professional photographers are credited as they appear. All others are by the author.

Because the subject matter draws from various academic disciplines, the book is written with inclusive language, avoiding the use of technical idiom arcane to any one field of professional practice. On occasion more extensive explanation is given to a term or concept that is essential to the text, but perhaps less familiar to some in the broader readership.

My interest in space and light began early in my professional career teaching the history of architecture, which gave insights that gradually redirected my teaching to a different plateau for understanding architectural design. Architectural history became more of a tool than a métier. I have repeatedly upheld that the "great" buildings from the past should be used as models for study and inspiration, to be investigated for their *principles of design,* not their stylistic image. In those celebrated buildings and reconstructions from ruins, I found a common substance: extraordinary spatial relationships, sensitively and interestingly illuminated. I refer to buildings such as the Alhambra in Spain; the Temples of Karnak and Queen Hatshepsut from ancient Egypt; the Pantheon and the Baths of Caracalla in ancient Rome; S. Vitale in Ravenna; Hagia Sophia in Istanbul; the great medieval cathedrals of Europe; Renaissance open courts and public squares; the Gardens of the Villa d'Este at Tivoli, Italy; the composite basilica and piazza of St. Peter's in Rome; the Paris Opera House; the Piazza San Marco and the entire city of Venice; many of the works of Frank Lloyd Wright; and numerous others. I have stood in those spaces marveling over their intrinsic capacity to stimulate mood, examining and cross-examining exactly what it was that made me feel good when experiencing them, making myself aware of spatial dimensions, time of day, angle of the sun, and the color and reflectance of their building materials. In their spaces I have spent many hours making notes, observing people, listening to what they said, and watching how they moved about. Those masterpieces became my workshops for analyzing the architecture of excellence. They provided the *design qualities*—not stylistic images—that I thought should be carried into the classroom and into the architecture of the future.

I have found equally informative and inspirational the "architecture" of Nature, my reliable classroom companion. As an avid hiker, I have taken therapeutic and educational walks through the great sequoias and redwoods of California, along mountain paths in the Rockies and Alps, into Polynesian jungle, through the rain forests of the Olympic Northwest, and into the Grand Canyon descending to its floor. I have taken profitable mental journeys inside seashells, corals, geodes, and wildflowers, again and again finding the enriching power of form, space, color, and light. In December 1984, I experienced a turbulent winter snowstorm and swirling winds on an upper rim trail when ascending out of the Grand Canyon. I witnessed an intense drama of shafts of colored light intermittently coming from above and piercing the darkened "sky" below me, opening and closing momentary glimpses into brilliantly lit and colorful subspaces of the inner canyons, first in one direction and then another. It was a consummate expression of space and light.

There were other catalysts. The first of importance was Prof. George Forsyth, Jr. at the University of Michigan who explained Gothic cathedrals in terms of space, and incited within me a desire to visit them. But most of all in his office one day he placed in my hands James J. Gibson's *The Perception of the Visual World,* and a new door opened. In turn followed Bruno Zevi's *Architecture as Space* and an invigorating discussion with its author at Cranbrook Academy in 1964. Those early paths branched to include the writings of Rudolph Arnheim, Gyorgy Kepes, Susanne K. Langer, Sven Hesselgren, Christopher Alexander, John E. Flynn, P. R. Boyce, David M. Egan, R. G. Hopkinson, William M. C. Lam, William H. Ittelson, and Julian Hochberg. Among those and other authors of related work there formed for me an invaluable hybrid of architecture, art, light, and the workings of the human eye.

This book is written in three parts, organized by subject matter to reach a wide range of design-related professions, and to provide a systematic understanding of space and light theory. Humanizing architecture involves investigating it through the behavioral sciences. To know how people see is to know how to design for them. Hence the reason for selected topics of visual perception in Part 1, which serves as the foundation and as continual reference for the remainder of the book. I sifted through publications by behavioral psychologists to extract the practical aspects of visual perception theory, which I

thought would be most helpful for designers, and on which I based and interrelated the chapters that follow. My own laboratory research in space and light theory is interwoven throughout the text and appears in the Appendix. Part 2 formally analyzes architectural space. The reader learns to define architectural space by its dominant boundaries, how they serve as backdrop for interior furnishings in form-space relationships, and how space is perceived by people moving through it. The segregation of space from lighting was done for analysis only, to make more clear its modification by light as shown in later chapters. Part 3 then examines the principles, and art, of lighting architectural spaces, integrating the contents of Parts 1 and 2, to make the process of designing with light meaningful with respect to behavioral responses of the human being.

In 1967, Gyorgy Kepes wrote:

The application of light to clarify and inform architectural spaces and complex cityscapes is not yet a discipline. . . . We know how to make illumination both adequate and comfortable. This has been the goal of illumination engineers who have learned all that physiology and physics can teach them concerning both natural and artificial lighting. But architects and planners realize that there are immense opportunities in lighting, and they demand more than just comfort and amplitude.

A great deal of research and publication has contributed to the development of that "discipline" of lighting architectural and urban spaces since Kepes wrote those words. An investigation of those contributions has added significantly to this book. If there is a notable concern through all of this, it is the challenge to designers of architecture and cities to carry a late twentieth-century message into the oncoming century as an acknowledgment of the continuing need to humanize our environment in a serious and mature manner.

Acknowledgments

I take this opportunity to express my gratitude to two special people who significantly influenced the outcome of this book. To Bruno Leon I am indebted for instilling in my teaching an understanding of architecture related to human living. As an architect and my first dean when I began teaching at the University of Detroit, he was a rich source of inspiration, and his words, thoughts, and friendship were truly filled with light. It was with John Loss that I shared an office in those early teaching years. Through daily discussions across our desks, he planted in my thinking values of architecture and life that have remained with me throughout my career. It was he who opened my eyes to the beauty and appropriateness of structural systems for buildings, but more than that, he structured my early teaching. Those two individuals are truly my mentors, and for their faithful guidance and treasured friendship there is little I can return.

Collectively I thank my colleagues at The University of Kansas, whose ideas nurtured my growth in architecture. To David Griffin, Gaylord Richardson, and Clay Belcher I am especially indebted for reading major portions of this manuscript, a task added to the already heavy workloads of their own careers. Their good counsel, suggestions, and criticisms were invaluable in putting together the main body of the text, and they should realize their thoughts became an essential part of this book. Moreover, their sincere friendship has made my years at the university a cherished experience.

Putting together this book that embraces different professional fields within the scope of architecture was not an easy task, but was made less difficult by the generous help of the reviewers of the manuscript. To ensure the content was examined from different points of view, I sought the counsel of nationally recognized individuals in the companion fields to architecture. I give special thanks to Ronald Helms, professor of architectural engineering at North Carolina A&T State University; to Robert L. Smith, professor emeritus of architecture at the University of Illinois and former columnist for *Lighting Design + Application*; to Andrea Daugherty, designer and professor of interior design at Louisiana State University; and to James F. Juola, professor of psychology and visual perception specialist at The University of Kansas. To them I am grateful for their constructive criticism and for pointing out errors that needed correction. I wish to thank Lorretta Palagi for reading the entire manuscript and making helpful editorial suggestions.

Although mentioned above as readers, I owe additional thanks to Clay Belcher, Ron Helms, and James Juola for their counsel and problem-solving visits to the Space and Light Laboratory, and for advice on lighting experiments and development of the laboratory's research facilities. I also thank Thomas E. Glavinich, chairman of architectural engineering at The University of Kansas, for technical advice and troubleshooting in the lighting lab.

Special recognition is due to Dennis Domer, dear friend, scholar, and administrator of the School of Architecture and Urban Design at The University of Kansas. He has been a continual source of encouragement, but I am even more thankful for our conversations that go far beyond architecture.

I am grateful to two other colleagues at The University of Kansas: to Hobart Jackson for his time and advice for solving problems of photographing architecture and lighting lab demonstrations, and to Brent Anderson, who did the computerized graphics that appear in Chapter 14.

I thank Kevin Skyat Kengingwiluya, who produced a number of the graphics that appear in this book.

Teachers are always indebted to their students. I express my deep appreciation to those whose hard work in my course in Space and Light Theory pioneered new territories and whose questions and laboratory investigations literally enlightened the basic content of this book. I am grateful to them for their diligence and perseverance on the difficult roads of research that sometimes lead to success, but at other times to dead-end streets. Some deserve special mention for their advanced research work in the Space and Light Laboratory that led to significant findings. They are Jennifer Hess, Kimberly Koile, and

Gregory Tice. I also thank Todd Brewood and Michael Andracsek, who blended knowledge of this subject with their crafts skills to help develop two new research/demonstration models for the lighting lab.

I give sincere thanks to Van Nostrand Reinhold for the grant that assisted me in bringing this book to a conclusion.

Thanks are also due to the following institutions who gave permission to reproduce photographs and graphics from their holdings: Aramco World; Art Resource, New York; the Chicago Historical Society; the Illuminating Engineering Society of North America; Johnson Wax Company, Racine; Metropolitan Museum of Art, New York; Ministero per Beni Culturali e Ambientali, Rome; National Gallery of Art, Washington, D.C.; Bibliothèque nationale de France, Paris; Österreichische National-bibliothek, Vienna; and The Solomon R. Guggenheim Foundation, New York.

Special assistance also came from industry. I thank the following companies for contributing photographs and laboratory support materials: ALKCO Lighting, Boeing Aviation, Cooper Lighting, Frank Paxton Lumber Company, Kansas City, GE Lighting, Lithonia Lighting, Lutron Electronics, Masonite Corporation, Munsell Color of Macbeth Corporation, Philips Lighting, Pittsburgh Corning Corporation, OSRAM SYLVANIA, Specialty Lighting Inc., SR Wood Inc., and Steelcase, Inc.

The material help given by institutions and industry is exceptionally valuable. There is a deep, inner help of another kind that is immeasurable, and can be given only through love and spiritual support. For that I give sincere thanks to Claude and Dorothy Norris, who through a close and loyal friendship gave me continual encouragement to complete this work.

But work of this kind cannot be accomplished without another certain kind of gift—that of time. Time for work. That was the priceless gift given to me by my children, who too often went without my attention when demands of a professional career pulled me in other directions. I thank you Kathie, Kevin, Diane, and Eileen, with a kind of love that only a father can give.

Lou Michel

Introduction

*From cradle to grave this problem of running
order through chaos, direction through space,
discipline through freedom, unity through
multiplicity, has always been, and must
always be, the task of education.*

*After a January blizzard, the boy who could
look with pleasure into the violent snow-glare
of the cold white sunshine, with its intense
light and shade, scarcely knew what was
meant by tone. He could reach it only by
education.*

　　　　　　　—The Education of Henry Adams*

Throughout human history the treatment of surfaces forming architectural space has been a revealing manifestation of lifestyles and cultural values. Paleolithic cave dwellers of northern Spain and southern France transformed their habitats by painting on the irregular cavernous walls red and yellow ochre figures of themselves and animals of the hunt. Light from small stone lamps fueled with tallow flickered across the natural stone surfaces enhanced by art, and gave visible shape to the space of communal shelter. What had begun was an irrepressible tendency to design the enclosing surfaces of the human environment. With the arrival of civilization sunlight described sculptural reliefs on temple walls, filtered through colonnades, illuminated the interiors of basilica halls, and reflected off mosaic floors in private houses. In the Middle Ages processions followed along ambula-

* From *The Education of Henry Adams, An Autobiography,* Boston: Houghton Mifflin, 1961, pp. 9, 12.

tories articulated by colored light through stained glass, and in the Renaissance arcaded loggias cast rhythmic shadow patterns on the pavements of palace courts. During subsequent periods the boundaries of space became stuccoed, bricked, glassed, draped, muraled, painted, paneled, and papered. In due time electricity dramatically altered urban life by extending the "day," and significantly changed the visual world of the home, workplace, and street. Electric lighting became the supplement to and substitute for sunlight, and the escalation of manufactured building materials and lighting systems gave to designers virtually unlimited resources from which to choose. The new industrial technology spawned the centrifugal pump and the elevator, which together literally gave rise to towering buildings shaping and shadowing the spaces of streets below.

Light is stimulating. Painters and architects have long realized its potential for moving the human spirit. In the

Baroque period painters such as Caravaggio, Rembrandt, La Tour, and Ribera utilized the spotlighting effects of tenebrism to dramatize the essence of human struggle and sanctity, set against contrasting dark backgrounds of space. Baroque architects used hidden windows to create a sense of mystical light streaming into religious interiors, and in England Newton was scientifically investigating how prisms disperse light into colors of the visual spectrum. Later the Impressionist painters discovered the atmospheric light of the open air, and turned from the stark contrasts of light and dark to subtle shifts of tone within a narrower range of the color palette. Orientals filtered light through paper screens to soften interior living space, and Islamic architects veiled daylight with intricately carved grilles to cast arabesque patterns of light on walls and floors.

Whether in painting, sculpture, or architecture, light reflected on surfaces links the visual environment with human feelings, creating mood. "This is the task of education," said the late Walter Gropius, "to teach what influences the psyche of man in terms of light, scale, space, form, and color. Vague phrases like 'the atmosphere of a building,' or 'the coziness of a room' should be defined precisely in specific terms. The designer must learn to see; he must know the effect of optical illusions, the psychological influence of shapes, colors and textures, the effects of contrast, direction, tension and repose; and he must learn to grasp the significance of the human scale."[1]

We do not see light. We see the effects of light. People stand in sentimental awe as they witness a breathtaking sunset caused by the reflection of sunlight on clouds and atmospheric dust, and in a spacious public atrium shoppers pass through geometric shadows created by a clearstory high above. Reflected light on walls, floors, ceilings, and furniture sends to the eye and brain a flow of information governing sensations of color, surface texture, highlights, and shadows. Brightness relationships assist us in judging distances, glare can cause physical discomfort, and we temper our personalities with the likes and dislikes of things we see in the illuminated world.

As architectural design is developed, space should not be thought of as a void as some writers have suggested; such a notion is too vague and intangible, and too often misused by designers and critics. I respect the ancient Chinese philosopher Lao-tzu's profound reference to the vacuum of a jar where only the void inside contains the truly essential, and Frank Lloyd Wright's sensitive declaration that the essence of his design for Unity Temple is the space within. Those are poetic, even philosophi-

cal accounts of space. They are worthy goals to reach, to elevate architecture to the status it should rightfully attain as a FINE art. But once past the inchoate, conceptual stage of the design process, space is much more manageable and easily comprehended when defined as the physical surfaces enclosing the void: walls, floors, ceilings, skylights, balconies, balustrades, colonnades, or adjustable office partitions. Those major surfaces are the visual boundaries that shape space. It is not the void, but the colored, textured, and patterned planes on which the human eye fixates. Inanimate surfaces, good and bad, animate feelings inside the viewer. When architectural space is tastefully created, to comfort and refine rather than merely to play with human feelings, then and only then is space raised to the dignity expressed by the metaphor of Lao-tzu's jar.

Space is generally measured in three dimensions: length, width, and height. So is sculpture or furniture. But whereas sculptural objects occupy space, architectural space itself is enclosed, either partially or completely, depending on the number of openings in the spatial envelope. To this must be added the fourth dimension of time, or movement through space and around objects—the kinesthetic experience of the total environment.

Post-Renaissance architectural practice has established praxes for design communication in the forms of floor plans, city plans, and vertical sections cut through buildings or public squares. As necessary as those conventions are for the practicalities and efficiency of communicating design, cost estimating, and fabrication, they are not representative of how the eventual users of space will see the setting around them. Seldom, and for but only a brief moment, is a building's facade or an interior wall seen full front as delineated on an elevation drawing. During the course of daily activities, 99.9% of the time people see the boundaries of space at a slant. Seen from varying angles, a wall or floor is visually altered because its slant presents to the eye a modified view of reflected light on its surface, which changes the appearance of its intrinsic color and texture. Moreover, the architectural environment undergoes highly significant perceptual changes for a person walking through connected spaces due to light or dark adaptation of the retina.

The appearance of architectural space is dependent on the quality and quantity of illumination, in combination with variations of surfacing materials. An urban square in morning light appears differently in the late afternoon, different again on an overcast day from what it was when bathed in direct sunlight, and more different yet in December from what it was in June. Imagine the destiny of that square when its boundaries change over time by the successive replacing of buildings with ones surfaced with "new" materials. The same is true for

---

[1] Walter Gropius, *The Scope of Total Architecture*, p. 33.

interior space. As the quality and quantity of lighting changes, and alterations are made to surfaces of the dominant boundaries, so changes the mood.

Lighting alone can create conspicuous change in the appearance of space. When the lighting is raised in a dimly illuminated room, it appears larger without any change having taken place in its physical size or the surfacing of its boundaries. Further, it is the quality and quantity of light that influences brightness adaptation of the human eye in interspacial conditions. Standing in a bright room while looking into another of lower illumination, the adjacent room can be made to look brighter—and larger—by dimming the lights in the room of the observer.

To create architectural space then is not to design with light, but to design with the *effects* of light. "We shape our buildings and afterwards our buildings shape us" as Winston Churchill once said referring to the re-modeling of the Chambers of the London House of Commons. We organize and design architectural spaces, determine the illumination, specify the finished surfaces, and they become the effects of light that influence and shape human behavior.

Architectural space should be considered integral to the total built environment, not just as interiors of buildings. Only at certain times are people preoccupied in a single room. Most often they are only partially enclosed, and have views out doorways to adjoining rooms, or have a window view to a neighboring or distant landscape, which the Japanese call "borrowed space." In the city, only in a few situations should a building be conceived as an isolated entity, such as a monument or other edifice of cultural prominence. Collectively, buildings shape urban space, just like walls shape interior rooms. An exterior wall not only defines the building's form and demarcates the spaces of its interior, but its elevation becomes one of the boundaries for the urban space it faces. Thus, a building's exterior walls serve a dual purpose, as a consequence of urbanization. Designers therefore should think along an interior to urban continuum. We walk out of one room and into another, down a corridor and into a lobby, out a door and into a street or plaza. Once outside, interior painted and paneled spatial boundaries have given way to exterior surfaces of concrete, brick, and glass. Lighted surfaces of the interior have given way to those reflecting sunlight or night illumination.

All of this is part of the fascinating interaction between light and space. Taken together, the two afford an integrated and meaningful approach to the design of the human environment, because that is how people see their surroundings. The composition of light reflected from the surfaces around us gives us cognizance of the architectural world, setting the limits and directions for how we move about in it, and in this way *light is the shape of space.*

CHAPTER 1

93 Million Miles of Effect

Lies the seed unreck'd for centuries in the ground?
lo, to God's due occasion,
Uprising in the night, it sprouts, blooms,
And fills the earth with use and beauty.
— *Walt Whitman*
*Leaves of Grass**

Reflections

A narrow arc of fiery red breaks above the darkened horizon. Dew-covered grasses and wildflowers glisten in the silent dawn. Streaming rays of early morning light streak through crimson clouds and lengthen across a slumbering prairie . . .

. . . pass through soft-lit curtains and come to rest on auburn hair splendent against a silken pillow. Facades of a dense metropolis gleam in the golden sunrise and compose themselves against a brightening sky.

In the sweltering afternoon, rays of light bend through narrow layers of warm and cool air hugging the arid valley floor, and a thirsting antelope looks into the glaring mirage at a lake that isn't there. High on an alpine slope a rampant river breaks as a majestic waterfall and continues its seaward journey. Great ocean swells roll above the deep toward a rocky coastline; pounding surf breaks against the rocks into sparkling sunlit spray. A sandpiper scurries across glistening sands . . .

. . . under the watchfull eyes of vacationers taking leisure in the shade of a beach house veranda. Shimmering white sails flick upon the whitecapped azure sea. Jetting waters of a fountain splash in a sunken court mirrored by the polished granite wall of a symphony hall. In a jeweler's window brilliant facets of diamonds and the fire of radiant opals attract the attention of passersby. Patches of shimmering light dance on a ceiling in concert with summer breezes rippling the surface of a nearby garden pool.

The earth turns its back to the sun and the darkening sky exposes the dusty Milky Way. A full midnight moon hovers above a mountain pass and washes the granite cliffs with blue-white light. Crests of luminous surf splash against the moonlit sands . . .

. . . while hand in hand two lovers walk ankle-deep in phosphorescent foam. Columns of an arcade cast rhythms of moon shadow across a timeworn pavement; a walker alone in thought passes through the alternating light and dark.

The blue planet reaches its appointed orbital mark, and an aspen grove turns to golden yellow. A field is patterned by the flutter of orange and black wings, announcing the southward migration of monarchs to warmer quarters. A reddened maple leaf floats downward . . .

. . . to alight on the garden path of a suburban villa. Shoppers step from a small boutique into golden light streaming through autumn foliage. A casement window frames the breakfast view over a leaf-strewn terrace to a browning landscape.

* From Kouwenhoven, John, ed. 1950. *Leaves of Grass and Selected Prose by Walt Whitman*. New York: Random House, p. 326.

Transient shadows of a low winter sun undulate across a blanket of white concealing lifeless grasses beneath the snow. Beads of melted ice trickle downward from a glacier's frozen edge to mold pendant icicles suspended in glassy light. The late afternoon sun draws long tree shadows on the snowy forest floor . . .

. . . and filters through a picket fence repeating its lengthened outline across a snow-covered field. A low brick ledge capped by puffy snow sweeps across the blanketed white lawn as a vivid red stripe. Colorful displays of store windows glare as impressionistic sketches on an icy street.

A spiraled fern head pushes up through the dampened soil, and multicolored crocuses accent the greening of the earth. On the stage of a grassland puddle a thunder-squall choreographs ordinary raindrops to bubble-dance in flickering light. In a swampy marsh an iridescent blue-green dragonfly sunbathes on a newborn pondweed spike. At the edge of an inland forest lake a fawn pauses in mirrored stillness; a raindrop breaks the water's silence sending light rings rippling outward . . .

. . . while in dim light of the cloudburst a secretary peers out an office window where March winds scatter rain patterns against the pane. An arcing rainbow paints its spectrum high above a village nestled in verdant hills. Iris and daffodils spring to color along the bordering balustrade of a weathered cedar deck. Laughing children gaze upward and shield their eyes to watch gay-colored kites swirl and dart in the twisting wind. Flowering dogwoods shade a river walk; bright balloons and colorful banners deck a terraced amphitheater for an afternoon concert in the park.

Each of these images is a commonplace tableau orchestrated by light from a single source 93,000,000 miles away—the sun. It is a powerful medium whose journey work illuminates the phenomena of nature and the efforts of humankind. The sun's design effects were discovered during the birth of art and architecture, and for millennia daylight has defined the beautiful and the ugly, the exceptional and the ordinary, the sacred and the profane, and the serious and the frivolous. Whatever the impact of those effects, subtle or dramatic, light is a potent vehicle for human expression. Yet, the sun is but *one* source. Imagine the opportunities—and the pitfalls—of attempting to supplement the sun with light from electric sources.

Our Planetary Clock

The terrestrial environment for plant, animal, and human life was set into motion when the earth cooled and was pulled into its assigned place in the solar system. The laws of time, as measured by the earth's axial rotation and its revolution around the sun, temper the biological existence and behavior of all living organisms in the ecological order. The span of the year regulates the highest and lowest angular path for the arrival of solar light, defining the texture of the planet's surface from mountain peak and urban skyscraper to pebbles strewn on a canyon floor. The year numbers the pages of our chronicles and walks us step by step through the scant breadth of time each of us was given by consequence of birth. The day/night cycle controls the duration and greatest contrast between light and dark. Just one turn on the earth's axis sets into motion the pace at which we conduct our private and public affairs, sensitively stated by the twentieth-century architect Le Corbusier (1967, 104):

> *Architecture, city planning,*
> *our happiness,*
> *the state of our consciousness,*
> *the equilibrium of our individual lives,*
> *the rhythm of our collective duties*

are all governed by the 24-hour cycle of the sun. The sun is in control. Of everything: thought, action, movement, functions, undertakings, obligations, all these are contained, inevitably, within the exact boundaries established by two sleeps. Each morning life begins afresh, and our energies are renewed; every evening, our eyelids close, and sleep performs its inexplicable miracle.

24 hours! That is the yardstick and the rhythm of human life; the unit to which everything must conform.

In combination with the earth's rotation, atmospheric conditions create still greater fluctuations in the quantity and quality of daylight and moonlight. Light penetrating the atmosphere strikes particles that partly absorb and partly reflect the sun's energy. Shifting weather patterns continually alter cloud coverage, sometimes within a daily cycle. By mid-morning, to the painter's and photographer's delight, the sun can induce convection to form white cumulus clouds made vivid against a deep blue sky. By noon, they can increase enough to dominate the sky and, by late afternoon, they may obliterate the blue completely. The atmosphere is a great filter between the sun and the earth, which continually modifies the visual environment in which we live. With the dimming of sunlight, we meddle with our living quarters, turning light switches on and off to make our tasks easier and to satisfy our moods.

Further changes in daylight result from geographic location on the globe. The distance of latitude north or south of the equator accounts for the specific angle at which sunlight strikes the earth's surface at any one locality. Important to every student and professional architect is the critical understanding of *where* a proposed building is to be placed with regard to the directional movement of the sun and predominant weather patterns.

Awareness of "where on the earth" with regard to time and place is cogently gained by personal experience when for the first time we are transported to a geographic area remote from the one to which we are accustomed. Such was the case of the youthful traveler who had been raised near the 40th parallel and was promptly educated to the difference of inclination of the sun while on a summer visit to Scandinavia, which is located near the 60th parallel. A sense of disbelief surfaced when stepping from a late-night restaurant in Stockholm to discover the first light of sunrise shortly after midnight. The difference between those 20 degrees of latitude was an instant revelation. In a similar event, a North American photographer on a first trip down the Nile was surprised to learn how differently the sun crosses the earth in the Sudan. Unaccustomed to the extraordinary brightness of the clear, crisp African sky, he was convinced his camera's light meter was malfunctioning while taking readings on a stone wall of an ancient ruin, receiving abnormal suggested aperture settings for the lens. Angle, duration, and quality of sunlight vary dramatically throughout the northern and southern hemispheres.

The impact of the seasons further modifies the visual effects of sunlight. It is not the relative closeness of our planet to the sun on its year-long orbital travel, but the tilt of the earth's axis that causes seasonal change. The earth is farthest from the sun in summer and closest in winter. The seasons are important references for considering differences of sunlight at any one specific location on the earth's surface. Our "planetary clock" therefore determines the quantity and quality of natural light and creates fluctuations in temperature. This clock is responsible for the greening or browning of leaves and the arrival of flowers or snow. It determines the length of stay for sunlight and shadow reaching longer or shorter into a landscaped plaza, midtown office, or private study. This is why daylight is fundamental to architecture, and the designer needs to be critically aware of how it strikes exterior surfaces and illuminates interior spaces.

Nature's Beauty and Light

Why have landscapes, sunsets, mountains, waterfalls, forests, deer, the human figure, and close-ups of flowers become regular subjects for the painter's brush and photographer's lens? Natural beauty, whether experienced directly or through artistic media, awakens in the observer feelings of romance, awe, tranquility, peace, and even worship. There is a biological interface between beauty in nature and the instinctive human drive to beautify the built environment. John Dewey (1958, 28) once said that "human hopes and purposes find a basis and support in nature." As part of those purposes, we can look to nature to better understand the qualities of beauty and let those qualities influence the things we create and put before the public eye. A measure of the popularity of natural beauty among the general public is its continued appearance in commercial advertising, sometimes to attract attention to products remote from nature itself. Although not all people admire natural beauty for its own sake, the merit of using such advertising imagery lies in nature's capacity to stimulate human reaction.

Designers, critics, and aestheticians have tried to tap the secret of beauty in nature and explain it through analytical processes. The fundamental approach is to single out attributes of form, space, color, texture, structure, proportion of the parts, and harmonious composition. Through these, parallels can be drawn rather easily between design in nature and design in human artistic endeavor. Out of any meaningful investigation of natural beauty comes the recognition of the role of light. Whether a rose is portrayed in direct sunlight or shadowy mist is a matter of interpretation, yet both hold visual interest and can be said to be "beautiful." In an art gallery people seeing a photograph of a rose dramatized by a single shaft of light may comment on the beauty of the scene and point out the feature of "interesting light." An analysis of architectural design may be approached accordingly, using the same attributes of form, space, and color. Just as in nature's beauty, light can be made interesting in architecture, and its principal role of *activating the visual world around us* can be exploited to stir human emotions.

Interesting light found in nature, however, by itself will not guarantee beauty even when dramatically photographed or painted on the artist's canvas. The rose in the previous paragraph is beautiful in mist or sunlight because no mention was made of its condition. Most people would have imagined it in natural beauty. What a contrast, however, when information is added to describe the rose as one with browning and missing petals, drooping on a broken stem in a neglected garden. In the same way beauty is not guaranteed by adding interesting light to architectural settings. People see only reflected light off the surfaces of their surroundings, and sometimes the condition of those surfaces conveys feelings of antibeauty, which resulted from impoverishment related to imbalance in the socioeconomics of human culture. For example, interesting light can be found in a photojournalism exhibition of urban slums or war, yet the subject matter stirs within the viewer feelings that are antithetical to human contentment or peace. So in this regard the human environment parallels the world of nature. A building in a slum crumbles into decay like a water-starved shrub deteriorates in a parched desert landscape. Light may "interestingly" describe both of those scenes, but the physical conditions of surfaces generate far different levels of appreciation for the viewer than would those of the freshly opened, dew-covered rose in the early morning sun.

The union between light and the character of the surfaces on which it falls is a key factor for determining the quality of design. But a deteriorating condition of a building does not necessarily mean the viewer will respond to it in a mood that prevailed while looking at the dying rose. On the Acropolis in Greece the Parthenon may have received more attention *after* it fell into ruin following the breakup of that once proud Athenian state. That is caused by Romanticism, which awakens interest in the glories of the past by dramatizing ruins that have survived the passing of time. Broken architectural columns lying in sunlight become seductive forms awaiting the sketchpad and camera lens. It is only a twisted sort of romanticism that finds the same interest in the broken walls of a poverty-stricken inner-city ghetto. True, dramatic photographs can be taken of shafts of daylight slicing through clouds to spotlight an abandoned, rusted-out car in a debris-cluttered alley, highlighting the signs and symbols of poverty and despair. Those photographs have value in an exhibit or magazine article to raise a call to correct the situation, but the appeal of such imagery awakens romanticized interest only if the viewer of the picture does not have to *live* in the ghetto. When assessing the pictorial qualities of such a scene, the word "beauty" is set aside.

Nature has its own impoverishment, as attested to by the dying rose and the desolate landscape, but it sustains an enduring renewal to hold before the human species infinite examples of inspiration and design excellence. Beauty was there in the natural environment in previous geologic ages, but needed the human spirit to discover its preciousness and opulence. The history of architecture and the fine arts is filled with examples of artists, musicians, poets, and architects borrowing from nature. Frank Lloyd Wright (1943, 347) said, "Integral ornament is simply structure-pattern made visibly articulate and seen in the building as it is seen articulate in the structure of the trees or a lily of the fields." Composer Richard Wagner (Curtis and Greenslet, 1962, 511) found the motivation for writing his orchestral overture to *Rheingold* while taking "a long tramp . . . through the hilly country, which was covered with pine woods." The American Transcendentalist Ralph Waldo Emerson (Miller, 1957, 177) said, ". . . the forms and colors of Nature have a new charm for us in our perception, that not one ornament was added for ornament." His compatriot Henry David Thoreau (1980, 167) said, "If I were

a drawing-master, I would set my pupils to copying these leaves, that they might learn to draw firmly and gracefully." Thoreau (1980, 98) told the story of a traveler asking Wordsworth's servant to show him her master's study, and she answered, "Here is his library, but his study is out of doors." It was the discovery of the clear, brilliant natural light in southern France that changed the canvases of Vincent van Gogh. After arriving in Arles he wrote to his brother Theo (Wallace, 1969, 100): "Those who don't believe in this sun here are real infidels." The list goes on. Architecture is the art of spatially composing surfaces "painted" by the arrival of light, and a building must be so well conceived and assembled that it offers to the human being the same pleasure and gratification that can be found in the beauty of nature.

Animation of the Human Environment

The search for beauty in design antedates recorded history, as evidenced by archaeological remains that testify to the basic human impulse to adorn habitats and domestic implements. An unearthed potsherd bearing geometric or floral decoration documents this inclination to bring organization and beautification to things formerly produced in an uncultivated manner. Long before the age of electricity, both occidental and oriental societies attempted to order and embellish their built environment through the expedient use of sunlight. Granted, a considerable amount of this most likely resulted from the functional distribution of light for the practicalities of daily activities. Yet what was happening long ago was the gradual development of artistic taste. Designers began to consciously control lighting effects in their surroundings by taking advantage of the daily and annual movements of the sun. This cannot be denied in light of the technical precision required for the planning and construction of the ancient Egyptian temple at Abu Simbel, where the rising sun glows on sculptured deities deep in its sanctuary for just a few moments only twice a year during the vernal and autumnal equinoxes, or the ancient Roman Pantheon, where the oculus in its dome controls the direction of a disk of light so that it directly strikes one altar in the morning and then moves ever so gradually across the floor to shine on an opposite altar in the afternoon. These environments are animated by the interaction of space and light and appeal strongly to human sensitivities whether in the ancient world or today. Those early examples were the genesis of *architecture,* and the transformation from mere shelter to art had taken place. Experiencing those interiors was refreshing and out of the ordinary. Architectural space, articulated by light, became alive.

As architects know, and at the risk of scientific heresy, the sun moves around the earth, painting each building on it with changing values of light. Keeping time with our planetary clock, the environment is continually animated by changing sky conditions of day, night, and the seasons. Design animation is also experienced when walking through a building or the city. Passing from corridor to gallery or from street to public square, the surfaces of the environment generally remain under constant illumination, but they undergo change in the way they *appear* due to light or dark adaptation of the eye. The designer's task then is to design for a moving sun and moving people, *designing with the effects of light,* as seen by human vision from a changing point of view.

Another way of animating the environment is the texturing and coloring of surfaces that shape space. Textured and nontextured materials behave differently under the influence of light, depending on their orientation to the source of light and the viewing angle of the observer. As the eye looks down the length of a wall at an acute angle, often the case when walking down a sidewalk or corridor, surfaces of smooth building materials may produce sheen or even glare. However, textured interior wall fabrics, stepped brickwork, rusticated stone, protruding moldings, architectural concrete, or tiered balconies on a highrise building—all enliven surface by the introduction of shadow. Texture modifies color, which shifts in value and brightness as various degrees of shadow are introduced or withdrawn. Contemporary building materials are offered and advertised in a variety of textures and colors, but all visually change when subjected to one or more of the various sources of illumination. Knowing how to select from such a palette of visual wealth and skillfully bring together surfaces that shape and animate space is the designer's art.

Poetic animation has long been achieved in the visual arts by *composing light and shadow in rhythms.* For centuries, the technique of alternating light and dark has been used in painting to dramatize the two-dimensional surface. The three dimensions of architecture and its construction process of assembling modular parts provide ample opportunity for creating rhythmic compositions of light and shade. Arcades, sun screens and window patterns, rows of luminaires and their electric light, and sequencing connected spaces of different brightness, all are rhythmic layouts that stimulate the eye and provide a cadence of accents along paths of movement through architecture. Similar to the beat in a musical score, rhythms of light can be strong or weak, long or short. Human response to rhythm is inborn, as natural as responding to the repetitiveness of night following day, season following season. Just as natural are the recurring rhythms of physiological movements in the human organism—the regularity of heartbeat or periodic inhaling and exhaling. The rhythms of human biology intricately mesh with those of the greater ecological order. The design of the human environment can gain by the incorporation of rhythmic visual elements that are in dialogue with that total natural system.

When proficiently assembled into a well-designed and illuminated architectural space, individual surfaces mutually interact to form a harmonious whole. When good lighting design is integrated with good spatial composition, and when psychological impairments to human comfort are eliminated, architecture comes to life in a meaningful and gratifying way. Walls abused by the overuse of color, texture, and ornament in a space that includes glaring reflections join to create a visual overload for the eye and brain, and the whole disintegrates into a confusion of discordant parts. The total effect can be offensive and disturbing. There is no "natural" beauty, and the word "architecture" is inappropriate.

Exemplary monuments to architecture have been erected by diverse cultures throughout the course of human history, winning the praise of succeeding generations. Why do individuals living in the modern world experience good feelings and enthusiasm when visiting a well-designed architectural environment produced by another culture far removed by centuries, language, and customs? Why do present-day travelers from the Orient step inside the Gothic cathedrals of Europe and stop in awe before the splendor of colored light streaming through stained glass? Why do Western tourists sense an immediate order and calm upon entering the enclosed court of a traditional oriental temple or Japanese garden? Why did a sixth-century chronicler (De La Croix, Tansey, and Kirkpatrick, 1991, 287) once document the experiences of Hagia Sophia in Istanbul with the words "One would declare that the place were not illuminated from the outside by the sun, but that the radiance originated from within . . . ", and why do visitors enter that same building and continue to praise its interior mystical light more than 1400 years later? There is good reason why people from different historical periods and different cultures respond to the qualities of space and light in that and other renowned masterpieces of architecture. In a physiological and artistic kinship, there is a special common bond between the designers from former historical periods and those of us who have followed. That bonding lies in a significant element of the human anatomy—the *retina*. Designers in the past brought forth new architecture of merit by *seeing*, then learning, from works that preceded them. When they stepped inside the Pantheon, Hagia Sophia, a cathedral, an oriental temple, or a forest clearing patterned by wildflowers, they were moved by what they came to recognize as something magnificent and praiseworthy. They knew what to emulate, what to improve on, and what to reject. Although early designers did not understand the physiology of the human eye as we do today, they had their own understanding of visual perception, and how human vision responds to the effects of color, texture, and light in architectural space. Herein lies the essence of "designing for people," the ergonomics of design, the orderly shaping of the environment in accordance with how it is perceived. *This is the humanization of architecture.*

Whether to design with only daylight as was the case before the Industrial Revolution or to augment daylight with the technology of electric illumination, invaluable lessons are to be learned from studying the activating influence of that celebrated instrument of design, the sun. Behind the earthly mask of changing atmosphere and seasonal itinerary, it stays out there as a permanent fixture in the sky, offering designers the plenitude, the luxury, and the excitement of its 93,000,000 miles of effect.

Part 1: Visual Perception and Light

CHAPTER 2

Visual Perception
for Architecture

O Star (the fairest one in sight),
We grant your loftiness the right
To some obscurity of cloud—
It will not do to say of night,
Since dark is what brings out your light.
                              —Robert Frost
                    "Take Something Like a Star"*

Introduction and Application to Design

How does human vision see the architectural environment? What practical aspects of visual perception can best benefit design professionals when creating that environment? Answers to these questions can be found among the wealth of publications in research psychology published during the twentieth century, providing invaluable design information regarding how people visually see the world in which they live. This book is process oriented and therefore a beginning is made by explaining selected components of visual perception that may lead to formulating design principles based on how the eye sees. Application of those principles will not only benefit professionals practicing design but, by extension of their work, also will physiologically and psychologically benefit the people who will come to live in the environments they create.

* From *The Poetry of Robert Frost* edited by Edward Connery Lathem. Copyright © 1977 by Lesley Frost Ballantine. Copyright 1949 © 1969 by Henry Holt and Co., Inc. Reprinted by permission of Henry Holt and Co., Inc.

Vision is part of a complicated network of the total human sensory system, and is closely related to touch and hearing. In this chapter, special attention is placed on vision as a direct avenue for investigating the relationship between architectural space and light. This is done because light in all its varieties manifests the shapes, locations, colors, textures, and reflections of surfaces in the physical world that are sent as messages to the brain. Recorded there, each new daily experience is synthesized in the ongoing learning process that conditions people's awareness of their surroundings, from clarity to clutter and from visual comfort to visual disturbance.

Visual perception, which takes place as the observer comes in contact and interacts with the visible surroundings, is externally oriented. Reflected off surfaces of the external world, light arrives in the eye where it touches off reactions of sensitive receptor cells in the retina. Those cells are the rods and cones that initiate *sensations,* which are neural responses that transduce electromagnetic energy into neural activity. This is the delicate process by which things seen are transmitted to the brain as things visually perceived. Through that dialogue between object and perception, we come to see and know the world around us, and find our way around in buildings and cities. Visual images build up over time, and are stored away in memory, each contributing to our perception of the visual world. The eye and the mind construct the total experience of one's lifetime, which tempers each new perception of the world and is unique to the individual.

Physiology of the Eye

One of the great wonders of nature is the human eye (Figure 2-1). Through it comes most of our information about the physical world. It is delicate and complex. Illuminated by light, the visual image of an object enters the eye through the *lens*.[1] Immediately in front of the lens is the *iris*, which automatically reacts to the amount of light entering the eye. The dark circular aperture in the center of the iris is the *pupil*. As illumination increases and surfaces appear brighter, the iris closes, reducing the amount of light that falls on the retina. When illumination decreases, the iris opens (dilates).

The *retina* (Figure 2-2) is a thin membrane surrounding the viscous fluids of the vitreous humor in the interior of the eye. It covers nearly 200 degrees of the total inside surface of the eye, and contains the light-sensitive receptor cells. The receptor cells in the retina are morphologically of two distinct types, *rods* and *cones*, so-named in the nineteenth century because of their cylindrical and conic appearance as observed in a microscope (see Figure 2-3). The rods and cones are highly specialized in terms of how they receive light. Cones function in daylight and increased brightness of artificial light; they number about seven million in each retina. Cones are also responsible for seeing color, as well as details of texture. Rods function in dim light (cones do not), operating at night and in darkened rooms. There are 120 to 130 million rods in each retina, greatly surpassing the number of cones. Rods respond to changes in brightness but not to color, presenting us with a view of the world in shades of gray.

Behind the vitreous humor and in the retina lies the *fovea centralis*, often referred to simply as the *fovea*. It is here where the image of what we are looking at is focused. Measuring only about 2 mm across, the fovea defines the visual axis of the eye, and is mechanically aligned with whatever is of interest to the observer at the moment. In the fovea, there are no rods, but they exist in profusion in the *parafovea*, the region of the retina around the fovea. The fovea is made up of the greatest number of cones, tightly packed together, and

[1] The human eye is often compared with the camera, noting the similarities in the visual mechanism of each. For an interesting article on this subject, see Wald (1950).

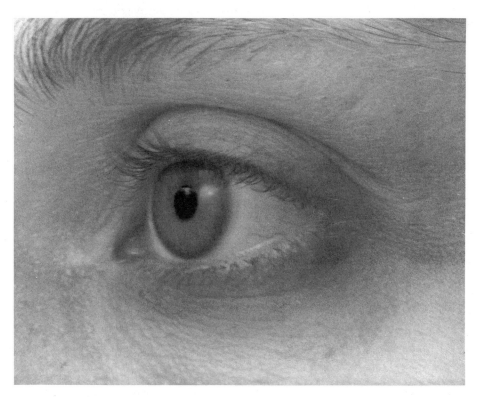

Figure 2-1. Through the human eye comes most of our knowledge of the environment.

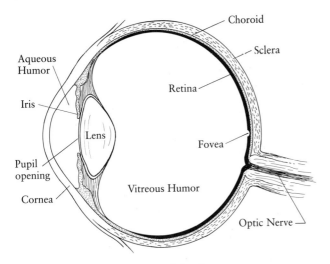

Figure 2-2. Cross section of the human eye.

falling off in number outward into the parafovea. The angle of vision in which focus occurs is extremely narrow. Sharp focus drops off 50% for any object only 1 degree off center from the fovea. For an object just 8 degrees off the line of sight, only 15% of maximum acuity is possible. Although retinal projections away from the fovea are not sharp in detail, they are very important for peripheral vision.

The actual layering of the photoreceptors in the retina is not organized in the way one would logically expect. Because the rods and cones respond to the incoming

light of the eye, it might be assumed they face the lens where the light actually enters. This is not the case. Figure 2-3 shows they are actually located in the layer of the retina opposite the direction of incoming light. This is a curious arrangement, because before light can activate the receptors, it must first pass through a series of other cells and blood vessels.

What is the path then, for the stimuli of light reflected off the objects in the visual world to actually *appear* as chairs, books, rocks, and flowers? Groups of rods and cones photochemically register the presence of lighted corners, edges, and surfaces, and then they relay their electrical messages to intermediate neurons (*bipolar cells*), which continue to pass the message to *ganglion cells*. The axons, or nerve fibers, of the ganglion cells form the *optic nerve*, which in turn transmits the visual message to the brain, where it is "correctly" inverted and "seen" right side up to coincide with the image before the eye.

"Turn on some more light" is frequently heard when there is difficulty reading or performing close-up tasks in a dimly lit room. This indeed should be done, but only to an extent. It was noted above that as brightness increases, the iris constricts and reduces the size of the pupil, which affects the resolving power of the eye. In the darkened room the cones are less active; the fine details needed for reading thereby lose their sharpness, and this causes a fall off in *visual acuity,* the capability of the eye to distinguish fine detail. As the lights are turned up, the cones take over, and details and patterns appear more crisp than they were in the darker room. Acuity is thus dependent on the amount of illumination, but there is a limit to the practicalities of continuing to increase the amount of light. As a general rule, an increase in absolute lighting levels over 10 fc has little effect on the ability of the eye to see an object better. John Boud (1973, 5) associated this with the "law of diminishing returns," particularly in terms of cost effectiveness of illumination levels. Figure 2-4 shows that as the amount of light increases from A to B, from B to C,

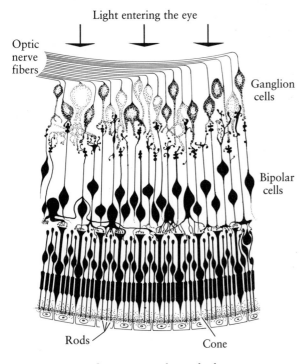

Figure 2-3. Cross section through the retina.

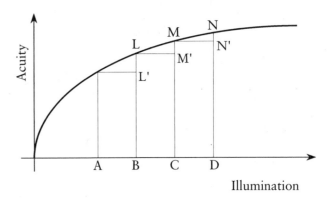

Figure 2-4. Increasing illumination versus acuity.

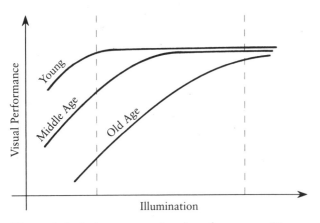

Figure 2-5. Aging versus visual performance. [From Boyce, P.R. 1973. Illuminance, visual performance and preference. Lighting Research and Technology 5(3):137]

and from C to D, the improvement in visibility decreases (compare the diminishing distance between L'L, M'M, with N'N).

P. R. Boyce (1973) writing on illumination, visual performance, and age, called attention to visual problems for the elderly. Older people encounter a reduction in the range of *accommodation*, the change in lens shape by flattening or bulging when an image is focused on the retina. This makes it difficult for the elderly to read distant signs and see environmental details. There is an increase in the absorption and scattering of light in the eye, which produces greater sensitivity to what is known in the lighting field as *disability glare*. As aging occurs, there is a gradual reduction of the pupil diameter at a given level of adaptation to light. Boyce says these physiological changes can be responsible for a threefold reduction in the amount of light reaching the retina of a 60-year-old person as compared with a younger person at age 20. Figure 2-5 shows how different age groups perform three types of performance tasks, from low (left column) to high (right column) illumination. These are important considerations for the design and operation of nursing homes and retirement centers.

Seeing Edges and Contours: Ordinal Stimulation

Why have edges and outlines been considered artistically important through the history of art and architecture? That question is answered most easily by analyzing the mechanism of the visual system. Psychologists tell us that, in object perception, edges and outlines of a form are seen *first*, then the eye scans the surfaces within

the outer contours. This is a noteworthy aspect of the visual process because it relates to *all* people, not just designers looking for the guiding assistance of "good" contours. Psychologists have also shown that when an object is viewed through some sort of framing device where only its surface is seen, not its outer edges, it is perceived quite differently when stripped of the impact of its peripheral contours. Understanding the process by which the eye perceives edges will produce invaluable design information and strategy for designing architectural form and space.

Receptors in the retina are stimulated according to a process called *ordinal stimulation*, which means simply that the physical energy from a stimulus reaches the receptors *in order*, or in succession. This is another way of saying a surface is perceived as a continuous gradient. Whether that gradient is smooth or rough, the eye sees it as smooth or rough texture flowing along a continuous surface. Figure 2-6 shows what happens when a continuous surface is broken, or when ordinal stimulation is interrupted. The eye instantly responds to the *abrupt* change in the gradient from A to B where the edge (E) is created. The foreground texture and density at t_1 breaks sharply as seen against the gradient of texture and density immediately behind the edge at t_2. "Abruptness," says Gibson (1974, 114) "seems to be the critical condition. . . . The retina is probably to be conceived as an organ of the body which is sensitive to grades of light, not points of light." In the continuous flow of ordinal stimulation from any surface, a sudden break of surface is perceptually dramatic.

Breaks in ordinal stimulation are not limited to the perception of physical edges of an object. A gradient can be interrupted by shadow, shape, or color patterns lying *on* the plane of a surface, creating edges perceived as changes in reflectance or brightness.[2] For example, edges or contours are formed by pattern shapes on a two-dimensional surface like the decorative details of a Persian rug, details on a wall mural, or bright patches of reflected sunlight and shadows cast on a floor by overhead truss work in an atrium or by sash patterns of a window pane.

Edges of patterns on a surface plane compete with the physical edges at the outer contours of the plane. When the surface pattern is one of great detail or complexity, particularly when high contrast exists between the pattern and background, the strength of the outer border is weakened. The eye becomes distracted by the interior surface pattern (see Figure 2-22). This can be observed by looking at visually complex walls bearing highly ornate wallpaper or fabrics, mirrors reflecting a cluttered room, or an overload of pictures and other

---

[2] For further information on the perception of reflectance, see Gilchrist and Jacobsen (1984).

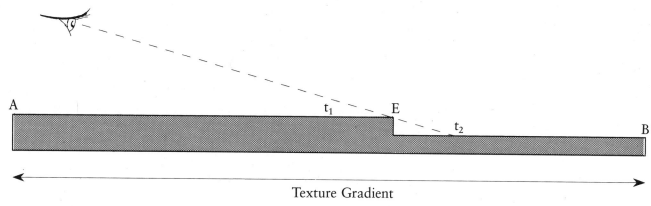

Texture Gradient

Figure 2-6. Ordinal stimulation.

hangings. In those conditions the edges of the wall are severely weakened as visual limits of the surface plane.

The importance of edge in visual perception is being made here because the very nature of architecture is a continuous array of connected spaces, joined by edges at corners, doorways, and windows. The more architectural surfaces appear visually "busy," the more edges connecting adjoining spaces lose their intrinsic strength. As will be shown amply in Part 3 (Designing with Space and Light), it is at the edges of spatial connections that reflected light plays a critical role, because at those edges the natural visual system perceives a spatial brightness-contrast, and at those edges the eye makes transitions between light and dark adaptation as a person moves from one space to another.

Brightness

The phenomenon of *brightness* is fundamental to the entire experience of viewing the world. It is introduced here not only as a basic component of visual perception, but as an essential part of space and light theory as applied to the design of the architectural environment. It is not to be confused with "luminance," which is the visual effect of light reflected off a surface as measured with a photometer. Brightness, as used throughout this book, is defined as the subjective impression of light illuminating one surface as compared with another surface. By this definition, brightness requires two or more surfaces or objects to consider one as brighter than the other.

The term "apparent brightness" sometimes is found in psychology and lighting design literature, and should be avoided. It is mistakenly used to refer to a change in brightness of a surface as caused by the presence of other illuminated surfaces. What is meant in those cases is "apparent luminance," where the actual measured lumi-

nance *looks* lighter or darker under the influence of a neighboring surface that is darker or lighter. The measured luminance stays the same; it just appears differently. According to the definition just given, there is nothing about brightness that is *apparent.* "Apparent" means how a surface looks, not how it is measured as luminance.

When the appearance of a surface differs significantly from its background, it is said to have *brightness-contrast.* In the next chapter, brightness-contrast is explained in numerical units of lighting, known as the *luminance ratio,* which refers to a comparison of two different surfaces by way of their light-reflecting qualities and the brightness that results. Comparative brightness is a means for establishing design relationships of color, texture, and location of surfaces in space and, most important, will be directly related to the location, quantity, and quality of the light sources in a room.

An interesting aspect of the perception of brightness is *gamma movement,* which influences the way we see a surface in spatial depth. It is another way of saying "brightness advances" and was given the label "gamma" by F. Kenkel in 1913. Size, texture, shadow, and color all convey some information about relative distance from the viewer, but when all other physical features are equal, a bright object will appear closer and slightly larger than a darker one. Gamma movement is independent of physical location in space. When subjected to increased light, an object brightens and appears to advance toward the viewer from its initial fixation point, and when the light is decreased it returns to its former position. This is easily demonstrated in the lighting lab. Photographed in the Interspace Model (see Appendix), Figure 2-7 shows two rectangular blocks of identical size, shape, and surfacing material, and both are at the same distance from the viewer. The frame through which the blocks are seen is given for reference. A controlled beam of light is cast only on the block on the right. Observers consistently pick out the brighter of the two blocks as the nearer,

Figure 2-7. A bright form advances in space.

and also report it as being larger. Easy as it is to observe gamma movement in graphic form or under laboratory conditions, the question may be asked, does this phenomenon happen—spatially—in the everyday world? The answer is yes. Studies in visual perception performed outside the laboratory verify this fascinating relationship between spatial depth and brightness. After illumination on an object is increased, subjects participating in these real-life studies evaluate its appearance as being closer and larger. In the everyday surroundings of architecture, most people are not aware of the effects of brightness advancing. But the designer should be aware of it, learning to use it when selecting the color and value of building materials during the refinement stage of design composition, and learning to avoid the phenomenon in unwanted circumstances.

Simultaneous Contrast: Reversal at the Edge of Light

When it comes to seeing brightness-contrast, the eye has a mind of its own. As artists and graphic designers have known for a long time, placing two areas of high contrast in adjacent positions alters the appearance of both. This is the effect of *simultaneous contrast,* which plays havoc in the architectural environment because of the frequent juxtaposition of light and dark surfaces created by natural or electric illumination.

Simply stated, simultaneous contrast is the change in the appearance of a surface caused by the presence of an adjacent surface that is much brighter or darker. Figure 2-8 illustrates this effect. Both center squares are the same middle gray, but the black surrounding field

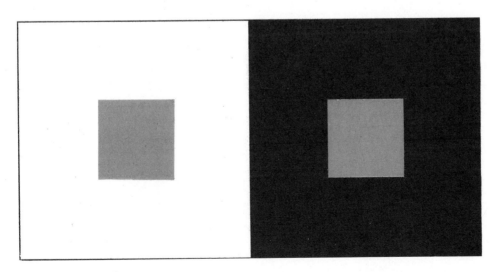

Figure 2-8. Simultaneous contrast.

Figure 2-9. Brightness as a function of background.

brightens the gray square, whereas the white field creates the reverse effect by darkening the gray.

Because art and architecture involve multiple variances of brightness, it is more useful to study the principle of simultaneous contrast over a range of contrast effects. This was done in Figure 2-9, which shows that the brightness of a surface is a function of its background, not the absolute light it receives. Each of the small interior squares has an identical middle gray value, yet each varies in brightness as the background changes in the sequence from black to white. That is to say, the central squares are equal in reflectance and luminance, but vary in brightness.

Simultaneous contrast is often encountered in exhibition design. Sometimes high contrast is used intentionally and effectively to dramatize part of a display. There are situations, however, where a contrast extreme is not appropriate, and steps can be taken to avoid it entirely. Figure 2-10 shows a gallery in Louis Kahn's Kimbell Art Museum in Fort Worth. The overall brightness value of the panel on which the painting is displayed corresponds to the average tonal qualities of the painting and its frame, preventing a high-contrast condition for the museum visitor. Visualize the surrounding display panel as exceptionally bright or dark. Either way would give greater emphasis to the work of art, but the contrast effects would modify the actual color tones of the painting in the perception of the observer, unintended by the artist.

Conditions of simultaneous contrast exist throughout the architectural world. One needs only to view the open bright sky through a window (Figure 2-11), especially where the opening is nearly flush with an interior wall. When looking out the window toward a bright field of view, the areas of wall adjacent to the window appear darker, and surface detailing such as wood grain on the window frame virtually disappears. That section of interior wall is often the location for ornate drapes or nearby wall hangings, which also darken and lose detail in the presence of high contrast. The sudden change from dark to light or vice versa is an extreme break in the flow of ordinal stimulation in the retina. Note the effect of splaying the window, which inserts surfaces of middle brightness values between the otherwise high contrast between the interior and exterior view. From this we can state a working principle: *The introduction of any surface at a brightness level intermediate between two extremes of contrast, either by splaying or any other means, lessens the impact of simultaneous contrast by creating a softer transition for the eye.*

Let's put this principle to work. Figure 2-12 shows a skylighted atrium in a public building, which had a high-contrast potential for people walking along the upper floors where opaque architectural edges would have been contrasted with the bright visual field of the sky. The square structural unit supported by the double cross beams was given angled side panels, which functionally reflect incoming sunlight down into the atrium. Those angled surfaces insert the intermediate brightness levels

Figure 2-10. Brightness compatibility of background. [Kimbell Art Museum, Fort Worth. Architect: Louis I. Kahn]

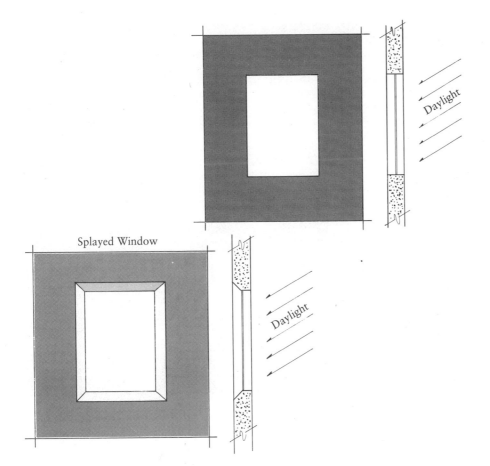

Figure 2-11. Ordinal stimulation at window openings.

Splayed Window

that eliminate high contrast in the upward view. Note how the undersides of the support beams and the central square unit appear in middle gray, and as such also contribute to the breakup of high contrast. How was that done? Those underside surfaces are nothing more than gypsum board, painted white. They take on a value of middle gray by receiving ambient light, and together with the angled panels create a pleasant—and ergonomic—field of view for people walking in those spaces. The angled surfaces reflecting daylight into the atrium space is only one function of that unit. It also houses a fan and exhaust system for smoke evacuation. The architects solved both problems at once, and at the same time, added to spatial aesthetics. A series of models was built to study the conditions of reflected daylight and air flow until a solution was found that created a "good fit" between the skylight design and the atrium it illuminates.

Patterns of Edges and Light

Architecture is filled with patterns of edges encountered as a normal part of our daily activities. Curtain wall construction, window frames, Venetian blinds, decorative grilles, louvered screens, and glass block configurations are just a few. For purposes of design, patterns should be analyzed according to the size of the parts. A composition of comparatively small units is generally perceived as a pattern. When the components stand out in high contrast, a pattern significantly changes the perception—and mood—of an environment.

Observe the contrasting patterns of light and shade in the view down the pergola in Figure 2-13. Taken in early morning light, the photograph shows the influence of rich patterning on the perception of architectural space. Note how the patterns of light and the scale of the units alter the perception of the colonnades. The columns on the left side read as a pattern of larger units, which is perceptually more simplified; they help to describe the three stages of the receding space, especially by their shadows cast on the pavement. But the right side is another story. The eye sees a multitude of edges, in high contrast. The units of patterns are much smaller in scale and more intricate. Trellis shadows cast on the columns run counter to the direction of shadows on the vertical flutes, adding pattern effects that are not seen on the left side. Some of the trellis shadows create perspective lines on the pavement; others intermingle with

Figure 2-12. Multiple problem solving. [U.S. Federal Building, Topeka, Kansas. Architects: Kansas Architects and Planners Associated. Photograph: © Paul S. Kivett]

Figure 2-13. Patterns of light and shade. [Paseo Pergola, Kansas City, Missouri]

all other micropatterns on the benches, greenery, and buildings behind. The patterns on the right side add visual interest by animating the scene, but they also make the perception of the space more ambiguous.

When certain patterns are rendered in high contrast, illusionary effects can occur at the intersections. This is known as the *Hermann grid effect* (Figure 2-14), an intriguing perceptual observation that was first recorded in 1870. Illusions of faint gray spots appear at the intersections of the grid, induced by the white lines set against the high contrasting black squares. It makes no difference if the "background" for the lines is black as shown, or white with black lines in front. The strong contrast and the proportionally narrow size of the lines generate the illusions. Of special interest is the fact that the gray spots appear only at those intersections that lie in the peripheral vision of the eye—the effect does not occur at any intersection on which the eye is focused. The Hermann grid shown in Figure 2-15 shows the dependency of the illusionary effects on the width of the bars and the resultant size of intersections at the corners of the squares. The larger the area of intersection, the less the illusions appear.

Under the right conditions Hermann grid illusions can be observed in design patterns of the day-to-day urban

Visual Perception and Light

Figure 2-14. Hermann grid illusion.

environment, appearing in the presence of high contrast and where the bars of a grid are proportionally narrow compared with their surrounding fields. Sometimes they appear on the silhouette of window mullions seen against a bright sky. They also can be observed on interior decorative grilles of dark wood or other material when the space behind the grille is brightly illuminated, or on grilles manufactured from light-colored materials like woods such as birch or ash, with a dark space behind. The pattern design, percent of opening of the apertures, and relative brightness of the grille can all create problems of illumination, which will be given special attention for practical application in Chapter 13. The size of the pattern components and high contrast are the critical factors.

Light and Dark Adaptation of the Eye

The first premise on which all decisions of architectural and lighting design are based is that architecture is not a static art. Following the circulation routes, people experience buildings moment by moment as they move through them. As that happens, the eye goes through its involuntary process of responding and adapting to changing brightness values of successive spaces. We move in and out of dark quarters, as well as in and out of the intense brightness of unfiltered daylight. Sometimes those changes in brightness are severe and occur suddenly, and the eye is forced to adapt accordingly. We

now take up the issue of how the humanistic designer handles those conditions of high brightness-contrast to which human vision must adapt.

Most everyone has experienced the temporary blindness of stepping from a dark movie theater into the bright sunshine reflecting off concrete pavements and neighboring buildings. Having been accustomed to the interior darkness of the auditorium, the eye requires time to adjust to the new brightness levels outside, and undergoes what perceptually is known as *light adaptation*. When the eye leaves the dark and enters bright surroundings, the iris contracts, letting much less light into the retina. If the viewer had been in total darkness for some time, a few minutes are required for adaptation to light.

Departing from a movie theater into the bright sunlight creates a design problem involving space, light, and time. Sometimes people shade their eyes when leaving a theater as a natural reaction to the retina needing to adjust to the brightness of the daylight outside. Here is where the sequence of architectural spaces from theater seat to parking lot should be *programmed with light*. The darkness of the auditorium is a given. The movie on the screen becomes visible like the star in the night sky, as poet Robert Frost said: "Since dark is what brings out your light." The shape and the lighting of the theater lobby is next in importance, because it is a transition zone that can assist the retina in undergoing adaptation to the brightness awaiting outside. Fortunately the lobby generally is the location of a gaily illuminated snack bar and lighted posters of coming attractions, and these provide the intermediate brightness values between the

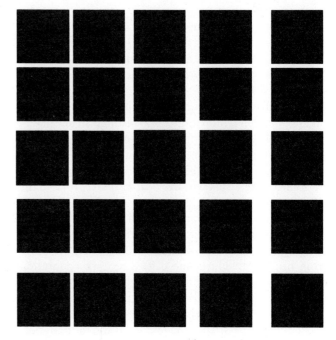

Figure 2-15. Illusion versus grid composition.

---

darkened auditorium and the bright daylight of the street scene. Even the floor dimensions of the lobby come into play, to provide walking time for retinal adaptation. Sometimes the density of a crowd leaving the theater at the end of the movie helps this process by slowing down the pace of the individual. This is not meant to suggest that the architect give inordinate length to the lobby that would require the few minutes of walk necessary for light adaptation to work. The order of the theater's spaces is noted here only to point out that the lighting values are to be sequenced from dark, to middle brightness, to bright daylight, each in turn conforming to the natural process of human vision.

In other buildings transitional zones of intermediate brightness are achieved in a number of ways. The lighting and brightness values of finishing materials used in foyers can help regulate the adaptive process, and so do entrance overhangs and sheltered porches, which provide the last segment of shade for the eyes just before a person walks from the interior into direct sunlight.

Light adaptation is equally a design concern for people entering brightly illuminated interiors from the contrasting darkness of night. Note the luminaires at each side of the entrance shown in Figure 2-16. They accomplish more than just night lighting for the street and attracting attention to the place of entry. From a perceptual standpoint, they increase the brightness of the wall around the door, which otherwise would appear dark by simultaneous contrast caused by the bright interior. For a person entering the building, that area of exterior wall joins with the reflected light on the pavement below and assists the retina as it begins light adaptation to the interior.

When entering darkness after having been exposed to bright light, the eye goes through *dark adaptation,* which in some cases can take about 10 minutes following an abrupt change, and up to 30 minutes or more to completely finish the process. Once the eye has become dark adapted, the fovea is much less stimulated; acuity decreases, making it more difficult to distinguish fine detail. The prolonged dark adaptation time is what hinders some people from finding their way in a darkened theater after entering from the bright outdoors. Only gradually do some of the visual features become perceptible in the darkness of the auditorium.

In most cases, the change from a bright to dark environment is not as extreme as entering a theater. However, in the normal daily routine of entering buildings from broad daylight, some degree of dark adaptation takes place depending on the overall brightness level in the *first* space encountered inside the building. Sometimes the brightness levels of the exterior can be extreme, depending on the orientation of the sun and the materials used for the building's entrance elevation and pavement underfoot, all contributing to retinal adaptation. Figure

Figure 2-16. Lighting for retinal adaptation. [One Portland Square, Portland, Oregon. Architects: Sasaki Associates, Inc. Photograph: © Steve Rosenthal]

C-1 shows the main facade of the West Wing of Boston's Museum of Fine Arts. The proportionally large facade of white Deer Island granite and the aggregate concrete pavement below progressively fill the field of view with high brightness with each step toward the entrance. If the door had been located flush with the facade wall, the change to the interior would have been abrupt and harsh. Instead, the architects penetrated the wall with an entryway, which begins the adaptation process by shading the vision of the entering visitor.

As we move through the lighted environment, whether from light to dark or the converse, the brightness of all objects and surfaces in the extended field of view shifts in appearance according to the state of adaptation of the eye. The intense light of a red "Exit" sign looks extremely bright inside a darkened auditorium, but that same sign may be only moderately visible in the daylighted street outside. The implications of light or dark adaptation offered here are not so much for the lighting design of singular architectural spaces, but for illuminating any space that participates in a sequence of lighted spaces, because the ease or difficulty of light or dark adaptation will determine the visual comprehension, pleasantness, or discomfort experienced by moving from one space into another. The architectural and lighting designer should avoid creating situations where the eye must adapt suddenly to excessive changes of light and dark.

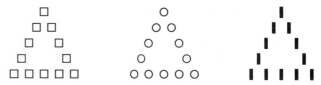

Figure 2-17. Gestalt transposition.

Gestalt Theory and Architectural Design

In the everyday urban environment, the mind is asked to process a myriad of complex visual stimuli such as signs, crowds, traffic, buildings inside and out, reflections, glare, minutiae of detail, and clutter. As part of the human visual perception system there is a dynamic self-organizational tendency to maintain a sense of equilibrium when the eye is confronted with scenes that might be considered *visual overload*. How this perceptual organization takes place intrigued a group of German psychologists in the 1920s and 1930s who sought to explain how the mind was able to "see" order amid all the intricacies and redundancies in the visual world. What they learned has come to be known as Gestalt psychology.

The central theory of the Gestalt process holds that the visual system tends to group perceptual stimuli into organized patterns. This was recognized around 1912 by Max Wertheimer, generally recognized as the founder of the Gestalt school, who became convinced that this process takes place as the human visual system sorts through the collective stimuli of the environment. Wertheimer's research took the lead in developing the theory of pattern organization by the eye and mind. His work was followed in the 1930s by Kurt Koffka (1935), who placed importance on how stimulus elements were organized into the most simple and stable relationships, and laid the groundwork for the formulation of "laws" of perceptual organization. By the late 1930s, Wolfgang Metzger, who has been considered one of the foremost authorities of the second generation of Gestalt psychologists, refined previous theory into what is now known as the *Gestalt "laws" of organization*.

According to Gestalt theory the mind arranges incoming groups of perceptual stimuli by *spontaneous organization*. The organizing of similar stimuli into the most simple relationships creates the opportunity for spontaneity, and gives relative stability to the perceived organized patterns. A "good Gestalt," as psychologists call it, is an organization of parts that is characterized by perceptual simplicity, neatness, and order, and has the smallest possible number of structural features required to form a larger pattern or shape.

Figure 2-17 illustrates Gestalt theory at work. Although made up of different units, each group of symbols is "read" as triangles. That is, the property of the *whole* transcends the shape of the individual parts. The image of the whole is made up of the structural relations of the parts, and the mind sees the group through what is called *transposition*. The squares, circles, and bars are transposed into the larger whole of a triangle.

The Gestalt "laws" of organization that follow were selected from psychology literature for their value in application to the design and criticism of the architectural environment.

Law of Similarity. In a perceptual field, elements that have similar visual characteristics of shape isolate themselves from dissimilar elements and tend to be seen as a set (Figure 2-18a). In the left group of Figure 2-18a, the repeating shapes of squares make them stand out from the circles. It is not necessary, however, for the shapes to be totally different. In the right group, all the elements have the same circular contours, but organize themselves by *similarity* of either hollow circles or circular solids.

The law of similarity has long been commonplace in architecture. In recent times it has been prevalent throughout the industrialized environment largely due to the mass production of standardized parts (Figure 2-18b). All the units in both buildings are geometrically rectilinear, but *similar* characteristics of glass panels, fascias, and precast concrete units immediately organize those three basic elements into distinct perceptual groups.

Law of Proximity. A number of elements that are spatially close together tend to form a subgroup. Figure 2-19a shows configurations of circles belonging to rows, because the spacing between the rows is greater than that between adjacent elements in any one row. Bruce and Green (1991) point out that this law is one of the most important for determining the visual organization of a scene and is a powerful factor for depth perception, where the distance between units closes as a series is seen receding in perspective.

The facade design of Figure 2-19b owes part of its perceptual clarity to the *similarity* of the window bays and structural units, but also to the law of proximity.

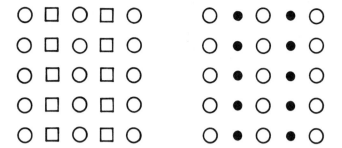

Figure 2-18a. "Law of similarity."

Figure 2-18b. [Photograph: © Paul S. Kivett]

The smaller alternating vertical units group themselves by proximity, because they are not separated too far from each other by the intersecting horizontal fascias. Note how their rhythmic flow (by proximity) continues through each floor, but is abruptly stopped by the broad horizontal bands at the top and below.

Law of Closure. This law states that only segments of a whole are necessary for shape identification, as long as they are organized according to the construct of the shape they tend to represent (Figure 2-20a). Any part of a figure may be missing as long as what is there is enough to clearly close off and complete a familiar pattern. The mind instantly fills in the missing parts. The diagram also illustrates a main tenet of Gestalt

psychology—that the mind seems to need a "whole" to restore a sense of completeness and equilibrium in the presence of incompleteness.

Figure 2-20b illustrates the law of closure in the design of the atrium lounge of a major hotel. Two low circular partitions are interrupted by steps, ramp, and an escalator, but enough of the "circle" is there to give identity to the central lounge. Its space is animated in design by the breaks in the circular partition and by careful placement of the elements that radiate outward from the center. Static symmetry is avoided by the straight low partition that joins the central "circle" at

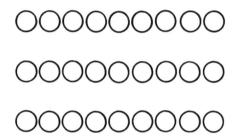

Figure 2-19a. "Law of proximity."

Figure 2-19b.

Visual Perception and Light

Figure 2-20a. "Law of closure."

Figure 2-20b. [Hyatt Regency Hotel, Dallas]

the left; its design behavior as a *line* directs the eye toward a sweep around the circle that the law of closure completes, in "good Gestalt," and in good design composition as well.

Law of Good Continuation. The direction of the pattern illustrated by Figure 2-21a is dependent on the obvious relationship of the elements in the set. The laws of similarity and proximity are also at work. As the name "law of good continuation" implies, the arrangement of the parts is such that the addition of one or more elements of the same kind, or even of a different kind, will continue the serpentine path that has already been established. The Gestaltists claimed, as Bruce and Green (1991, 112) tell us, that this "perceptual organisation will tend to preserve smooth continuity rather than yielding abrupt changes." Note how words like "flow," "stream," "course," "cadence," "progression," "rhythm," "melody," "arpeggio," and even "infinity" all depend on continuity, and contain the principle of good continuation as elements proceed on their way, but we

don't know where they are going until we are given a clue by some part of an organized pattern.

Applied to design, this law helps to hold parts together in a visual flow, and is exceptionally useful for creating and maintaining harmony of elements in spatial composition. This principle is a strong design motif for architecture. Figure 2-21b shows the restaurant of a baseball stadium. In the foreground, the two rows of tables begin a straight line of movement away from the observer. The rows of stadium seats just outside the far end of the room then curve to the left and follow around the stadium in *good continuation*. The outdoor seats just below the restaurant at first parallel the dining tables, but then continue their sweep around the space of the playing field. Tables, seats, and the window mullions, all are different shapes, but when combined with proximity, they assemble in the mind to give stability and harmony to a spatial composition that obeys the law of good continuation. That detailing of the whole provides smooth continuity, where here again "good Gestalt" contributes to good design.

To anyone practicing in any discipline of visual design, the Gestalt "laws" are invaluable working principles for structuring and ordering composition. The obvious needs to be stated: Note how each of the laws is easily visualized, and how each is spontaneously organized in the mind of the viewer. Whenever "style" is used by a designer—classical, Gothic, Victorian, modern, or postmodern—the stylistic details are perceived as visual stimuli in patterns, and will be subjected to Gestalt organization as part of the human visual system. The designer needs to remember this basic human process, which is timeless and to an extent even cultureless, belonging to the natural working relationship between the eye and the mind. Independent of style, any design in which the details are organized to conform with the theme of a greater composition takes advantage of the natural organizing forces endorsed by Gestalt theory. When composed into a meaningful whole—creating "good form"—related parts perceptually organize themselves, and swing the pendulum of design away from confusion and formlessness, and toward equilibrium and order.

It is interesting to contemplate the emergence of Gestalt theory in psychology in the 1930s. Two decades later it was readily appearing in books on art and architecture, most notably by Rudolf Arnheim (1969), and became valuable theoretical support for teaching design. As if following the behavior of modern-day fads and fashions, in recent times Gestalt has appeared less in design literature and the classroom, but not so in scientific research. Humphreys and Bruce (1991) tell us the work of psychologist David Marr showed that light patterns traced in the retina follow a perceptual process of pattern organization similar to the Gestalt "Laws of

Figure 2-21a. "Law of good continuation."

Figure 2-21b. [Kauffman Stadium, Kansas City, Missouri. Photograph: © Paul S. Kivett]

Organization." Considering how Gestalt principles have been pushed into the corner of the art and architectural classroom in recent times, it appears that the attention span of designers has lapsed, whereas the research psychologists have stayed focused on the job.

A certain amount of caution surfaces in an attempt to apply the findings of the research psychologist to design aesthetics and criticism. There is greater intellectual comfort in approaching Gestalt theory through the eyes of the scientist, but to take it further by saying

Gestalt "laws" render design creations as pleasing and satisfying to the human emotions remains an artistic value statement. Nevertheless, those Gestalt laws are good to keep in mind while composing and coordinating elements of design. We live in an urban world where streets are lined with buildings of good and bad design, or of no design, all reflecting the diversified tastes of our pluralistic culture. Moreover, the visual clutter caused by neglect, disrepair, and gaudy overdetailed commercial advertising displays are plentiful in our cities.

Visual Perception and Light

Rejuvenating ongoing urbanization can benefit from adding to the visual environment new and remodeled buildings and other cultural products that *are* pleasing and satisfying. Gestalt laws come to the aid of that mission, in a natural process of human vision. Kreitler and Kreitler (1972, 88–89) tell us those Gestalt laws provide organization that "makes possible an efficient and relatively effortless grasp of information from the external world, and thus provides the basis for orientation in the environment in which we live. As a means of orientation, the perception of gestalts may be assumed to be pleasurable by resolving the tensions of disorientation evoked by chaos." There, precisely, is the value of Gestalt theory for design—benefiting the people who use the products of designers. Quite simply, as the Kreitlers add, "organization in terms of gestalt laws makes for economy in the encoding of information, and allows us to grasp maximum information through a relative minimum of means and effort."

Perceptual Simplicity

The structural properties of any one percept that the eye sends to the mind determine how easy or difficult it is to see what lies before us. The more visually complex the environment, the more difficult it is for the mind to spontaneously organize Gestalt patterns. It has already been shown how the eye responds to edges, caused by the abrupt break in ordinal stimulation (see Figure 2-6). The stronger the impact of detail on a surface, the less is the influence of the surrounding edge. Compare the two rectangles of Figure 2-22. The one at left is perceptually more simplified, because the mind has much fewer stimuli to process than is required for the one on the right. From this we can state the principle: *The simplest surface to see is the one with the smallest amount of detail.* The corollary to this is *the more complex the surface pattern, the weaker the influence of the outer border.* These perceptual principles of object recognition are helpful for determining how shapes and surfaces of

objects resting in space are seen against their backgrounds. This is explained further in Chapter 4.

How much can the human visual system be taxed as it searches for order in a complex scene, and what is easy for it to remember? When it comes to how much information the mind can process and remember easily, George A. Miller (1956) proposed a limit for what he called the "span of absolute judgment," setting the extent of data that can be relatively easy to recall from memory at "the magical number seven." With reference to vision and memory, Miller said the span of absolute judgment "can distinguish about seven categories and that there is a span of attention that will encompass about six objects at a glance." In practice, the spontaneous comprehension of a visual group is demonstrated by Figure 2-23. How many *spaces* are easily read between the vertical lines? Four lines (and obviously less than four) create a three-space pattern that is simple to comprehend. When a fifth line is added, the grouping is altered, but the spaces are still easily picked out as four. Six lines set up five spaces, and once a center one is recognized, it establishes a balance as the remaining spaces instantly conform to a symmetrical pattern. When a seventh line is added, the eye tries to make a "quick read" of the pattern organization just as it does for fewer lines, but finding no simple, recognizable pattern of spaces, it tends to move back and forth among the lines and the mind begins to count. But comprehending the number of *lines* (not spaces) is a different matter. With seven, a centerline can still be found rather easily, and once done, the groups of three on each side of the centerline quickly fall into symmetry. For most people, if the spaces are being sought, six lines appear to be the maximum range for ease of recognition. If the quick search is for lines, seven appear to establish a visual *simplicity comprehension limit.*

For application to architecture, no case is being made here to limit the number of elements in a visual field. The exterior of a highrise can have a composition of hundreds of windows, but, if present, the Gestalt laws of similarity, proximity, etc. can preserve a quality of simplicity and order. It is the increasing number of *different kinds* of elements that begins to bring about visual confusion and is often detrimental to the quality of architectural design.

A critic was dining in a new restaurant and observed that the physical space was structurally ordered, but the total environment appeared visually cluttered. He made a studied count of the prominent interior surfacing materials, which reached 17. All were different, and all competed with each other in color and reflective qualities. A short time later, the critic was at a party where the same restaurant came up in conversation. A young couple complained about the "busy feeling" they experienced from the design of the eating area, and said, "It looks

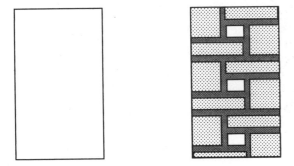

Figure 2-22. Surface simplicity and outline.

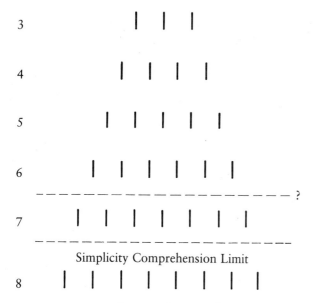

3
4
5
6
7

Simplicity Comprehension Limit

8

Figure 2-23. Simplicity and comprehension.

like a plastic version of a storehouse for a gypsy bazaar." A bystander interjected, "That sounds like my teenager's room!"

Perception of Spatial Depth

Knowledge of the depth cues in visual perception is important for understanding spatial perception, and provides key elements for designing architectural space.

There is disagreement among psychologists regarding the actual number of depth cues (sometimes called "clues"), varying from just a few to about a dozen depending upon the source of information. Those described next are generally agreed on by most authorities, and were selected for their application to the perception and design of architectural space.

1. *Linear perspective.* This is one of the most dynamic of all the cues, and one of the strongest for use by designers. It is sometimes known as *convergence,* and some authorities list both terms independently. When they do so, convergence is the physiological cue to depth, and refers to the angle of vision made by both eyes when fixated on an object, which is inversely related to the distance of the object from the eyes. A geometric definition of linear perspective is the constant distance between two points that subtend a smaller and smaller angle as sets of points recede into the distance. It is most easily visualized as parallel curbs of a straight street or railroad tracks appearing to meet at a "vanishing point" in the far distance.

Figure 2-24 shows the interior of an airport terminal, which at first glance creates a propelling visual move-

ment into the receding space. A number of the depth cues make this happen. The converging lines of the ceiling, service counter, and bases of the piers create exceptionally strong lines of linear perspective that generate a powerful spatial move away from the camera.

2. *Relative size.* When the general physical size of an object has been learned through experience, its distance from the observer is detected by its apparent size. The farther an object is from the observer, the smaller it appears, because it is casting a smaller image on the retina. Note how in Figure 2-24 the gradual reduction of size of the people standing at the service counter and also the diminishing size of the structural piers add to the appearance of spatial depth. Their images are proportionally reduced in retinal size the farther they are down the field of view. When diminishing size combines with convergence of linear perspective, the thrust of visual space becomes exceptionally strong.

3. *Texture gradient.* Seen on a slant, a textured surface forms a gradient. The steeper the slant, the greater the compression of texture. This cue is most effective when the surface has deep texture, such as a stepped brick or stone wall (Figure 2-25). In the far distance, a

Figure 2-24. Depth cues in architectural space. [Des Moines Municipal Airport. Architects: HNTB Corp., Kansas City, Missouri]

Figure 2-25. Loss of texture as depth cue.

textured wall or pavement will appear smooth. This characteristic of gradient is always at work as the eye sees textured walls or other surfaces that are angled in a spatial view.

4. *Superposition.* When one object or surface is overlapped by another, the one with the continuous outer contour appears to be in front, and closer. Figure 2-26 shows the importance of the unbroken outline in principle. In the left diagram, a diamond appears to be in front of a square. But if the "square" is only partial, and its outline coincides with that of the diamond, both figures appear to lie on the same plane. When the partial square is moved to overlap the diamond, it assumes the closer position and shows its true shape. Other terms for this cue are "occlusion," "interposition," and "overlay."

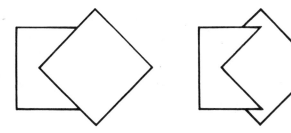

Figure 2-26. Depth by overlap.

Superposition also influences the perception of object size. This is demonstrated by holding one hand straight up at the end of your arm, and the other hand straight up at only half the distance of the other one. Then move the near hand over so that it partially covers the other, and it instantly appears much larger. Move it back and it appears reduced in size.

Observe how superposition conveys spatial depth in Figure 2-24. Each of the people and the structural piers occlude what is behind them. Those people or objects that do not have their peripheral contour broken at all clearly stand in front of what is behind them.

5. *Motion parallax.* In contemporary perceptual theory, this and other cues involving movement of the observer are referred to as "dynamic cues." When the eye is moving, nearby objects in the field of view appear to move at faster speeds than those in the distance (Figure 2-27). While riding in a vehicle, objects just outside the window flash past the eye rapidly, while a tree off in the distance tends to remain motionless. Objects at a middle distance move at half the speed. The same is true for moving through architectural space and passing by furniture or other interior furnishings. Those close to the eye rapidly sweep past in the field of vision.

Parallax conditions also relate to movement of the head. By holding up a finger close to your face while focusing on another finger at arm's length, moving your

Movement of Observer

Figure 2-27. Motion parallax and depth perception.

head back and forth makes the near one shift in position. As the head moves, the leading edges of near objects progressively occlude the scene behind, while trailing edges disocclude the scene. For all their realism, the absence of parallax prevents images on television, movies, still photographs, and computer monitors from conveying the spatial depth that the human eye sees; objects on television screens do not occlude or disocclude what is behind them when the viewer's head moves from side to side.

6. *Angle of location.* The degree of angle that the line of vision makes with a plane horizontal to the ground is a cue for depth perception. An object located in the far distance requires the eye to make little change of angular vision from the horizontal plane, but a sharp downward angle is created when looking at an object resting on the ground near the viewer, or a sharp upward angle for an object located above and near the viewer. Sometimes this cue is called the "angle of regard."

7. *Relative brightness.* We saw from our earlier discussion on gamma movement that brightness advances (see Figure 2-7). When all other cues are equal, the brighter of two objects will appear closer. This is an important depth cue for architectural and lighting designers.

8. *Shadow.* The shadow cast by an object gives information about its distance when it is compared with shadows cast by other objects closer or father away. Surface shadow, or "shading," is also an important cue, which gives the appearance of solidity and the third dimension. An image drawn or painted by an artist will appear flat until given dimension by adding shadow. Cartoons drawn with lines only lack shading and appear flat. The direction of light illuminating an object also provides information about spatial depth. We seem to take for granted that light comes from above, which most of the time it does in the natural and architectural world, so we have learned to interpret the bottom and undersides of an object by the presence of shadow under protruding parts.

As established by the next cue (aerial perspective), light is scattered in the distance, and that breaks up shadow to highlight relationships on objects lying in the far distance. Shadow also relates to size of texture for conveying spatial depth. Even inside buildings, surface detail diminishes on surfaces in the distance, tending to merge the smaller highlights and shadows into a generalized area of brightness. In Figure 2-24, clear shadow details are visible on the woman's clothing in the foreground, but the figures at the far end of the space have lost surface detailing and textural effects.

9. *Aerial perspective.* This term refers to the effects of air on vision. Objects at great distances are seen through haze, resulting in loss of surface detail and color. The presence of fog amplifies this effect, as shown along the Oregon coast in Figure 2-28, where receding outcrops of rock and surf fade from view and vanish toward the horizon. The same happens to buildings and other objects of the urban scene when fog, rain, or snow obscures their surface details and dulls their otherwise crisp outlines. With the loss of highlights, shadow prevails, and under excessive conditions color is obliterated. In *The Mirror of the Sea,* Joseph Conrad described the gray water of the sea in a storm as "lustreless, dull, without gleams, as though it had been created before light itself."

10. *Accommodation.* The lens mechanism of the eye refracts entering light according to the distance away an object lies. When the eyes converge to focus on the object, the lens of each actually changes in physical shape. The eyes do not converge as much when looking at objects in the distance, and consequently are more relaxed. But when they focus at an object nearby, they accommodate to the greater convergence, and the lens actually thickens from the front to the back. The flexibility of the lens in the eye sometimes creates problems, and this is why accommodation is often more difficult for older people, whose muscular control of the lens has grown weaker through aging.

11. *Disparity of binocular image.* This cue is the physiological result of sight with two eyes, and is some-times called *stereoscopic vision.* The retinal image of the right eye is different from that of the left, and the difference between the two gives information about depth. It can be demonstrated by holding a finger about 10 inches from the eye, and focusing on an object across the room with one eye closed. By opening and closing both eyes alternately, the finger shifts in position relative to a distant target. This illustrates how binocular vision is receiving two different views, which are simultaneously coordinated in the brain. The specific views are therefore different for each eye when vision is focused on objects nearby as compared with the two different retinal images of objects seen on the distant horizon.

What the designer of the environment must be aware of is how those cues influence the perception of spatial depth, and how they can be used to change the appearance of architectural space. For practical application to design, review the list of cues as listed earlier. Note how 1, 2, 3, 7, and 8 can be controlled by the designer when shaping architectural space. Number 4 (superposition) possibly could be included, because the designer does have a say about placing some things in front of others, but because people move about freely in their environment, the designer lacks full control over that cue. The remaining cues on the list, 5, 6, 9, 10, and 11, are largely physiological, and although important for spatial vision, they are really out of the designer's jurisdiction. But what is strikingly clear, is that at least *half* of the depth cues can be manipulated by designers to modify the appearance of architectural space as it will be perceived by people using it.

Relative size as it relates to perceptual constancy is a good example of practical application of the depth cues. When Colin Fletcher (1967, 72) hiked the treacherous and (for him) unexplored territory at the bottom of the Grand Canyon, he observed: "A rockface that from a distance looks like something you might have to lift your pack over turns out to be high as a house. As compensation, though, a ledge that promises no more than a handhold may be wide enough to drive a bus along." Fletcher quickly learned to use the *size* of the agave (century plant), which in the Canyon grows to about three feet tall, to provide a "rough-and-ready scale for judging the height of distant rockfaces." Anyone who has experienced the Grand Canyon by hiking to its floor and into its inner canyons knows its vast scale is often deceiving and plays tricks on the mind. The key word regarding size as a depth cue is *relative*. In the vast scale of the Canyon, sizes of agave plants and other natural elements that maintain perceptual constancy do help judging distances and locations. The same is true for the urban environment. Errors regarding relative size are often made by designers or others responsible for select-

Figure 2-28. Atmosphere and loss of detail.

ing components for an architectural environment. Furniture, lighting fixtures, office furnishings, the size of characters used on signage, or wall hangings are too often over- or under-sized for the room they occupy or the exterior they adorn. Working against other natural depth cues, misfit details give a false feeling for the true space of which they are a part. Sometimes those out-of-place details upset the "good fit" of all the parts into a wholesome composition in ways that historically the great masters of design had the talent for creating.

As discussed earlier, linear perspective is an exceptionally strong spatial cue, and can be made forceful or weak by designer's choice. Figure 2-24 makes this point clearly. Intentionally or not, it was a design decision that created the strong linearity in the ceiling and other details that create the powerful perspective lines. The rows of lights also enforce spatial depth. Sometimes the creation of strong perspective lines is inappropriate and can contribute to psychological discomfort. Think of an accident victim in pain and on crutches hobbling down an "apparently long" hospital corridor toward an x-ray room that looks farther away than it actually is. That long corridor might be optically shortened by simply avoiding detailing that emphasizes the linear thrust forward. Visualize how dark, contrasting base moldings or prominent edges created by walls meeting ceilings in high color contrast set up strong perspective lines down a corridor. How many times have raked mortar joints of a brick wall been written into building specifications by office custom rather than by study of what the stronger perspective lines of shadow will do to the perception of spatial depth?

Interrelationships among depth cues relating to the perception of architectural space have been studied by Tommy Gärling (1969; 1970), who found that accuracy of depth judgments of exterior spaces and interior rooms needed full-cue conditions. The designer needs to keep in mind the additive effect of each decision, which builds up until full-cue conditions are reached. At that point, perception of spatial depth is at full strength. Teodor Künnapas (1968) found "with successive increase of the number of perceptual cues, that range and the discrimination of perceived distances increase and improve in accuracy." From studies like these we learn how the architectural environment is perceived. What a challenge it is for designers to shape and proportion architectural spaces when once they are aware of the influence—and counterinfluence—of how the depth cues contribute to the perception of spatial depth.

Visual Fields for the Designer

Considering the intricacies of the human perceptual system as it processes the unlimited amount of visual stimuli that surrounds us in our daily activities, how does the designer contend with those complexities to stay in control of organizing and detailing the surfaces that become the architectural environment? Within one space alone there is obviously a notable difference between the view from any one station point as it compares with spatial percepts made from other locations. All lighted

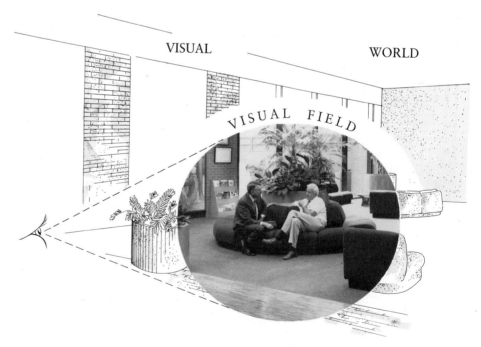

Figure 2-29. Visual fields in the visual world.

surfaces and depth perspectives continually change in appearance as the observer moves from place to place.

To assist visualizing an architectural space as it is being developed and refined, we can borrow from the perception theory of James J. Gibson who distinguished between *visual field* and the *visual world*. The visual world is what architects call the total environment. Gibson (1974, 3) described the visual world as all the solid objects and slanted surfaces seen about us. It is "extended in distance and modelled in depth; it is upright, stable, and without boundaries; it is colored, shadowed, illuminated, and textured; it is composed of surfaces, edges, shapes, and interspaces; finally, and most important of all, it is filled with things which have meaning." The visual world is perceived as the head and eyes move and as the person moves through the environment. It has no center (no central vanishing point) and is panoramic in character.

A single, stop-action view in that visual world is what Gibson called a *visual field*. It is virtually theoretical, because it is difficult to keep the eyes trained in a certain direction for very long. Looking straight ahead with the eyes fixated on a central point, the contents of the field are taken in with a single glance. Unlike the boundless visual world, a visual field has boundaries, although they are not distinct. The scene is "bounded" to contain only what is seen when the head and eyes are fixed in position. From that station point, the field is sharp and detailed at the center, and progressively becomes less detailed and vague outward in peripheral vision until the hypothetical boundaries establish its limits.

The use of a visual field is a good procedural practice to assist the development and refinement of spatial composition. It is mentally moved about from viewpoint to viewpoint in a single room or toward spaces openly connected in sequence. It may be thought of as stop-action or freeze-frame as in motion photography or television. The stopped photographic print or slide is the same idea, but remember, of course, that the camera has no retina and only monocular vision. The visual field provides a mental check, taken at carefully selected positions on a floor plan, in a section drawing, or a stopped frame in a *CAD* perspective sequence. At those station points, the designer *pre*visualizes the shapes of space, and contemplates the effects of light that will take place on the major surfaces in that particular field, seeking answers to perceptual questions such as the following:

- What are the significant depth cues that work from here?

- Will the cues be strong or weak, depending on how surfaces are detailed?

- How have major surfaces changed in perspective shape?

- Where are the dominant connecting edges and contours?

- How would texture appear on this wall, and would it weaken because of slant?

- Where are the light sources as seen from here?

- Are they exceptionally bright, and do they dominate the field of view?

- Have glares been created due to reflections?

- What are the effects of shadows, and do they influence spatial depth?

- How do colors and textures appear on walls due to light quality and direction?

- What is the probable light/dark adaptation of the eye at this point?

- What brightness-contrast is most visible from here?

- What new views open as a viewer looks generally ahead?

- Where would I be prompted to walk from here?

From these rapid-fire evaluations the successive visual fields are assembled into the perceptual visual world, the living spaces of architecture. From station point to station point, the exercise of seeing in visual fields begins to detect design errors and problem areas. Subtleties begin to suggest alternative avenues toward design refinement. If the perceptual problems are solved, the architecture is becoming humanized as spaces are put together.

The visual field is an *elliptical cone of vision*. For Gibson (1974, 27) perception of a visual field encompasses a view that is generally oval in shape, 180° laterally, and 150° vertically (Figure 2-29). This horizontally oriented elliptical view is a natural result of the human being having two eyes, located side by side on a horizontal plane in the head. In later chapters the implications of this biological fact are discussed in relation to the experience of horizontality and verticality of architectural spaces. In traditional architectural practice, however, the cone of vision has been conceived as more narrow, and literature on this subject shows that architects and critics vary in what they believe is the "proper viewing angle" for looking at a building. The cone of vision for architectural design can vary from 60° to 90° on the horizontal, and from 18° to 90° on the vertical, depending on the book in hand. This is confusing to architectural designers. The differences in interpretation stem from personal preference of pictorial view at a station point considered to provide the "best" or "proper" viewing angle. But how often are the users of a building or walkers through a city actually *at* such a key location to see their environment at "the proper viewing angle?" Chapter 4 discusses this delicate issue, taking into account high information stimuli located at the center of attention and in peripheral vision that attracts the eye as a person moves through the built environment.

Although the visual field is generally horizontal, when looking in the direction of any one visual field, the eye adjusts its vertical range. This is caused by the simple fact that the eye lid operates from above the iris. When brightness and/or focus of attention dictate the amount of opening or closing of the pupil (such as lowering the eye lid in conditions of extreme brightness), this automatically changes the vertical dimension of the cone of vision. Because the thesis of this book is predicated on how the eyes see lighted architectural space, the visual field will be taken from the perceptual point of view (i.e., 180° horizontally and 150° vertically).

As a person moves about, the eyes adapt to light and dark, the surfaces that shape space change in relative brightness, depth cues are modified, and object-background relationships shift in architectural space. The construct of a visual field is therefore helpful for the designer, whether at the computer monitor, the drawing board, or using architectural models. In any one field, light sources can be mentally moved about and windows cut in, removed, or adjusted in size to visualize the resulting light effects on the surfaces involved from that one viewpoint. Important edge lines that connect spaces can be given emphasis or diminished by selection of the surface materials that frame spatial views to adjacent rooms. Glares and extreme brightness-contrasts can be eliminated, depending on dominant viewing angles from workstations or along normal circulation routes. In short, the visual field is a spot check for creating *humanized* spaces in architecture and the city.

CHAPTER 3

The Effects of Light

. . . he struck a light—two inches of sallow, sorrowful, consumptive tallow candle, that burned blue, and sputtered, and got discouraged and went out. The porter lit it again, and I asked if that was all the light the clerk sent. He said, "Oh no, I've got another one here," and he produced another couple of inches of tallow candle. I said, "Light them both—I'll have to have one to see the other by."

—Mark Twain
*The Innocents Abroad**

Reflecting off one surface to another and scattering about, light defines our visual world. Once struck by illumination a wall responds with certain effects depending on the quality and quantity of the light itself and the properties of its surface materials. Texture modifies its color, and the angle at which light arrives alters its brightness and so does the viewing angle from which the wall is seen. One of the finest features of light is the shadows it creates, modeling and activating the surfaces around us. Shadows, like highlights, await the designer's artistic touch, to be cast into the environment in a calligraphy of patterned light and shade. When light passes through a translucent medium such as diffused glass or colored liquids, it orchestrates a metamorphosis of substance that the eye long has found appealing. One time Galileo delightfully described wine as "light held together by moisture." Light can be softened for the eye, for instance, when it passes through the paper wall of the Japanese *shoji,* or when it is reflected off a ceiling as indirect illumination. It can be refracted through lenses of luminaires or the images of stained glass to "paint" the environment with artistic patterns of luminance. It can be reflected in brilliance off the intricate facets of cut diamonds and crafted crystal, but also as blinding glare off the gloss and glaze of highly reflective surfaces. These are the effects of light, ranging from the subtle to the powerful, all modulating the mood of the observer, all affecting the quality of the architectural experience and influencing the quality of human life.

In Chapter 2 we looked at the architectural environment the way the eye and mind see it. We now turn our attention to the visual behavior of light. As we do, we need to keep in mind the two means by which architecture is illuminated, either by natural light reflecting on its exterior and interior surfaces, or by adding electric light. We must take precaution, however, when employing that second method, which implies that there exists a physical framework called architecture, and we simply put light into it. Light and architectural space interact, each influencing the other. From the outset we need to alter a traditional or conventional approach to the task of lighting architecture, by formulating a design philosophy that states "Do not design with light, *design with the effects of light.*"

* From Neider, Charles, Ed. 1966. *The Complete Travel Books of Mark Twain.* Garden City: Doubleday & Company, Inc., p. 409.

Illuminance and Luminance

Understanding the behavior and character of light paves the way toward proficiency in designing with the effects of light. Visible light is only a small part of the total energy spectrum from a source. Although emitted in waves as the physicist tells us, for the practical purposes of design, light travels in a straight line until it is reflected, absorbed, or refracted by a surface lying in its path. *Illuminance* (Figure 3-1) is the light energy arriving at a surface at a certain rate. *Luminous intensity* is the amount of light emitted by the source, traveling in a given direction. Intensity of illumination is measured using the unit *candela* (cd), which has replaced the older term *candlepower* (cp).

Illuminance obeys the *inverse square law,* one of the most important characteristics of light for application to design. This law states that the quantity of light arriving at a surface depends on its distance from the source. That quantity varies inversely with the square of the distance between the source and the surface receiving its light. The farther a surface is from a source, the less light it will receive. If the distance between the lamp and surface is doubled, the amount of light reaching the surface will decrease to 25%, or by a factor of 4. The relation between illuminance and distance is easily demonstrated by moving a lamp closer or farther from an object and observing the change in brightness on the object's surface from what it was.

The reflected light that appears on a surface as seen by the eye is *luminance,* and this is one of the most important aspects of lighting for the architectural and interior designer. Technically, luminance refers to the light leaving a surface after it is reflected, but it is used here as the visual appearance of a surface when illumi-nated. Luminance is dependent upon the reflectance quality of the surface material and the amount of illumi-nance it receives.

For application of luminance to design, the essential principle to keep in mind is that *luminance is not affected by a change of distance between a lighted surface and the observer.* An illuminated surface will have the same brightness for two people viewing it from different distances (Figure 3-1). For a person looking at an illumi-nated street poster, its image will have the same lumi-nance regardless of how far away it is, so will the luminance on the background against which the poster is seen. Therefore, from a block away the poster and the wall on which it is attached will appear as bright in relation to each other as they will up close. The appear-ance of the luminance of a surface is therefore a most important characteristic of lighting as the designer com-poses brightness relationships of all the elements in a visual field. Always keep in mind: *Design with lumi-nance; do not design with illuminance.*

Luminance Ratios and Brightness

As illuminance is increased or decreased on an isolated object, its surface will obviously change in brightness compared with its surroundings. In the preceding chapter *brightness* was defined as the appearance of the lumi-nance of one surface as seen in comparison with another (Figure 2-9). To compare two surfaces of different lumi-nance, the term *luminance ratio* is used. Figure 3-2 shows a vase at one luminance (L_1) as seen against a luminance background (L_2). If the vase is given a luminance of 16 cd/ft^2 and the surface behind has a luminance of 8 cd/

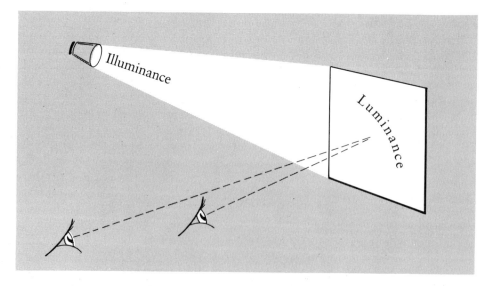

Figure 3-1. Illuminance and luminance.

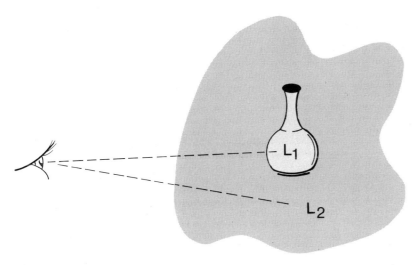

Figure 3-2. Contrast and luminance ratio.

ft², its luminance ratio is 2 : 1. Luminance ratios, however, are not reliable for making design decisions regarding the brightness difference between two surfaces or an object against its background. Studies have shown that there is no correlation between perceived brightness and actual measured luminances.

To see how different luminance ratios compare, return to Figure 2-9, which shows the same middle gray value for the small interior squares compared with the background scale of grays from black to white. That series was exposed to broad illumination in the lighting laboratory to determine the luminance ratios created by the smaller interior squares with their respective backgrounds. Each of the interior middle gray squares was measured at 41.7 cd/ft². Table 3-1 gives the luminance ratios they set up with their backgrounds, given in order from black (position 1) to white (position 7). The background for position 4 is identical to its interior square, which was outlined to make it visible.

Chapter 2 explained that it is simultaneous contrast that makes the interior squares change in brightness as they progress across the series, even though their luminance remains the same. The measured luminance ratios of the sets illustrate that brightness involves perceptual factors other than luminance alone. In seeing three-dimensional objects in the real world, other things influence brightness, such as texture, proportions of highlight to shadow areas, color values, state of adaptation of the retina, etc.

To illustrate how brightness-contrasts relate to luminance ratios, two pieces of sculpture were selected in the Nelson-Atkins Museum of Art in Kansas City. The first is an example of a bright figure seen against a dark background. Figure 3-3 shows an ancient Roman sculpture carved from white marble, which is exhibited against a variegated black marble background and illuminated from above. Graduated luminance readings were taken of the background niche from top to bottom, and averaged to compare with average readings taken on the figure. The average luminance ratio of the white marble figure against its background was found to be 27 : 1.

The second example (Figure 3-4) shows the reverse contrast relationship, this time of a dark figure seen against a brighter background. The large seated Buddha at the Nelson-Atkins Museum is placed on a stair landing in front of a vertically ribbed background. The aged gilding on the figure's surface has lost most of its luster, resulting in its dark appearance. The average luminance ratio of the brighter background to the Buddha was found to be only 2.42 : 1. Looking at the photograph, and at the figure at the site, it would appear that the luminance ratio between the two would be much greater.

Both of these museum sculptures demonstrate that numerical luminance ratios do not truly communicate the perception of comparative brightness. But there are some luminance ratios that serve as helpful starting points for the designer to visualize potential brightness relationships:

Table 3-1. Luminance ratios of Figure 2-9

Position Number	Background Luminance (cd/ft²)	Ratio of Interior Square to Background
1 (black)	4.68	8.9 : 1
2	15.87	2.63 : 1
3	27.02	1.54 : 1
4 (middle gray)	41.7	1 : 1
5	64.46	.65 : 1
6	88.58	.47 : 1
7 (white)	113.0	.37 : 1

Figure 3-3. High-contrast, high-luminance ratio. [The Nelson-Atkins Museum of Art, Kansas City, Missouri]

2 : 1	Easily perceived brightness difference between two surfaces.
3 : 1	Will create a significant focal area in the environment if all other background materials are of similar brightness. For comfort of prolonged task performance, it is also the maximum contrast for a bright paper on the working surface of a desk. (A white sheet of paper creates a 6 : 1 ratio on a teak desk top, and 8 : 1 on a walnut top.)
10 : 1	Will create an exceptionally strong focal area as a dominant visual force in the environment.
25 : 1	Northern clear sky as seen against varnished, nonstained oak window frame. Simultaneous contrast will make the frame appear extremely dark.

Some books on lighting and lighting design give various luminance ratios beyond the 25 : 1 contrast level as limits that should not be exceeded in the visual environment, yet in the everyday world there are numerous examples above that ratio. Recall the marble youth seen against the almost black background in Figure 3-3 as having a 27 : 1 luminance ratio. That contrast draws attention in its museum setting, but is not too bright for the eye to casually examine its details. What many of the luminance ratios in excess of 25 : 1 refer to, especially as high as say 100 : 1, are the light sources themselves and materials reflecting glare. The human eye can tolerate a number of intense light sources in the visual world, but tolerance should not grant liberty for placing excessive brightness contrasts in the built environment. What is important is *where* in architectural space a brightly contrasting element is located, and what is its size in proportion to all the surfaces in the total space. William Lam (1977, 48) stated this succinctly when he said: "Contrary to most current thinking in the field of lighting, high brightness ratios are not inherently undesirable, as long as the eye can perceive and justify the cause of the high brightness ratio. A brilliantly illuminated crystal chandelier is a pleasure to behold, regardless of the high brightness ratios which it may engender in a space."

Other than the 2 : 1 ratio, the luminance ratios listed above apply mostly to strong contrast conditions, but the art of designing with lighted surfaces calls for sensitive control of brightness and color compatibility within lu-

Figure 3-4. High-contrast, low-luminance ratio. [The Nelson-Atkins Museum of Art, Kansas City, Missouri]

minance ratios of a much more narrow range of 3 : 1 and even 2 : 1. For this reason, a Luminance Brightness Rating (LBR) System of building materials is introduced in Chapter 5. Mistakes are made by trying to design with illuminance, which does not take into consideration the nature of surface reflectances of the materials on which it lands. Light reflecting from a surface has been transformed by the material's reflectance quality and color, so by itself illuminance does not provide the necessary latitude to achieve effects of brightness subtleties. Therefore, it is luminance that becomes the most effective aspect of lighting in the hands of the designer. It is luminance that the eye sees. Designing with luminance is designing with the effects of light, and to understand this further it is necessary to examine the properties of reflectance.

Reflectance and Reflections: The Surface Action of Light

Light travels in rays through empty space, and would continue indefinitely unless interrupted by an object. When light strikes a physical material (Figure 3-5), any or all of three surface actions take place: (1) It can be *absorbed* by the surface, normally transformed into heat; (2) it can be *reflected* back into space in a direction other than that from which it came; or (3) it can be *transmitted* (refracted) through a medium to continue onward on the other side. With these properties of light, designing with the effects of light begins.

Figure 3-6 illustrates the surface action of natural light interacting with building materials. Some of the sunlight is *absorbed* by the glass block, making it feel warm to the touch. Some is *reflected* internally and across its surface, creating a visual movement like reflections on rippling water. The glass diffuses the view out (a good design strategy for when the outward view is undesirable), but the remainder of incoming light is *transmitted* through the glass and reflects on the textured brick wall.

Animated effects of light are easily achieved with electric illumination made possible by the numerous designs of luminaires available on the markets. The sunburst patterns in Figure 3-7 are created by incandescent light transmitted through the glass and reflected by the angled facets of crystal globes. The luminaires are mounted just under a projecting surface on which the reflections blaze in decorative radial patterns, fitting for the theater in which they were placed. What a difference there is between making design decisions regarding the luminaire itself or the effects of light it creates. Both look good in the isolated view of this illustration (as lighting fixtures often appear in sales catalogs), but when making choices of products, the designer must ask the question of what does this luminaire do? Where will its light go, and what will its reflections look like? Further, the designer needs to exercise caution when inserting the luminous action similar to Figure 3-7 into an environment that is already decoratively patterned by other surface designs, creating competition among too many design elements in proximity, and thereby creating a perceptually complex scene.

Not all the light that strikes an opaque surface is reflected back into space. Even in the case of high-gloss mirrored surfaces, a small amount of light is absorbed into the material itself. *Reflectance* is therefore defined as the percentage of incident light that bounces back into space after striking a surface. A perfectly reflecting surface would reflect 100% of the light reaching it, but that rarely exists in the visual world. A good white reflects about 85% of the light it receives. Even the darkest, flattest black surface still reflects about 4%. Most people would perceive a surface as "black" when it reflects up to 10%, and a very dark gray reflects only about 14%. Between 14% and 85% lies the continuum of reflecting grays and equivalent color values.

Reflectance does not change when the amount of illumination changes. The ratio of light absorbed by and reflected off a surface is the same percentage of the arriving incident light whether the illuminance is increased or decreased. For a polished aluminum nameplate (reflectance 60%) attached to a mahogany wooden door (reflectance 10%), the ratio of reflectance will be 6 : 1 regardless of the quantity of light arriving to illuminate both surfaces.

For purposes of developing architectural space and light theory that this book promotes, a distinction needs to be made between two different grades of surface texture before proceeding with an analysis of how surfaces

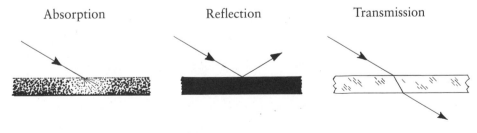

Figure 3-5. Surface action of light.

Figure 3-6. Animation effects of light. [Photograph: © Paul S. Kivett]

Figure 3-7. Light patterns by design. [Ordway Music Theater, St. Paul. Architects: Ben Thompson & Associates. Photograph: © Steve Rosenthal]

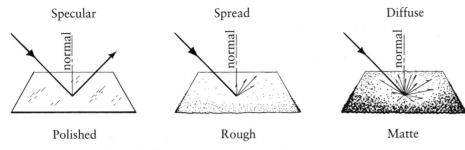

Specular   Spread   Diffuse

Polished   Rough   Matte

Figure 3-8. Quality of reflectance.

reflect light. We first need to examine the nature of light reflecting off materials at a *microscale,* those that are more two dimensional and are characterized by smooth or only slightly textured surfaces. In most lighting books, that kind of reflectance is illustrated similar to Figure 3-8. Examples include the relatively smoother surfaces of many building materials such as glass, plastic laminates, finely cut and polished stone, smooth and brushed metals, sanded woods, painted smooth surfaces, and fine to moderately textured vinyls and wall fabrics.

The *macroscale* of surface texture includes those materials that emphasize the third dimension of a surface, which visibly interacts with light to produce prominent highlights and shadows. That group includes a range beginning with wall fabrics and vinyls that have deep indentations and protuberances, runs through those surfaces of still greater dimensionality such as architectural concrete, stepped brick walls, and on upward in relief to include a building facade dominated by balconies. The reason for making this distinction of macro surfaces is not so much how they reflect light, but how they cast shadow. As we will see later, it is the shadow effects of texture that are important for surface definition and brightness. In reality, microscale surfaces also cast shadows, but they do not dominate. Even smooth glass will appear as pebbled on the surface if seen through a microscope or in microphotography. But the eye perceives flat glass as a very smooth surface, sometimes reflecting glare. Macroscale surfaces and their accompanying shadow effects can be used to articulate the surfaces of architectural space, as Chapter 8 shows.

For microscale surfaces of less textured building materials, Figure 3-8 illustrates the three types of reflectance that are conventionally used in the lighting field: specular, spread, and diffuse. A highly polished surface lacking texture is said to have the quality of *specular* reflection, where very little incident light is absorbed, and the far greater percentage is reflected back into space on the same side of the surface. The most obvious example of this condition is the mirror, but also to be mentioned are other materials that have good but slightly less perfect image reflecting capability. These materials include smoothly polished or anodized aluminum, nontextured glass and plastics, chrome, polished marble, porcelain,

and gloss enamel paints. On such surfaces, a law of physics states that the angle of incident light is equal to the angle of reflected light. Those angles are measured with reference to a theoretical plane called the *normal* (Figure 3-8), which is perpendicular to the illuminated surface. Depending on the observer's viewing angle and the angle of the reflected light, specular reflection can easily cause intense glare.

A rough or partially textured surface creates *spread* reflection. This refers to surfaces on which the incident light rays are only moderately disturbed (spread), and are thus incapable of reflecting mirror-like images. Examples of such surfaces are those that are etched, brushed, burnished, or sand blasted. The irregularities create micro highlights on the surface, and although almost unnoticeable, minuscule shadow detail is introduced. For centuries artisans have used this quality of reflectance by roughening surfaces by sanding or burnishing to create a desired sheen or to soften glaring reflections.

When a surface is textured enough for shadow to play a stronger role in its visual appearance (although still micro in scale), *diffuse* reflectance is taking place. Materials of this kind are more coarse grained or granular, and any ray of light striking one of the protruding surface particles or crystals follows the law of the angle of incidence equaling the angle of reflectance, and hence some of the spread rays are reflected back in the direction of the incident light (Figure 3-8). Diffuse reflectance thus scatters light in all directions and creates a matte surface. On these surfaces tiny pockets of shadow are larger and more abundant, and highlights are proportionally less than in spread reflectance. Flat paints, unfinished white plaster, porous unfinished woods, concrete, and rough bricks are all good examples of diffuse reflectance.

Two or all three of these types of reflectance (specular, spread, or diffuse) can coexist on the same surface of many contemporary architectural building materials. Numerous conditions also exist where all three are found individually on different materials in the same environment. With the ongoing introduction of newly developed materials, these types of reflectance are helpful guides for the designer to stay in control of the appearance of

Figure 3-9. From ceiling to floor and back. [CIGNA Corp., Bloomfield, Connecticut. Architects: The Architects Collaborative. Photograph: © Steve Rosenthal]

surfaces that will ultimately render brightness differences in the composition of architectural space.

Where light goes after it is reflected is important for lighting architectural space. Figure 3-9 shows the employee's lounge of a corporation, where the total space of the room is illuminated by a method that is not at first obvious. Light sources are recessed in the ceiling, and their light descends to reflect off two major surfaces below: the tables and the carpeted floor. On the return trip to the coved ceiling sections, it reflects again, this time on fabric, creating a soft luminance in the field of view. The total ceiling area of the space is therefore not dominated by the intense brightness of the light sources themselves.

The design potential of the surface action of light is enormous. In the hands of the competent designer it is converted from reflectance, to reflections, to art. The space of the small court in Figure C-2 is defined by only three exterior walls and the lawn in front. In the center is a magnolia tree whose presence is heightened not only by its full bloom, but by the fact that the building materials shaping the space were kept to a minimum: grass, brick, and glass. The conoid glass wall behind the tree receives the sunlight that is concluding its 93,000,000 million mile journey and transmits some of it to the building's interior; but the glass wall also reflects a pattern of hourglass images that gradually move across the

wall on the right as directed by the sun. Compare this photograph with Figure 3-7. The principle is the same: Light is reflected into patterned reflections. In both instances, the effects of light became art.

In the Shadow of Light

An object lying in the path of illumination not only redirects the rays of light by surface reflectance, but creates the phenomenon that lies at the basis of visual perception and artistic representation: shadow. When struck by light, the object itself is instantly modeled in dimensionality and solidity by shadows affixed to its surface, and simultaneously casts a shadow on other surfaces that it blocks from the oncoming light.

When that light returns and strikes our surroundings, it creates two kinds of shadow: attached and cast. The inclination of an object to the source of light determines which faces or facets receive direct light, while others receive various degrees of indirect light reflected from other surfaces in the proximal environment. The surfaces facing away from the light source and receiving indirect illumination are said to have *attached shadow* (Figure 3-10). The angle or corner separating one face that receives direct light from another delineated by attached

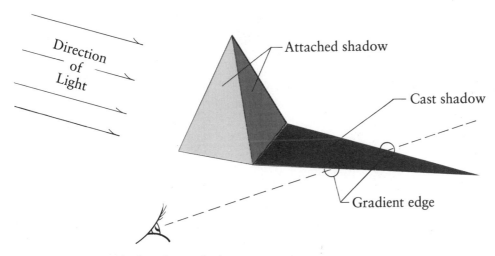

Figure 3-10. Attached and cast shadows.

shadow produces an exceptionally strong edge as perceived by ordinal stimulation in the retina. Borders between nearly all other shadowed faces are still effective communicators of change of inclination to light no matter how slight the difference of angle might be. Research has shown that at very low ratios of reflectance between two adjoining surfaces, even as small as 1%, that difference is still enough for the human eye to perceive the presence of an edge. In the case of undulating surfaces such as on curved areas of sculptures or the human body, where sharp edges are absent, the gradual change from highlighted to shadowed regions imparts the feature of contours.

A *cast shadow* is one that an object throws on another surface as the former stands in the path of light. When cast shadows are crisp, they provide perceptual information for spatial depth in a number of ways. As objects diminish in size as they recede in space, so do their shadows, providing an additional reference for distance away from the eye. The lines of shadow are subject to the laws of perspective just as the lines of tangible things in the environment. The difference of visible detail inside and outside the shadow also provides information for depth perception. Just as under low illumination, those details lying in shadow cannot be brought into focus easily, so the lesser detail inside the shadow compared with that outside combines to convey spatial depth of the scene. Another perceptual quality that relates to shadow is surface gradient. As Figure 3-10 illustrates, the line of vision from the eye across an area on which a shadow is cast forms a gradient, along which dramatic edges of shadows are signaled to the brain.

Probably no other artistic element is more responsible for the animation of art and architectural design than the combination of light and shade. Shadows are created by the simple act of placing an object in the path of the light source, but the affinity between object and shadow it casts gives still greater importance to the de-

sign quality of whatever it is that casts the shadow. A glance back at Figure 2-13 shows how the roof trellis of a pergola casts patterns of shadow on the pavement below, animating the pathway down the terraces. It becomes a different space on an overcast day, when the shadows are removed. The principle of designing with the effects of light can now be expanded to include its corollary: design with the effects of shadow. Skylights over interior courts or atria need to be designed for more than just meeting structural requirements—they need to be designed for the shadows they cast. In those shadows, people walk and are subjected to good or bad shadow design. In his stimulating book *In Praise of Shadows*, Juníchiro Tanizaki reminds us of the elegance and life-relatedness that shadows can bring to the built environment, which for centuries has been so skillfully manipulated by the Japanese. "The quality that we call beauty," says Tanizaki (1977, 18), "must always grow from the realities of life, and our ancestors, forced to live in dark rooms, presently came to discover beauty in shadows, ultimately to guide shadows towards beauty's ends."

Texture as Surface Definition

In the preceding discussion of reflectance, the distinction was made between the microscale of texture that applies to the relatively flat surfaces of most common building materials and the macroscale of texture, which is better used for critiques of architectural form and space. The macroscale of texture on objects or entire walls gives the greater dimensions of architecture a dimensional pattern made up of distinct units repeated regularly or randomly, and a surface is therefore characteristic of those units.

Texture and brightness accompany one another. The light that falls on a highly textured surface brings out rich contrasts of highlights and shadows, and the relative

Figure 3-11. Brightness related to texture.

size and density of the units raise or lower brightness according to the proportional effects of shadow. This is illustrated by the three panels of varying texture shown in Figure 3-11. The one on the right was slightly surfaced with sand, the center with crushed granite, and the left with an aggregate of marble chips. All three were sprayed at the same time with the same neutral gray paint. The influence of texture is dramatic. The three different values of gray (as with any other color) shift in brightness significantly.

In addition to the aspect of gradient, experiments have shown that the size of the units of texture figures prominently in the perception of slant and consequently spatial depth. H.E. Gruber and W.C. Clark (1956) tested individuals for their perception of variously textured surfaces, and slant judgments were shown to have been affected by the size and density of the units, as well as the viewing distance between the viewer and the surface. The researchers determined that depth judgments were most accurate when the surface was composed with the largest unit elements and the coarsest texture, and when seen from the closest viewing distance. This perceptual feature of texture often has application to real-life situations. As a visual device for determining scale, texture was used by Colin Fletcher (1967, 64) while hiking in the Grand Canyon (Figure 3-12). He was well aware of the influence of texture and size on the perception of distance:

You know too that your eye is suffering another illusion. An illusion of space and texture. For the Esplanade is above all a land of textures. Of textures and colors. You live under a smooth blue sky. Raised white clouds scurry across it. Off to the left your world is bounded by fine-grained cliffs, white and far away. Below them curves burlap talus. Then the red rock begins. First, as fine-grained as the cliffs. Then, when distance no longer hides the whole truth, coarsening. And finally, in the last half mile, slashed and fissured and crumbled into a chaos of ledges and clefts and massive boulders. And this final close-up reveals how smoothly the distant textures have lied.

The composition of different textural effects is interesting for the way it defines form and space, whether in the immensity of the Grand Canyon or on faces of the smaller gifts of Nature. The asteroid seastar (*Asteroidea*) shown in Figure 3-13 illustrates how various grades of texture respond to the arrival of light, lively articulating its countenance. The protruding spinal bosses cast the strongest shadows away from the direction of light. It is their larger size and that of their shadows that dominate the overall surface and create visual activity along the periphery of the star-shaped form. The myriad of tiny pits (hydropores) gives microtexture to the surface. The cell-like groups in which they are clustered vary in degrees of shadow, which modulate the surface contours and suggest the very movement of the former living organism.

Shadowed texture also gives visual "weight" to form, a design aesthetic particularly applicable to architecture. We have seen that a minimal amount or no texture can yield sheen or even glare to a surface, and when an entire wall lacks texture it tends to appear lightweight. At the other extreme, a heavily textured wall (with its proportionally greater shadow) will appear heavy. This latter effect has continually appeared in Western architecture, which critics and art historians refer to as "heavy at the

Figure 3-12. Texture and spatial depth. [Grand Canyon, Arizona]

base." That design quality visually anchors a building to the ground, giving it a sturdy base as support for its vertical rise. The artistic weight that shadow creates was well known by European Renaissance architects who varied the texture of exterior stone walls to achieve ef-

Figure 3-13. Texture defining surface undulation.

fects of visual weight or weightlessness. The Palazzo Medici (Figure 3-14) in Florence, Italy, was given a heavily textured (rusticated) exterior wall on the lowest floor, medium texture on the middle floor, and a smooth upper floor capped by strong shadow under a projecting cornice. With this textural composition the building appears firmly planted on the ground, lightens as it rises, and then is suddenly stopped by the dark shadowed edge of the cornice. The theory of this visual weight by texture can also be observed by turning Figure 3-11 on either side.

Islamic architects were masters of the art of texturing architectural surfaces. Figure 3-15 shows the Court of the Myrtles in the Alhambra at Granada, Spain. What a design decision it was to texture the panels over the arches at the end of the court. The delicately carved stucco ornament was given a small size of unit that creates a feeling of lightness, particularly important considering the proportional size of the slender columns supporting the arcade. Compare that stucco pattern with the size of the rusticated masonry blocks conveying the heavy base of the Palazzo Medici in Figure 3-14. It is not the building material (stucco versus stone) that communicates the difference of visual weight between the two buildings. It is the size of unit texture, plus shadow. Now compare both buildings with the texture of the seastar of Figure 3-13. The pitted surface of the seastar is a more soft surface, like the carved stucco of the Alhambra, and the larger spinal bosses add visual strength to the form,

Figure 3-14. Shadow and visual weight. [Palazzo Medici, Florence, Italy]

Figure 3-15. Composing texture in space. [Court of the Myrtles, Alhambra, Granada, Spain]

like the rusticated base of the Palazzo Medici. Keeping the size of texture in mind, the Alhambra's Court of the Myrtles' design harmony arises from the fact that texture was not applied indiscriminately, but was used spatially, taking advantage of "the effects of light." Note the narrow band of roof tiles above the arcade. The tiles are also small in unit size. Also note the decoration on the wall under the loggia. The diagonally laid tiles give that strip of wall a reading of texture at a unit size that harmonizes with the texture of the myrtle hedges along the pool, the stuccoed panels of the arcade, and the roof tiles above. Another key decision was to texture the elegant entry arch in the foreground. Its units also are proportioned in size to the scale of decoration used throughout the court, and welcomes the entering visitor like an operatic overture.

We have been analyzing texture mostly from the standpoint of how it generates expressiveness of building materials or the surface planes of architecture. Choice locations in a building may call for a greater role for texture, beyond the mere patterns of building materials, to employ the surface action of light to define sculptural art. Recalling the days of ancient Egypt and Babylonia,

bas-relief brick sculpture is once again enjoying popularity, advanced and promulgated by the Brick Institute of America at Reston, Virginia. Figure 3-16 shows the entry foyer of a clay products company where the textural art of sculpture greets the visitor to the building. Jack Curran's 8-ft × 8-ft brick art "Double Eagles with Fish" is illuminated by electric light from above and daylight through a floor-to-ceiling glass entrance wall, and light acts on the relief surface that elevates an ordinary brick wall to meaningful art.

Glare

The effects of light are not always comfortable for human vision. An excessive amount of light cannot be tolerated by the human eye. If an extreme amount reflects off a smooth surface and is angled directly toward the eye, the abusive quality of *glare* is produced. At some time or another most people have experienced the extreme discomfort of looking into oncoming headlights while driving at night, or walking in the direction of blinding sunlight reflecting off snow or water, or walking down a dimly lit corridor toward a window framing a brilliant rising or setting sun. It is difficult if not impossible to focus on a given task performed on a highly pol-

Figure 3-16. Texture as surface art. ["Double Eagles with Fish." Sculptor: Jack Curran. Endicott Clay Products Office, Fairbury, Nebraska]

ished tabletop that reflects a bright light overhead. These are conditions of glare, causing people to shield their eyes, squint, or look away, and prohibiting the eye from functioning at full efficiency.

Glare is produced in the interior of the eye. When the observer has been subjected to darkened surroundings, the iris is wide open. At that time, any sudden and direct light enters freely, is scattered about the eye's interior, and casts a photochemical veil over the retina. This interferes with the previous dark adaptation, and reduces contrast for the retinal image of an object on which the eye is trying to focus. Glare is a greater problem for the elderly, because the eye becomes increasingly more sensitive to glare as a natural part of aging.

The lighting industry and visual perception psychologists distinguish among different types of glare: blinding, disability, and discomfort. When the amount of light is excessive and comes to the eye at an angle close to the line of vision, the veiling of the retina reaches extreme proportions, and totally reduces visibility. This condition is defined as *blinding glare,* caused by light being so intense, and for an appreciable length of time, that objects cannot be seen at all.

The state of *disability glare* occurs when the retinal veiling makes object visibility nearly impossible, and greatly reduces visual task performance. It is disability glare that occurs during night driving, when the beams of oncoming headlights reach the eye and veil the retinal

images formed by the prior field of vision. This condition limits discrimination of surface details on the surrounding roadway and becomes a major cause of accidents. Disability glare also is experienced when departing from a dark movie theater and intense sunlight is reflected into the eye off automobiles or other highly polished surfaces.

When glare is disturbing to the observer, but not severe enough to prevent visual performance, it is called *discomfort glare.* This occurs when the light source or its reflected light in the field of view is intense, but does not create the extreme brightness contrast as that produced by blinding or disability glare. In the interior architectural environment, discomfort glare is most often caused by lighting fixtures that appear excessively bright in the visual field. Other examples include high light levels of exposed bare filament lamps and unshielded luminaires seen in high contrast against a dark ceiling; views toward a brilliant sky framed by a window in a darkened wall; a bright window glaring off a highly reflective corridor floor or stair landing; or highly polished surfaces or objects that reflect bright light into a task performance area. The closer any such glare is to the line of sight, the more the observer will experience discomfort glare.

It is sometimes questionable as to what constitutes glare and what are the lesser reflections that are a normal part of the visual world. There is obviously a line between the physiological limitations for vision that accompanies blinding, disability, and discomfort glare and the undisturbing reflections that are normative for the architectural environment. Sometimes glare is only temporal in the field of view for a person walking from one place to another. Such are the glaring contours at the top of the columns on the right side of the corridor in Figure 3-17. The photograph, however, is somewhat misleading. It is the chemistry of film that makes them more glaring in the photograph than they are at the actual site. The linear highlights on the floor are not as intense as those on the columns, because the flooring material has less percentage of reflectance. If the light sources in the corridor were exposed to view, they would create glaring, mirrored images of themselves on the polished floor. Decisions for design of such spaces involve a trade-off between the quality and placement of light sources and the materials that will reflect their light.

The bottom line statement about glare is that its control is essential for the ergonomics of architectural and interior design and for the creation of an overall humanized environment. When bright light sources in the visual field are less visible, and the surfaces surrounding the light sources are reduced in luminance contrast with the source itself, glare will be reduced. Most overhead manufactured light sources that are located for task performance are very bright. A reduction of their contrast with surrounding surfaces might suggest that all ceilings should not be dark in appearance. This need not always be the case. When interior design choices require high-intensity light sources, yet ceilings or any other background surfaces should be dark in luminance, glare can be mitigated by keeping the luminaires proportionally

Figure 3-17. Reflections versus glare.

smaller in unit size relative to the total ceiling area, and also by selecting luminaires that are sufficiently recessed or screened to prevent the lamps themselves from appearing excessively bright in the visual field. The spatial distribution of luminance—designing with the effects of light—is a continual challenge for the designer, who needs to introduce light into the environment and at the same time eliminate the problems of light.

Brightness and the Angle of Slant

We have seen how the amount of texture and shadow on a surface determines its level of brightness, but that assumes it is seen from a stationary viewing point. When that surface is seen from different viewing angles of slant, its brightness changes. That happens because the surface is perceived as a textural gradient (recall Figure 2-25), and seeing it at a steeper and steeper angle compresses the surface texture, and less shadow is visible in areas farther down the viewing plane.

It is a different situation, however, when a surface changes in angle to the light source. A glance around a room whose walls are all painted the same color or surfaced with the same material will show how the brightness of a surface is dependent on its angle of slant to the arriving illumination. The effect of a surface slanted to the direction of light is illustrated by Figure 3-18, which shows three Kodak Neutral Test Cards photographed under controlled light conditions. The three were positioned at different angles to a light source, and no other lights were on in the room. The camera takes the place of the viewing angle of the observer. As the photograph demonstrates, brightness depends on the orientation of the card to the direction of illumination.

The three Neutral Test Cards differ in brightness dramatically, but that is because there was no other light in the room. This is obviously not the case with surface planes in the day-to-day architectural world. In interiors especially, light tends to come from a number of sources, much in the form of reflected light off other objects and surfaces. That reflected light is known as *ambient light*. The word *ambient* means surrounding or encompassing. If the three cards were subjected to additional light sources, and surrounded by other light-reflecting surfaces, they would change in brightness as they receive ambient light. They would also change in brightness levels relative to each other.

The architectural and lighting designer needs to develop proficiency for predicting how illumination will determine the visual appearance of surfaces shaping the human habitat. There are specified reflectance percentages of building materials published in texts and manufacturers' literature that serve as design references and also color value measurement references (e.g., Munsell

Figure 3-18. The influence of slant on brightness.

notations). But once a surface is located in space, it is slanted toward direct and ambient light, and will take on a particular level of brightness accordingly. So if brightness is to become a significant factor in the design and composition of illuminated architectural space, as we shall see in the remainder of this book, using specified reflectance alone will not predict how bright a surfacing material will look in the context of architectural space. But before we can design space, and illuminate space, we must have additional help in making those predictions of brightness, and this is done in Chapter 5.

Transformation of Space by Reflected Light

The reflective surfaces of the dominant boundaries of architectural space are most important in terms of how a space is perceived. Choices of building materials and the locations of light sources can significantly transform the finished space from the design that had been conceived. Sometimes surfaces of high reflectance can illusionistically shift the physical relationships of spatial boundaries once the environment is illuminated and the surface action of light goes to work. Under certain conditions, light and reflections become modifiers of the "real" space, and reshape it into a different view that the observer actually sees.

Figure 3-19a shows a corridor leading to executive offices of a major insurance firm. The wall surfaces of the corridor are modular panels that provide access to spaces and storage behind. The panels were surfaced with light-colored Formica, which produces a sheen that

gradually increases in mirror effects down the length of the space. The contrasting brightness of the distant perpendicular wall and the colorful painting reflect off the Formica, and nearly dissolve the actual spatial boundaries near the end of the corridor. The impressionistic reflections extending deeply into the walls transform the space by breaking up what otherwise would be an unembellished and commonplace corridor. The corridor walls actually become art in this merger of painting and architecture.

The effect of transformation adds spaciousness to the corridor, which is further enhanced by reflections of the recessed down lights on the corridor walls, twice on each side. Carpet on the floor prevents further (and unnecessary) reflections in the visual field, and saves the space from visual overload. The perspective view down the corridor is spatially interesting for its interchange with the sitting area at the end. The converging lines of the corridor ceiling lights and the dark linear recesses where the walls meet floor and ceiling create strong spatial movement toward the focal climax: the painting. But much of the effect is relative to the position of the viewer. The brightness of the walls increases in the peripheral vision of the viewer with each step forward, gradually providing light adaptation for the retina. By the time the end of the corridor is reached (Figure 3-19b), the eye has been prepared for the brightness that comes next, making a pleasant and humanistic transition from dim corridor to the brighter executive offices.

There are times when illusionary effects of space and light are so subtle, and so intriguing, that they create pleasant surprises awaiting the perceptive eye. This occurred at Thorncrown Chapel at Eureka Springs, Arkansas. Figure 3-20 shows the glass wall on the right side of the nave, where a natural mirror condition occurred when the architecture and a portion of the site came together causing illuminated crosses to glow in the dark terrain outside the chapel. The clear glass of the nave wall in front of the terrain created a natural mirror condition. Reflections are seen of the specially designed cross luminaires that line the nave on the opposite wall. They hover like an apparition in the darkness of space, and the effect is mystical. Enchantingly spiritual. Was it planned? No. The crosses were discovered when the glass was installed. Both architects Fay Jones and Maurice Jennings admit it was as much a surprise to them as it is to visitors today. While they were "trying to accomplish other things" in the design of the chapel, the cross reflections "just happened," and Thorncrown is all the richer for it.

For centuries landscape architects have exploited the use of water for the aesthetic and psychological effects of its reflective qualities. The 'floor' of a space formed by a reflecting pool disappears when mirroring the environment behind it or overhead. As shown earlier in the

Figure 3-19a. Reflections transforming space. [American Republic Insurance Company, Des Moines. Architects: SOM, New York]

Figure 3-19b. Spatial transition by reflected light. [American Republic Insurance Company, Des Moines. Architects: SOM, New York]

Figure 3-20. Reflected images hovering in space. [Thorncrown Chapel, Eureka Springs, Arkansas. Architects: Fay Jones and Maurice Jennings]

Figure 3-21a. Potential enlargement of urban space. [Williams Square, Irving, Texas. Architects: SOM, San Francisco]

Figure 3-21b. Urban space enlarged. [Williams Square, Irving, Texas. Architects: SOM, San Francisco]

Alhambra's Court of the Myrtles (Figure 3-15), the spatial effect is doubled when the surface of the water is perfectly still, which it is most of the time because of the enclosing walls blocking out the wind. The appeal of water reflections has been common to many cultures worldwide. The mirroring effect of reflected light on water's surface has been a hallmark of the traditional Japanese water garden, which demonstrates how quiet water becomes a superb design feature for creating a tranquil habitat conducive to contemplation and peace. The water is at rest. The mind finds repose in its stillness. When wind or spray from a fountain ripples the water, it becomes textured, and the scattered light joins to create an impressionistic rendition of what is reflected when the water is still.

Williams Square in Irving, Texas (Figure 3-21a), offers a large-scale example of the influence of reflecting water on urban space. The building facades are the dominant boundaries shaping the space of the public square. The small lake in the foreground of the picture lies about a block away from the site. At the time the photograph was taken, an energetic wind was sweeping across the water, whose moving surface gives only faint reflections of the square in the distant view. Overnight, a calming of the wind and direct sunlight transformed the actual space into what is shown in Figure 3-21b. The quieted water doubles the shape of the space by illusion. Direct sunlight and the smooth water sharpened the reflections,

replacing the diffused images that were there the day before. Notice how the square appears closer in Figure 3-21b than in Figure 3-21a. This happens because of a perception of the buildings' surfaces where gamma movement causes brightness to advance, and also because the reflected crisp and clear images of the buildings are now virtually at the feet of the observer.

The transformation of space by reflections that create illusions is an intriguing design technique, but also brings up a delicate and timely issue. The popularity of reflective glass and metallic surfacing materials that has persisted since the mid-twentieth century has resulted in a proliferation of mirroring surfaces in the urban environment. Unfortunately, that practice oftentimes has doubled the views toward traffic congestion or undesirable sections of the city, like gaudy displays of rampant commercialism in the form of tasteless advertising signage and the cluttered visual residue of misguided business ventures. Often this happens as a result of "selecting building materials in the abstract," which means that a building's exterior gets covered with a reflective material for the only reason that it is fashionable or has esoteric value to the design firm or client. That abstract decision fails to take into consideration how the building will relate to its urban surroundings, and the images it reflects will be those of the tawdry and the impoverished, instead of the beautiful "effects of light."

CHAPTER 4

Seeing Form-Space Relationships

. . . in looking at an object, we reach out for it. With an invisible finger we move through the space around us, go out to the distant places where things are found, touch them, catch them, scan their surfaces, trace their borders, explore their texture. It is an eminently active occupation.

—*Rudolf Arnheim*
*Art and Visual Perception**

To isolate space as a component of architecture is advantageous for design analysis, but by itself is incomplete for a visual study of the built environment. Under normal living conditions, it is rare for spatial enclosures to be experienced without the infill of interior furnishings. Offices, sales rooms, lobbies, and living rooms may be initially conceived as empty shells, but as viable constituents of the human habitat they become complete only with the inclusion of their contents—the life support equipment that fills those spaces. A room's enclosing walls or partitions, therefore, are rarely perceived as singular experiences, but are most often interrupted by occluding furniture, office equipment, sales counters, or display cases. To facilitate a more tenable approach to the design and lighting of architectural space, consideration needs to be given to the interrelationship between freestanding objects and their enclosing spatial boundaries. For this reason, the study of architectural space must include the perception of *forms in space.*

* From Arnheim, Rudolf. 1969. *Art and Visual Perception.* Berkeley: University of California Press, p. 33.

The Perception of Form

Searching through books on design theory, aesthetics, and visual perception for definitions of *form* and *shape* confirms the fact that there is little agreement among designers, art critics, and psychologists as to how either word should be used or to what situation either should be applied. Some speak of buildings or furniture as having form; others speak of their shape. The word *form* is used here to designate three-dimensional material objects resting or moving in the free volume of space. As it relates to object perception, the definition of *shape* is reserved to designate the peripheral contour of the object, and to define any two-dimensional configuration of a surface, such as one side of an object. We may speak of the triangular *shape* of a facet on the *form* of a diamond or one side of a pyramid. The term *shape* will also be used to define the composition of the peripheral boundaries that establish the enclosure of architectural space. A room has shape, but a table in the room has form.

Lighting plays a critical role for form perception. Under weak illumination, the all important outer edge (or shape) of an object may be all the information that the eye is able to send to the brain, and surface texture may not be visible at all. But as illumination is increased, details of outer contour and surface become more visible, and consequently the object is more comprehensible. The murex shell in Figure 4-1 was illuminated and photographed to dramatize its form, and to illustrate the theory of edge and surface perception. Seen against the prevailing darkness, brightness contrast makes its irregular outline crisp and sharp, giving it instant identity as a former inhabitant of the sea. Most of the outer contour shouts in brilliant white, but note the upper right portion of the shell that is cast in shadow. There, the eye sees no surface detail on the shell, but the protruding edge of a single spine appears as a darkened silhouette by its contrast against the only visible light in the entire background, and that solitary edge is enough to give added information about the total form. Contrast of texture, over the total shell, heightens the dimensionality of its form. Striations of light and shade etch the coarse outer surface in contrast to the smoothly flowing white entrance to its interior, serenely toned in soft shadow.

Before moving on to an analysis of architectural form, it is helpful to expand on the subject of how surface properties of an object generate its specific character. To accomplish this, we turn to the fascinating world of microbiology. Beautiful and penetrating interpretations of natural design and structure were given to us by D'Arcy Thompson from his scientific, Jules Verne-type odyssey into the sea by way of the microscope. In his exemplary work *On Growth and Form* (1961), Thompson's studies of radiolaria (marine protozoa) are veritable classroom exercises for inquiry into the "architecture" of form, chiefly because the organic designs of their structure express inherent life systems. It is the action of surface structure that endows the form of these organisms with architectural interest. Figure 4-2 shows three drawings of radiolaria taken from Thompson's publication. Perhaps influential for the conception of the modern geodesic dome, *Aulonia hexagona* (left) takes its name from a pattern of hexagonally shaped cells that give visual order to its spherical structure. In the drawing, those cells render the surface in relatively shallow texture compared with the other two examples. By comparison, the funnel-like capsules of *Ethmosphaera conosiphonia* (right) give a totally different surface expression to the overall form. The individual cells and the deeper texture they create seem to emanate from living growth within rather than enclose life as the former example seems to

Figure 4-1. Light and the perception of form.

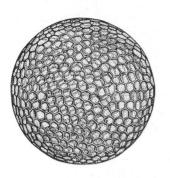 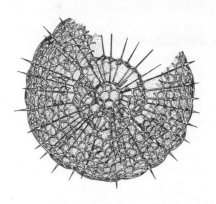 

Aulonia hexagona   Actinomma arcadophorum   Ethmosphaera conosiphonia

Figure 4-2. Radiolaria. Left: Aulonia hexagona. Center: Actinomma arcadophorum. Right: Ethmosphaera conosiphonia. [Reprinted with the permission of Cambridge University Press]

do. The capsules suggest slow inward expansion, exhaling as it were, and the greater degree of texture increases the interplay of light and shadow on the surface. The surface action is totally different for *Actinomma arcadophorum* (center), whose form is energized by the presence (and life force) of the proportionally thin spines radiating outward as if in a sudden burst. All three radiolaria have the common denominator of the perfect sphere, and note how all three have good configuration, thanks to the Gestalt laws of similarity, proximity, good continuation, and (applicable to the incomplete drawing of the center figure) the law of closure. Yet each is so distinctive in its individual character. Each is alive with surface action, but of a different kind. Their forms are animated. Exciting. Studies in the surface action of light. Lessons in the principles of design.

Visually reading the forms of radiolaria is like reading the forms of architecture, and as we saw with the microorganisms just discussed, surface details play a major role in communicating the character of form. To evaluate architecture perceptually, L. Wright asked the question "How many bits?" referring to the surface detailing of buildings. He used the amount of detailing as a factor for determining what makes one facade appear visually simplified when compared with another that is visually complex. To provide a means for assessing the amount of surface detailing, Wright put to use what is known in the field of perception as "simplification/amplification" theory. He established a continuum of design complexity with the style of Modern architecture at one end and Victorian at the other (Figure 4-3) to demonstrate their comparative ease or difficulty for visual comprehension. Basing his method on the information theory of M. Kiemle, Wright takes his stand that the human mind is able to comprehend only a limited amount of details when a person looks at a scene. "This information," he writes (1973, 251), "is more or less standard for all observers, is quantifiable and is expressed as 160 binary units (or bits) per 10 seconds. This is all the short-time-memory-store can hold." Applying this theory to viewing a building, said Wright, if its exterior form has a complex (numerous) amount of detail, the mind sees it as "interesting." If it is oversimplified and lacking surface detail, it is seen as "dull." As examples of facade detailing, he

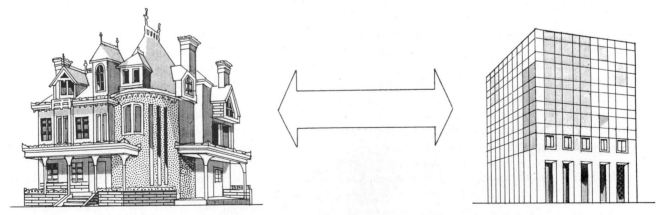

Figure 4-3. Surface detailing and the perception of architectural form.

used what he called "groups of signs" such as windows, quoins, and gables. The fewer number of different kinds of signs that appears, the more perceptually simple the form; the greater the number, the more complex. How any one group of such signs (e.g., windows) registers in the mind of the viewer relates to the frequency with which the sign is repeated in the scene. When all the different elements in an architectural visual field are counted in perceptual bits, and the computation falls below the 160-bit level, the mind of the observer comprehends such a view in the direction of "simplification." When the number exceeds 160, an evaluation of the scene moves to the other end of the continuum, toward "amplification," indicating that the scene is more perceptually complex. Using this method of visually assessing building facades, the Victorian style came out high, or "interesting," in contrast to Modern facades, which rarely reached the 160-bit level. But, as we will see below, Victorian buildings may have gone too far, even though they are "interesting." As Wright says,

. . . buildings which are interesting are not necessarily excellent. . . . The "simplification/amplification" theory of perception suggests that what, more than anything else, makes a building or a scene "easy on the eye" is a marriage between complexity and coherence. There must be "plenty to see," but the act of seeing must be made easy by coherence between the parts.

Wright concludes that the difficulty of visually comprehending Victorian architecture is that it represents "a mere agglomeration of features." It has too many different elements for the eye to know where to look next in its simplifying, amplifying search, whereas Modern architecture has too few surface elements to arouse visual interest. The reader is reminded that Wright's interpretations of architecture were based on visual perception, not the popularity of style, from the perspective of "the man in the street," not the design critic.

There have been other studies done to ascertain public reaction to architectural design. J. Bortz (1972) conducted studies[1] to evaluate how people subjectively perceived buildings according to their outward appearance. He selected examples having areas of plain walls (small and large), roof details, windows, balconies, decorative elements, and greenery. He found that people rated facades negatively if they had a high frequency of relatively plain wall surfacing, but positively if the plainness of facades was broken up by balconies or greenery. This seems to conform with L. Wright's views that building form tends to become more interesting with more surface

detail. What about too much detail? Bortz's findings showed that older houses having many different kinds of window forms were evaluated negatively, suggesting a preference by those people studied for perceptual simplicity.

Martin Krampen sought a connection between subjective evaluations, such as those used by Bortz, and objective facade measurements. Krampen (1980, 77) studied facades of older buildings constructed prior to 1900 and those of the Modern Movement of architecture, and found that "Facades constructed before 1900 were generally rated more friendly and irregular than their modern counterparts." Once again, it seems that although the human mind finds it easier to comprehend more perceptually simplified facades, people prefer buildings that have more "interest" than Modern buildings with plain and sterile surfaces.

From these studies the question arises of just where along the "simplification/amplification" continuum does a design become perceptually better, and also appealing to the general public? We saw above that Victorian design can be found to be interesting, but also perceptually complex. Wright (1973, 252) said the problem with Victorian is that "the parts do not really fit together." He adds:

The eye is not presented with an orderly sequence and therefore does not know where to turn next in its simplifying, amplifying process. Not knowing where to look next, it gives up. It turns away, leaving the building uncomprehended and leaving the mind with an impression of mere chaos.

Architectural historians know that some Victorian buildings do not give the impression of chaos, but many did, in part if not in whole, including their interiors. The intent of presenting these studies of building complexity is not to stir stylistic debates, but to construct a vantage ground for assessing architectural design from a perceptual point of view. The issue of perceptual clarity lies not necessarily with the *number* of parts comprising a whole, but the number of *kinds* of parts, and the *correlation among the parts*. Returning to the examples of radiolaria (Figure 4-2) the surface cells of all three represent a great number of parts, but they are correlated into the total form. The most complex radiolaria and the one with the greater number of different parts is *Actinomma arcadophorum*, whose surface is indeed one of action compared with the other two. But the number of different kinds of parts is not excessive. It is time to recall George A. Miller's "span of absolute judgment" as grounded on "the magical number seven" (p. 23). The number of different surface features of *Actinomma arcadophorum* is but half of that, if the count includes (1) the spines, (2) the irregular cell outlines taken as a patterned

---

[1] English summaries of the German publication of Bortz can be found in Krampen (1980), from which the findings explained here were taken.

group, and (3) the slightly textured surface of each cell. Yet its surface is vibrantly animated, and its form communicates a visual energy that a simple sphere does not have.

The preceding studies all seem to confirm that "How many bits?" is a valid question to keep in the forefront of architectural design thinking. Too many different visible details lead to complexity and create difficulty in comprehension; too few lead to monotony and lack of interest. These are important considerations for the study of form, and as we will see later, are equally important for the study of architectural space. Inscribed on an ancient temple at Delphi is a maxim that was known to every educated Greek: "Nothing too much." Whether for radiolaria or architecture, the simplification/amplification theory is a good one to keep in mind for the study of surface definition of form.

Figure-Ground in Space

Basic to introductory studies of the visual arts is the study of what traditionally has been known as "figure-ground," by which students learn how to render an image in artistic clarity by not giving undue emphasis to its background. The topic of figure separation from a visual field has also been a subject of interest in psychology, pioneered in 1915 by the Danish psychologist Edgar Rubin. His research and that of his successors became influential for application to both two- and three-dimensional art. How singular elements (*figures*) are seen against the *ground* of other parts of a greater composition is fundamental to the design and placement of forms in architectural space.

The spatial boundaries of exterior urban spaces and those of the interior of a room are most often the background for the freestanding forms (figures) occupying space. When placed in a room, furnishings alter the spatial perception of the space in two ways. First, they interrupt the views toward walls, floor, and ceiling because their opaque surfaces occlude what is behind them. Secondly, they add form, color, and surface brightness to the scene, and in so doing, furniture and other implements move the perception of a room further toward the complex end of the simplification/amplification continuum. This happens as a natural result of the furnishings adding more stimuli for the eye to see and the mind to process, adding to the two-dimensional figure-ground relationships created by pictures or other hangings on the walls. For a realistic study of architectural space,

Figure 4-4. Figure-ground perception in the urban world. [Seattle, Washington]

therefore, it is necessary to understand how objects in an environment assemble into figure-ground percepts that the eye sends to the mind.

Successful design of a total architectural environment is made easier by understanding figure-ground relationships, but Gibson (1974, 39) counseled us that everyday scenes "do not divide up neatly into figures and background. In most of them it is a relative matter whether a given area be regarded as a figure or as a background. One object may be the background for another nearer object, and another larger object may be the background for the first." This is a recurrent perceptual dilemma encountered in the visual complexities of the urban landscape. The dense city center of Seattle (Figure 4-4) provides a good example to begin the analysis of figure-ground perception. In the near foreground is the Space Needle, once a feature attraction of the 1962 World's Fair and now an urban landmark for the city. Notice how relatively easy its form is picked out at first glance of the photograph, even if the viewer had previously been unfamiliar with its image. The Space Needle has high perceptual characteristics of figure. Its structural form and uncommon image make it stand out against the aggregate architectural environment (the composite ground). When the eye moves to focus on other buildings, one at a time, then each in turn becomes a figure, and even the Space Needle becomes part of the collective background.

Contrasting and bright color enhances figure qualities. Even in the black and white photograph, the white of the Space Needle separates it from the other buildings, most all of which appear darker. Greater size also contributes to figure. Photographed from Queen Anne Hill in Seattle, the camera's viewing angle makes the Space Needle look like the tallest structure in the city. It isn't, but its size *apparently* towers over the other buildings, and that adds to its figural quality. Identity and familiarity also add to figure. For the residents of Seattle and frequent visitors to the city, the mere mention of the Space Needle's name brings to mind its image—as figure—set against the mental background of other visual thoughts.

Regularity of pattern or a plain surface is especially important for surfaces intended to serve as background for forms having fluid contours. A good illustration of this is the setting for the Picasso sculpture in Chicago's Daley Center Plaza (Figure 4-5). The geometric grid of the facade behind the Picasso is in stark contrast to the flowing lines of the sculpture's contours, which actually enhances the interplay of figure and ground as the eye focuses back and forth between the sculpture and the background building. A curvilinear or irregular pattern behind would visually compete with the sculpture. The principle of camouflage works exactly on that principle—to reproduce on the figure itself the same

Figure 4-5. Figure-ground identity by design contrast. [Daley Center Plaza, Chicago. Sculpture: Picasso]

pattern configurations that would be found in background images. In such cases, figure-ground relationships are broken down as the figure is visually absorbed into its surroundings.

Focus is a physiological component of figure-ground analysis. When the eyes are focused on an object, for example, on one of the lesser buildings in the photograph of Seattle (Figure 4-4), that building is in sharp focus because it is centered in the fovea of the retina, and the others are less sharply defined by being outside the fovea. Thus each building that is the moment of attention is perceptually segregated from all the others and becomes figure. Focus also requires accommodation of the two eyes, and that important depth cue supplies distance information, directly related to figure-ground perception.

Figure, Ground, and Brightness

For the design of the luminous environment, the role of light in establishing figure-ground relationships raises the question of how ratios of brightness levels are spatially perceived. By definition the brightness of an object depends on the appearance of its luminance compared with other objects in the vicinity and with those luminances comprising its background. As a reminder, the reflectance of a surfacing material does not change with an increase or decrease in illumination. It reflects the same percentage of the light it receives, whether bright or dim. One would think then that it would be a relatively simple task to isolate figure from ground by calculating luminances in a ratio of one surface as it will be seen against another. Generally, this is true, but measured luminance ratios will not provide the true appearance of one surface when perceived in relation to another. We saw earlier that simultaneous contrast changes the brightness relationship between two surfaces in a way not expected by their measured luminance ratio.

To learn more about brightness and figure-ground perception, Stanley Coren investigated cognitive factors in the laboratory. Of all the variables determining how certain objects are perceived as figure, he demonstrated that meaning "is one of the most potent." When we are looking for something specific in the visual world, its meaning alone makes it figure even though it may not stand out in terms of brightness. Most interesting of Coren's findings (1969, 521) were demonstrations showing that *perceived* brightness (a subjective experience) differs significantly from the *measured* luminance of an object in figure-ground relations. He said his findings "make it quite clear that brightness contrast is not simply determined by brightness differences in adjacent areas. Cognitive factors, such as whether the test patch is seen as figure or as ground, produce large differences in the amount of perceived brightness." Using what he calls an ambiguous figure paradigm, where subjects have the freedom to see a test patch either as figure or ground, Coren said his "experiments indicate that there is more [brightness] contrast when the test patch is seen as figure than when it is seen as ground. The magnitude of this difference can be quite large, amounting to 20% more contrast when the patch is seen as figure than as ground. . . ." What this means for lighting architectural spaces and furnishings is that using brightness to create figural emphasis is not an easy procedure. Luminance contrast ratios (see Chapter 3) are helpful initially, as long as we remember that those ratios are not fixed absolutes from the standpoint of how people perceive brightness.

To illustrate some of these issues, Figure C-3 shows the interior of a bank where the suspended chandelier stands out as perceptual figure by its form and brightness. Its effectiveness is heightened by the relatively subdued luminances on the surrounding architecture. The windows and the indirect light on the ceiling behind are indeed bright, but it is the chandelier that stands out in the visual field from the position of the camera. It stands out because it has rich figural qualities. Its exposed lamps combined with the intensity and incandescent color of its illumination make it unique in its environment. The

character of its design in contrast to the architecture around it make it a feature that could also be used for directional reference. Its standout image in both shape and brightness can serve as an interior feature that locates the escalators when seen from distant points in the public spaces of the building.

The computer stations shown in Figure C-4 demonstrate the relation between figure and brightness in another way. The white curvilinear shapes of the individual working surfaces create strong perceptual figures in the space, made visually stronger by the darker backgrounds of carpet and the lower walls around the room. Although connected, the four curved peninsula shapes each are dominant figures as seen against their surroundings. A key design factor making this happen is the proportion of their brightness and that of their accompanying light-colored computers. Normally, the computer monitors would be strong perceptual figures in a space because of the luminous images on their screens, but here their screen size is proportionately small, and the computers are comparatively few in number distributed around the room. This makes the flat working surfaces dominate, and their bright shapes clearly demarcate the work-stations.

Establishing figure-ground relationships is helpful for organizing architectural space. Selected locations for significant forms or major surface areas can be previsualized early in the design stage. Later they can be refined when color values are selected and specific illumination requirements are determined. Freestanding objects or furnishings can be emphasized, and if necessary, their backgrounds deemphasized, by anticipating the perception of their figure to ground. These are practical applications of figure, background, and brightness ratios. The illumination of figure-ground situations, as lighted forms in space, is developed further in Chapter 12.

Interspace

Architectural spaces are not always defined as full-scale volumes that appear as rooms, halls, atria, or urban squares. Frequently found in the built environment are the lesser but clearly identifiable spaces that result from placing major forms in the greater space. The forms set up new visual relationships in the overall composition, and establish new circulation routes for people. Because of the frequency with which those minor spaces occur in architecture, the designer needs to deal with them to take advantage of how they can add to the enrichment of the architectural experience.

The term *interspace* is introduced here to provide a means for analyzing the more intricate aspects of form-space relationships. An interspace is the interval between two or more forms or partial boundaries that are part of a larger architectural space. Interspaces are more like "space potential" rather than "space enclosed." This results mostly by forms in space related to movement of the eye or movement of the observer. That movement changes the viewing relationships between forms and the greater spatial boundaries to which they relate. When they are well designed and kept to minimums, interspaces make aesthetic contributions to the larger space. On the other hand, the cluttered spaces we encounter in our daily lives suffer from too many visually diversified objects coexisting in the same environment, and uncoordinated in design.

Figure 4-6 shows the principle of interspace as found among the natural forms of Monument Valley in southern Utah. Interspaces are defined by relationships among forms in space rather than by greater surface areas of boundaries that express an enclosure of space. The first interspace always begins with the location of the observer. In this illustration it extends to the stoic windswept tree, then to the dominant butte to the left, then to the one at the distant right. Interspaces seem momentary, shifting in configurations and dimensions as the eye mentally scans the panorama into the distance. Here in Monument Valley, the design coordination of the buttes that shape the interspaces is responsible for maintaining Nature's own aesthetics. The characteristic upward thrusts of rock and the disintegrating taluses at their angled bases unite their forms in the scene. Even though the tree

adds a new element to the composition, the aesthetics of the triangular interspace is kept in tact by the forms giving it definition. The buttes are harmonic in design, and the tree fits the character of the parched landscape. That character communicates the ongoing passage of time: the land forms in eons, the perishing tree as a reminder of life's brevity.

The principle of interspace offers a strategy for creating design relationships in the architectural environment. To begin we return to Chicago's Daley Center Plaza (Figure 4-5) where we observed the Picasso sculpture in an active figure-ground relationship with the building it contrasts. The space of the plaza is shaped by highrise buildings surrounding the square, and the sculpture is its focal point of interest. Taken from the lobby of the Richard J. Daley Center behind the sculpture, the photograph of Figure 4-7 changes the viewpoint, where the idea of interspace enlarges the form-space relationships into a completely different spatial experience. Like the tree at Monument Valley, the thin lines of the curtainwall and the men sitting in the foreground screen the view to the Picasso. That screen sets up an interspace, joining the one on the other side of the sculpture, giving greater spatial dimension to the field of view. Once again the design character of the parts contributes to spatial aesthetics. The lines of the curtainwall in front are compatible with those forming the geometric grids of the buildings outside. Just as we saw in Figure 4-5, the strict geometry reinforces the contours of the sculpture (and

Figure 4-6. Interspaces created by forms in Nature. [Monument Valley, Utah]

Visual Perception and Light

Figure 4-7. Interspatial connections in architecture. [Daley Center Plaza, Chicago]

the men in the foreground), further activating the fluid movement of curvilinear form. The seated men actually contribute to a double set of interlocking interspaces. Their forms set up one with the Picasso; the thin mullions of the curtainwall in the foreground set up another with the grid across the plaza. The interlinkage of the two creates spatial interest that would not be expected in the presence of the dominating geometric patterns.

When well done, the locations and dimensions of interspaces instill dynamics to architectural space. To observe how this happens let's return to Williams Square in Irving, Texas, shown in the preceding chapter only from a distance (Figures 3-21 a and b). The setting is serene, but the dynamics take place when stepping into the square (Figure 4-8). On center stage the visitor finds "The Mustangs of Las Colinas," created in bronze by wildlife sculptor Robert Glen. Symbolizing the freedom wild horses once enjoyed in the openness of the Southwest, the equestrian group appears to have just run from between two buildings to splash across a meandering "river" running diagonally through the abstract "plain." Just inside the loggias of the buildings are shops and reception areas. From there, as the photograph shows, viewing angles toward the sculptures create an atmosphere for the group of yet another kind, one that separates the world of the spectator from the primitive abandon of the wild horses. This is made possible by the

landscaping, with trees flanking two sides of the square. From the walkways, the position of the observer sets up a first interspace with the overhanging branches. Another interspace separates the branches from the sculpture, and then another continues from behind the group to the trees on the other side. The foreground branches frame the eventful view of the mustangs thundering across the square, isolating the spectacle for the viewer to imagine a scene that once was commonplace prior to the encroachment of civilization on the Great Plains.

Interspaces are common to architectural interiors, often set up by positioning permanent features like fountains in hotel lobbies or kiosks in shopping malls. But many are created by the simple act of selecting and arranging furnishings. Figure 4-9 shows a visitors' waiting area in the lobby of a corporation building. The space of the room is clear and distinct. The walls are adorned by only two paintings, and the space is softly illuminated by recessed lighting in the coffered ceiling. The pieces of furniture establish interspatial relations that are not intended to convey visual excitement, but communicate a relaxing environment appropriate for the room's function. This interior and the examples given earlier demonstrate how the principle of interspace can be manipulated for designing the infill of the larger voids of the built environment, and to control figure-ground relations for fine tuning the total experience of architectural space.

Figure 4-8. Interspaces creating dynamic viewing relationships. [Williams Square, Irving, Texas]

Figure 4-9. Interspaces in architectural interiors. [American Republic Insurance Company, Des Moines. Architects: SOM, New York]

The Mind in Visual Search

The contemporary urban environment is composed of an infinite number of objects and detailed surfaces seen at varying distances. It is a complex collection of surface planes, contours, textures, colors, and levels of brightness. The observer's capacity for searching through such stimuli for meaningful comprehension of the environment is limited, because as we saw earlier in the perception of form, the mind can sort out, process, and remember only a finite amount of perceptual data. When a person turns the corner in a downtown street or enters a complex interior space for the first time, the eye sees a myriad of new perceptual stimuli that the mind must encode to comprehend a sense of place. When creating or remodeling architectural forms and spaces, knowing how that visual stimuli is processed in the mind gives the designer an understanding of how comfortable or complicated a proposed environment will become.

Saccadic Movements. When the eye looks about the visual world, casually or intentionally, it moves in a series of small, intermittent and rapid jumps or tremors known as *saccades*. The term has linguistic roots in Old French, where "saccade" means "flick of a sail." The eye searches about an environment flicking from one fixation to another. As it does so, it successively displaces one area of focus in the fovea with the next one on which the eye has momentarily stopped. When the eye moves to a new position, the feature that caused the displacement then in turn moves into the fovea. This can be experienced by simply looking about the visual world, and being cognizant of each saccade the eye makes. It is nearly impossible to voluntarily scan the environment in a steady, even flow of vision. Scientists have studied these physiological movements of the eye to determine the rate at which saccades are made. In a very rapid surveillance of a visual scene, an upper limit for saccadic movements has been found to be between four and five saccades per second, with the minimum saccadic interval being about 30 to 80 milliseconds.

It is possible for the eye to move in a continuous flow, but only when it receives the assistance of some feature in the external world. This happens when the eye follows a moving target. An adjustment of the ocular system then takes place, and the eye moves very smoothly, not in the sudden saccadic jerks. Scientists refer to this movement of the eye as *pursuit*, which keeps a moving object locked in the fovea where focus is taking place, and also applies to fixating on an object while the observer moves. The smooth following of a moving target can be demonstrated by holding a finger at arm's length from the eyes, and focusing on the finger as it is swept across the field of view. No saccades will be experienced. While the image of the finger stays focused in the fovea, the background appears as one continuous blur.

Scanning. In the human visual system, the eye and brain coordination continually samples the stimuli of the visual world by what is known as *scanning*. By this process the eye looks at various optical stimuli in succession, moving from fixation to fixation, separated by saccades. The information received in any one fixation often determines where the eye will look next. The visual data picked up along the way is then sent to the brain, where it is assessed, assembled, edited, stored, or ignored. How then is all the visual information comprehended? This is explained by a cognitive mapping process that takes place in the mind as the eye scans the environment in search of visual recognition.

The Cognitive Map. Day to day and moment by moment experiences are evaluated in the mind and assembled into our comprehension of the world by what is known as *cognitive mapping,* sometimes referred to as *schematic mapping.* David Stea (1974, 158) describes this function as the human-environment interface:

> . . . *with an environment that is rich, diverse, uncertain and overwhelmingly informative; and with a human being having a limited capacity for holding information and limited time to make decisions, who is capable of storing in his brain the nature of events and objects repeatedly encountered, and who groups information into classes which are categorical and schematic. One kind of stored information consists of networks of mental representations, or images, of recurring objects and events, and these networks come close to what we term cognitive maps.*

Over time, individuals build up their knowledge of the physical world through this process. Cognitive maps become mental pictures of the environment. They undergo continual change as the individual develops in age and learning, and serve as a reference base for behavior. In new or strange situations, cognitive maps provide stored information that suggests how to get from here to there, based on former experiences. While looking at Figure 4-4, imagine a first-time visitor to Seattle. The newcomer begins to sort out all the new urban imagery by referencing it against what had been previously experienced in other city centers like Miami, Minneapolis, or Oshkosh, even if those cities had been seen only in photographs and television, or having been heard about in conversations. Each singular experience provides intrinsic information contributing to the ongoing development of cognitive maps.

The designer needs to know, however, the features in the environment that arrest the scanning eye in its saccadic travels. Where in all the stimuli of the architectural world does the eye pause before making its next move? If we know about that process, we will learn more about how to compose visual relationships in the design of architectural form and space.

Selection in the Visual World

A recurring theme in this book is the difference between the environment as *designed* and the environment as *perceived* by the people who experience it. In this chapter we have been analyzing form-space relationships, particularly those of spatial figure-ground, but questions arise as to how this might be applied to the architectural world, in light of the fact that it is filled with any number of objects or surfaces that at one time or another have enough visual significance to become figure. We therefore need to examine the inherent visual characteristics by which certain elements in the visual world attract the saccadic stops in the scanning process of human vision.

There are *focal accents* in the environment, elements that in a given situation have greater attracting power for the eye than others. They are of different kinds and are ranked in a hierarchical order according to their potency to stop the scanning eye even if for just a brief moment. They exist in the architectural and natural world. A focal accent can be a three-dimensional free-standing object or a prominent element on a wall, ceiling, or floor. It can be animate or inanimate. It can be moving or still. But what makes it an accent is that it becomes the terminal resting point for any one saccade of the eye, whether voluntary or involuntary. People can be looking *for* something, or idly glancing about or daydreaming, but the eye continues its natural saccadic movements stopping here and there as attracted by the focal accents. Even when looking for something specific, some other accent may arrest the scanning by exerting its own presence, becoming another stopping point in the saccadic search. The pause at any one point or place may be so brief that we are not even aware a fixation has taken place. Whether perusing a beautifully designed room or the clutter of a littered street, the nature of human vision maintains this instinctive process, which we will call *selection in the visual world*.

Information about how the eye selects saccadic targets in a field of view has come from researchers who have investigated the scanning patterns traced by subjects looking at flat surface planes of pictures. Research of this kind dates back to the 1930s, but more recently Mackworth and Morandi (1967) conducted such experiments where subjects were presented with unfamiliar pictures, and their eye movements were charted to observe their responses to various stimuli in the picture. While the subjects perused the pictures, their fixations were electronically measured and averaged at 300 milliseconds each. Although the researchers found that there was no particular order as to how subjects examined the pictures, they did observe that most often fixations were centered on high-information parts of the pictures, meaning those parts that could be recognized on another occasion. Fixations did cluster in certain patterns, and it was noted that high concentration took place in regions that tended to have significant variation of pictorial content.

The Russian A. L. Yarbus (1967) conducted similar experiments to study eye movements, relating them to how an observer's attention is held by certain elements in a picture. Using I. E. Repin's "An Unexpected Visitor" (Figure 4-10), Yarbus first gave subjects the opportunity to examine the picture freely (see scanning trace #1), and then observed their scanning patterns after they were asked specific questions about the scene. For example, subjects were asked to give the ages of the people in the picture (trace #3), and what they thought the family had been doing before the "unexpected visitor" entered the room (trace #4). The questions prompted the subjects to fixate on some of the picture's elements more than others, but with or without previous instructions, the electronic traces show that Yarbus' subjects clearly established fixation patterns that centered on visual nodes, while some features in the picture drew minimal or no attention.

The activity of these visual searches lies deep in the human nervous system. Scanning the visual parts of a picture or a piece of graphic art relates to the interest level and attention span for eye-mind coordination. It is simply a matter of time, a very brief time indeed, before the mind tires or is interrupted while looking at a single fixation. In his excellent book on visual design, *Language of Vision*, Gyorgy Kepes (1969, 44) speaks of two limitations applied to what he calls a "field of attention." He says attention depends on "its limitation in the number of optical units it can encompass," and "its limited duration in time to focus on one optical situation." We know that except for situations when certain tasks have special interest or require concentration, the saccade made for each element in any one visual field has a short life in the scanning process. Applying that knowledge of eye movements and attention span to the visual arts, Kepes (1969, 52) made the point that a successful composition requires a distribution of eye-attracting nodes or interest centers that must be skillfully arranged in order to hold the viewer's attention. Referring to a static relationship among individual optical units that are found in pictures, he says:

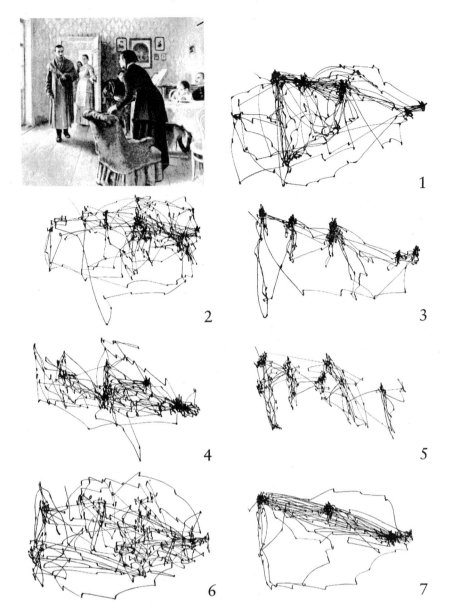

Figure 4-10. The scanning studies of A. L. Yarbus. Patterns of subjects' eye movements varied according to questions asked about the picture they were viewing. Each line corresponds to one saccade. (1) Free examination of the picture. Before the subsequent recording sessions, the subject was asked to (2) estimate the material circumstances of the family in the picture, (3) give the ages of the people, (4) surmise what the family had been doing before the arrival of the "unexpected visitor," (5) remember the clothes worn by the people, (6) remember the position of the people and objects in the room, (7) estimate how long the "unexpected visitor" had been away from the family. [From Alfred L. Yarbus (Ed.). Eye Movements and Vision. 1967. Plenum Publishing Co.]

The image as a living experience cannot long exist in a frozen structure. For the image to remain a living organism, relationships within it must be constantly changing. The eye and the mind must be fed with changing visual relationships. Only this changing variety can provide the stimulation necessary for holding attention upon the picture surface.

The great masters of the visual arts understood very well how to compose interest centers in a painting, and doing so they towered over the lesser artists. They knew how to enrich the component parts of a composition, and knew precisely where to insert certain visual content to keep the mind of the viewer involved in the subject. In this regard much contemporary pictorial art fails, including a great deal of modern abstract art, which offers little beyond the initial reaction to the whole, and does not invite scrutiny of the parts. Content, human interest, or mind-engaging elements may not be present or adequately composed to provide the stimulation necessary for holding the viewer's attention the way Kepes described. This theory is valid for the graphic arts and also applies to viewing the architectural environment. The design of architectural space often fails because there are too few or too many interest centers, or those that are present are poorly composed in space. In the normal scanning of a room the eye does not fixate on any one object very long, because, as Kepes said, the mind is being fed by changing visual relationships. It is now time to answer the important question: As long as the eye searches the environment by moving from image to image, where does it stop . . . ?

Hierarchy of Focal Accents

What catches the eye as it scans an environment are *focal accents* created by objects or surface details that are high perceptual stimuli and those having novel features. The degree to which those features stand out in the visual world will largely determine the power they have to attract—and distract—the eye. As certain accents dominate the scene, the eyes will dwell on them longer, as long as they are not offensive, such as when disability or discomfort glare results. Personal expectations, desires, and past experiences all influence the scanning process, but any object or surface having exceptional visual attributes' will create focal attention and become a saccadic stop for the eye. If any one element is not the star of the show at first, it will step into the scan as an intruding if not petulant side stop for the moving eye as it selects in the visual world.

To experience how human vision is attracted by focal accents as high informational stimuli, the reader is asked to close the eyes and face away from this page. Being especially attentive, open the eyes. What was the *first* thing seen? What was the *second*? It makes little difference which one of the two came before the other, but in most circumstances the ones contending for attention were most likely those that sent to the brain high visual stimuli as focal accents. Reviewing the scene in which the test was made, what were the features of the other elements in the scan that were not able to compete with those that were selected first? Try it again, this time after turning in a different direction. Try it still again, but this time with eyes open. The results are usually similar. Such exercises demonstrate how focal accents participate in the natural process of selection in the visual world. Not only are certain accents highly perceptible amid the welter of details in the built environment, but they partake in a rank order according to their power for claiming our visual attention. This creates a hierarchy of the way human vision generally responds to focal accents among the forms and surfaces in the architectural world:

1. People

2. Movement

3. Brightness

4. High contrast

5. Vivid color

6. Strong pattern (when it exists as a single stimulus)

—to which must be added:

Meaning, and

Combinations.

Knowledge of these focal accents for their power of attracting vision as people respond to their environment lies central to creating a humanized architecture. Each of them has intrinsic properties to which the eye responds. The designer has control over most of them when developing and refining architectural space. Knowing where to place those accents and where to avoid them cultivates an ergonomic approach to architectural design.

People. Basic to the entire human nervous system is a person's awareness of the presence of another human being. This most likely applies to the animal kingdom as well, not just animals being sensitive to the presence of humans, but also to their own kind and members of other species. Animals and people need recognition for mating, and detection of other species as suitable prey or likely predators is important for survival. For people this apprehension of others may belong to anthropological behavior that took root in primitive life. If a person is in a room, even in very dim light, he or she will immediately draw the attention of another person entering the room. The human form is unmistakable. One can walk into a darkened storage room of a department store or museum and be startled by a mannequin. Human recognition was apparent in the scanning studies of Yarbus. Most traces by his subjects centered on the images of people in Repin's picture. When subjects were given certain instructions such as "give the ages of the people" or "remember the clothes worn by the people," their scanning would naturally focus on the human figure for answers, but when given free examination of the picture (trace #1), it is clear from the trace patterns that people focused primarily on people.

It is not only quite natural for the eye to be attracted by the human figure, but usually focal attention is drawn directly to the face. Experiments have shown that facial details are registered with high acuity. Gibson suggests that psychological motives are a part of scanning the face of another person, especially when that person is conveying some sort of active or unusual behavior, such as pacing up and down. In such a situation, Gibson (1966, 260) noted the observer will search the face of the other person to

. . . scan its fine details, with minute fixations superposed on the pursuit fixation, identifying a smile, and observing whether the other person does or does not look directly at him. The optical information for this environmental fact—being or not being looked at—is extremely subtle, consisting of form relations in the light reflected from dark pupils and white scleras of the eyes in proportion to the form of the face. . . . Men learn to watch the eyes of other men so as to detect their motivations.

The intention here is not to dwell on the suspicious side of human behavior, but only to illustrate how fundamentally the visual system works in the context of human culture, and for this reason people are ranked the highest on the list of focal accents, independent of whether or not they might be moving, what colors they are wearing, or if they are seen in bright light.

Figures C-5a and b show the entrance lobby and receptionist station for corporate offices, and it is an interesting exercise to ponder both photographs that are identical except for the fact that one includes people. The difference is a total change of atmosphere of the space, demonstrated by a few glances back and forth between the two pictures, observing how difficult it is for the eye not to be drawn to the people seated. With the exception of movement, all the other focal accents on the hierarchi-

cal list given earlier are present in the scene. Looking at the photographs is a much more casual experience than walking into the actual room, where the social interaction most people experience in public would immediately have the eye targeting even more intensely on the woman behind the desk or the man sitting in the chair. Visual searching eventually would move to other focal accents, shifting back and forth among them, but like the scanning traces recorded in the Yarbus studies, saccadic stops would continue to build up in number on the two people sitting in the room.

For design purposes, for now we are not analyzing how the eye scans a gathering of people in an environment, but only how it is attracted by just a few or even one. The point is to emphasize that the human focal accent is a strong visual force, an exceptional target for saccadic movement of the eye. Note particularly its application to the location and design of certain functional nodes such as receptionist stations, sales checkout stands, librarian desks, lecterns and pulpits, and information booths. Their effectiveness is weakened when sight lines to such functional centers in a building include other high activity centers as seen from a major circulation route or a predominant viewing angle.

Movement. When was the last time you experienced sitting in a darkened room or entering a dark garage, and suddenly whipped your head in the direction of a dark, running mouse or other animal or insect? Difficult to see as they are when standing still and camouflaged in their dark surroundings, they become highly visible when darting across the floor. The quick movement of someone's arm, a falling object, or a bird suddenly flying overhead, all will draw immediate attention even if occurring in extreme peripheral vision. These visual intrusions illustrate the importance of movement as a focal accent.

What is responsible for movement quickly attracting the eye, even under poor illumination, is the activity in the retina. Whatever the magnitude, reflected light from a moving object sets off reactions of an initial set of receptor cells, and instantaneously causes a series of successive reactions in neighboring receptors. By ordinal stimulation, areas of the background are rapidly occluded at the leading edge of a moving object, and disoccluded at the trailing edge. This high level of retinal activity caused by a moving figure seen against a stationary ground is known to link with attention systems in visual perception. When movement is combined with high illumination, it is an exceptionally powerful attraction for the eye. Flashing or moving lights will virtually guarantee the eyes and head to turn in their direction, to be fixated in the fovea until discomfort or another focal accent turns the head away.

Brightness. Exceptional brightness of any object or surface in an environment will always become a high focal accent. Remembering that brightness is determined by a significant difference in luminance between two surfaces, the greater the brightness of an object, the more it will assume a powerful role in attracting the scanning eye. Once again perform the test of closing your eyes, turning to a new direction, and opening them. At the instant your eyes are opened, be critically observant of any bright objects or surfaces in the scene. Often it will be a bright light source, glare, or a white object or piece of paper lying in the field of view.

Considering that the designer has little or no control over the first two hierarchical accents of people and movement (except for the obvious cause-effect relationship of locating circulation routes and movement patterns in a building or room), *brightness becomes one of the most dominant design components influencing how people will perceive the architectural environment.* Brightness is the result of comparative luminances, but luminance as brightness varies with the reflectance qualities of a surface and the quantity and quality of illumination. In the next chapter we will learn how to estimate the brightness of building materials, to assist the designer in predicting the appearance of brightness areas in the illuminated environment.

The designer must learn how to distribute brightness areas or centers about architectural space, whether in the form of the light sources or high levels of surface brightness produced by the arriving light. Decisions need to be made regarding when and where bright focal accents should be created, and where they are to be eliminated. In the bank interior of Figure C-3, the brightness of the ceiling behind the structural piers helps illuminate the space below, but it is also a focal accent, as are the distant windows. The two play a major role of giving identity to the space they help define. But as we saw earlier in the discussion of figure-ground, the incandescent chandelier in the foreground uses its brightness and contours to become a dominant element in space, a decorative as well as a bright focal accent in the visual field. The computer stations of Figure C-4 take on their identity by brightness shaping the work spaces as they curve around the room. They are perceived immediately, due to brightness as a focal accent, accompanied by the fluidity of form.

High Contrast. By its very definition, high contrast strongly differentiates one surface perceived against another. The greater the contrast an object creates in the visual array, the more it will achieve status as a focal accent. Notice how all the above accents depend on strong contrast for their effectiveness: people against inanimate objects, movement compared to being stationary, brightness against dim surrounds. Contrast can therefore be created through different means, but it is placed in the hierarchy of focal accents because objects of similar brightness still can be contrasted by altering their other physical attributes such as size and shape. Objects having unusual or novel features are highly contrasted when seen against a more common backdrop, as evidenced by the form and contours of Seattle's Space Needle and the Picasso sculpture in Chicago's Daley Center Plaza, both of which are highly contrasted against the shapes of their backgrounds.

Specifically related to lighting is the difference between two highly contrasted surfaces created by their luminance. Some brightness values will stand out much more than others in an environment; it depends on the degree of contrast. As we saw from the preceding chapter, luminance ratios of 3 : 1 set up a significant brightness contrast, and as a general rule, brightness will draw attention as a focal accent when the luminance of an object or surface is a minimum of three times that of its surroundings. A contrast above that 3 : 1 ratio will create an exceptionally strong visual attraction in the field of view, and when it reaches 10 : 1, it will be a dominant visual force.

It is not only high contrasting luminances that become focal accents, especially glare, but the light sources themselves can be potent elements of the highest order in the visual world. In darkness, exposed light sources might be the *only* focal accents in the field of view, even overpowering the accents of people and movement as is the case when disability glare blinds the eye for visual performance. As a fundamental principle for lighting design, *bright light sources are going to attract the scanning eye whether or not intended by the designer,* and in certain circumstances they can be highly distractive and destructive to the overall aesthetics of environmental design, let alone discomforting to a human being.

High brightness contrast as a distracting element in the environment has been demonstrated experimentally. In the late 1950s, Hopkinson and Longmore used a hidden camera and variable light sources to test observers' reactions to brightness while trying to perform a visual task. The researchers found that when placing a small light source of high illuminance in the field of view, subjects made a series of quick eye movements toward the source and then away from it. "Sometimes," Hopkinson observed (1970, 190), "the eyes moved only part of the way towards the source and back to the visual task. Presumably this eye movement pattern was associated with the glare discomfort which resulted from the source of high luminance." Those demonstrations are reminders that brightness in high contrast is a focal accent that not only attracts the eye of the observer, but often creates physical discomfort.

Vivid Color. When a color appears intensely bright as an isolated element in the environment, its vividness will attract the scanning eye. Under the same illumination, white, beige, and the saturated yellows, oranges, and reds will appear brighter than the darker blues, greens, and browns.

The two people in the lobby of Figure C-5b were analyzed as primary focal accents chiefly because of their human forms. Notwithstanding personal interest an observer might have regarding the gender of the two, the receptionist stands out in the visual field by the vivid color of her dress. Her attraction as a focal accent is heightened by the relatively subdued colors elsewhere in the scene. It is difficult to scan other parts of the photograph without being aware of the powerful draw toward the bright color. This demonstrates that a vivid color needs to be contrasted to be effective as a focal accent. If the carpet, furniture, and walls were the same hue and similar value of her dress, there would be an omnipresence of vivid color that would reduce her image for focal attraction. It is easy to visualize the woman and man changing places, where the vivid color of the woman's dress would remain a focal accent, but merely shift in location to the back of the room.

Vivid color can be used to compose multiple centers of attraction, as long as each unit is seen against a contrasting surround. In such cases, multiple elements are effective as focal accents in spatial distribution. Figure C-6 shows a cafeteria made festive by its bright atmosphere, accented by the colorful images of fruit and floral patterns composed about the space. Here vivid color joins with high contrast created by the predominantly bright walls and ceiling. The people compete as other focal accents in the room as perceptually they should, but this illustration shows how strong color can be used not only to attract the scanning eye, but to carry that scan through the dimensions of space.

Strong Pattern (as a single stimulus). Neurophysiological research has shown how pattern organization is basic to visual perception, and considering that the everyday natural and architectural environment is rich in pattern imagery, it comes as little surprise that configurations of pattern create focal accents. Russell and Karen De Valois (1988, 337 ff) have explained that cell reaction in the human visual system occurs as periodic recording in the retina (called "periodicities") of edges or bars of different widths, which are perceived as surface and spatial patterns. The researchers remind us that since the origin of the human species, botanical and biological patterns have been abundant in the natural environment, commonly found in the organized spacing of leaves and flowers in a great variety of plants, and in the periodic repetition of feathers and scales in rows and other formations in the animal kingdom.

More recently in anthropological time, countless relationships of regularized patterns have existed in the world of architecture and cities in the form of bricks, shingles, siding, windows, and row housing, to go along with stripes, plaids, and embroideries on clothing. As the eye scans the visual world, distinct, dominant patterns of visual units will stand out in a visual array, especially in one containing other less noticeable regularities. A dominant pattern, taken as a single stimulus, will create specialized identity and will draw focal attention.

Using the black and white photograph of Figure 4-11, and thereby eliminating color as an accent, the urban park is dominated by organized patterns that create focal centers. The steps read as a distinct pattern, as do the terraced water steps of the fountain. The pattern of windows enhances the rectangular form of the background building, increasing its drawing power; the two decorative patterns at the tops of both elevations also draw attention to those parts of the building. The triangles of metal structure and fabric have their own identity, achieved by patterns of a different kind. The groups of trees—as pattern—have their own individuality. Note how all the focal accents are at work. People are easily perceived, not only by their images, but for how their activities arouse curiosity for what they might be doing or where they might be going. High contrast of light and dark separates the steps of water from those of concrete. The brightness of the waterfall to the right, despite its location far from the center of the photograph, draws attention even while the eye scans the remainder of the field for a second or third time. The waterfalls are exceptionally strong as focal accents in the real life photographed, because in addition to creating patterns, the water moves. The Gestalt principles of similarity and proximity organize the different patterns throughout the scene.

Meaning. With this next category, we take up a focal accent of a different nature. The accents discussed so far draw attention to isolated parts of the visual world, but psychologists tell us that properties of identity and meaning are foremost in perceptual search. Once something has meaning to a person, it easily becomes a focal accent in applicable situations. When visiting a new city for the first time, street signs and traffic signals are already familiar, and their meanings associated with personal safety momentarily rank them very high in the hierarchy of focal accents for a person about to cross the street in a crowded downtown intersection. In the urban park of Figure 4-11, the people in the scene take high priority as accents for scanning, yet to the visitor they are strangers. But let us assume the man sitting alone near the top of the steps at the left is your dearest

Figure 4-11. Patterns as focal accents. [Central Park Mall, Omaha]

friend, whom you haven't seen for a long time, and who said he would meet you on the steps above the waterfall. His identity, and the situation, give him meaning as the most important focal accent above all others in the scene.

Other than commonly accepted identities such as traffic signals at a busy intersection, people give their own meanings to objects and places. A piece of old furniture sitting in the corner of a room may not attract the attention of a visitor, but as a treasured family heirloom it is a most important object for the owner. Two lovers like to return to "their booth" in a restaurant. A clock in a train station is a focal accent of highest regard for people eagerly waiting the arrival of a dear friend. Aside from these highly personal images, there are generalized meanings belonging to common knowledge that are of importance for the designer. In most situations, building entrances (when designed to be recognized as such), receptionist desks, elevator stations, and bus stops are all focal accents at times when they are meaningful for people engaged in personal activities related to those places. So the design and the location of such visual centers should be conceived as nodes in the overall composition of the architectural environment, where their designs announce their presence as focal accents in the social and visual world.

Combinations. Any object or segment of the environment achieves greater dominance when it combines two or more of the focal accents. An easy example to visualize is the flashing red light on a speeding emergency vehicle. Its effectiveness is created by a combination of four of the top five in the hierarchy of focal accents: movement (of the vehicle itself and the alternating on and off of the flashing light), brightness (particularly at night), vivid color (red), and contrast. The focal accent of people is added by the associative meaning of danger or tragedy (human concern). It is the combination of accents of people, brightness, vivid color, and contrast that creates the high focal center of the receptionist in Figure C-5b.

The question might be raised about why the focal accents are presented in a structured hierarchy when at times one accent positioned down on the list may override the attracting power of others ranked above. We noted that personal meaning attributed to an object can rank it higher than the other accents, and the intense brightness of a light source at night can obliterate all the other accents. In average scenes, the top three of people, movement, and brightness are going to attract human vision very quickly, even if held in attention only

Visual Perception and Light

momentarily. Any one of the accents below those top three can be manipulated by a skillful designer to make them change positions on the list. For example, a novel form or pattern highly contrasted in space could draw attention greater than another surface or object of vivid color. The top three will normally maintain their strength for drawing vision over the others, but taking all as a group, selections from the list can be made to build up focal areas and interest centers in the design of form-space relationships. Keep in mind that an overuse of the focal accents in an immediate vicinity or distributed in a spatial sequence can easily cause a visual overload for perception. This underscores a basic design principle that has been around a long time—plain or minimally embellished surfaces need to be distributed among the accents, and adequate voids need to be composed among accented forms in space.

During the design process, the hierarchy of focal accents is not only helpful for creating centers of attention, but also can be used as a checklist against design error in architectural space planning. Visualize a classroom, meeting room, or church where a requirement is to feature a place for a speaker, a panel discussion, or an altar. Assume within a visual field that centers on a podium that there is a nearby corridor that is visible through a glass opening. For those sitting in the room, people walking in the corridor combine the top two focal accents, and distract attention from the speaker at the podium. Or consider the task of designing an information booth in the lobby of a public building. The very fact that a person will be present contributes the highest rank of focal accents—the human figure. Any of the other accents of brightness, vivid color, contrast, or decorative pattern will amplify the booth design as a visual center, as long as the spatial background does not include a preponderance of competing focal accents as seen from the entrance of the building. Focal accents that are out of place can create havoc in the urban environment. It is easy to understand why cities have ordinances against flashing lights for commercial signage. In the heavy flow of dense night traffic, flashing lights at the sides of streets distract drivers' attention from the direction they—and other drivers—are going.

Because the hierarchy of focal accents is natural to the viewing process, it becomes a convenient structure for making design decisions. Most architectural spaces do not call for a single center of attention. Some require none at all. But by keeping the order of accents in mind, the designer takes heed of how people, movement, and certain effects of light, color, and pattern can articulate and punctuate the spaces being created. Good composition of brightness and color is essential for the successful design and lighting of the built environment. To learn how to control those basic design features as perceived on the surfaces that shape architectural space, we now turn our attention to the luminance brightness of building materials.

CHAPTER 5

Luminance Brightness of Building Materials: The LBR System

All five floors of the hotel were now illuminated and made the road in front of it bright from one side to the other. Automobiles were still careening along the road, although more intermittently, looming into sight more rapidly than by day, feeling for the road before them with the white beams of their headlights, which paled as they crossed the lighted zone of the hotel only to blaze out again as they rushed into the farther darkness.

—*Franz Kafka*
Amerika*

In Chapter 3 the effects of light were shown to be dependent on the reflectance of a material's surface and on the quantity and quality of illumination with which it interacts. That creates its *luminance*. The visual appearance of that luminance is modified by how the surface is angled to the direction of light, and also by the angle of slant it makes with the observer's line of vision. Placed in architectural space, it is perceived in relation to all other surfaces in the field of view, and its comparison with those surfaces determines its relative *brightness*. The total architectural environment thus becomes a spatial tapestry of brightness values, an array of color and reflectances all affected by the sources of light, their kind and location.

The noteworthy studies of John Flynn and his colleagues (1973) conducted at General Electric's research center at Nela Park demonstrated how the illumination on walls influences the visual perception of a conference room.[1] When the walls were washed with light, the room appeared more spacious and affected other behavioral responses from observers participating in the study. Adding illumination to the walls increased their luminance, and consequently their brightness. If light were held constant in such an experiment, brightness could be increased in another way, by painting or surfacing the walls with a color of higher value. Conversely, the walls can be reduced in brightness (and the room reduced in spaciousness) by resurfacing them with a color of lower

---

* From Kafka, Franz. 1946. *Amerika*. Garden City, NY: Doubleday, p. 121.

[1] Application of Flynn's research to space and light theory appears in Part 3 of this book, and is given specialized attention at that time.

value. The brightness of the walls, floor, ceiling, and furniture is therefore the result of the surface quality of the building materials and the lighting of the room.

Given the abundance of contemporary manufactured products keeping pace with society's changing fads and fashions, the designer faces the ongoing problem of choosing from the new surfacing materials and lighting systems that steadily enter global markets while abandoning certain favorites that fall to obsolescence. This reflects our pluralistic culture, which calls for the "new and different," stimulated by the business world in which manufacturers of products compete in the free enterprise system and flood the markets with "something better" or "something unique." Subjected to this dilemma of choice many designers succumb to making selections of products in the abstractions of personal preference, guesswork, or for novel effects to personalize their client's image.

When creating space and selecting the building materials that shape it, it is difficult for the designer to maintain control over the appearance a room eventually will take, and much of this stems from the very nature of how most architectural environments come into existence. Let us begin, as most buildings do, with the part played by the architect, interior designer, contractor, or anyone else responsible for initiating the empty shells of space. Interior rooms, circulation routes, and public spaces are basically shaped by the location of walls, floors, and ceilings as demarcated by lines on drawings or other construction documents.

Now consider what happens next. Granted, some designers create architectural space by thinking intuitively of shaping a room in terms of color and light, but in many if not most cases, a basic shell of space is first conceived, and then surfacing materials are applied and light is added as later steps. This refers to surfaces that will be painted (what color?), paneled (what species of wood?), or veneered (what wall fabric, vinyl, or tile?), and so on.

Who makes those decisions? Who selects the finishing materials? Who selects and designs the lighting? Who is the artist standing in front of the plain white "canvas" and "paints" the spatial shell with the colors and brightness levels that will become the users' field of view? Any combination of activities will determine the final outcome of what the surfaces will look like in illuminated space. One designer will modify the input of others, and the activities of all will interface to produce the final scene that comes into existence. In *Moby Dick* Herman Melville wrote of "the last featuring blow at events" when describing the work of a South Seas mat-maker, who was inattentively striking with his shuttle the marline lines he was weaving while idly looking out over the rolling ocean, not being aware of the character he was giving to the weave. So it is with illuminated space.

New lighting is installed and changes the color and brightness of a material. On the other hand, a new surfacing material is applied to a wall, and immediately is changed from its 'normal' appearance by the lighting already there. Whose work comes last? Is it the designer specifying a color of surfacing material, or the illuminating engineer adding light? Of importance is *only* the appearance of the major surfaces in space that comes about by what Melville called "the last featuring blow at events." It is that last interchange between surface and light that will give to a building material its color value and brightness that will influence the users' visual perception of their surroundings.

A persistent challenge for designers and lighting engineers then is to predict how the physical surfaces of building materials will appear once they are assembled to shape architectural space, and how they will appear on interior furnishings when placed in a room. Because light and spatial location are the concluding factors that determine the appearance of a material, and because quality architectural design is dependent on a harmoniously organized composition of all the luminous surfaces in an environment, it is advantageous during the stages of design to be able to *previsualize* how the color and texture of surfacing materials will ultimately appear to the human eye at various levels of brightness.

Some system is therefore needed for choosing from the myriad of available building materials and light sources, and from the continuous flow of new products that inevitably will show up in future markets. This chapter introduces such a system, the Luminance Brightness Rating (LBR) System of surfacing materials, determined not by just the material itself nor the lighting that falls on it, but by the simultaneous interaction of surface and light, which gives a material its relative brightness in architectural space.

The LBR system is based on a gray scale of brightnesses. The human eye does not see the total world in black, white, or gray, but the gray scale provides a means for assessing and controlling the appearance of color values in terms of brightness as seen on surfacing materials when subjected to illumination.

Before examining that system, a word on its practicality is in order. Because of the many implications of brightness in the visual perception of space, we must first recognize the nature of one color as it appears lighter or darker than another color. It is easy to visualize a light yellow as brighter than a dark blue. But unless color naming is accompanied by a visual color sample, it is not so easy to compare "pallid jasmine" with "blue mauve," and virtually impossible when encountering commercial labels like "Mesa View" or Talisman." What is needed, therefore, is a visual scale of segmented brightness zones that will accommodate the vast range of color names and scientific notations (present and future).

Further, the scale must contain a small number of easily manageable brightness steps for a designer to hold in memory or in hand while composing color relationships and organizing brightness levels in space.

Prior to explaining the LBR itself, we must first develop the scale with which the system can be used. A finishing material can then be positioned on that scale, based on its LBR. Considering the infinite number of color possibilities in manufactured paints and other surfacing materials, the theory of working with brightness becomes more simplified by initially avoiding color altogether. This can be done by visualizing color values by brightness alone, as they would appear in zones of brightness on a gray scale. For an understanding of this visualization process, we take a page out of the professional photographer's notebook.

Photography and the Gray Scale

A technique for visually measuring pictorial brightness levels is readily available in the field of black and white photography. It is a method of seeing the world in shades of gray, and has become a sophisticated approach to exposing film known to photographers as the "zone system." It was developed by the renowned master of photograpic art Ansel Adams, and was developed further by his followers including Minor White and others. By the chemistry of black and white photography, colors are converted to values of gray—in zones of brightness—when exposed on black and white film and photographic prints. A black and white photograph removes the impact of color, and becomes a convenient device for concentrating on brightness alone to examine how the luminance of a surface relates to others in a visual field.

The photographer needs to be attentive to more than just visualizing how any one surface or object of interest will appear as a particular shade of gray. It is necessary to "see" the whole scene about to be photographed as a total composition of different shades of gray. A judgment must then be made to estimate as closely as possible how that one surface or object in the scene will appear in relation to the brightness of all other elements in the composition. This is because when film is exposed to feature one element in a visual field, other surfaces often shift in values of gray due to the chemistry of the photographic process. The zone system therefore requires a *gray scale* to measure the brightness appearance of all possible surfaces in the scene, from total dark to total light. Some examples of gray scales used in photography, science, and industry are shown in Figure 5-1.

The manufacture of photographic products is founded on sensitometry, the scientific study of the chemistry of

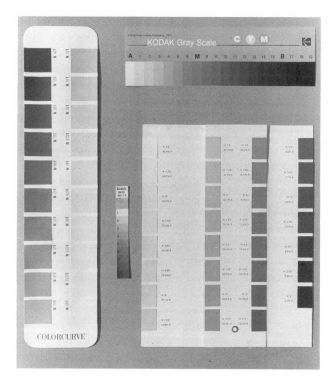

Figure 5-1. Gray scales for photography, science, and industry.

light effects on the characteristics of photographic film and paper. The zone system of the photographer is based on the principles of sensitometry, but is essentially a visual procedure. For professional photographers, the gray scale is an everyday working tool, and it is a system held in the memory as the photographer studies a scene and previsualizes how the various details will record on film once the shutter is snapped. Holding the gray scale in memory is made easier by the presence of a key zone midway between the two definitive ends of pure black and pure white, known as *middle gray*. Because middle gray is an important visual reference for photographers, Kodak manufactures a Neutral Test Card, sometimes simply called a "gray card," that is an indispensable tool in the traveling bag of the serious photographer. As a standard reference, the appearance of the gray card in both sunlight or electric light tells the critical observer how all other visible surfaces will relate to that middle gray, or how they will be located—in zones—toward the white or toward the black end of the scale. As we will see, this system of seeing the environment in terms of grays (brightness levels) is advantageous for decision making by the architectural and lighting designer.

How photographers use the zone system is shown in Figure 5-2, as often illustrated in handbooks on photography. The cafeteria shown in the photograph is a composition of brightness levels running the full scale from black to white. The illumination in the room is a mixture

Figure 5-2. *Gray zones measured in a photograph.*

of overhead fluorescent lighting and reflected sunlight from a court outside the windows. As they appear in the photograph, all surfaces have been rendered along the gray scale according to their orientation (angle of slant) toward the light sources and toward the observer (camera). A gray scale was used to measure the brightness of surfaces in the picture. The underside of the structural ceiling beam just right of the cross beam appears in zone 5 (middle gray), while near the windows where it receives more reflected light from the floor it brightens to zone 7. That change in zone shows how a surface responds to both light and spatial location. It should also be observed how glare radically increases the brightness of some surfaces, shifting them to zone 9, where surface details are nearly obliterated.

The theory of the photographic zone system is important for anyone associated with the visual arts for the basic fact that brightness levels rendered in a photograph remain *in a given order* on the gray scale. In simple logic, that means a surface brighter than middle gray will always locate toward the white end, and one darker than middle gray will locate toward the black end. It is the *order* of grays that is significant, the logical sequence of step-by-step increase in brightness from black to white. Now consider the proportional amount of surfaces in one brightness zone relative to all the others in an entire field of view. *How, where, and what proportion brightness levels occur is the essence of controlled composition for space and light design, regardless of the actual color of surfaces.* This is demonstrated in Part 3 of this book. Seeing the designed environment according to a gray scale to study the amount, proportion, and location of brightness patterns has validity for previsualizing what an architectural space will become once it is built and receives color and light.

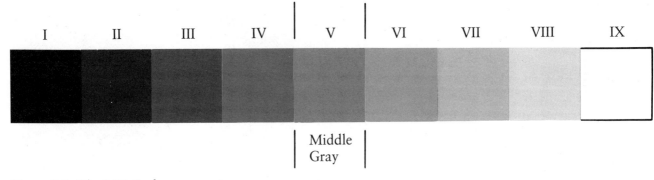

I   II   III   IV | V | VI   VII   VIII   IX

Middle
Gray

Figure 5-3. The LBR Scale.

A Nine-Zone Brightness Scale for Designers

The LBR Scale (Figure 5-3) was developed for the design and fabrication of the illuminated architectural environment. It is intended to serve as a visual measuring instrument for judging the relative brightness of a building material, and as a measure for predicting proportional shifts in brightness when the material is subjected to changes in illumination and angle of slant in architectural space. The scale is organized to meet two essential requirements: (1) a limited number of zones to aid the memory during the process of design and (2) the specification of gray values for the zones according to human visual perception. The zones were assigned Roman numerals for better distinction when combined with the Arabic mathematical notations of the LBR, which will be demonstrated later.

The LBR Scale was derived from the 1987 edition of the 31-step (matte) Munsell Neutral Value Scale (Figure 5-1), which according to Munsell "is a standard scale of neutral grays . . . in steps that look equal to the eye under standard viewing conditions." The Munsell system was used because of its ongoing tradition for the scientific and artistic study of color, its availability through the Macbeth Corporation in New Windsor, New York, and its ease of use in design, industrial production, and scientific research. For the reader preferring one of the other color systems, it is a simple matter of matching the gray zones of their system with those of Munsell.

The LBR Scale has nine zones, because as we shall see, they can be remembered without difficulty. The commercial gray scales having more steps (Figure 5-1) were produced to serve different purposes. A greater number of steps makes possible greater precision of measurement, but only as long as the physical scale itself is readily

at hand. The disadvantage of too many steps is that it works against the functions of memory for most individuals. A small number of steps is much more manageable for contemplating the luminance brightness of building materials during the process of design, and during consultation sessions between designers and sales representatives of product manufacturers. It is appropriate at this point to remember the advice of George A. Miller, and consider "the magical number seven" for recall as the "span of absolute judgment."[2] It is impractical to ask the human memory to recall the appearance of a brightness level of, say, a zone 17, let alone one of zone 63. The LBR Scale was therefore limited to nine zones, to include the two extremes readily found in the natural and architectural environment: absolute darkness and absolute lightness. Just as they are on the photographic scale, they establish the two bracketing ends of a continuum from black (zone I) to white (zone IX). Between the two is "the magical number seven."

The principal reason for developing an odd-numbered series of zones for the scale was to provide a middle value to serve as an internal reference between the two ends of black and white. That central value is middle gray, which assumes its symmetrical position as zone V (Figure 5-4). Middle gray was determined on ergonomic grounds, based on the human visual system. Known to visual perception psychologists and other scientists, a reflectance of 30% is middle gray *as seen by the human eye*. This was the justification for selecting Munsell notation N6 (exactly 30% R) as middle gray for the LBR Scale, which now conforms with human vision.

The completed LBR Scale as described in Munsell notations is given in Table 5-1.

[2] See Chapter 2, p. 23.

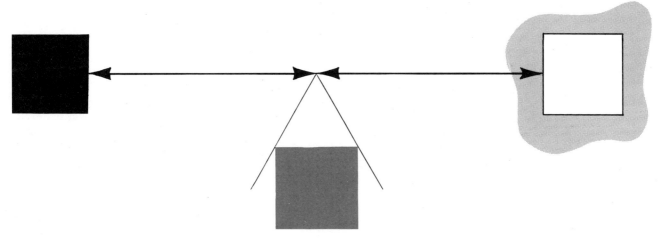

Figure 5-4. Constructing the LBR Scale.

Determining the Luminance Brightness Rating

To place a building material in a zone of the LBR Scale to be able to compare its brightness with other materials, it needs to be given a luminance brightness rating (LBR). The LBR is a two-part numerical notation of its brightness relative to all other architectural surfaces. One places the material on the LBR Scale as a *visual reference* for its comparative brightness. The other is a *percent notation,* which can be used for calculating the illuminance required to change its position from zone to zone. This is the line of communication between the designer who conceives the desired visual appearance of a surface in space and the lighting engineer who calculates the required illumination to create that desired appearance.

To make the system workable, LBRs were developed first for the zones themselves (i.e., for each of the Munsell notations selected as the mean brightness level for each zone). From the LBR of the seven internal zones between

Table 5-1. Munsells used for the LBR scale

Zone I	N2	3.1% R
Zone II	N3	6.6% R
Zone III	N4	12.0% R
Zone IV	N5	19.8% R
Zone V*	**N6**	**30.0% R**
Zone VI	N6.75	39.5% R
Zone VII	N7.5	50.7% R
Zone VIII	N8.5	68.4% R
Zone IX	N9.5	90.0% R

* Middle gray.

black and white, numerical boundaries were computed to establish the limits of the zones. So defined, the zones then can accommodate the placement of any building material on the scale according to its own LBR. The process used for determining the LBR of the Munsell notations will illustrate how the system works and how the LBR is calculated for any given material.

Calculation of the LBR of the zones begins with that of middle gray, zone V. As the midpoint of the LBR Scale, it becomes the standard reference point to which all other brightness levels are compared. The LBR of a building material in another zone is then derived as a percent differentiation indicating how far away its luminance appears from the mean of middle gray, either darker or brighter, in a standard situation.

The first question that needs an obvious answer is what should be the standard luminance of middle gray, the Munsell N6 located at the center of the LBR Scale. It would be invaluable if there were a national survey revealing the average luminances of the major spatial boundaries of office, residential, commercial, and industrial spaces. There are recommended reflectances, but not recommended luminances. This is due to the infinite possibilities of luminances resulting from the great number of surfacing materials and lighting techniques that are available on the market covering the whole spectrum of brightness levels across the entire LBR Scale. IESNA's *Lighting Handbook, Reference & Application* (1993, 518) recommends reflectances for walls at 50% to 70%, ceilings at 80% or more, floors at 20% to 40%, and furniture at 25% to 45%. As will be shown in Chapter 11, walls are major luminous boundaries of space, and as such they play a major role in determining the overall character of spatial design. To set a working luminance for the LBR System based on the IESNA-recommended wall reflectances, 10cd/ft^2 was chosen as representative of wall luminances in typical office environments. This luminance figure was assigned to the Munsell N6 gray card as the control standard for the LBR System.

Research in the Space and Light Laboratory was then conducted to develop the LBR for each of the remaining Munsell surfaces flanking middle gray on the LBR Scale. Brightness comparisons and photometer measurements were made in the laboratory's Luminance Viewer.[3] To perform those critical tests, subjects were chosen from the professions of architecture and interior design. Each tested the Munsell surfaces for zones II, III, IV, VI, VII and VIII to compare them in brightness with the N6 standard control panel (zone V) when it was illuminated at 10 cd/ft^2. The procedure used for those tests and the subsequent derivation of the LBR for the zones are as follows.

The Luminance Viewer has two side-by-side, independently illuminated chambers for comparing the brightness of two test panels under variable light. The N6 control panel was set in the left chamber, and was illuminated to create the standard control luminance of 10 cd/ft^2. The Munsell panels for the remaining LBR zones, each having the same specularity (matte), were inserted in the right chamber for testing. Each was first measured with a photometer under the same illumination that created the 10 cd/ft^2 for the N6 panel. The different reflectance of the test panel created a different luminance, and naturally a different brightness. The measurement of the test panel when illuminated at 10 cd/ft^2 established its entry luminance on the LBR Scale, and that luminance

determined the mean for each of the zones between black and white.

For each test panel, subjects were then asked to raise or lower its illumination until they judged the surface to have a "brightness match" with the N6 control panel displayed in the left chamber. A photometric measurement was then taken of the test panel, showing how much increase or reduction of illumination was required to move it from its entry luminance to match the brightness of the N6 panel. Fifty tests were made of each panel. The grand average was used to compute the LBR (see the example shown in Figure 5-5). The percent difference of luminance change from the material's entry luminance to its brightness match with the N6 control standard is its *luminance brightness rating*.

Because the LBR was computed with reference to middle gray, each test material was given a + or − percent rating. This means a material of dark value has an LBR of + percent because it requires that much more illumination necessary to brighten its appearance to match the value of N6 middle gray at zone V when illuminated at 10 cd/ft^2. Conversely, an LBR of − percent means that the material must be reduced in illumination to match the brightness of N6 middle gray. The LBRs of the Munsell materials used as the *mean* for each of the zones are given on Table 5-2.

Upon reviewing the luminance readings taken on the Munsell surfaces after they were illuminated to create a brightness match with the N6 control standard, at first it might be expected that they all should be 10 cd/ft^2 if the matches were accurate. This is not the case, either with the Munsells or any other surface, as we shall see later with tests of the LBR System applied to wood spe-

---

[3] For a description of the Luminance Viewer, see the Appendix.

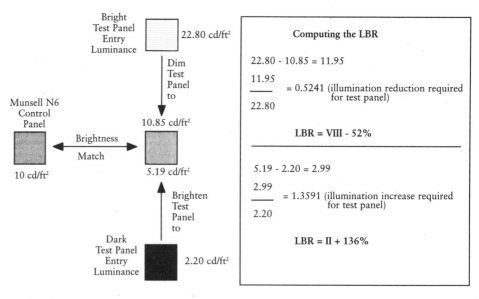

Figure 5-5. Computing the LBR.

Table 5-2. LBR of Munsell notations used for LBR scale

Value	Munsell Notation	Entry Luminance (cd/ft^2)	Brightness Match (cd/ft^2)	Difference	LBR Notation
Black	N2	—	—	—	I (end)
	N3	2.30	5.19	2.89	II +126%
	N4	4.00	5.96	1.96	III +49%
	N5	6.60	7.05	0.45	IV +7%
Middle gray	N6	10.00	—	—	V 00.0%
	N6.75	13.25	8.23	5.02	VI −38%
	N7.5	16.71	9.44	7.27	VII −44%
	N8.5	22.84	10.85	11.99	VIII −53%
White	N9.5	—	—	—	IX (end)

cies. Nor are the physical step measurements of the Munsell surfaces to be monotonic as might be expected. To account for this, we must turn to perceptual explanations.

The Weber-Fechner Law. In 1834 the German physiologist E. H. Weber observed that subjects made relative judgments of discrimination tasks instead of absolute judgments. The amount of change in a stimulus that they observed was proportional to its magnitude. Weber found that change is more easily observed at low levels of illumination than at high levels. As an example, people can notice an overall increase in brightness when a single lamp is added to a group of about 15, but not when 1 is added to a group of 100. Weber's work was followed up by the German physicist and experimental psychologist Gustave Fechner (1860), who published *The Elements of Psychophysics*, in which he gave a scaling method for measuring subjective brightness. Like Weber, Fechner found that subjective observance of absolute change in brightness was less at greater intensities of light. The principle of the Weber-Fechner law states that at high levels of illumination, a substantially large increase in luminance is required to perceive a noticeable change in brightness. This helps account for the differences in change in the LBR notation column of Table 5-2 comparing the Munsells below N6 with those above that middle gray standard. Further, in experiments in the Space and the Light Laboratory, it is frequently found that students have far greater difficulty making brightness judgments in conditions of high illumination of simulated architectural spaces.

The preceding procedure used for the Munsell surfaces is the same as that used for determining the LBR of any building material. Its *LBR notation* is the combination of its LBR Scale zone (Roman numerals) and its ± luminance rating (Arabic numerals). This is the dual notation of the LBR. It places the test material in one of the LBR Scale zones for visual comparison with the entire LBR Scale in which brightness ratios can be quickly judged. It also provides the percent difference from a standard illuminated middle gray for mathematical comparison to calculate the illumination required to give a surfacing material a desired brightness level as it will appear in architectural space.

The entry luminance of a surfacing material can be determined without elaborate laboratory viewing equipment. If the reflectance of the surface is known, the entry luminance can be calculated as a ratio of the LBR control standard Munsell N6 (30% reflectance) at 10 cd/ft^2. If the reflectance is not known, a simple studio light box can be constructed, one with a dimmer-controlled light source, and having balanced luminance levels in the viewing area. A small sheet of Munsell N6 matte paper can be purchased from the Macbeth Corporation in New Windsor, New York, and taped directly on the surfacing material. Place the material in the viewing box. Using a photometer, set the illumination at a level where the Munsell patch reads at 10 cd/ft^2. Without changing the illumination, take a luminance reading of the material immediately adjacent to the edge of the Munsell paper. That reading will be the surfacing material's entry luminance, which will fall somewhere between any two zone boundaries listed below. Several tests of the material should be done, each time verifying the 10 cd/ft^2 luminance of the Munsell. Power surges may give slight differences for each test, but normally they will not be severe.

With or without the known reflectance of a material, the second part of the LBR notation (the percent of change required for a brightness match with the N6) requires an elaborate laboratory testing system, especially for varicolored patterns of wall fabrics, vinyls, and carpeting. More is said about this later.

Numerical Boundaries for the Zones

Using the entry luminances of the Munsell surfaces, the numerical limits for each of the zones of the LBR Scale can now be established. With that done, the entry luminance of a building material will place it in one of the zones, and its comparison or contrast with other zones can be quickly visualized.

The two end zones of black (N2) and white (N9.5) are not considered means. They are ends and, as mentioned, are intended to represent all surfaces that appear as either extreme darkness or lightness in any environmental scene. The Munsell notations used for the seven internal zones are means.

The borders between zones II, III, IV and VI, VII, VIII were interpolated from the entry level of the Munsell gray used for each zone. Half of the distance between the LBR for zone II and zone III was used to establish the border between the two, and that figure was used for the border between zone II and zone I. The same was done for the border between zones VIII and IX. At the dead center of the LBR Scale, the numerical mean for zone V is 0.0. The boundaries for the zones are given in Table 5-3.

Given the infinite varieties of manufactured surfacing materials currently available and those forthcoming on future markets, many will fall close to the border between two zones. For example, two species of wood or two wall fabrics of similar color/pattern may be very close in LBR by percent notation, but fall into adjacent zones on the LBR Scale. This creates no major problem. The designer observes the location of a material near the border of a zone, and can simply visualize its brightness value as midway between the two zones flanking that border. The lighting engineer calculates the illumination from the luminance percentage of the LBR notation, independent of its proximity to a border, and that calculation is what is important for the ultimate appearance that the material will have in architectural space.

Figure 5-6. Colors and patterns of fabrics in a gray scale of brightness.

Table 5.3. Numerical boundaries for LBR zones

I	00.0—1.30 cd/ft^2
II	1.30—3.10
III	3.10—5.30
IV	5.30—8.30
V	8.30—11.85
VI	11.85—15.30
VII	15.30—19.85
VIII	19.85—25.75
IX	above 25.75

Luminance Brightness of Design Patterns

When samples of building materials are placed in the Luminance Viewer, most are comparatively easy to perceive as having an overall brightness, particularly painted surfaces, plain vinyls, even-grained wood species, and many wall fabrics and rugs of relatively simple patterns. Many other surfacing materials, however, are not that easy to evaluate, due to more complex design patterns and colors. It is difficult but not impossible to judge the overall brightness of materials bearing multicolored patterns. For this reason, professional laboratory testing is required where the rigors and exactitude of scientific procedure can be applied. Several of the leading manufacturers of wall fabrics and other materials contributed samples of their products to the Space and Light Laboratory for use in the research that spawned this LBR System.

Many fabric designs have a variety of colors in multiple hues and patterns, yet most of those tested in the Luminance Viewer did render a general brightness level that was manageable for LBR evaluation. Figure 5-6 shows two rows of swatches from a manufacturer's line of fabrics, and even though each has a pattern of contrasting light and dark hues, when viewed as a group they do indeed fit into a brightness scale. For some fabrics (Figure 5-7), it is a greater problem measuring the luminance than it is for subjects to visually match their brightness with the Munsell N6 control standard. For those patterns, photometric measurements can be taken in two ways. First, the dominant color/patterns are measured with a narrow-beam photometer and averaged, and then a wider angle photometer is used to include a cluster of the component color patterns. The two methods are averaged for an overall luminance of the fabric. This same dual method was required for some of the wood species, such as zebrawood (Figure 5-7), which has an irregular array of lights and darks in its grain pattern. A second method requires sophisticated laboratory equipment such as a rotary mechanism, in which a complex pattern is spun under variable light, which has the effect of averaging the lights and darks of the design.

LBR of Wood Species

The LBR System was applied first to woods for the simple reason that although there are numerous species of wood around the world, and that from time to time some have enjoyed a popularity or cost advantage more than others, they do not go in and out of style as rapidly as do wall fabrics and vinyls. Moreover, the widespread use of wood for flooring, wall paneling, architectural grilles, and furniture—major surfaces appearing in architectural space—suggested that an LBR for the wood species would be a significant contribution to the practice of architectural and lighting design.

Figure 5-7. The brightness of patterns.

Figure 5-8. Wood Index forming a gray scale.

A "Wood Index" has been compiled in the Space and Light Laboratory, displayed as a comprehensive collection of the more common woods used for architecture worldwide. Nature has given many of the woods a variety of hues within a species, such as white, medium, and red oak. Subspecies like those are considered standard for application to architectural and furniture design and therefore were given their own LBR. The wood samples used for LBR evaluation were finished with two coats of satin polyurethane varnish, because in an architectural environment wood surfaces most commonly have some protective finish. As wood finishers have long known, each of the species darkened from its pure cut and sanded state as the clear varnish was applied. Figure 5-8 shows a sampling from the Wood Index in the lab, and illustrates how a variety of woods form their own gray scale, from dark species like wenge, ebony, padauk, black walnut, and Carpathian elm burl at one end, to basswood, cottonwood, white pine, and birds-eye maple at the other. Some species that have deep reddish hue appear quite dark, like padauk, amaranth (purpleheart), and bubinga. Some are deceiving. Dark red lauan, which might be expected to appear at the dark end of the scale, actually appears near the middle. It is recognized that variations exist within some species. As much as possible, individual samples for the Wood Index are considered average for the species.

To determine the LBR of a sample material, refer to Figure 5-5. Using the wood species alder in Table 5-4 as an example, its entry luminance (11.75 cd/ft^2) places it in zone V. The difference (1.81 cd/ft^2) between its entry luminance and its brightness match (9.94 cd/ft^2), with the N6 control standard divided by the entry luminance, gives the LBR notation of V −15%. As explained earlier, the minus percentage means alder needs 15% less illumination to match the N6 standard at 10 cd/ft^2.

Table 5-4 lists the LBRs of the Wood Index alphabetically.[4]

Stain and other protective finishes modify the color value of the natural surface of the wood, changing its brightness. Consequently, that change can shift its location from one zone to another on the LBR Scale. Figure 5-9 shows white pine panels that have shifted in zone as the natural wood responded to darkening stains. Manufacturers of wood stains have their own color identification names, so for practical purposes each wood species must be tested with a variety of stains to learn how the brightness of the finished panel will result, and how its position on the LBR Scale will have shifted.

Memory and the LBR Scale

Remember that the LBR Scale was conceived to have only nine zones to make it easier to remember and to make it a practical device for designing and illuminating architectural space. When first attempting to use the scale for referencing the brightness of a surface compared with others, most people would have difficulty trying to remember the shades of gray for the interior zones be-

---

[4] This is only a partial list of the Wood Index being assembled in the Space and Light Laboratory in the School of Architecture and Urban Design at The University of Kansas. Accumulating good specimens of additional wood species native to the United States and worldwide is an ongoing process in the lab. The species listed in Table 5-4 are those that have been tested for their LBR at the time this book was published.

tween black and white. To solve this problem, the middle gray value of Munsell N6 needs to be memorized, and once that is done with reasonable consistency, it will be easier for you to recall the darker and lighter zones flanking the middle as we shall see.

Memorizing the value of Munsell N6 as middle gray for zone V comes through practice, when giving full visual and mental concentration to its brightness compared with common surfacing materials. In the photographer's work, frequent use of the photographic gray

Table 5-4. LBR of wood species

Zone ± LBR Notation	Species	Habitat	Entry Luminance cd/ft²	Brightness Match cd/ft²	Luminance Difference cd/ft²
V −15%	Alder	United States	11.75	9.94	1.81
III +116%	Amaranth (Purpleheart)	Brazil	4.30	9.27	4.97
VI −8%	Anigre	Africa	12.03	11.09	0.94
VI −17%	Ash	United States	11.88	9.84	2.04
VII −45%	Basswood	United States	15.34	8.38	6.96
V −11%	Beech	United States	11.27	10.08	1.19
VI −26%	Birch, yellow	United States	13.72	10.14	3.58
III +129%	Bloodwood (Cardinalwood)	Brazil	3.67	8.39	4.72
III +97%	Bubinga (African rosewood)	Africa	4.42	8.69	4.27
IV +67%	Cedar, red	United States	6.20	10.35	4.15
V +19%	Cherry, light	United States	9.39	11.19	1.80
IV +64%	Cherry, medium	United States	6.02	9.89	3.87
II +454%	Cocobola	Panama	1.77	9.80	8.03
II +263%	Cordia	Mexico	2.48	8.99	6.51
VII −43%	Cottonwood	United States	17.73	10.11	7.62
VI −32%	Cypress	United States	14.74	10.08	4.66
II +563%	Ebony	Africa, East Coast	1.31	8.68	7.37
II +351%	Elm, Carpathian (burl)	Eastern Europe	2.37	10.68	8.31
IV +90%	Gum, red	United States	5.82	11.06	5.24
IV +77%	Imbuia	Brazil	5.73	10.15	4.42
IV +94%	Koa, Brazilian	Brazil	5.47	10.63	5.16
V +15%	Lauan, dark red	Philippines	9.71	11.18	1.47
IV +61%	Mahogany, Honduras	Central America	5.63	9.08	3.45
VII −38%	Maple, bird's-eye medium	United States	17.35	10.68	6.67
V −18%	Maple, hard	United States	11.81	9.68	2.13
VI +27%	Maple, soft	United States	14.04	10.20	3.84
III +158%	Moradillo (Morado)	Bolivia	3.63	9.36	5.73
V −7%	Oak, red	United States	11.16	10.43	0.73
VI −22%	Oak, white	United States	12.51	9.78	2.73
III +239%	Padauk	Africa	3.47	11.75	8.28
V −16%	Pecan	United States	11.05	9.32	1.73
VII −43%	Pine, sugar white	United States	19.77	11.21	8.56
VII −44%	Pine, "knotty" white	United States	19.03	10.62	8.41
VI −31%	Poplar, yellow	United States	14.93	10.23	4.70
IV +45%	Rosewood, Honduras	Central America	5.82	8.41	2.59
V +21%	Sapele (African mahogany)	Africa	9.71	11.71	2.00
VI −13%	Sassafras	United States	12.19	10.59	1.60
IV +36%	Teak	Southeast Asia	5.59	7.62	2.03
II +182%	Walnut, black	North America	3.08	8.70	5.62
II +562%	Wenge (Panga Panga)	Africa	1.57	10.40	8.83
IV +77%	Willow	United States	5.35	9.47	4.12
IV +25%	Zebrawood	Africa	7.54	9.43	1.89

Figure 5-9. Staining woods for brightness.

card while taking light readings enables recognition of surfaces of similar brightness in a scene. The competent photographer can walk through a woods of filtered sunlight and pick out a plant leaf or tree bark that at the time is illuminated to give it a brightness level of middle gray. This can also be learned by professional designers and lighting engineers using the Munsell N6. A few sheets of the Munsell N6 (8½-in. × 11 in.) can be dry mounted on a firm panel and displayed in the studio in carefully selected locations where they receive common or average illumination. Two can be hung on walls at right angles to observe the shift in zone created by angle of slant to the light source and to the observer. If hung on a wall that receives sunlight or fluorescent illumination, the surface needs to be protected from ultraviolet light to prevent fading. The nineteenth-century French painter Delacroix hung a color circle in his studio as a constant reminder of color relationships. In like manner, displayed Munsell N6 cards should become permanent fixtures in the design studio or illumination workplace, serving as a continual reminder of the middle gray value of zone V under certain light.

How is the rest of the LBR Scale memorized? Let us return to the two ends, zone I (black) and zone IX (white). All architectural surfaces that fall into those two zones appear to the eye as extreme darkness or lightness, and have no visible surface details. Acuity is poor or nonexistent, because the eye has little or nothing on

which to focus. Zone I includes all areas of total darkness in the environment, those deep in shadow with very dark textureless surfaces where generally no details are readily noticeable. At the opposite end of the scale, zone IX includes all extremely light surfaces, such as textureless, pure white plaster and white painted walls facing direct, intense illumination, including direct sunlight on a bright day. Zone IX includes all intense light sources in the field of view, such as exposed lamps in luminaires and extremely bright reflector or diffusing panels. It also includes bright surfaces on which it is very difficult for the eye to focus due to high simultaneous contrast. Glare, which obliterates surface detail or fine texture, also belongs in zone IX. Note that these surfaces are high on the list of focal accents,[5] which arrest the saccadic movements of the eye as it scans the environment.

The next two zones inward from both ends are easily identified as those extremely dark or extremely light surfaces on which moderate texture appears. Zones II and VIII contain all materials that appear very dark and very bright, respectively, but differ from the two end zones by showing surface texture or faint detail. Examples for zone II are dark brown, blue, green, or gray carpeting, and all very dark colored wall fabrics and vinyls that make their presence known under dim illumination by exhibiting some surface characteristics that are

[5] See Chapter 4, p. 23.

not observable in the textureless or apparent textureless surfaces of zone I. The same theory applies to zone VIII, which includes textured, matte white walls, white ceiling tiles, or sprayed plaster ceilings.

At this point, note how easily five of the nine zones can be recalled from memory:

- the two ends of black and white (extreme darkness or lightness, no apparent texture)

- the next two inward zones (showing texture or faint detail)

- middle gray (once its brightness value has been learned).

The remaining zones, only two on each side of middle gray, can be learned by bringing to mind a few standard building materials or natural elements for each one, especially representative materials that are commonly used by an individual designer or design firm. From Table 5-4 of wood species, teak helps to define zone IV; yellow birch, zone VI; and so on. Once the LBR System is adopted by industry, memorizing the four interior zones flanking middle gray gradually will become reinforced by the day-to-day experiences of working with building materials. Laboratory tests will determine their brightness zones and percent LBR, both of which will appear on identifying labels of new and standard products, and their use in conceptual design and illumination calculations will develop a working familiarity of the complete LBR Scale.

Shifts in Zone by Texture and Slant

In Chapter 3 we show how the surface qualities of texture and reflectance determine how bright a material will appear under illumination, and also note how a surface will change in brightness as a result of its slant to the light source and to the observer. The physical surface characteristics and spatial orientation are therefore important attributes of building materials for working with the LBR System.

Varying the amount of texture on a surface modifies its brightness, and if texture is increased or decreased substantially, the appearance of a material shifts to another zone on the LBR Scale. Let's return to Figure 3-11, which shows three panels of different texture, all sprayed with the same gray color value as Munsell N6, middle gray on the LBR Scale. The three panels reduce in brightness as the amount of texture increases. The slightly textured panel on the right was measured in the laboratory to remain in zone V after being sprayed with N6 gray. The middle panel shifted one position, falling into zone IV, and the most heavily textured panel on the left shifted to zone III.

Wall fabrics and vinyls should be scrutinized for their textural qualities when selecting them for installation. As we shall see later, the direction of weave or other textural patterns should be studied for how a wall covering will be rendered in highlights and shadow resulting from its orientation to light after it is installed. Based on texture alone, unless a material's entry luminance on the LBR Scale is very close to a border between zones, only in the case of very coarse texture or high surface relief will a fabric or other surfacing material shift in zone.

Shifts in zone resulting from slant are another matter. The three Kodak Neutral Test Cards shown in Figure 3-18 clearly illustrate how the same color value and reflectance factor change in brightness as they change in slant to the light source. The angle of slant also affects visibility of surface detail. Figure 5-10 shows three views of a smooth, polished slab of petrified wood, photographed with the slab rotated to the light source. In the middle view, the average brightness of the slab places it in zone V, and the agate patterns appear most clearly. In the top view, glare begins to eradicate the surface details, and in the bottom view, the agate patterns lurk in shadow. This demonstration of brightness and surface recognition related to slant shows what happens to smooth walls, ceilings, and floors in the everyday world of the architectural environment.

Contemporary fabrics used for wall coverings and furniture are manufactured in a wide range of design patterns and weaves. The interlacing of warp and filling create a variety of weave constructions, known in the textile industry as plain, twill, satin, basket, rib, piqué, jacquard, and others. In some fabrics, that interlacing exposes different yarns in different directions to a light source, which changes how the same material looks when seen at different angles of slant (Figure 5-11). The result is a shift in brightness and a change in the appearance of the pattern. This demonstrates how a fabric can change in appearance once it is veneered to a wall and seen from different viewing angles.

Figure 5-12 shows the same fabric of Figure 5-11 mounted on two panels that are slanted to the light source. This demonstration shows how the texture and weave of a fabric can change the brightness by a full zone (or more) on the LBR Scale. It is a simple illustration of how a surfacing material changes in brightness and pattern once installed in architectural space, based on the location of the light sources.

These demonstrations of brightness related to texture and slant show that it is not a material's diffuse reflectance that will determine how it will appear in three-

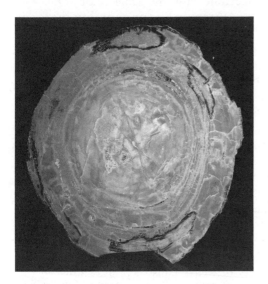

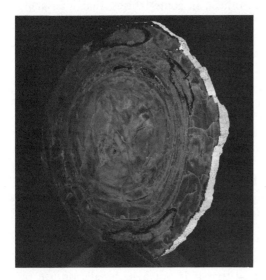

Figure 5-10. Slant, brightness, and surface detail.

dimensional space. Diffuse reflectance is important only as it establishes a material's entry zone on the LBR Scale. The LBR Scale is a reference guide for learning the behavior of building materials as they render brightness appearance in spatial perception. The key to using the LBR System is the recognition of the entry zone of a given material. That is to say, in an average condition (at a certain zone of gray) that material will appear at a given brightness when compared or contrasted with the entry zone of any other material that would be placed at that same spatial location. That appearance will change according to the quantity, quality, and direction of illumination, and to the viewing angle of the observer, but it will do so proportionally to materials in other zones with which it is being compared. Knowledge of brightness relationships, and how they are created by light, reflectances, and viewing angles is paramount for analysis and design of architectural space.

Application to Design and Industry

When the lights are turned on in a room, all the visible surfaces respond according to the surface properties that create their luminances. If working independently, the architect, interior designer, or lighting engineer may work counterproductively in their efforts to create the specific values of color and brightness of those surfaces. The LBR System is most helpful for regulating the overall design effects of an architectural space by focusing attention on the major space-defining surfaces. They are the ones that comprise the *spatial envelope,* which is analyzed in Parts 2 and 3 of this book. The LBR System is a quick and easy guide for selecting and illuminating the finishing materials to be used for that spatial envelope. The system can also be used for selecting the more subsidiary surfaces such as those that appear as furniture, room dividers, architectural grilles, or other significant elements of a total environment. In professional practice, the LBR System brings together the designer, lighting engineer, and manufacturers of building materials in a way that coordinates their activities and capitalizes on the expertise of each to bring into existence a well-designed architectural space.

USE OF THE LBR BY DESIGNERS

It is the architectural or interior designer who initially shapes architectural space and decides on the color and appearance of its major surfaces. As has been done for centuries, the designer thinks pictorially, and distributes

Figure 5-11. Brightness change on fabric by direction of weave.

colors in spatial composition by selecting the surfacing materials. As we have seen, illumination and angular location will produce the brightness levels of those materials based on their intrinsic color. It is here that the application of the LBR System becomes an effective procedure for the development and refinement of spatial design.

To begin, visualize a wall as a major surface defining an architectural space, and let's say the desired color for that wall is blue. What is important is the value of the blue, because its luminance will deliver the brightness

level of that surface. If the surfacing material of that wall is textured, the blue will be reduced in value relative to the density of the texture and the quality of illumination. If the material is a patterned, multicolored fabric, what is important is how much the blue dominates over the presence of other hues in the pattern.

The LBR System is a method for controlling the brightness levels in that total composition. With a sample of paint, fabric, or wood paneling in hand, the designer makes note of the LBR of that sample *by zone,* and visualizes its location on the LBR Scale. This is the entry

Figure 5-12. Brightness change by angle to light source.

zone for that building material, and that is the first step in working with the LBR System. That entry zone is then visualized relative to the entry zones of other materials being considered for the remaining major surfaces of the total design.

Now consider what will happen to a material once it appears in the illuminated spaces of architecture, that is, how it influences "the effects of light" that we saw in Chapter 3:

1. It brightens, darkens, or changes *value of hue* depending on the quantity and quality of illumination.

2. It darkens the more the surface is *textured* as a result of illumination creating more shadow.

3. It brightens or darkens depending on its *angle of slant to the light source(s),* including direct and/or indirect daylight from windows or skylights.

4. It brightens or darkens depending on its *angle of slant to the observer.*

This means that the material shifts in zone on the LBR Scale as any one or a combination of these conditions takes place. The designer (and lighting specialist) can stay in control of the first three points above, and those three are the most critical for creating the visual character of a space. Point 4 is another matter. People move around in space, and the ever-changing brightening or darkening of a surface due to its angle of slant to the moving eye is simply natural to the human use of the environment. There are situations, however, when that fourth point should be given special consideration, such as when some of the major surfaces will be seen at prevailing angles of slant common for most uses of the space. An example is a corridor's walls, ceilings, and floor, which generally stay at the same angle for people walking through. It also applies to staircases and to rooms where certain surfaces are angled to fixed seating arrangements.

The value of the LBR System is its effectiveness for comparing two or more surfacing materials when taken through each of the four "effects of light" listed above. From its entry location on the LBR Scale, any one material will shift to other zones according to those "effects of light." Other materials under the same lighting conditions will also shift, but in a direction and number of steps from their own entry zones. This is how the brightness levels in space are controlled: by the designer selecting materials by their color values and then using the LBR Scale as a guide for anticipating how the materials will be modified under variable illumination and the surface's spatial location.

A second design function of the LBR System is its application to perceptual analyses of seeing forms in space as presented in Chapter 4. This refers to the visual perception of furniture and other freestanding elements in the architectural environment in the all important design task of establishing spatial brightness ratios. The theory is illustrated in Figure 5-13. The brightness value of the Munsell N6 chip in the foreground sets up a brightness ratio with any one zone of the LBR Scale in the background. The zones represent brightness means for accommodating the natural woods and the unlimited number of manufactured materials available in present and future markets, when those manufactured materials are assigned an LBR zone. The zones into which materials will fall offer a quick reference for visual brightness ratios when contemplating spatial design concepts.

With continued use of the LBR System, designers in an office that frequently works with certain wood paneling and furniture materials will eventually learn to recognize how any one kind of wood or other materials will appear in brightness ratios under certain lighting. Figure C-7 shows how different wood species can be selected according to how each responds to light, and participates in a carefully composed, well-crafted composition. Each wood species is going to fall somewhere on the LBR Scale, as do dark, medium, or light brick and all other construction materials, exterior and interior. In time, the relative brightness of different standard materials will be learned. During design development, the brightness appearance of a freestanding surface in space can be previsualized in brightness ratios that it will make when compared with the estimated brightness of the dominant surface areas in a room. Visualizing the appearance of a material as it shifts in zones in the realities of architecture must be done by learning how its brightness is modified by light, and how it appears in the third dimension of space, not according to how it appears in a photograph—including the illustrations in this book—and not by how it happens to appear as a manufacturer's swatch lying on a design or conference table.

USE OF THE LBR BY ILLUMINATING ENGINEERS

Whatever the circumstances that account for light entering the built environment, it is the quantity and quality of illumination that modifies the brightness and color appearance of building materials. There are times when interior designers or architects create certain lighting effects as an integral part of their designs, but it is the professional lighting designer and illuminating engineer that have the expertise to render in light specific appearances of a surfacing material as it is located in architectural space.

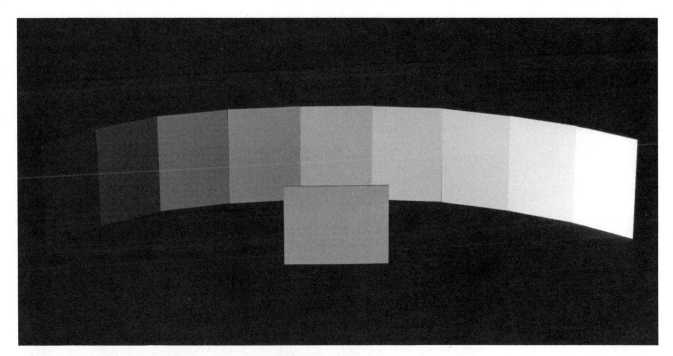

Figure 5-13. Luminance/brightness ratio with the LBR Scale.

40 W

75 W

Figure 5-14. Zone shift by lamp power.

Figure 5-15. Zone shift by inverse square law.

Other than the material's surface characteristics and the color of illumination, it is the *quantity* of light that is most responsible for a material's brightness. This takes place by a combination of the power of the light source and its distance from the surface. Figure 5-14 shows two Munsell N6 cards under incandescent light sources of different wattage (one 40 W, the other 75 W), each the same distance away. Figure 5-15 illustrates how brightness changes as a function of the inverse square law, as the light sources are set at different distances from the N6 cards. Such changes in brightness based on power and distance of illumination belong to common knowledge. What the LBR System offers are guidelines for creating and controlling the brightness of surfaces. The lighting specialist or whoever is responsible for the kind, quantity, and location of illumination that is put into architectural space can use the LBR Scale to develop and refine the final appearance of the major surfaces. This is done by working with the LBR of a material at its entry zone on the LBR Scale, that is, how it compares in brightness with the middle gray of Munsell N6 under the same illumination.

Decisions regarding the quantity of light with reference to brightness have far-reaching implications. The issue is energy savings. The brightness—and spaciousness—of a room can be increased in ways other than by adding more illumination, which adds to installation costs and operating budget. Manufacturers offer many lines of interior building materials in the form of paints, fabrics, vinyls, and wood paneling. A surfacing material with an upper-middle to high entry zone on the LBR Scale brightens the room with no increase in illumination. Further, laboratory demonstrations have shown that sometimes wall coverings with a high LBR take on an interestingly distinctive appearance under illumination that is reduced from what might be considered average lighting conditions. The final outcome of a room's appearance is a give-and-take situation between the designer selecting the surfacing materials and the illumination engineer giving them light. This requires further application of space and light theory for creating the mood of an illuminated environment, which will be done in Part 3.

USE OF THE LBR BY INDUSTRY

For purposes of working with the LBR System, luminance studies to compare the brightness of a building material with that of Munsell N6 can be done in the workplace of the designer, illuminating engineer, or the manufacturer originating a product, but many of the contemporary styles and multicolored patterns of wall coverings require sophisticated laboratory methods for assignment of an accurate LBR. This can be done by independent testing laboratories, but it is industry that should assume the responsibility for the visual evaluation of their products just as they do for tests and ratings of "flame spread."

The manufacturers' designers or product developers initiate the surface characteristics that will determine the brightness of building materials. They conceive the surface colors, textures, patterns, and finishes that eventually will respond to light in architectural environments. It is important for manufacturers to be aware of what their new materials will look like under variable light. How those materials are conceived and under what kind of light they are created are critical. If a material is being developed on a computer monitor, the designer must remember that its image is only a simulation created by light coming from behind the monitor's screen, and is unlike the physical product that will be produced and illuminated in architectural space. Imagine how many times discussions take place regarding evaluations of a new product design from its inception in the mind of the manufacturer's designer, through development meetings and marketing studies, until the final product rolls off production machinery and is packaged for shipment. It is interesting to contemplate the kind of lighting that illuminated the workplaces in which each of those discussions took place.

The very advantage of having available a wide variety of product designs is the fact that they take on different appearances when installed in different illumination and spatial conditions. This provides the architectural and interior designer the opportunity for making more critical selections to refine spatial composition by color and brightness values. A point of concern is that when a product line or style is chosen for a specific architectural space, sometimes there is a gap in the selection possibilities in terms of color and brightness values that should have been filled instead of creating too many designs of similar brightness in or near the same zone of the LBR Scale. The LBR System helps manufacturers' designers and market analysts to make those decisions. When there is a comprehensive distribution of brightness levels within a series of designs in one style, the architectural and lighting designers have greater control over the composition of brightness values in the spaces they create.

Between the manufacturer and the architectural designer lies the role of the sales representative. Traveling from office to office and to merchandise marts, representatives bring out their samples in whatever illumination happens to be at hand. Those products are instantly modified by the quality and quantity of light in the room. These situations prompt restatement of the most fundamental law for choosing a product: *Select the material under the same illumination that will exist in the architectural environment where it will appear.*

The LBR System provides a common visual language between the sales representative and the architectural and lighting designer, making more efficient the steps toward achieving specific design goals. Sales representatives who are knowledgeable about how their products respond to light can offer the consultation that designers want to hear: "This is how this fabric will raise in brightness when seen at 30° or 45° angle of slant for a person walking down that corridor" or "For the effect you want here, try these samples of this line, which have a lower (or higher) LBR."

The manufacturer should assume the responsibility of assigning the LBR to each new product and to each of their standard and present products. Attached to catalog swatches or menus of the actual material is a company's label identifying the product's name, style, color, backing, size, flame spread, and other information the designer requires. Manufacturers need to add one more item of information on that label and in related technical literature: *the LBR of that specific product.* It is time for the designers and manufacturers of the built environment to strive toward minimizing approximations and guesswork regarding the lighting effects on the surfaces of architectural space. This is a challenge to each industry that considers itself a leader in providing designers and illuminating engineers with a more informed use of their products for the design of the human habitats of the twenty-first century.

CHAPTER 6

Color Theory for Architectural Space

You may have thought that it was all talk and
no reality; but now that you are in the canyon,
and in a shadow, look about you and see if
there is not plenty of color there, too. The walls
are dyed with it, the stones are stained with
it—all sorts of colors from strata of rock, from
clays and slates, from minerals, from lichens,
from mosses. The stones under your feet have
not turned black or brown because out of the
sunlight.

—*John C. Van Dyke*
The Desert*

The fields of science and the visual arts benefit from an abundance of published color theory. Understanding its application to architecture is essential for the designer because color influences the lives of people in their everyday environment. Created by light, color induces mood sensations, stimulates feelings, and influences behavior. Research has shown that human response to color is both objective and subjective, and to create a truly humanized architecture, the technical, physiological, and psychological characteristics of color must be integrated throughout the design process. Books and articles pertaining to the chromatic aspects of architectural design too often treat color as a mere appliqué, like a painter approaching a plain, gessoed canvas ready for the brush. If color is applied to a building at a time when it is virtually completed as a structural assemblage of barren forms and

volumes, it is little more than a decorative afterthought. Many recent architectural books published with color in their titles are not much more than collections of color photographs of buildings. To reinforce the scope of this book that presents architectural space as the environment perceived by human vision, this chapter focuses on selected components of color theory taken from the fields of design, lighting, and visual perception so we can lay the groundwork for the practical applications of color to architecture that is done in Part 3.

The very mention of the word *color* breeds about as many different points of view as to how it should be explained as there are colors in a kaleidoscope. Consistently clear communication across scientific and artistic lines suffers from the lack of a universally adopted language of color theory and application. The difficulty with the various color systems and different approaches to color research is the lack of standardization. Problems stem from the differences of color in illumination, the color of surfaces (*object color*) on which light reflects,

* From Van Dyke, John C. 1980. *The Desert.* Salt Lake City: Peregrine Smith, p. 210.

and the *perceived color* in the retina. The perception of color varies from individual to individual, and about 8% of the male population and 0.5% of females have some form of color blindness. The quality and quantity of illumination are especially important for the appearance of color, particularly as they apply to the lighting of architectural space. For a good condensed version of the essential properties of illumination related to color, and for an additional bibliography, the reader is directed to Chapter 4 of the 1993 edition of the *Lighting Handbook, Reference & Application* published by IESNA. A convenient 44-page quick reference for color and lighting is *Color and Illumination,* also available through IESNA.

Attributes of Color

For use in science, industry, and the arts, descriptions of color are based on three attributes: *hue, saturation,* and *value.* At times their application to design becomes confusing to the student, especially in the presence of overlapping terminology such as *lightness* and *brightness.* To provide a workable and generally accepted vocabulary for use in space and light theory for architecture, the attributes are illustrated in Figure C-8. It is the same as the Munsell system, except that Munsell uses *chroma* instead of saturation. The term *chroma* causes difficulty at times because it lacks a clear counterpart as a verb or participle; it is easier to speak of "saturating" the hue of a given material or the "saturating" influence of illumination. Moreover, the term *saturation* often appears as an attribute in color literature.

Hue is the more precise term for what most people call *color* in everyday conversation. It is the attribute for describing one sensation of color in the retina as it differs from others, such as red compared with green. In the physics of light the dimensions of wavelengths define the primary hues of yellow, red, and blue, and the secondary hues of green, orange, and violet. For most practical applications of color, hue by itself is insufficient for describing the unlimited appearances of color sensations existing in the visual world. Within the range of what most people call "red," we hear of red apples, crimson sunsets, vermilion flowers, carmine bracelets, scarlet clothing, ruby lips, and maroon automobiles. It is clear that additional attributes other than hue are required for working with color in design analysis and practice.

Saturation refers to the purity of a hue and is dependent on how much gray it contains as a result of its proportional content of black or white. Figure C-8 shows that the farther away a hue is from the influence of the gray scale at the vertical column, the more pure it becomes. Red is more saturated than maroon and pink. Sometimes the term *intensity* is used to describe the satu-

rated appearance of a hue, but that again becomes confusing because of its association with *light* and *illumination.* The best way to remember the saturation of a color is by its content of gray, and as it moves farther outward from the gray-scale column of Figure C-8, it becomes more saturated.

Value is the third attribute for color analysis, greatly contributing to the degree of its brightness as dark or light. From Figure C-8, a change in appearance of value can be visualized by sliding a saturated hue up or down the column between black and white. When applying the meaning of this attribute of color to the illumination of architectural space, it is easy to see why the term *lightness* is being avoided for definition of hue and saturation, as just mentioned for the term *intensity.* The same is true for the term *brightness.* A shift in value does brighten or darken a hue, but so does saturation. Whereas saturation refers to the *quantity* of a gray in a given hue, value refers to the *quality* of the gray, in a range from black to white.

To see how all three attributes interrelate, imagine a middle value of a highly saturated red, positioned well outward from the gray scale. Move it inward toward the vertical column, and it will progressively dull and darken as it picks up gray content. Then slide it down. Near the bottom and close to the value column, its original saturation (pure red) is virtually annihilated. Slide it up and away from the column of grays, and its change in value and saturation will make it appear brighter as it leaves the dark reds and maroons and enters the pastels.

Psychophysiological Response to Color

People have likes and dislikes for certain colors, but clinical and research psychologists have learned that men and women react to color in psychophysiological ways beyond their subjective preferences as expressed in artistic and decorative tastes. Color affects brain activity and biorhythms, influencing our moods and feelings. Although it is unclear at the moment as to exactly how it occurs, we know that the pituitary and pineal glands interact with the electromagnetic energy of color, and it appears certain that nonvisual cells near the retina may activate photobiological sensations that supplement hormone activity in the body.

Exposure to red light is physiologically stimulating, and has been known to raise blood pressure and increase respiration and heart rates, but under certain conditions of prolonged exposure to red, the body may actually reverse the excitation response and function below normal. The human eye must make adjustments when receiving red light waves, which actually focus behind the retina. For sharp focus on red, therefore, the lens of the eye changes to a greater convex shape, which draws the red light waves forward. This creates an illusion of red surfaces appearing closer and larger than they actually are.

Blue behaves just the opposite of red. It causes the lens of the eye to flatten compared with the more convex shape it takes when exposed to red, tending to make a blue surface recede in spatial distance and appear reduced in size. Physiological experiments with emotions have shown that exposure to blue generally has a calming effect, reduces pulse and respiration rates, and lowers blood pressure. But like the reversal nature of red, prolonged exposure to blue can also have an opposite effect, in this case causing the body to respond above its normal functions.

Along with red and blue, the third primary color is yellow. It is cheerful and high-spirited, and carries feelings of happiness and vitality. Yellow abounds in associations with sunny days, many of nature's flowers, and inspiration. Impure mixtures of yellow that reduce saturation and drop value can strip the hue of its geniality and gaiety. This can be observed in the swatches of Figure C-10, from the more 'pure' yellow of the farthest right in the second row from the top (Munsell 5Y 8.5/14) diagonally downward to the lower left area of the Munsells.

The secondary colors of green, violet, and orange also generate psychological responses. Like the season of Spring, green is refreshing and rejuvenating, suggesting the fertile and renewing powers of nature. Green is a relaxing color, and like blue can instill feelings of calm. In the physiology of the eye, green light waves focus directly on the retina, and for this reason green is most restful for human vision.

The psychological effect of purple is interesting because it is a mixture of the two opposites, red and blue. For this reason the slightest change in value can make purple appear warm or cool.

Orange, like its neighboring red, is stimulating and exciting, and borrows the spirit of cheerfulness from its other neighbor, yellow. It is positively associated with energetic, social, extroverted, and jovial personalities.

During the past 30 years, a number of formal studies have been carried out investigating the psychophysiological effects of colored surroundings on behavior. Ifan Payne (1969) reported a study conducted in the late 1960s at the Bartlett School of Architecture in London, which correlated arousal of feelings with measured change in pupil size of fourth- and fifth-year architectural students viewing color slides of model rooms. Subjects showed greater response to rooms colored red and blue than one colored white. Note, however, that observers were studied while looking *at* photographic images of colored space, not while being *in* the colored rooms. Still, the impact of red and blue was significant.

Because of their influence on personal mood, certain colors are valuable for surroundings in medical facilities. Consultant Frank H. Mahnke (1981) advised the use of selected colors for hospital interiors, based on their psychophysiological effects. Corridors by their function as circulation routes for patients and concerned loved ones should be painted with cool or warm colors to create a calming atmosphere. Known for their tranquilizing effects, aqua and lower saturated greens or blue-greens are appropriate for intensive care units. In physical therapy rooms the influence of aqua reduces muscular tension, and in occupational therapy rooms of pale orange or yellow contribute an atmosphere of cheerfulness. Mahnke suggested a colorful environment of warm hues for pediatric wards. Other types of public space could likewise benefit from colors that generate relaxing effects, such as waiting areas for departing passengers in airport terminals, where some people experience an unsettling fear of air travel.

The Munsell Color System

A color system having a wide range of application to science, industry, commerce, and the arts is the Munsell system (Figure C-9). Developed by the American Albert H. Munsell (1858–1918), its organization specifies colors by hue, value, and chroma (saturation). It too is a three-dimensional system with a gray scale of black to white forming a vertical axis. Radiating horizontally outward from the axis like spokes of a wheel are the hues, with their chroma (saturation) determined by their distance outward from the axis. Value notations relate to the vertical gray scale.

The *Munsell Book of Color* is an atlas of color chips available in both matte and glossy surface. Figure C-10 shows a typical page taken from the atlas, where yellow chips are arranged by their Munsell notations. The chips located diagonally upward and farthest right increase in value and saturation. They lose their purity as they descend diagonally to the lower left corner of the page. Recalling the earlier discussion of the psychological response to color, the cheery and high-spirited nature of the more pure yellow contrasts the murky appearance of the deep graying of the hue in the figure.

As a visual and numerical system, samples of manufactured or natural materials can be matched in color with the chips and referenced with a Munsell number. We use the Munsell system for reference throughout this book, and it was adopted for development of the LBR System described in the preceding chapter. The advantage of the Munsell system is that it is easy to learn and teach, easy to work with for art and architecture. The atlas, other linear charts, and computer programs of the system are available from the Munsell Color Company, c/o Macbeth Corporation, New Windsor, New York. Munsell computer software provides exact color specification in *continuums* of hue, value, and chroma (versus the *step* notation of the *Munsell Book of Color*), making possible the selection of any color that exists. The designer may specify a desired color appearance for a building material by hue, value, and saturation, and the lighting engineer can then use that notation to create with light the effect the designer wants. There are other systems than Munsell for specifying color, and most are computerized for unlimited application to industry and the arts. Notations from one system can be converted to another.

The Color Circle and Hue Organization

The color circle (sometimes called a color wheel)[1] as a system of hue organization has been a central component of color theory for a long time. Its purpose is to interpret the basic hue interrelationships according to the principles of color perception. Art and design students traditionally have been introduced to the circle to learn the interaction of hues for mixing pigments and for composing contrasts and harmonies. It is a helpful tool for design of architectural space, because it facilitates the distribution of color in spatial connections and for establishing chromatic compatibility or contrasts when composing form-space relationships.

Making the color circle functional for designers resurrects the same problem confronted in the preceding chapter when we were dealing with how many values of gray should comprise the LBR scale. How can the basic hue relationships be committed to memory, for quick recall in design practice? For most people this is not going to happen with a circle of 24 or 64 steps that exist in some versions. Figure C-11 follows the organization of a color circle by Johannes Itten (1973, 35). It is a 12-step system constructed with Munsell notations. It is developed from both the primary and secondary hues, and organized such that if forgotten, it can be easily reconstructed. The primary and secondary hues manifest themselves in a

[1] For a brief, illustrated history of the color circle, see Faber Birren (1969, 9ff).

simple, logical rationale. Forming a triangle at the center are the three primary colors: yellow, blue, and red. Mixing any two of the primaries in equal amounts produces the secondary hues of orange, green, and purple, which take natural positions in the outer triangle. Each of the interior primary and secondary hues connects with their locations as steps in the outer circle. Intermediate steps of equal mixes of adjacent primaries and secondaries are inserted to complete the logical order of the hue relationships. From this arrangement, the meaning of *complementary hues* is understood from their positions on the circle. Two colors are complementary when, upon mixing them as *pigment* (not light), they yield the appearance of gray. The organization of this color circle makes it easy to remember the complementary hues. Red/green, blue/orange, and yellow/purple all are complementary sets, lying as direct opposites on the circle. Those same opposites produce *retinal simultaneous contrast,* which is discussed later.

The steps of the color circle of Figure C-11 are described by Munsell notations. The key positions are yellow (Munsell 5Y), yellow-red (5YR), red (5R), purple (5P), blue (5B), and green (5G). Between those steps are the Munsell notations as indicated on the diagram. This organization of the fundamental hues provides a reference for design composition and visual perception of surface colors as pigment. Their appearance will change under different illumination. But before discussing the interaction of surface color and light, other perceptual phenomena of color need to be considered—how contrasting colors interact.

Simultaneous Contrast and Afterimages

A color's appearance is significantly modified by simultaneous contrast that takes place in the retina. In Chapter 2, Figure 2-8 introduced the perceptual phenomenon where the same value of gray square darkened when surrounded by a white field, and brightened when surrounded by a black field. Figure C-12 shows the principle applied to color. The surrounding influence of a black field makes the red and yellow disks appear brighter and more intense, whereas the white background makes both hues appear darker.

Simultaneous contrast also goes to work when color contrasts color, demonstrated by placing a primary or secondary hue in a contrasting situation with its complementary color. Using the color circle of Figure C-11, simultaneous contrast will be the greatest when juxtaposing two hues that lie as polar opposites on the circle.

This is a physiological phenomenon that takes place in the retina. When the eye is focused on a given color, the retina automatically inserts its complementary hue. In that condition of greatest contrast, the color on which the eye is focused will appear more true. This is demonstrated by Figure C-13, which shows a yellow disk appearing in its most pure state when surrounded by purple. Because yellow and purple are complementary hues, there is little interference from the rest of the color spectrum. When surrounded by a yellow-orange background, the same yellow disk is influenced by the complementary of the orange, giving the disk a slightly blue tint.

The effect of the retina compensating for focus on one color by reflexively supplying its complement is easiest to demonstrate when using a neutral surface. The two gray squares in Figure C-14 are of identical value, but appear to be different under the influence of their contrasting backgrounds. As expected from their positions on the color circle, the surrounding red field induces its complementary greenish tint over the gray square, and the blue field generates the tint of its opposite, orange. The effect is strongest when the contrast-inducing color is most saturated.

Another retinal phenomenon related to simultaneous contrast is that of *chromatic afterimage*. Staring at a red disk under good light for about 30 seconds will build an image of the complementary hue in the retina; shutting the eyes will gradually bring about the same shape in green, hovering in the black void of closed vision. In like manner, staring at a purple disk will create a floating yellow image after the eyes are closed. These afterimages have a life of fractional moments or several seconds depending on the intensity of the inducing light and the duration of focus. They are caused by the sensation of incoming color stimuli interacting with the color-sensitive cones in the retina.

Chromatic afterimages are sometimes thought of as only curiosities or interesting conversational topics in the visual arts, but there are practical applications. Mahnke and Mahnke (1987, 28) described a factory production-line environment in which workers complained about suffering from migraine headaches and seeing green spots in front of their eyes while checking purple pills. The problem was solved by placing green screens in the vicinity of the workers. When looking up from their work, the green afterimages of the purple pills disappeared into the green screens. The authors also remind us of former times when clinical white dominated hospital operating rooms. White sheets and surgical gowns reflected the intense illumination required for surgery. Temporarily looking away from the red of blood and tissue created disturbing green afterimages for surgeons and attendants. That problem too was solved by changing the color of walls, cover sheets, and hospital gowns from white to green or blue-green. In addition to its function of resolving problems of afterimage, the blue-green also exerts its psychologically calming influence, which is appropriate for the operating room.

The Brightness of Colors

For the designer of the illuminated environment, it is imperative to keep in mind that colors are perceived as values of brightness. Color therefore can be introduced into architectural space as a means of controlling the composition of brightness levels, an important factor that influences decisions regarding the quality and quantity of illumination. In the preceding chapter, it was noted that the entry luminance of a building material in the LBR System is the initial consideration for composing brightness levels in space. Entry luminance refers to how its color in the three attributes of hue, value, and saturation compares with the color attributes of another building material.

Which is the brighter surface color, red or green? The missing information in that question is color value and saturation, depending on the specific red or green that came to mind when the question was asked. If the red and green were of the same value and saturation, and of the same reflectance and texture, you were correct if you answered they would render about the same brightness.

Using the color circle of Figure C-11, the translation of the hues into grays (brightness levels) will render the red opposite green at approximately the same brightness. Purple and yellow create the strongest contrast, and blue and orange are moderately contrasted. A good exercise is to visualize each hue adjusted toward the others by modifying its saturation and value to change its brightness. The structure of the Munsell system (Figure C-9) is helpful for visualizing change of brightness for any given hue, by moving it vertically in value, horizontally in chroma (saturation), or combinations of both value and chroma.

Color and brightness are two principal components of space and light theory for architecture. In the preceding chapter, we studied how colors of building materials translate into brightness values (see Figures 5-6 and 5-9). Because brightness influences the perception of spatial depth and the apparent spatial location of objects, the *brightness of color* becomes a major design consideration. With enough illumination, dark colors can be raised in brightness high on the LBR Scale. But that is an inefficient use of electrical power, and is unnecessary when brightness can be achieved by working with the attributes of value and saturation of a hue, requiring less illumination to achieve feelings of greater spaciousness.

For now, when it comes to comparing color relationships simply as they are seen in spatial composition, a preliminary principle can be stated: *Brightness difference is as important as color difference in the visual perception of architectural space.*

The Color of Light

The color of the architectural environment most often begins with the color selection of its surfacing materials, but once in place the appearance of those surfaces is altered by the color of the illumination that makes them visible. For this reason it is essential that special attention be given to the color of light itself.

Purity of Hue. The attribute of saturation applies to physical light much as it does to the object color (luminance color) of a surface. A hue is fully saturated at its most pure wavelength as located on what is known as the *luminosity curve*, where the component hues of white light are located by the strength of their wavelengths. Those hues are called *spectral colors.* In our everyday surroundings, however, we seldom encounter a light sensation of any one hue in its pure state, other than for specialized purposes of commercial or theatrical effects where monochromatic colors are desired. The saturation of a hue of light is diminished when mixed with others, or its purity may be diluted or "washed out" with white light to obtain tints or shades of a color.

When white light dominates, only a tint of the saturated hue may be noticeable. Such is the case with some fluorescent lamps, which look white but give off a slightly blue, yellow, green, or pink light.

Mixing Colored Light. Combining two or more hues of light does not produce the same results that happen when pigments are blended by a painter. Red light mixed with green light will appear yellow, far different from mixing red and green paint. Blue light mixed with green will look cyan, and red light plus blue will appear magenta. Physicists refer to mixing colored light as *additive,* which increases the luminance on a surface. When a green light is mixed with red as shown in Figure 6-1, the additive nature of the combination increases the brightness in the area of overlap. Note, however, that the luminance of the mixture is not the sum of the luminances of the two light sources. As measured with a photometer, the green (21.4 cd/ft^2) plus the red (19.6 cd/ft^2) did not create 41.0 cd/ft^2 of luminance as might be expected, but only 29.9 cd/ft^2.

When light is modified by colored filters, both absorption and transmission take place. A blue filter placed in front of a light source transmits blue because the filter *subtracts* green and red. The effect of a blue filter on illuminated surfaces is that green and red objects will appear darker, whereas blue ones appear brighter and more intense. Red has the reverse effect, subtracting green and blue, and intensifying the reds.

An interesting observation can be made from mixing illumination of different hues, namely, that it is nearly

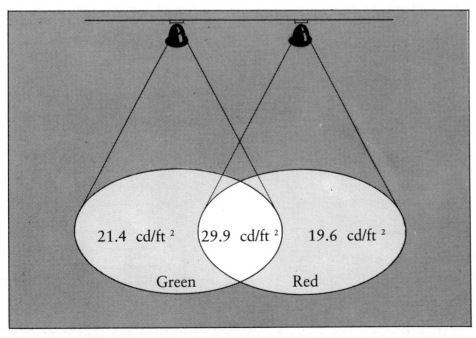

Figure 6-1. Mixing colored light increases luminance.

impossible to create a bad or distasteful color of light, unless a person has a preconceived dislike for a certain hue. Mixing colors of light is quite different from mixing pigments. Mixing red, blue, and green light produces white. As the school child quickly learns, mixing a variety of colored paints (as pigments) produces a muddy brown, quite a contrast from casting a variety of colored lights on a white surface, which normally creates a pleasing visual experience.

Temperature of Light and the Color Rendering Index (CRI). The color of light is related to its temperature. *Color temperature* is measured in degrees Kelvin (K), at which a *blackbody* (a theoretically perfect radiator) would have to be heated to render in color the same appearance of a light source. This is observed by watching iron change in color when subjected to increasing heat, first glowing in red, then becoming orange and yellow, and finally becoming what is called "white hot." Color temperature is applied to rating the color tint of a light source.

The expression *color rendering* refers to the effect of a light source on the color appearance of a surface. The physics and chemistry of lamp production has created a wide variety of colored light, and for purposes of comparing the physical properties and hue of one source with another, the *Color Rendering Index* (CRI) has been devised. The CRI is a numerical expression of a light source for its capacity to render color as compared with a standard reference source. That reference is based on natural daylight, which has a CRI of 100. A CRI of 100 is an exact color match with the reference. The color rendering properties of any two light sources should be compared only if each has the same correlated color temperature. The influence of temperature Kelvin is most applicable to light sources that are thermal radiators

such as incandescent lamps. For gaseous discharge sources (e.g., fluorescent lamps), temperature Kelvin serves only as a guide for the warm or cool appearance of light. As a general guideline, the higher the CRI, the better it will render the "true" color of a surface. The temperature of a lamp is difficult to control during the manufacturing process, and lamps produced on the assembly line can vary by as much as 500 K from the data given on their packaging labels. Table 6-1 lists the CRI of selected lamps at the temperature Kelvin shown. This list of electric light sources is only an illustration of variations of lamp quality and their color rendering properties and cannot be considered a standard list. That is because of the rapid changes taking place in the lighting industry in America spurred by the long overdue passage of the National Energy Policy Act of 1992 (EPACT). Lighting in America accounts for up to 25% of the electricity used and can reach as high as 50% for commercial installations. The goal of the EPACT is to greatly reduce the amount of energy consumption. The response by the lighting industry has been to replace many of what in recent times have been considered standard light sources. The transition from old to new types of lamps will generate more efficient conversion of electricity into light for private homes and public spaces. Some incandescent and fluorescent lamps are becoming obsolete and new sources are steadily appearing on the market, a trend that will continue into the twenty-first century resulting from technological lighting research and production. New products mean changes in the CRI. Designers in fields related to architecture need to keep abreast of those changes that will sweep across the markets in the years ahead. Maintaining contact with lighting industry literature and sales representatives is essential. In addition to specifying lamp efficacy and cost effectiveness, those responsible

Table 6-1. CRI of selected lamps

Lamp Source	CRI		Color Temperature (K)
Incandescent	99	at	2700
Deluxe cool white fluorescent	89	at	4100
Natural white fluorescent	86	at	3600
Daylight fluorescent	76	at	6300
Deluxe warm white fluorescent	74	at	2950
Metal-halide high-intensity discharge (HID)	70	at	3200
Cool-white fluorescent	62	at	4200
Warm-white fluorescent	52	at	3450
Mercury, warmtone, HID	52	at	3300
Mercury, clear, HID	22	at	5900
High-pressure sodium HID	20	at	1800

for decisions on the appearance of the built environment must stay focused on the basic design criteria for lamp selection: the quantity and *color* of light.

Spectral Distribution. The CRI is but one method of color rendering measurement used by industry. The manufacture of different light sources, particularly fluorescent lamps, varies with regard to the relative strengths of their component hues. Some are more rich in the reds, others in greens or violet. Standard cool-white fluorescent sources have greater energy output in the yellow-green region of the spectrum, and it is there where the eye is most sensitive to brightness. But standard cool-white fluorescent lamps have a comparatively lower CRI, and therefore do not have the property for rendering good color as do incandescent lamps. From this it may seem that incandescent is a far better light source. It may be for color, but not for efficiency. The visible light emitted from incandescent lamps generally found in households is only 10% to 12% of the radiation those lamps produce; the rest is lost as heat. What this means is that for certain tasks, some color rendering lamps are better than others.

Lamp manufacturers are continually striving to produce light sources that combine good color rendition and cost effectiveness. Figure C-15 shows the Wayne Towne Center Mall in Wayne, New Jersey. To attract customers, the management of Daffy's retail store wanted to display their designer clothes in warm, natural colors, that would contrast the general lighting of the mall itself. To do this, white SON high-pressure sodium lamps (Philips Lighting) were installed. Normally, high-pressure sodium HID lamps have a very low CRI and are therefore poor for color rendition. The SON sources have a high CRI of 80 (2700 K), and have good color rendering quality. They differ from the standard high-pressure sodium lamps by containing all the colors of the spectrum, are much brighter, and last significantly longer than incandescent light sources. The illustration shows the bright, warm light of Daffy's display windows enhancing the retail clothing, and standing out from the more washed out appearance of the mall itself.

Surface Color Under Light

It is the reflected light on the surfaces of the environment that we perceive as the everyday chromatic world. When the illumination that strikes an object is a mixture of wavelengths, some of the hues are absorbed into its surface, and the rest are reflected. Therefore, differences in the color of light will change the color appearance of a surface as it is seen under daylight, incandescent, fluorescent, or other type of illumination. We noted above that the additive process of mixing red and green light produces yellow, but mixing red and green pigments can produce a murky brown, and if blue were added the result may be a dark gray. Mixing surface pigments is known to chemists as the *subtractive* nature of color. The wavelengths (hues) absorbed by the surface material are subtracted from the total coming from the source. When white light (containing all the spectral hues) falls on a blue-painted surface, the red and yellow wavelengths are all absorbed by the chemistry of the paint, and the predominantly blue part of the spectrum is what is seen as reflected light. But surfaces are not selective in reflecting only pure, fully saturated hues. As blue is located between violet and green in the spectrum, some of those two adjacent hues can also be reflected depending on the physical properties of the surface. Likewise, an orange surface absorbs the green and blue while reflecting orange light waves, but proportions of the neighboring yellows and reds may be included. Therefore, we rarely see pure, monochromatic colors; the environment is filled with tints and shades, as a result of the different properties of reflective surfaces responding to different colors of light.

The dilemma facing all of us is that the appearance of the things we see is not their "true" colors because they are influenced by the color of light. Under certain types of illumination, surface color changes radically. HID lamps are good examples, which include mercury-vapor, high-pressure sodium, and metal-halide, Sodium vapor at low pressure produces a yellow monochromatic light. The demonstration shown in Figure C-16 shows the drastic change in color by low-pressure sodium (right) compared with incandescent light (left). Mercury-vapor lamps appear as bright, bluish-white light, and standard varieties have a low CRI, making them poor in color rendering. They emit predominantly yellow and green light waves, with a small percentage of blue and violet. Red wavelengths are absent, so red surfaces appear dark brown or dark gray. These lamps have been improved, and a version called mercury-vapor deluxe has reasonably good color rendering properties. High-pressure sodium lamps also create significant color change. Like mercury-vapor, they too lack red and give off a warm yellow light, and have a low CRI. The metal-halide sources resemble the more white light of mercury-vapor, but the addition of the halide chemical compounds increases their color rendering capacity. The advantage of HID sources is that they have a proportionally much longer life compared with conventional incandescent and fluorescent lamps. This important cost-saving feature is what has increased their popularity for many industrial and commercial environments, and for night lighting out of doors. The lack of red in mercury-vapor and high-pressure sodium makes them acceptable for lighting the exteriors of buildings and streets, where their predominantly yellow emission finds a compatibility with the color of stone and concrete. But in a parking lot illuminated by high-pressure sodium sources, the unsuspecting shopper accustomed to looking for his or her familiar red automobile must learn to look for the brown one.

Change of pigment color takes place under different qualities of fluorescent light as well. Figure C-17 shows the bluish cast of cool-white fluorescent lamps (right) compared with warmer fluorescent (left). Caucasian flesh looks poor under cool-white fluorescent light, but much more "healthy" under warm fluorescent. Most people are unaware of these differences until suffering the disappointment of purchasing an article in a store illuminated by one kind of electric light, and then seeing it in a different light at home.

Metamerism. Two samples may appear to match in color under one light source, but not under a different colored source. This phenomenon is called *metamerism*. The color of the two surfaces may appear identical when placed side by side in daylight, but when both are viewed under incandescent or some other quality electric light, the samples no longer match. This is caused by the dissimilar spectral reflectance of their surfaces, each responding differently to light sources of varying color. A *metameric match* is said to be made when two surfaces of different spectral characteristics appear to match in color when viewed under the same light source.

Problems of metamerism can arise for the architect and interior designer when making color selections for interior surfaces that are subject to two different light sources. To be sure of a metameric match, two samples should be viewed under more than one source of illumination, preferably one daylight or daylight fluorescent, and another incandescent. This can be done easily in the designer's studio using a viewing box with a painted white interior that is equipped with two overhead light sources inside the box. General Electric recommends the incandescent to be two 40-W silvered bowl lamps, and the daylight simulated by two F20T12D fluorescent lamps. Both sources should be switched independently, and turning them on and off while viewing two different materials inside the box will reveal whether or not the colors are a metameric match.

Color of Reflected Light. An important component of color theory for the design of architectural space is the behavior of illumination reflecting off one surface to another. The physical properties of materials in turn modify the color of light as it is reflected off their surfaces. Illumination arrives in a mixture of hues, then picks up the dominant color tints or shades of the surface that it strikes. This can be seen in Figure C-18, which shows a lounge illuminated by recessed canisters in the ceiling. "White" light is cast downward and reflects off the red carpeting, and returns to "paint" the white ceiling pink. This feature of reflected light tinting another surface is often noticeable in the environment once the observer becomes aware of it, although it is not always as strong as that caused by the red carpet in the illustration. Note the brownish tint on the ceiling over the tile floor in the foreground. In visual perception, there is the phenomenon of *color constancy*. The brain stores in the memory what certain colors should look like even though they may appear differently under various light qualities or in shadow. Color constancy will communicate the lounge ceiling as white to those who know it is white, and from viewing areas outside the red carpet area where the ceiling appears closer to its actual color. But for people in the room and for those entering the lounge from the camera angle shown in the illustration, the ceiling is pink.

According to studies conducted to evaluate individual responses to illumination quality, there is no *best* color for light sources by popular preference. People's perceptions and tastes differ from designers' choices. Studies in the 1970s showed that substantial segments of the population like the appearance of each of the more common types of incandescent and fluorescent lamps. Helson and Lansford (1970) surveyed people's perceptions of objects seen under different popular light sources, and found if a color was liked under one, it was liked under another. C. W. Jerome (1972; 1973) tested individual likes and dislikes of fluorescent lamps (warm white, cool white, etc.), and learned that not one of those light sources was widely preferred. These findings are not to imply that designers are to proceed without regard to the interaction between the color of light and surface. Competent designers are aware of how light will tint or shade a building material, and they learn to incorporate into design refinement the cause-effect nature of illuminance and reflectance on the colors of surfaces.

There is a cardinal error in color selection that must be avoided by all individuals who sell, purchase, or choose the materials that will eventually color our architectural surroundings. What is that error?: Making selections from color samples or swatches as they lie on desk tops, drawing tables, or park benches, or in sales rooms, merchandise marts, living rooms or any place where the color of the light at the time is *not* the color of light under which the material will be seen in its final placement. Error after error is made by paint merchandisers, where differences in the color of lighting varies from store to store, or during rearrangement of sales rooms when sample color chips are displayed at one time under the store's fluorescent luminous ceiling, another time under the influence of a nearby incandescent display, or under daylight from a street window where the colorful rack of paint samples was moved to attract passersby. The error is common throughout the commercial world. Unaware of the interaction between colored light and colored surfaces, a buyer purchases an "irresistible" article of clothing displayed in a store, and later is surprised and dissatisfied upon wearing it for the first time in daylight or in a workplace where the lighting is significantly different from that of the store in which it was purchased. A sample paint chip or fabric swatch is picked out for the bathroom with joint approval by a friend at lunch under incandescent lighting of a restaurant, or under the cool-white fluorescent lights of the kitchen. Soon after comes the inevitable cliché: "I just don't like the color—it looked a lot better on the sample than it does on the wall." Error made in color selection of building materials can be avoided by simply following the fundamental law: *Select the material under the same illumination that will exist in the architectural environment where it will appear.* An apparatus similar to the Multiluminator (see Appendix) belongs in every architectural design office, where chambers with interchangeable lighting are readily available for designers and visiting product sales representatives. A Color Modulator (see Appendix) can also be used to demonstrate the effects of changing angles of slant. Paint, fabric, carpet, tile, furniture, and paneling stores should maintain carefully located display booths equipped with different kinds of the most popular light sources.

Appearance of Color in Shadow

The architectural and lighting designer needs to remember how colored surfaces behave under the influence of varying quality and quantity of light, and also how they appear when subjected to the dimming consequence of shadow. The quotation at the beginning of this chapter lays open the observations of John C. Van Dyke (1980, 210) describing color he saw in shadows in the canyons and deserts of America's Southwest. Leaving his professorship in art history at Rutgers University in 1898, he turned his trained eyes from the criticism of art to what he called "sensuous seeing" in the beauties of nature. He studied the colors of the earth bathed in shadow and the color of shadow itself produced by reflections from the sky. Inquiry into the nature of color in shadow is another aspect of design aesthetics. In the shadow of light, colors become subdued, lose their intensity and luster, but gain from shifting into a fusion of chromatic softness and quiet. Colors in shadow blend into harmonious tonalities intermediate between light and dark.

The continued interest in bringing daylight into contemporary architecture makes the study of color in shadow all the more relevant. Depending on geographic location, time of season, site orientation, and atmospheric conditions, many daylighted interior spaces carry a high percentage of major surfaces that are shadowed for a predominant part if not all of the day. In those spaces special attention should be given to hue, value, and saturation to create environments that are warm and appealing. Color selections should be done after determining how many of the dominant boundaries of a space, and its furnishings, are subjected to shadow for the proportionally greater amount of time. The theory of this can be illustrated by visualizing the space of Figure C-19. The beige color of the wall in shadow has dropped in saturation and value. In spaces of this kind, if the path of the sun were parallel to the longitudinal dimension of such a space, most of the walls and floors would rest in shadow most of the time.

For practical application to color selection, the designer needs to consider the influence of cast and attached shadow (recall Figure 3-10), and the shadow effects of texture (Figure 3-11); all reduce the value and saturation of a surface color from its appearance under normal lighting conditions. When direct daylight or electric illumination is intense, shadows tend to be strong and dark, and significantly alter the color appearance of an object or surface on which shadows are cast. The same is true for attached shadows, those on surfaces not facing the light source directly. Where two walls of the same color meet at a corner, the one facing the light source appears brighter and more saturated, and the attached shadow on the neighboring wall will lower the color value and saturation. Where necessary, compensations for these conditions can be made by the designer when it is known a surface or object is destined to occupy a place where shadow will prevail. For choosing a color for surfaces that will be seen predominantly in deep shadow or in conditions of unfavorable contrast (e.g., a wall next to a bright window), R. G. Hopkinson (1963, 111) recommended the following working rule: Select a Munsell notation that is two steps higher in value, and four steps higher in chroma (saturation). More needs to be known about color adjustments for shadowed surfaces of architecture, and is a subject for which more research is to be encouraged.

Color Adaptation

As the eye adapts to the brightness level of the space it is in (see Chapter 2, p. 17ff), it also adjusts to a dominant surrounding color and undergoes *color adaptation*. When a person is walking down a corridor that is dominated by a certain color, the retina adapts to the overall color field created by the spatial envelope. Figure C-20 shows the reception area of IBM's Marketing and

Technical Support Center at Westlake, Texas, where the walls and barrel vault overhead are painted blue. The eye is surrounded by the overall blue to which the retina adapts. The strength of retinal stimulation by the surrounding blue surfaces determines the level of color adaptation, and at places where the dominant color is strong, the appearance of other hues in the visual field is affected. In the view of Figure C-20 the door opens to a yellow entrance way, which in turn leads to a red passage space (seen through the door) connecting the exterior court. When the eye has adapted to the blue vaulted hall, what it fixates on next will temporarily come under the influence of the complementary orange. Through good color selection by Mexican architect Ricardo Legorreta, who designed the sequence, the yellow and red surfaces outside the door are perceptually compatible with the complementary orange supplied by the retina when adapted to the blue interior.

Lighting plays an important part in color adaptation as space and light theory is applied to architectural design. When a space is shaped and monochromatically colored so that it creates retinal adaptation, the lighting technique of wall-washing will intensify the dominant hue, increasing color saturation on the wall below the light source. If such a space is a corridor or some other connecting space that is dominated by a single hue, sufficient walking time must take place for color adaptation to occur, just as we saw with the general conditions of light or dark adaptation described in Chapter 2. It is the proportional amount of the surrounding inducing color that is important, and when it dominates, color adaptation will come into play.

Increase of color value and saturation by wall-washing is illustrated in Figure C-21, which shows a waiting area at the Harvard station of the Boston transit system. The red tiles at the back of the seating area are most intense near the light source, and reduce in value and saturation as they descend toward the middle of the wall, but increase again as they approach the bright reflections off the seat. Are the woman and man experiencing color adaptation to the expanse of red around them? Not to any significant degree. The shallowness of the space in which they sit does not supply enough red field in their peripheral vision, although red reflections off the wall behind them tint the pages they are reading. Note the reddish tone on the woman's face, reflecting off her newspaper, just as we saw earlier with the red-tinted reflected light painting the ceiling pink in Figure C-18. For a person standing in conversation close in front of them, the tiles would stimulate color adaptation the more the visual field is filled with red. The bright seat and signage strip work to reduce adaptation to the red, and diminish the chance for the complementary color of green to tint the people sitting.

Color and Spatial Effects

Published color theory for the arts most often has been directed toward the two-dimensional media of painting and graphic design. But color studies as illustrated on flat surface planes are perceived far differently in the third dimension of architecture, where they are subjected to a wide range of illumination and reflections, and can be seen from an infinite number of viewing angles. Those spatial factors modify the value, saturation, and brightness of the hues, particularly as color appears on the building materials of architecture.

Lois Swirnoff (1988, 36) who studied with Josef Albers at Yale University set up experiments to observe "dimensional color" interaction in a spatial context.[2] Using what she called "the window problem," Swirnoff investigated the appearance of hues when looking at them through an aperture of contrasting color. Her subjects peered through a 3-inch window in a card of varying color toward a card of another hue located 9 inches behind the opening, with both cards under the same illumination. When the window was white, an orange-red located behind the aperture not only appeared to advance, but after prolonged exposure (30 to 60 seconds) the red appeared to be located inches in front of the window. A cooler red did not appear to advance as much as the warmer red. A fully saturated blue at first seemed to advance toward the window, but then "resolved" its location behind the frame. When red and blue were observed together, equal in proportion and adjacent to each other at the same distance behind the window, the blue was seen as appreciably more distant than red. Yellow interacted with the frame, and appeared to expand radially rather than advance. When a dark gray window was used, yellow behind the frame increased in brightness, and appeared to advance. Bright hues tended to advance toward the gray window more than they did through the white.

What was happening in the Swirnoff demonstrations of the brightest hues advancing from distant positions was *gamma movement* as explained in Chapter 2. This is the brightness advances principle, here applied to color theory. E. H. Johns and F. C. Sumner (1948) tested the relation between apparent distance and the brightness of hue and found that brightly colored objects appear closer to the eye, whereas darker colored ones appear to recede. Other studies have shown that fully saturated hues will advance more than those that are less saturated.

A study conducted in the Space and Light Laboratory at The University of Kansas counterposed gamma movement of color values with the depth cues of linear perspective and diminishing size. A series of "gates" (Figure

[2] See her Chapter 3, "Color-Space and Time."

C-22) of diminishing size and sequenced color values were set up under equal illumination. Two series were angled to the observer's line of vision so that two different sequences could be seen and judged at the same time. The receding corners of the gates created linear perspective, one of the strongest perceptual depth cues. Size reduction of the gates added a second prominent depth cue, further increasing the illusion of the space into the distance. Within that physical structure the theory of gamma movement was inserted.

Because high color value and saturation create brighter renditions of hues, the brightness advances principle was applied by organizing the color values of the gates in sequences of brightness. This allowed a progression of color values to follow the two depth cues into receding space (1) by putting the darkest values in the most distant position or (2) by placing the brightest values at the end where they would perceptually advance in countermovement against the receding depth cues of linear perspective and diminishing size. As expected, when the values of the colors were arranged in order from brightest in front to darkest in back, the progression of diminishing brightness aligned with the depth cues of linear perspective and diminishing size to create a strong visual movement into the distance. When the order was reversed, placing the brightest value at the end, the length of the space shortened as the brighter values worked their way forward by gamma movement. Changes of apparent spatial depth created by reversing the brightness sequence occurred for all colors tested.

The brightness of the different hues also had its impact. Using the order of the darkest value in back, to create the maximum spatial depth for each hue, the blue series appeared deeper than red and yellow, and the green appeared deeper than yellow. When red was compared with green (opposites on the color circle), both spaces appeared the same in spatial depth. Using the order of the darkest value in back for all hues (Figure C-23a and b), the greatest spatial depth was created by blue, followed by green, red, and yellow.

Advantage can be taken of the perceptual and behavioral effects of color as it is programmed through architecture. Figure C-24 shows a series of hues in spatial sequence through the Shore Country Day School at Beverly, Massachusetts. A two-level bridge was designed to link an existing school building with a new addition that includes a library on the upper level (behind the camera). The space is relatively short, and it was the intent of the architects to make the bridge itself "an event" when passing between the two buildings, heightening the experience of movement through space. The colors were not chosen indiscriminately, but were selected for both their design and behavioral influence. The headmaster of the school offered a concern about overactive children pro-

ceeding too zestfully from the higher activity spaces of the classrooms in the existing building to the more passive and quiet environment of the library. Cool colors of blue and green were therefore applied to walls leading toward the library (the back sides of the walls shown in the photograph), and warm colors reverse the mood in the movement back to the active classrooms. In either direction, there was no attempt to program the different hues by way of their progressing from "most active" to "least active" or vise versa, but only to allow color to impact a change of feeling when moving across the bridge.

The colorful walls serve a number of functions. Structurally, they support the two-level bridge as well as a barrel vaulted skylight that follows the space below. The walls were also positioned to create a curving perspective to enrich the experience of space. The green protective guardrail on the upper level moves in Gestalt good continuation and contributes to the flow of space, especially on the right side where the walls momentarily move out of sight.

In the view shown in the photograph, the walls are interesting perceptually for the spatial effects of color. The total length of the bridge is only about 20 feet, but the distance it spans appears farther. One of the reasons is the depth cue of linear perspective created by the railing and the corners of the wall openings similar to those in the laboratory gate study already described. Another reason for the apparent depth is the *diminishing brightness* of the hues, beginning with white on the foreground doorway and overhead soffits, then orange—red—purple—dark, in sequence. The hues were not necessarily programmed with the intent to perceptually lengthen the space, but only to maintain a warmth of color in the direction of movement shown. The application of a different hue for each wall was a design decision to create a change of feeling upon encountering the space. The different brightness levels of the hues—in the order they exist—nevertheless contribute to the perception of spatial depth. Here, in this small but visually active space, the behavioral and perceptual effects of color are combined, and they heighten the experience of moving across the bridge, just as the architects intended.

Color theory for architecture must include the influence of the light sources. Cited earlier was the research of H. Helson and T. Lansford (1970), which investigated people's reactions to color, background, and illumination with respect to perceived pleasantness. In the article cited, they published tables of notations for Munsell color chips as viewed against various background hues. In most cases they found that chromatic and brightness-*contrasts* of colored objects seen against colored backgrounds were more important than the quality of the light source in its spectral power distribution. They observed that brightness-contrast was the most important factor determining the pleasantness of color combinations, and that contrasts of brightness were more decisive than contrasts of hue and saturation. Their findings are now recommended by the IESNA (Rea, 1993). To enhance the pleasantness of object color, background colors should be either very high in Munsell value notation (8 or 9), or very low in value (1 or 2) and also very low in saturation (chroma). Highly saturated colors are preferred for object colors. Neutral colors rank lower for object color, but are better for backgrounds.

Helson and Lansford left us with a final note concerning the influence of illumination quality on the perception of hue, value, and saturation. They pointed out that it is the complex interaction between the quality of lighting and the appearance of color that helps to account for the conflicting opinions on color harmony, often found in the literature of aesthetic theory.

This chapter focuses on selected aspects of color theory that are applicable to the perception and design of architectural space. As a conclusion to Part 1, its contents can be seen as an overlay for the chapters preceding it, which topic by topic establish a framework for analyzing the complex nature of perceiving the colored world we inhabit.

The design and fabrication of the human environment is not a one-profession affair, but is the result of combined activities of architects and engineers, interior and lighting designers, landscape and urban designers, manufacturers and sales representatives, contractors and subcontractors. In practice, the work of one is often counterproductive to the input of the others. Those professions speak a common language of design and color systems, specifications, floor plans, and sections. But people do not live in plans, sections, and design systems. *People live in the spaces of architecture and the city.* There is where they perceive their colored surroundings, and where the surfaces of the environment influence their feelings and moods. We therefore now turn to a formal analysis of architectural space, to formulate a natural and practical meeting ground on which the diversified professions can communicate to effectively and meaningfully shape the human environment. To begin, we focus on the design and organization of the material surfaces brought together in light—the *spatial envelope.*

Part 2: Analysis of Architectural Space

CHAPTER 7

The Spatial Envelope

*Most of the channels through which we glide
are narrow as compared with their length and
with the height of the mountain walls of the
islands which bound their shores. . . . While
we may be gazing into the depths of this leafy
ocean lane, the ship, turning suddenly to right
or left, enters an open space, a sound decorated
with small islands, sprinkled or clustered in
forms and compositions such as nature alone
can invent. The smallest of the islands are mere
dots, but how beautiful they are!*

—*John Muir
"The Alaska Trip,"
Wilderness Essays**

How is architectural space defined? By its boundaries. Space would be a limitless void without some sense of enclosure or visual reference that communicates a sense of place. To organize the functions a building is to serve, the designer customarily represents space by the use of scaled and dimensioned drawings—floor plans, sections, and elevations. Those conventions locate spatial boundaries in the forms of walls, floors, ceilings, and other major surfaces. A composite set of those boundaries at any one place comprises the *spatial envelope,* a working mechanism for the design, analysis, and lighting of architectural space. The envelope is a conceptualization of a space, stripped of movable or temporary furnishings. This theoretical segregation of shell and contents facili-

tates control of the color and brightness relationships created by all reflected light in the total environment once the furnishings are added. The envelope carries the dominant areas of stimuli for visual perception, and thereby establishes the major surface planes forming the physical limits of space as seen by human vision. The objects set within the boundaries are space modulators. As visual stimuli themselves, those furnishings will be perceived against the lighted spatial envelope when the space is complete, and that's where form-space relationships of color and brightness take place.

When a spatial envelope is almost totally confining, such as a simple interior room where the only view out is through a door or small window, its space generally is characterized as static. In other situations, space may be more dynamic or ambiguous, depending on the composition of the surrounding boundaries. A spatial enve-

* Muir, John. 1980. *Wilderness Essays.* Salt Lake City, Utah: Peregrine Smith, Inc., p. 40–41.

lope might be only partially confining; it might open to join one or more neighboring spaces, i.e., it might make connections with one or more contiguous spatial envelopes (Figure 7-1). In the outdoor spaces of the city, spatial boundaries are the facades of buildings, pavements, lawns, or the "ceilings" of sky or overpasses.

Conceptualizing an architectural volume as a spatial envelope groups the boundaries that appear in floor plans and section drawings into spatial rather than planar organization, which coincides with the perspective array as seen by human vision in the real environment. By its panoptic nature, the total envelope brings together the isolated elements of floors, walls, and ceilings. The spatial envelope affords a convenient "everything at once" view of architectural space, providing an instant impression of the volume of a room or urban setting. In design practice, the envelope is an operational scheme for previsualizing and analyzing the desired character and mood of a space that can be expected when all surfaces eventually are brought together in light, all working as a whole. The spatial envelope becomes a convenient and practical vehicle for discussions among members of the various design disciplines and the users of space.

Cutting into and through the envelope creates visual interest by spatial articulation and by the connections that are formed with other spaces. Articulation can be achieved by enhancing the facial surfaces of the envelope,

animating the space with the influence of texture, pattern, and color. Putting freestanding objects or furnishings inside the envelope sets up figure-ground relationships, brightness ratios, and color relationships. The spatial envelope then provides a vantage ground for evaluating perceptual simplicity, complexity, Gestalt patterns, mood, and, most important, the locations of light sources and their resulting luminance effects. The spatial envelope is an invaluable design tool for sorting out irregularities as they occur, for avoiding an overload of visual stimuli, and for the development and refinement of lighting design.

Boundaries for Spatial Definition

A spatial envelope is best identified by the *dominant* boundaries that shape a clearly defined volume functioning as a full or partial enclosure. The easier it is to single out those and only those boundaries, the more distinct is the definition of architectural space. As a simple illustration from nature, Figure 7-2 shows Meteor Crater, Arizona, carved out of the earth's surface by the violent impact of meteoritic action some 25,000 years ago. It appears like a giant amphitheater illuminated by early sunrise. Its generally flat floor and the sweeping uninterrupted concave boundary of its inner wall form its spatial

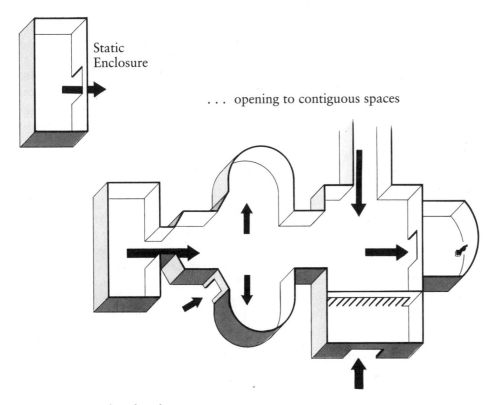

Static Enclosure

. . . opening to contiguous spaces

Figure 7-1. Enclosed and contiguous space.

Figure 7-2. The natural spatial envelope of Meteor Crater, Arizona.

envelope and shape its great spacious "room." Looking into its interior, the space is confined and static. Looking upward and away, its space is liberated, opening into its contiguous space and stretching to infinity between desert floor and sky.

Spatial envelopes are also formed by grouping related surfaces that are not joined in a continuous surface flow like the wall of Meteor Crater or the walls of a room in architecture. Instead, they establish *partial* envelopes that set up a series of spaces. Again turning to nature, the monolithic forms of Utah's Arches National Monument (Figure 7-3) conjure associations with New York's Park Avenue bounded by massive skyscrapers. The shapes of major and minor envelopes create a series of contiguous spaces reaching far into the distance. The stalwart forms to the right and the vertical surface of the butte to the left shape the foreground space occupied by the observer. In that first "room" can be found a number of small alcoves and terraces that articulate the greater volume as small but visually interesting subspaces. A *subspace* is one formed by its own spatial envelope, but it also clearly relates to a larger space in a role of articulation. A second, partial spatial envelope is visible in the middle ground, marked by the slender pinnacle resembling a pylon gateway, which begins a third space straight ahead. The series of envelopes is joined by the light on their common floor, which directs a visual movement

to the distant horizon. All the spatial boundaries are characterized by the same texture and color, giving harmony to the whole sequence. The interplay of light and shadow moves about the scene like a visual sonata, orchestrated by the sun and its "93,000,000 miles of effect." The interaction of the series of envelopes draws the eye forward. The sequential quality of the scene invites exploration and makes walking a tempting solution to satisfy the curious mind of what nature has reserved in the "rooms" that lie ahead.

In the context of the city, urban spatial envelopes are formed by the facades of buildings and pavements describing the outer limits of the void between them. Sometimes urban space is clear and organized, sometimes it is not, but for spatial definition it is only necessary to locate those facades or other major surfaces that are prominent enough to be considered dominant boundaries. Like the series of spaces at Arches National Monument, urban facades also do not have to be physically connected or totally enclosing to define space. A clear spatial envelope is present when the organizational placement and sizes of the boundaries determine a relatedness that makes evident a given volume of space. Figure 7-4 shows the distinct spatial envelope of the popular Williams Square in Irving, Texas, analyzed for its interspaces in Chapter 4 (see Figures 4-8 and 3-21). The envelope is formed by the inner facades of just three

Analysis of Architectural Space

Figure 7-3. Lessons from nature: sequencing spatial envelopes. [Arches National Park, Utah]

Figure 7-4. Urban spatial envelope. [Williams Square, Las Colinas, Irving, Texas. Architects: SOM, San Francisco]

buildings and the pavement base on which they rest. Coordinated landscaping with trees and commonness of detailing on the buildings contribute to spatial clarity.

The size of the spatial envelope is significant. Urban spaces do not have to be large and imposing to gain human appeal. When the envelope is small, and rendered in perceptual clarity, an environment can be characterized by a warmth and intimacy of mood. This is illustrated by Figure 7-5, which shows Acorn Street in Boston's historic Beacon Hill area. The envelope is sized and proportioned to human scale, and the space is closed off visually but not functionally by the perpendicular row of houses at the end of the street. The surface detailing and compatibility of building materials in brick and stone strike an accord with the cobblestone street, giving the spatial envelope a disposition that preserves the charm that once prevailed in Emerson's day.

Interior spatial envelopes are relatively easy to identify when applied to simple rooms or to larger spaces that are enclosed for the specialized purposes of group activities. Walls, floors, and ceiling most often coalesce into a single visual field, or are perceived in spatial relations by a sweep of the eye about a room. Like the public space of Williams Square shown in Figure 7-4, oftentimes an

interior space is also defined by only partial enclosure, yet a clear spatial identity is maintained by the presence of an organized envelope, limiting and describing the volume of space for a specific function. The small exhibit alcove shown in Figure 7-6 opens freely to a larger gallery behind the camera, but is instantly perceived as an ordered space of its own, made clear by its envelope of three walls, and vaulted ceiling. The compatible surfaces communicate a perceptual simplicity of background that gives visual emphasis to the paintings, plants, and visitors' seat, which clearly state the conceptual function of the space: a museum.

These examples are given only to illustrate the identification of the basic spatial envelope as defined by the dominant boundaries of space. For now we bypass the role played by objects or furnishings fixed or moving within its confines, a subject to be taken up later. It is the envelope that receives the broadest areas and patterns of reflected light, which are transformed into the colors and textures to which an observer's vision will adapt. The spatial envelope is an expedient design device that coincides with spatial perception natural to human vision.

Visual Perception of the Envelope

In most contemporary cultures, seeing architectural space as enclosures with boundaries begins in the formative years of life. We are told by the eminent Swiss psychologist Jean Piaget (1954) that in the first 18 months of life, the physical environment strongly influences learning and development. From 3 to 6 months of age, the child recognizes objects as forms and perceives the displacement of one object by another. By 6 to 12 months, the child has advanced in the visual construction of spatial depth. From birth on, modern cultures impose on the child various experiences of being enclosed in configurations of bounded space. Newborn infants are placed in cubical receptacles in maternity wards, taken home (in cars) and laid in bassinets, and in time creep around the small "room" of their cribs (Figure 7-7). Charles Burnette (1974, 174) has called the crib an infant learning environment where the infant experiences sizes and shapes that make for easy exploration and comprehension. These crib "rooms" are the spaces that provide early exercises for gradually sharpening the total senses. Burnette calls the crib a bounded domain that serves as a stable background and helps the infant to concentrate on a limited number of objects and to learn their spatial location related to sight and touch. For the infant and toddler these initial experiences begin the visual perception of spatial enclosure as a natural occurrence in human living.

Figure 7-5. Envelope size and human scale. [Acorn Street, Beacon Hill, Boston]

Figure 7-6. Interior spatial envelope. [Kimbell Art Museum, Fort Worth, Texas. Architect: Louis I. Kahn]

For now we are not interested in the artistic design of the boundaries, but only in how the surfaces carry perceptual stimuli and how physical boundaries form a spatial envelope. That is how the eye sees environmental spaces; that is how the brain comprehends them. The boundaries are the limits of the envelope for visual perception, no matter how close or how far away they are, as long as they are visible. Whether it is a stuccoed wall close enough to receive our own shadow or a highrise facade looming in the morning mist several city blocks away, if its surface is cognizable, then it can be said to contribute to the shaping and dimensioning of architectural space.

We can learn much about the perception of space by first observing how a singular boundary contributes to the formation of the total envelope. As an entity, each wall, floor, ceiling, or exterior building facade is rarely seen full-front at a 90° angle to the line of vision. In the visual perception of architectural space, each boundary is almost always seen at a slant. As we saw in earlier

chapters, slant influences spatial depth, and changes the value of a surface's color, texture, and brightness.

In Part 1, we saw that edges and contours are strong activators of the photoreceptors in the retina by breaking the flow of surface gradients. Edges therefore are highly important for the communication of spatial depth, because the dominant edges and corners of the planes bounding architectural space are nearly all seen at a slant, heightening the effect of perspective views. This was shown by the studies of Tommy Gärling (1970, 138), who investigated the perception of spatial depth in architectural settings. Figures 7-8a and b show two sets of four perspective drawings used by Gärling, one set delineated with surface details, and the other providing only the dominant edges of the same surfaces. When shown to subjects, the drawings having only edges (Figure 7-8b) proved to be as reliable for spatial depth judgments as those with the added surface details. In both sets of drawings, spatial envelopes are easy to identify, and it is clear that the importance of edges and corners

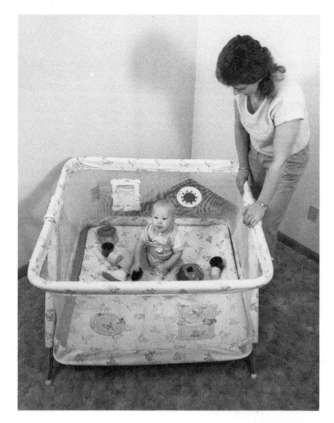

Figure 7-7. Spatial perception and infant development.

source for glare. If carpeted, the floor absorbs much light, but still can reflect some to the walls and ceiling as we are reminded by Figure C-18. The floor and ceiling (if seen as an uninterrupted flow) serve another important role. Returning to the example from nature in Figure 7-3, the landscape "floor" and "ceiling" are the principal agents for connecting a series of spaces, linking the sequence of individual spatial envelopes.

Spreading its great canopy over our visual world, the sky in exterior space is the ceiling of the urban spatial envelope. Even though some cloud types such as cumulus or cirrus may be considered white patterns with edges seen against the upper reaches of the blue atmosphere, perceptually the sky is considered a textureless background against which buildings (as the walls of urban space) are seen. On a cloudless or totally overcast day, the sky is free of surface information for visual perception. The panorama of the sky serves as "ground" for the "figure" of buildings seen in front of it. In this regard, the words of the Brazilian poet/archbishop Dom Helder Camara (1981, 37) come to mind in his short stanza:

> I was afraid
> that with their blocks of concrete
> the skyscrapers might wound the
> dawn.

The perception of urban space is greatly influenced by the changing brightness of the sky. Even on an overcast day, the luminance directly overhead is about three times brighter than that on the horizon. Obviously we have little control over this fickle and ever-changing "luminous ceiling" spread over an outdoor spatial envelope. As far as the sky should be considered as a spatial boundary, designing urban space is like trying to act out a part on stage while the person responsible for lighting the set is reading from a different script. In short, the sky is simply there . . . up toward which we send the walls of urban space whether or not we "wound the dawn" with architectural imagery.

Paramount for good design of architectural space is the concern for size and human scale. We saw the importance of this in the intimate spaces of Boston's Beacon Hill (Figure 7-5). That quality can be found in urban neighborhoods, and in some of New York City's "vest-pocket" parks or the small piazzas of Venice. Designing with the concept of a spatial envelope is a more realistic means for visualizing volumetric proportions than traditional floor plans and section drawings, where in architectural practice spaces are designed but sometimes misconceived by overlooking the *interaction* of length, width, and ceiling height. Proficient architects and interior designers have an innate sense for scale, dimensions, and proportions related to human activities. Good fictional authors (as designers of the written word) have

cannot be overemphasized. This is not to imply that designers should necessarily dramatize edges and corners of buildings and rooms; perception alone will take care of that. They need to be aware of the organization of major boundaries for the edge relationships they create in their role of communicating architectural space.

There is a tendency to identify architectural space primarily by its enclosing walls, but special attention needs to be given to the perception of floors and ceilings. People are terrestrial animals, and have acclimated to traversing the natural and built environment with keen awareness of the lower portion of the visual field as filled by the terrain. Awareness of this natural process places emphasis on the floor, either out-of-doors or inside, as a primal component of the spatial envelope. Like the other boundaries, the floor too is seen consistently at a slant. The designer influences the perception of spatial depth by selecting patterns and textures for the floor or by leaving them unadorned. In the illuminated environment, reflectance must also be considered. Because most light comes at some angle from above, the reflectance of flooring materials is a major factor for how they will influence perception of the rest of the spatial envelope. A polished floor scatters light on neighboring boundaries, and because it is seen at a slant, is oftentimes a

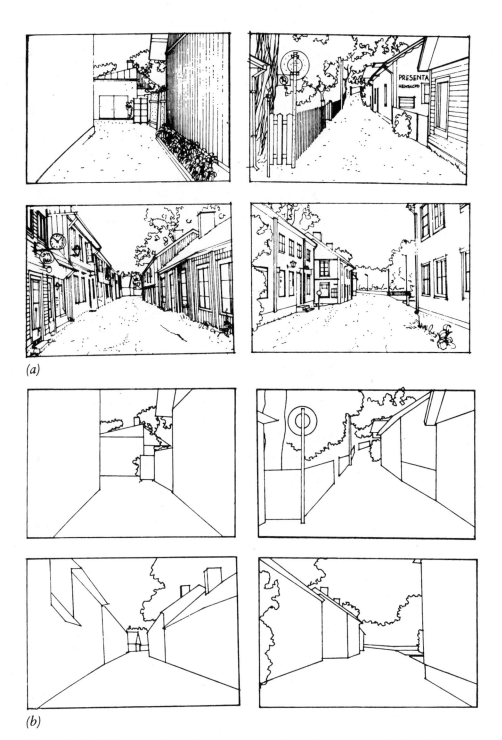

(a)

(b)

Figure 7-8. Gärling studies of perceived depth. a. Drawings with detail.
b. Drawings without detail. [Permission granted by Scandinavian University
Press. From Scandinavian Journal of Psychology, *Vol. 11, 1970 pp. 139, 141.]*

that same understanding, being able to plant in the mental vision of the reader an appropriate image of scale. In his travel books, Mark Twain crafted vivid descriptions of architectural size without ever mentioning feet or meters. In *Roughing It,* on the Pacific Ocean en route to Hawaii he once described the dimensions of the ship as being "long as two street cars, and about as wide as one." His readers also learn the exact size of his shipboard cabin, which was so small "One might swing a cat in it . . . . but not a long cat." In his *The Innocents Abroad,* he was equal to the task of conveying the magnitude of the interior space of St. Peter's basilica in Rome:

I could believe the story that ten thousand troops went to St. Peter's once, to hear mass, and their commanding officer came afterward, and not finding them, supposed they had not yet arrived. But they were in the church, nevertheless—they were in one of the transepts.

From both descriptions, the spatial limits of cabin and basilica are easily comprehended, and anyone who has stepped aboard a nineteenth-century oceanic sailing vessel or into that Vatican showpiece knows that Twain's sense of scale was accurate, at least as measured by human sensitivity, if not by architect's dimensions.

The Character of Space

We talk about spaces as having mood. That is the essence of architecture in its capacity to work on our feelings. Wherever you go over the next few days, be mindful of the interchange between the architectural environment and your personal, intuitive response to its mood. Just like people, architectural space has character, and that character is conveyed by the collective imagery that we perceive as a living room, office, shopping mall, or one of those special places we like to visit. The character of spaces in which we move ranges from the satisfying and peaceful to the stressful and depressing. They include the appealing and the exciting, the distasteful and the deplorable. The spatial envelope is a principal conveyor of the character of a space. The freestanding contents in a room further describe its individualism, but the intent here is to continue to isolate the spatial envelope to facilitate analysis of the space it defines. Furniture can be replaced or rearranged and litter picked up, but the surface complexion of the boundaries of a room remains more stable and in prominent view, influencing our feelings. The appearance of those boundaries affects us much as the countenance of other people. Style and condition of clothing, skin modified by cosmetics, hair combed or uncombed, posture poised or slouched, an eyebrow raised or lowered, a grin or a frown—all communicate a person's character and mood. The surfaces of walls deliver similar messages. They can be harsh or soft, tattered or trim, upright or leaning, monotone or colorful, bright or shadowed.

The visual appearance of boundaries can be deceiving in their capacity for conveying the character and mood of an environment. Figure 7-9 shows an award-winning adaptive-use restoration of a narrow space left between two old buildings. Small shops are located just behind the windows. The surfaces of the two walls were left in their state of deterioration at the time of renewal of the site and are little more than random broken-away

Figure 7-9. Old surfaces shaping a new space. [Passageway, The Old Market, Omaha, Nebraska]

patches of stucco over old brick. The principle of how the mood of a space depends on the character of its boundaries is here speciously misleading. The small cafe, the leisurely attitude of the people, their dress and demeanor, planters and greenery, and the swept floor all counteract the intrinsic influence of the time-worn walls, which in their "new" role impart a romanticized vestige of former times, not poverty and social blight. Visualize the same space with the same walls, but add broken pavement, the litter of paper and aluminum cans, a broken shutter hanging from a window with shattered glass, a rusted bicycle wheel, a derelict or two, and the space communicates an urban slum.

The age of boundary surfaces is but one factor contributing to the character of architectural space. Familiarity is another. When the boundaries are visually read like a well-known book and impart recognizable imagery popularized by movies, television, or common knowledge, the character of the space is instantly conveyed. Figure 7-10 shows the picturesque urban square of the

Place Plumereau in Tours, France, one of many such vestiges of old Europe. The compactness of the fifteenth-century brick-and-timber framed houses shapes the spatial envelope, and the buildings' exterior surfaces create the visual impact that promptly stamps the square with its medieval character. The composite historic facades pattern the spatial envelope with part timber, giving harmony to the space, in spite of the unfortunate white intruder seen at the right. The clarity of the space is being carried by Gestalt factors. Common elements like the gables, windows, diagonal framing, brick patterns, chimneys, and color—all unite to recall the medieval past. Consider the "intruder." Note how its gable, chimney, and windows impart Gestalt factors of similarity, proximity, and good continuation, all of which appear on the medieval buildings. However unfortunate was the poor choice of its contrasting white surfacing along aesthetic grounds, those visual laws of Gestalt perception are the saving grace that allows its presence to at least border on acceptability. It is the *visual appearance of the spatial envelope* that dominates the scene, and when stepping into the square, the character of the space greets the visitor as vintage Old World.

By way of contrast to times past, one current of modern architectural design philosophy produced austere interior spaces (as well as exterior forms). With its emphasis on pristine, carefully proportioned cubic volumes, the spatial envelope of interiors was held in restraint as background for a few paintings or wall hangings and furniture. Historicism and lavish ornamentation were taboo, and incoming sunlight often came to rest on the purity of white walls. The most representative of this philosophy of design was the "less is more" practice of the modern master Mies van der Rohe. Interiors of his 860–880 N. Lake Shore Drive apartments in Chicago are patent examples (Figure 7-11). Unless significantly altered by the people living in them (as many did), the character of those spaces exemplified a type that Bruno Zevi (1957, 31) called "architectural nudism." The mood of the space is muted, serene, "pure." To be added to this group is Le Corbusier, who in some of his works combined mathematical proportions with cubic volumes to achieve an architecture he called "the purity of white." Many architects and interior designers pursued this philosophy of minimalism to its limits until the postmodernists broke the austerity with the introduction of more sensuous color, decorative use of materials, and whimsical forms and spaces. In the process, some postmodernists often went to the other extreme, overstepping the line of visual simplicity comprehension limits (see Chapter 2), and destroyed spatial clarity entirely with excessive architectural detailing and spacial infill.

Are architectural spaces that are bounded by undecorated and monochromatic surfaces destined to create spatial character that is dull and prosaic? Not at all. Size, shape, and proportions of the spatial envelope can

Figure 7-10. Vertical boundaries characterizing urban space. [Place Plumereau, Tours, France]

Figure 7-11. Austerity of the spatial envelope. [Interior of apartment at 860–880 N. Lake Shore Drive, Chicago. Architect: Mies van der Rohe. Photograph: Chicago Historical Society, HB-13809W5]

be made interesting and very livable even if only one surface material is used throughout an entire human habitation. This is attested to by the centuries of cultural dictates that brought about and sustained the "white towns" in southern Spain. Towns like Cordoba, Rhonda, Tolox, and Mijas (Figure 7-12) possess a rich variety of interesting spaces, even though the boundaries of their streets and interior courts are totally white. By custom, the inhabitants whitewash all exterior walls of their homes and other buildings, and neighboring facades are not in stylistic competition. Spatial envelopes are clearly developed. Streets and pedestrian paths change levels, pass under arches, and open into small plazas. Naturally formed spaces interconnect, offering glimpses into neighboring spaces with the turn of nearly every corner, and the spaces encourage exploration by visitors. The only decoration amid the ambiance of white is an occasional punctuation by colored doors or window blinds, flowers, or black wrought iron grilles. Uniform in character throughout the town, the boundaries belie the opinion that the absence of multiple styles leads to monotony, sterility, and boredom. It is the variety of shapes, sizes, and proportions of the spatial envelopes that give these towns their spatial richness and architectural interest. The same principle of common spatial character as cre-

ated by simplicity of monochromatic boundaries can be found in the native Indian adobe villages of America's southwest, the island settlements of Greece, and cities of the Middle East and North Africa, yet they too are affluent in spatial appeal.

Distortion of the Spatial Envelope

The spatial envelope can be conceived in any shape, proportion, or character to produce ergonomic architecture, but it can also be responsible for the distortion of space, which can be physically upsetting to the human nervous system when the shapes and organization of the dominant boundaries deprive people of the basic human need for equilibrium. A moderate but demonstrative example is a space at New York's Kennedy Airport. Connecting the TWA terminal with the boarding areas for incoming and departing international flights is a long tunnel whose spatial envelope is curved in length, forcing people to walk the concourse along a bowed floor while surrounded by curving walls and ceiling. Little needs to be said about its effect on weary or airsick

Figure 7-12. Spatial character independent of surface color. [Arched street, Mijas, Spain]

passengers returning from a long and exhausting transatlantic trip.

Distortions of interior space sometimes occur when one or more of the spatial boundaries create compositional and psychological imbalance with the others as a result a structural member serving two different spaces. Such is the case if the underside of a roof is a ceiling that malforms the upper section of an interior spatial envelope, or a wall that is insensitively angled in one room because of a function it was created to serve on the other side. Some deformations of space come about by the intent of the designer from the outset, for the simple purpose of wanting to create a novel spatial effect. A look through the architectural journals of the last few decades of the twentieth century will provide a number of examples of either method. This is not to make a case that all architectural spaces should be bounded symmetrically and characterized as static, but to point up how a breakdown of good spatial composition occurs when an unusually sloped or twisted boundary creates a discordant part of the spatial envelope, violating spatial aesthetics. Even worse is when it is a violation of ergonomics, contributing to the dehumanization of architecture. People require a sense of balance, and extreme distortions of our visual surroundings are disorienting and unsettling.

It is from the very attempt to enliven a space that distortions often occur. The designer must always be aware of how one elevation works with another, influencing perception of the space as a whole. In Figure 7-13, an enclosed public atrium is faced by interior elevations that generally give a rectilinear shape to the volume of space. The upper level offices on the left are glazed flush with the horizontal fascias, but the offices on the right step back as they ascend toward the roof. The vertical piers on the left are also flush with the boundary plane, but are answered on the opposite side by vertical niches in the upward terracing. Overhead structural members and skylights aesthetically compete in an attempt to bridge the two opposing elevations. Reflected images of the horizontals over the central space appear on the glass of the left side, creating a labyrinth of reflected versus real structural members, a visual experience that contrasts the right side. The visual field as seen from the floor gives the feeling of a distorted upward tilt.

Even though the spatial envelope may be organized in a balanced composition, the space that it actually defines can still be obscured as a result of excessive detailing in the visual field. This has been an ergonomic problem with many high-tech structural installations. By the nature of its assemblage of multiple parts, those construction systems greatly increase the amount of perceptual stimuli over and above what will come later when all other furnishings are added. Moreover, a high-tech network oftentimes makes a poor visual backdrop for the perception of form-space relationships.

Figure 7-14 shows a public atrium that is a major circulation route connecting two office towers. Most of the basic spatial envelope (nearly everything but the

Figure 7-13. Distorted spatial envelope. [Dallas City Hall]

Figure 7-14. Excessive stimuli and vagueness of space. [Leadership Square, Oklahoma City]

floor) is an assembly of high-tech truss work and other members of a rational structural system. An abundance of glass incorporated into the spatial envelope creates an array of reflected light patterns throughout the atrium, one that obscures the actual boundaries of space. Sections of the envelope in the left-central and upper left sections of the photograph are diffused by a veil of stacked rows of mesh screens sprayed in different colors and suspended from the open trusswork. In itself the screening effect is interesting, but when interposed between the viewer and a spatial envelope already perceptually weakened by the overload of stimuli of structure, light, and glare patterns, much of the aesthetic effectiveness of the suspended colored screens is lost. The end product is a space that is perceptually vague, one where the spatial envelope and its appendages enshroud the visual presence of offices scarcely visible on the right, and to an extent even the escalator. Those elements that could be used for orienting the visitor and enriching the total spatial experience are obscured amid the welter of visual details.

The two atria just discussed are mild examples of spatial distortion when compared with what some postmodernist designers have put into the urban landscape.

One need only to review some of the designs by Peter Eisenman, most notably his Koizumi Sangyo Building in Tokyo on which tilted cubes "appear to have been shaken by an earthquake,"[1] and his Greater Columbus Convention Center in Columbus, Ohio, both of which willfully distort the human environment, inside and out. As reviewer Joseph Giovannini reports on the Convention Center,[2] its interior of curved and listing walls, tilted columns, complex intersections, and "walls gridded at the angle of the Titanic in her final hours" produced some disorienting interior environments that were so strong "that some optical illusions have caused visitors to leave seminar rooms." In private environments and Disneylands such "spatial entertainment" is acceptable. In public spaces where people have little choice to avoid the environments they encounter, it is a deplorable imposition on human living. The designers who subscribe to such practices and the editors who flaunt their works in the professional journals perpetuate the dehumanization of architecture.

[1] See *Architecture*. Sep. 1990. pp. 80–85.
[2] *Architecture*. May 1993. pp. 52–63.

Clarity of the Spatial Envelope

Organizing the dominant boundaries of space for perceptual clarity is an essential step toward achieving visual order and architectural beauty. Remember that we are still analyzing the spatial envelope *per se*, not yet including its interior furnishings. It is obvious the clarity of a room is disrupted when it contains disharmonious or clashing objects, but the disarray is further magnified when the boundaries themselves are optically cluttered. Such an environment is a conglomerate of excessive visual stimuli, overloading the perceptual tasks for the retina, and stifling the ease of comprehension for the mind. To enrich a space, a major surface may deviate from the others as a designed accent, but the more the individual boundaries are differentiated by dissimilar surface pattern, color, or appendages, the more the clarity of the overall space is weakened.

Figure 7-15 shows a minor spatial envelope of a public park sunk beneath street level. An overpass partially frames the scene in the upper left corner of the photograph. In the field of view, there are only two constructional building materials: the concrete of the embankment and the brick on the building showing above. There are only two natural materials: water and greenery. The concrete and brick contribute to the spatial character as rigid, unpliable surfaces, but the softening influence of the natural materials counteracts the harder boundaries. The spatial envelope has clarity, because it is not excessively stepped, penetrated, patterned, or colored. That is the reason the waterfall, trees, and illumination bollards along the sidewalk are visually unhampered in their roles as accenting forms in space. The person walking along the footway is not overpowered by excessive visual stimuli, and the sound of the falling water adds its human appeal.

Perceptual clarity breaks down the more design character varies from boundary to boundary of the spatial envelope. Put into traditional design language, this means unity of the parts contributes to harmony of the whole. When the boundaries of the spatial envelope correspond in similar form and surface pattern, and when discordant parts are absent, clarity of the spatial envelope is heightened. As the number of different *kinds* of component shapes and surface variations increases, clarity of the envelope deteriorates. By intent, no discussion is made here concerning human responses to such spaces as being "static," "boring," or "uninteresting." For the present, only the principle of perceptual clarity is the focus of attention. How interest is added and maintained during design development without the breakdown of clarity and order is explained in the next and subsequent chapters.

The advantage of conceptualizing the enclosure of architectural space by Gestalt factors is that they are fundamental to human visual perception, making them universal and free from cultural variants and historical time periods. Applied to an example from the past, the spatial clarity of Michelangelo's renowned Campidoglio in Rome (Figure 7-16) clearly relates to the presence of Gestalt principles, whether observed in photographs, drawings, or by viewing the actual site. Three vertical

Figure 7-15. Perceptual simplicity in urban space. [Central Park Mall, Omaha]

Figure 7-16. Campidoglio, Rome. [Engraving by E. Dupérac. No. inv. F.N. 12060. Permission courtesy: Ministero per Beni ambientalie Culturali. Instituto Nazionale per la Grafica, Rome]

boundaries shape the space. A fourth is the horizontal pavement, inscribed with an elliptical inlay pattern of white marble, which sweeps around and mutually interacts with the three vertical facades, and its major axis coincides with the flow of space to the open end. The proximity of the three buildings at one end allows the Gestalt factor of closure to take effect, enhancing the spatial envelope, but the buildings are just far enough apart to prevent feelings of confinement. The absence of a building on the open end breaks what otherwise might be a static, enclosed space, and the elevated site provides a panoramic view to a lower piazza and street below. The proximity of the boundaries simplifies the function of two other Gestalt factors: similarity and good continuation of the detailing, allowing the eye to scan the space with perceptual ease. The fact that the detailing on the buildings is classical is not essential for perceptual clarity (compare Figure 7-4). Visitors to the space do not have to know classicism, Renaissance theory, or what constitutes good design. They will perceive the space in a state of order.

The same perceptual theory applies to contemporary design. Figure 7-17 shows a small, generic shopping court that has spatial clarity and is ordered by Gestalt principles. Its spatial envelope is defined by a series of small shops recessed under a surrounding loggia, and by entrance pavilions that step into the space. The factor of similarity contributes to spatial clarity by way of repeating rectangles of loggia openings and structural piers and the semicircles of the upper windows on the two entrance facades. The circular patterns of windows perceptually group with the circular organization of landscaping and lampposts in the center of the space. The ensemble of circular elements diminishes a static quality of the space by contrasting the prevailing rectangularity. The narrow proportions of brick piers allow the horizontal fascias of the second floor to pass visually through their vertical pattern in good continuation, paralleling the fascias at the roof line. Spatial clarity is also maintained by the limited kinds of building materials and the minimal number of shapes forming visual patterns. The mind easily comprehends a sense of place.

Clarity of the spatial envelope is independent of the size of the space, and whether it is urban or interior. The grand lobby shown in Figure C-25 is located in an office building that has been a controversial design for the city of Boston, mainly due to the design of its exterior and interior that is overladen by excessive use of expensive materials. The lobby is still impressive, and most likely will appear so for most visitors. That is because of the perceptual clarity of the spatial envelope, and its proportions that convey the character of a grand public

Analysis of Architectural Space

space. The clarity is achieved by the design pattern of the skylight and the shapes of surface penetration that articulate the upper walls. Gestalt factors simultaneously unite to make an immediate impact in the panoptic field of view for a person stepping into the space, but that applies more to the upper floors than to the ground floor. The design of the shops at pavement level strikes a discordant note; they seem to belong to another building, perhaps even to another era. Nevertheless, this space is a good demonstration of the value of the spatial envelope as a device for space perception. In the "everything at once" view of the human visual field, the patterns on the upper floors carry the rhythmic harmony that flows around the space, and are largely responsible for the spatial clarity that is there.

In summary, the design of a clear spatial envelope is dependent on a minimal number of dominant boundaries, and a minimal number of similar surface elements spread throughout a space. The more the boundaries share similar design qualities, the more they will be tied into stable relationships for visual order. To enrich, enliven, and animate the boundaries is the most critical stage of design development, because that means multiplying the effects of reflected light and shadow throughout the totality of a space. Animation of the boundaries is a means for putting life into architectural space, but should not be overdone. In the end, the envelope itself must maintain integrity.

Proportioning the Spatial Envelope

The composition of the dominant boundaries and the distance between them establish the basic proportions for space. Some architects set up spatial proportions by shaping and dimensioning floor plans and sections. Modern master architect Le Corbusier (1931, 47) said "The plan is the generator. The eye of the spectator finds itself looking at a site composed of streets and houses. It receives the impact of the masses which rise up around it." In that simple explanation, he brought together the designer's creative act and the end result of what observers will perceive as their environment. We are told Frank Lloyd Wright had awareness of total spatial coordination as he designed. He was sensitive to the shape and proportions of a first floor room, while intuitively knowing how it related to another room located diagonally upward from it on the second floor. Not all designers have that gift. Designing with the concept of the spatial

Figure 7-17. Clarity by perceptual simplicity. [College Metcalf Plaza, Overland Park, Kansas. Architects: The Hollis & Miller Group, Inc.]

envelope does not negate the role of conventional building plans and sections, but they alone cannot fully communicate architectural space. They cannot provide the "everything at once" view for human vision, which needs to be sustained in the designer's mind as space is developed and refined, as plans and sections are drawn.

The proportions of architectural space are volumetric, not two dimensional. As planes, the boundaries themselves are normally shaped as squares, rectangles, or other curved or planar geometric shapes, but their proportional configuration as a group sets up a controlled volume, which determines spatial perception.

A study conducted at the University of Washington in Seattle (Thiel, Harrison, and Alden, 1986) investigated the interrelationships of the boundaries of interior space for the way people respond with feelings of enclosure and openness. Using a series of line drawings depicting various angular views of a rectangular room, Thiel and colleagues tested subjects for how they would perceive the degree of enclosure relative to the proportional amount of boundary surfaces in a visual field. They concluded that the floor is the least significant surface for communicating spatial enclosure, the walls have an intermediate effect, and the ceiling is most important. But this must be put in context of the proportions of the total spatial volume. When walls are separated by great dimensions such as a large room with a low ceiling, the walls are far in the field of view, and the ceiling—by proportion—is the dominating member of the spatial envelope. The researchers for the Washington study acknowledged the limitations of their work in that they used two-dimensional drawings and not real spaces of architectural rooms, but their findings make us aware of the importance of ceiling design as finished interior space is perceived. It is at or near that surface plane of the envelope where most electric support lighting is located, often introducing patterns of intense brightness by exposed luminaires (as well as other visual stimuli in the form of mechanical support equipment). This has serious design implications for lighting interior space, as is shown in Chapter 11.

Much is to be learned about proportions of the spatial envelope from studying the grand spaces in historical architecture. The vertical spaces of Gothic cathedrals are excellent examples (Figure 7-18). Granted, their enormous size is a major contributing factor to their grandeur, but the ratio of height to width of Gothic naves and side aisles creates *dynamic* architectural space. Fundamental design theory states that a rectangle engenders greater linear movement the more it is lengthened. The same is true for proportions of space. Stepping into the nave of a Gothic cathedral, the observer immediately is awed by its soaring verticality. Much of the vertical effect is created by the preponderance of linear elements of piers and colonettes, which the eye tends to follow from floor to keystone. But the impression of verticality is enforced by the relatively narrow proportions of space, with the longer dimension of the nave cross section oriented upward in the field of view. The height-to-width ratio of the nave of French cathedrals averages 3 : 1. Shown in Figure 7-18 is Reims Cathedral, whose nave height is nearly 3 : 1 of its width. The impact of the rising vertical space of the cathedrals is set up by the comparatively low covered narthex, experienced by visitors just before entering the nave. The question may be asked, "What makes the visual impression of Gothic naves appear not only as vertical, but as dynamic?" Some of this may be answered by contrasting the *vertical* orientation of Gothic interiors (Figure 7-19) with the *horizontal* orientation of the human visual field, an elliptical shape with the major axis horizontal. With the two eyes in their natural horizontal position, the major axis of the elliptical visual field runs perpendicular to the verticality of the Gothic nave, increasing the vigor of perceptual response through countermovement.

Figure 7-18. Verticality of Gothic space. [Nave facing west, Reims Cathedral, France. Photograph: Foto Marburg/Art Resource, NY, S0032928 182595]

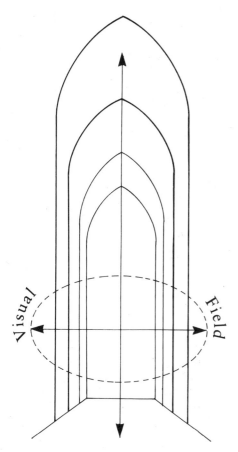

Figure 7-19. Visual field and the dynamics of space.

In a study to learn more about how people perceive proportions of contemporary interior space (Holmberg, Kuller, and Tidblom, 1966, 1967), an experiment was set up in which observers walked in and around a series of six full-scale rooms, whose volumes varied through changes in the floor area. The first was a "standard room" of 1:1 ratio in plan (a square), and each of the others lengthened to ratios of 1.5:1, 2:1, 2.5:1, 3:1, and 3.5:1. The rectangular rooms were entered from one of the narrow ends. Two experiments were conducted. In one, subjects viewed the rooms only from the door. In the second they were allowed to walk around in the rooms, and were also allowed to walk back and forth between the rectangular rooms and the "standard room." When people were allowed to walk around in the rooms, they were less affected by the spatial proportions. The researchers suggest a possible reason for this might be that the distance of the walls from the observer is critical for volume perception, and that when standing in the room, the viewer never perceives the entire volume in one glance. They couldn't have been more correct. As their subjects walked around inside the rooms, they were perceiving the boundaries of the total spatial envelope

in changing relationships. That is a quite different experience from perceiving a room as seen from just inside the door. From there, boundary edges of walls, floor, and ceiling enhance depth perception by linear perspective, creating the elongated, directional character for the spaces of the longer rooms.

The designer must be on guard for the use and abuse of the generally accepted idealized proportions for a singular surface plane. The traditional "golden rectangle" is a case in point. Designers have dimensioned walls in rooms and floor plans using its 5:3 ratio with the security of its being a "perfect" proportion. Remember, however, that the boundaries of the spatial envelope are rarely seen full-front, i.e., in their true geometric shape. This is supported by the study of Holmberg *et al.* where the influence of any one wall was diminished for people perceiving the total room while walking about. People perceive space as created by the assemblage of *all* of its definitive boundaries, not just one or two, and they see them at slant. Using ratios such as the golden rectangle is useful only if the area lies in a prominent field of view, or if the area contributes to similarity by relating to other areas of the spatial envelope. *The humanization of architecture is an issue that must differentiate between the intellectualizing of design and the natural process by which people normally see and experience their environment.* Calling that very problem "the architectural polemic," Albert Bush-Brown (1959, 150) denounced the abstracting of design, saying "rigorous theories of proportion are doomed to failure. In search of absolutes, Le Corbusier or Francesco di Giorgio fashioned yardsticks, but they willingly threw them away, as they admitted. . . the moment their eyes saw that colors, materials, light, exits, and entrances affect the apparent proportions of a space as much as arithmetic and geometry."[3] The functional requirements for human living should never be sidestepped in favor of applying rigid abstract design theory to environmental design. Not only are the boundaries of interior space rarely seen in their pure geometric shape when perpendicular to the line of sight, but it is equally as rare for them to be seen unobstructed. Walls are cut into with windows, doors, air vents, or stairs, and are occluded by sofas, desks, file cabinets, or plants. Le Corbusier *did* recognize the improbability that space could be created with all the spatial boundaries dimensioned in preferred proportions. He knew the shapes of some walls simply would be less than artistically desirable as the total architectural scheme is worked out. He solved that problem by distracting vision from poor proportions in a room by "dynamiting the bad

[3] Bush-Brown's reference to Le Corbusier and di Giorgio ("as they admitted") is taken from Henry Millon. 1958. The architectural theory of Francesco di Girogio. *Art Bulletin.* XL 3:257ff.

walls" with paintings and graphics. He intuitively knew and took advantage of the natural process of human vision, what in this book is called *selection in the visual world*, related to the natural scanning process of visual perception. The saccadic movements of the eye will be stopped momentarily by a colorful painting or graphic, overlooking the fact that the wall it adorns may be poorly proportioned. Le Corbusier (1948, 99) said, "The mural paintings brightened only the most unpleasing walls of the house. The 'good walls' remained white."

The Color of Architectural Space

The predominant surfacing materials of the spatial envelope determine the prevailing color of an environment. Once a decision is made to designate prominent walls as brick, concrete, or wood left in its natural state, the coloring of space has begun. Those boundaries not intended to remain in natural hues are subjected to secondary surfacing of paint, veneer, or other appliqué, each affecting the developing mood of a space. The same is true for ceilings, floors, and other major components of the total envelope. Ceiling panels, floor tiles, or carpeting add large areas of color. Over time, the major boundaries may be changed by surface remodeling and lighting modifications, and new colors assert their expressive impact. The color of the spatial envelope will serve as the greater field against which all other colors will be perceived after wall appendages and interior furnishings are added. *The color of space should be anticipated as the spatial envelope is conceived,* and rationally controlled throughout design development.

The principles of color theory developed in the preceding chapter apply directly to the perception of the boundaries of the envelope, all slanted to both the observer and the sources of light. Variations of reflectance and texture cause hues to shift in value and saturation. All the walls of a room may be of the same color, and even though their different angles of slant change their appearance where they meet at a corner, the dominance of their basic hue remains, wrapped around the spatial envelope.

The amount of surface area of the total envelope is significant for the way various hues influence the quality of spaciousness. Brighter colors tend to make a room appear larger, and darker colors make it appear smaller. If one wall is to vary in color from the others, its size is important for how it compares *in proportion* with the other boundaries of the envelope. What needs to be questioned is how color will influence spatial perception based on how much appears in a typical field of view. Will the majority of the dominant boundaries be of a certain hue, and will its specific saturation and value create a very light pastel causing the room to appear more spacious, or will those attributes be darker (lower on the LBR Scale) mitigating the effect of spaciousness?

Color of building materials also affects spatial perception of exterior spaces. It is an important decision when specifying either dark red or light buff brick for walls that will enclose a small exterior court. Not only does each influence spaciousness in a different way, but in turn, the color of those boundaries is exceptionally important if that court is to be enhanced by the addition of landscaping elements. The intrinsic color values of the exterior building materials influence the choice of appropriate planting materials, which will be visually absorbed or vividly contrasted when seen against the background of the spatial envelope formed by the brick walls of the building.

A sequential walk through a world of multicolored spaces awaits the visitor to the Italian island village of Burano (Figure C-26) off the mainland of Venice. In vivid contrast to the "white towns" of southern Spain, the exterior stuccoed walls of houses and small shops of Burano are painted in full color, trimmed with accents around windows and doorways. Like its neighboring Venice, the village is a network of small neighborhood piazzas connected by pedestrian paths between buildings and along a main canal. Spatial envelopes of every conceivable size, shape, and proportion are formed by the configuration of connected buildings, each individualized by pastel or deep hues from pavement to roof. Sometimes three houses bound a small yard forming a unified chromatic envelope; elsewhere a group of differently colored houses creates a mosaic as rich as pigments dashed on an artist's palette. Walking the streets of the town is like experiencing a slowly moving kaleidoscope, with one color momentarily centering itself in the fovea of the retina while others enter in peripheral vision. Chromatic and spatial discovery awaits every turn of corner. At one time the observer is surrounded by deep maroons and mint greens in full sun, and around the next corner the eye is shadowed in a walkway of dimmed blues or ochres. The entire village becomes a chromatic improvisation when washed by the orange light of the setting sun. So fascinating is this adventure, the desire to explore can easily absorb the visitor to the point of finally returning to the seaside pier too late to catch the departing vaporetto back to Venice.

A medley of colors distributed about the spatial envelope is a means for enlivening interior space. The school library of Figure C-27 shows a spatial envelope that maintains clarity by its major boundaries—roof, clerestory wall just below, floor, and distant wall. Polychromatic color characterizes the composition of spatial surfaces (including the colorful array of the books themselves). The stability and clarity of the spatial envelope and the arrangement of the interior furnishings maintain visual order, without which, the environment would suffer from an overload of stimuli by a combination of multiple surfaces and multiple colors. But controlled spatial and chromatic design rewards the visitors to the library, in this case, children, who are greeted by the refreshing and stimulating array of colors and the invitation for spatial exploration.

The colors in the library space were not indiscriminately applied. The architects developed and followed a rational program that called for the hues of the classrooms to be neutral, but other rooms and circulation spaces colored to provide orientation. The colors selected for the library not only enliven the space, but conform to a color program used throughout the school. Structural columns, beams, and trusses are blue. Lighting fixtures are burgundy. Electrical conduits, ducts, etc., appear in other colors. That color coding was intentional, as "didactic color," by which children can learn to identify architectural parts and functions.

Like the design of the spatial envelope itself, the function of a space should form the premise for color selection. In Figure C-20 it was the architect's choice for a monochromatic environment, a blue vaulted entrance hall to a corporation's marketing center. In the school environments of Figures C-24 and C-27, children benefit from the spirit arousing nature of colors as they encounter them through the course of the school day. It was the culture of Burano, Italy, that determined its polychromatic walkways and piazzas, and designer's choice that enriched a children's library with a variegated interior. Color selection should be appropriate to the space in which it appears, and how it contributes to the clarity and character of an environment is closely tied with the shape of the spatial envelope.

The concept of the spatial envelope provides an effective means for analyzing how space is shaped, how it is illuminated and colored, and how it connects with neighboring spaces. As a tool for design, the envelope is more than just the positioning of walls, floors, and ceilings. It is a framework for the maturation of a *space aesthetic*. We speak of certain buildings or urban areas as having "good spaces" or "beautiful spaces," and designers strive to emulate and improve such models. Other than a few exceptions in the historical development of cities, great architectural spaces do not just happen. They have to be designed.

To avoid the potential sterility or confining quality that may be suggested by bringing together surfaces that envelop, we now need to focus on how to bring an architectural environment to life by taking the spatial envelope into the next phase of analysis, the articulation of its dominant boundaries. This is done by adding to or subtracting from the major space-defining surfaces, while ensuring that each step is one toward enrichment not destruction of a desired spatial character, and certainly one that maintains and does not destroy spatial clarity. Modification of the boundaries by adding and subtracting is not an easy task, but it is a way to create visual interest, animating the spaces in which we live. The enhancement of the spatial envelope is the reach into the spatial aesthetic, and the design of the boundaries should be so well done that the assembled composition would applaud the entry of light.

CHAPTER 8

Articulation of the Spatial Envelope

The winter sea was a mirror in a cold, half-lighted room, the summer sea is a mirror in a room burning with light. So abundant is the light and so huge the mirror that the whole of a summer day floats reflected on the glass. Colours gather there, sunrise and twilight, cloud shadows and cloud reflections, the pewter dullness of gathering rain, the blue, burning splendour of space swept free of every cloud. Light transfixes ocean, and some warmth steals in with the light, but the waves that glint in the sun are still a tingling cold.

—Henry Beston
The Outermost House*

We have seen how the comprehension of architectural space is dependent on the clarity of the spatial envelope. Further, the character of space was shown to be dependent on the overall visual impression of its composite dominant boundaries. Striving for perceptual clarity tends to suggest a pendulum swing toward plain surfaces and away from ornate or other surface characteristics capable of generating design vitality. Using that line of thinking, it might be argued that clarity of space requires visual simplicity produced by plain, undecorated surfaces, but it is well known that architectural design of that kind leans in the direction of visual boredom. When taken in the context of the psychophysiological workings of the eye and mind, the meaning of simplicity is quite

* Beston, Henry. 1971. *The Outermost House*. New York: Ballantine Books, pp. 153–154.

different from its interpretation often given by critics of the visual arts. In visual perception, simplicity of surface means there is less complex stimuli to be encoded by the brain, and hence contributes to a visual environment that is easier to comprehend. To design the envelope with clarity does not imply that the boundary surfaces must remain plain or simple. Historical periods of architecture have provided enough examples of interiors that are dominated by richly patterned and colorful interiors. Clarity of space, therefore, can be achieved even with multiple visual stimuli on the spatial boundaries. As buildings are put together by a process of assembling fabricated parts, the patterns formed on the singular boundaries can activate the surfaces, but need to be joined together into a good composition for the whole. This is the *articulation* of space, and to make that process successful, we need to reiterate this principle: *Clarity* of architectural space depends on the distinctness and intelligible order of the entire spatial envelope. Regardless of whether it is plain or ornate, the envelope must be visually comprehensible and must possess design integrity. When the eye is confronted with multiple stimuli on the boundary surfaces, the mind can find order through the organization of the spatial boundaries and cohesiveness of their detailing. But when the envelope itself breaks down and loses clarity, and the boundaries are overdetailed and lack uniformity, then order and organization of space dissolve.

To enrich and animate architectural space while at the same time maintaining its clarity is the mark of quality design. The major spatial boundaries and their organization need to remain a focus of attention for designers when working through the stages of design development and refinement. Boundary surfaces may be textured, ornamented, or left plain; they may be penetrated for sunlight or for views opening to contiguous spaces. But as each boundary is attended, the composition of the spatial envelope must remain in a state of *perceptual* simplicity, remembering that this does not mean plainness or the omission of surface decoration. "Elimination," Frank Lloyd Wright (1943, 144) believed, "may be just as meaningless as elaboration." To him, simplicity was basic to his philosophy of organic architecture: "Only as a feature or any part becomes [a] harmonious element in the harmonious whole does it arrive at the state of simplicity." The boundaries of space—as they compose into a spatial envelope—are those features or parts to be integrated into a harmonious whole. Their design and detailing, as they are perceived in the panoptic view of human vision, need to be harmoniously designed and coordinated so that they are linked together in a visual flow like rhythmic stanzas of a poem or passages of a beautiful symphony.

Patterning the Dominant Boundaries

Combining an interesting composition for the spatial envelope with pattern detailing of its boundaries is an excellent way of animating space for human appeal. Figure 8-1 shows a small sunken court that connects the lower offices of a public building with a street above. A spatial envelope is shaped by the pavement, the stepped waterfall and low retaining walls leading to the stairs, and landscaping. The retaining walls and steps conform to the shape of the waterfalls, giving order and clarity to the envelope. The stepped walls are a pattern in themselves, and their surfaces are patterned by the texture of the rippling water. Visual effects of sunlight and shadow

Figure 8-1. Luminous walls animated by water and sunlight. [Lincoln Plaza, Dallas]

convert the walls to sparkling luminous boundaries, changing through the course of the day with the movement of the sun. The waterfall visually activates the space, making the court a pleasant amenity for people pausing to sit and for those just passing through. Sounds of traffic and other urban noises at street level are blocked out by the vertical boundaries, and the chamber of space fills with the continuous sound and refreshing aroma of falling water. The spatial character is one of tranquillity, conducive for personal thought and social intercourse.

As a perceptual phenomenon, *pattern* belongs to the "hierarchy of focal accents" and attracts the eye scanning the visual world. That is what makes it an effective means for animating architectural space. Note how it makes an immediate impression as a space-defining boundary for the historic cast-iron Pergola in Seattle (Figure 8-2). The glass roof assumes prominence by its grid pattern of iron framework and panes of glass. As the glass transfuses the daylight, it renders the dark iron in high contrast and emphasizes the grid. At the sides, repetition of the iron columns forms a pattern; the columns set the limits of width for the spatial envelope, and show how little is actually required for space definition. But it is the high-contrast, patterned glass that is the dominant visual boundary, and that is enough to direct the flow of space around the corner. The Pergola was originally built in 1909 to shelter people waiting for the trolley, and today still serves as an amenity for the city. The overhead screen shades passersby from the sun, and park benches under the Pergola provide places to sit in the soft

Figure 8-2. Patterns of light shaping space. [Pergola, Seattle]

light permeating the glass. The combination of minimal pattern and diffused daylight here defines and articulates space, establishes direction for movement, and offers attractive shelter for Seattle's rainy days.

The perceptual strength of pattern for its attraction as a focal accent plays into the designer's hand for spatial articulation. As pattern draws attention to one surface in a visual field, it also draws the eye to another, and becomes effective for uniting the boundaries of space. The actual shell of the lobby of Figure C-28 is a simplified volume—walls, floor, and ceiling—but pattern on the walls and floor animates each of those boundaries through enrichment by detailing. The geometric inlay work simultaneously articulates the boundaries and the space as a whole. The ceiling receives indirect light, and its plain surface passively submits to the visual activity of the walls and floor. It is ambient light that illuminates the lower part of the spatial envelope, which attracts attention not by dramatics of lighting, but by pattern organization on the boundaries. A linear pattern also is at work, by the inlaid horizontal rectangles at the top of the walls and the lines of the stepped cove just above them. The doorway to the left opens the space, where the linearism of the black marble base along the floor

continues into the adjacent room helping to unite both spaces.

Too often the ceilings of public spaces are a complex collection of visual stimuli, including intensely bright light sources often intermingled with random structural members and various appendages of environmental equipment. That is quite different from the courtroom of Figure C-29, whose ceiling area was articulated to give spatial and symbolic interest to the room, while integrating the structural, mechanical, and electrical systems. The room was designed as an end of a "ceremonial axis," which begins with neighboring governmental buildings, proceeds through the main entrance and lobby of the building, and finishes here with a focus on the judges' bench and state seal. Structural beams and wall supports create a linear perspective that reinforces that focus. The square perforations in the beams are coordinated by shape with windows and other apertures used throughout the building. It was the square as "having something to do with equality" that prompted the architects to add that symbolic geometry to the character of the room. The ceiling and walls are only painted surfaces, but become expressive by light as it defines patterns of structure and perforations. On the roof immediately above, daylight is reflected off the red brick of the building, enters the courtroom through skylights to visually activate the ceiling, and tints the neutrally painted walls with various shades of red at different times of day. Electric support lighting also generates spatial interplay of the structural forms and penetrations. The room is thus animated by the interaction of structure, space, and pattern, achieved by good articulation of the spatial envelope, and without the visual distraction of discordant mechanical and electrical features.

When the opportunity presents itself and when ergonomically justified, the lower portion of the spatial envelope is a viable place for the introduction of special features. Figure 8-3 shows a sunken garden in a public park where the activity of water animates the entire floor of the envelope. Both trees and concrete barriers close off extraneous urban noises and outside visual distractions, and thereby establish the relative seclusion fitting for a sunken garden. The general quiet of the space is broken by the steady resonance of the splashing water. Again returning to the list of attributes comprising the "hierarchy of focal accents," a combination here articulates the space. The fountains combine water and sunlight to create sparkling accents of pattern, brightness, and movement, three of the six focal accents that attract human vision. The lower boundary of the envelope immediately draws the attention of visitors walking in the park above. The vertical boundaries minimize the distracting sounds and sights of the city, and their perceptual simplicity creates a passive backdrop for the activity

Figure 8-3. Pattern, brightness, and movement on the spatial floor. [Water Garden, Fort Worth, Texas]

of the fountains. The continuous drizzle of water dancing in sunlight provides the audiovisual magic that the play of fountains always seems to have. The space in the water garden is successful because of good control over the vertical boundaries of the spatial envelope, which work to feature—not compete with—the performance of the fountains.

Among the innumerable surface treatments designers use to add spatial interest to architectural interiors is that of mirrors. Sometimes they are applied to walls as mere novelties to create illusion, other times to consciously add to spatial dimensions. In the tight confines of elevators, they add spaciousness in ways helpful for people with claustrophobic tendencies. A narrow strip mirror around the top of elevator walls expands the ceiling and the feeling of space without people seeing their own reflected images. The use of mirrors in other interiors, however, is often abused, with problems stemming from the visual scenes they reflect. The considerations surrounding the use of mirrors always need to be checked for their appropriateness. From the most common viewing angle, do the mirrors reflect a portion of the real space that already is a distorted spatial envelope, and do they multiply glaring luminaires? How do the mirrors contribute to the overall spatial clarity, if at all, and how can they enhance the articulation of space?

Figure 8-4 shows a mirrored wall reflecting the very small and compact lobby of a commercial building. Upon first entering, the viewing angle does not permit the visibility of the observer's own image, and a first quick impression is one of a larger room containing a small pool with figurine and plants. The total space is created partially by the reflected spatial envelope behind the visitor. The plants are strategically placed. Their foliage is reflected as more of the same, which generally occludes the reflected image of the floor on which the observer enters. The office walls reflected in the mirrors contribute to spatial clarity, because in their real positions they form a perceptually simplified segment of the spatial envelope. The geometric pattern of the luminous ceiling reflects in a continued linear perspective that originates overhead, uniting the real and the reflected space, and is greatly responsible for the spatial illusion that characterizes the room.

Another way to enliven the spatial envelope is the protrusion of prominent surface elements *on* the dominant boundaries. An example is an exterior space bounded by facades studded with balconies (Figure 8-5). In Chapter 4 we saw how balconies enhance building form, based on the investigations of Jürgen Bortz (1972). Respondents in Bortz's study were most impressed by facades with balconies, and least by those

Figure 8-4. Extension of boundary patterns by mirrors.

Figure 8-5. Balconies "texturing" a facade.

having large wall areas of undecorated surface. The visual appeal of facades with balconies or other protruding elements is largely the result of pictorial qualities created by the added dimension to the surface plane, which increases textural effects by the play of light and shadow.

Penetration of the Spatial Envelope

The most simplified architectural space is a volume of near total enclosure by plain surfaced, two-dimensional boundaries. Spaces of that kind can be found in interior rooms devoid of windows, or tightly bound exterior spaces shaped by relatively flat elevations. The nature of those spaces is self-confining and can be characterized as static. They invite little or no movement of the observer. Articulating such spaces by animated detailing of their boundaries begins to break up the static quality, but that technique is not nearly as effective as actual penetration of the greater spatial envelope by windows, doorways, grilles, or other openings that connect adjacent spaces or subspaces. When openings are cut into the boundaries, two visual phenomena are happening simultaneously. The first is the introduction of additional stimuli in the form of all reflected light on surfaces visible through the opening, diminishing the power of enclosure for that section of the envelope. The second is the perceptual phenomenon of *ordinal stimulation* (see Chapter 2) created by the edges around the opening. At those edges high retinal activity takes place, due to the sharp contrast of visual stimuli in gradient size, texture, and color on the surface around the opening as differentiated from the stimuli in the distant scene. Both of those phenomena dramatize depth perception, which draws the space of the observer outward through the openings. For the design and lighting of architectural space, the quality of penetration of the spatial envelope is exceptionally important for composing interspatial color relationships, and most of all, for the brightness ratios created by reflected light on the surface around the opening as contrasted with something lighter or darker seen through the opening.

In direct sunlight, surface penetration is potent for activating exterior form-space relationships. In the facade of Leon Battista Alberti's Renaissance church of Sant' Andrea in Mantua, Italy (Figure 8-6), the openings provide a vivid illustration of how reflected light and shadow animate the major facade plane, and also how they integrate the open space in front of the building with its interior. Doorways and niches penetrate the facade, creating sharp edges and changes in brightness that stimulate high retinal response. Alberti knew where to begin

Figure 8-6. Spatial interaction by surface penetration. [Sant' Andrea, Mantua, Italy. Architect: Leon Battista Alberti. Photograph: Alinari/Art Resource, NY]

and where to stop penetration of the elevation, how to proportion the openings, and how to cast shadows. Light and shadow vitalize the facade, which is masterfully articulated by the penetrations. They make clear where to enter the church, and at the same time do not destroy the boundary plane where the facade openings interact with the space of the piazza in front. Interior and exterior spaces are brought together. See these aspects of facade animation as principles of design, based on human vision and locomotion, and they can all be achieved with modern design, without resort to the "classical" design vocabulary of Alberti's day.

The proportional amount of penetration of the spatial envelope relates to feelings of enclosure. Figure 8-9 shows a theoretical model of a small room, which progressively increases in spaciousness the more the envelope is penetrated, without increasing floor area or providing direct views to an outside environment. The demonstration does not presuppose unnecessarily thick walls, but serves only to illustrate an evolutionary shift from tight enclosure by uninterrupted boundary surfaces (Figure 8-7a) to the greater spaciousness that results when the envelope is amply penetrated and the interior

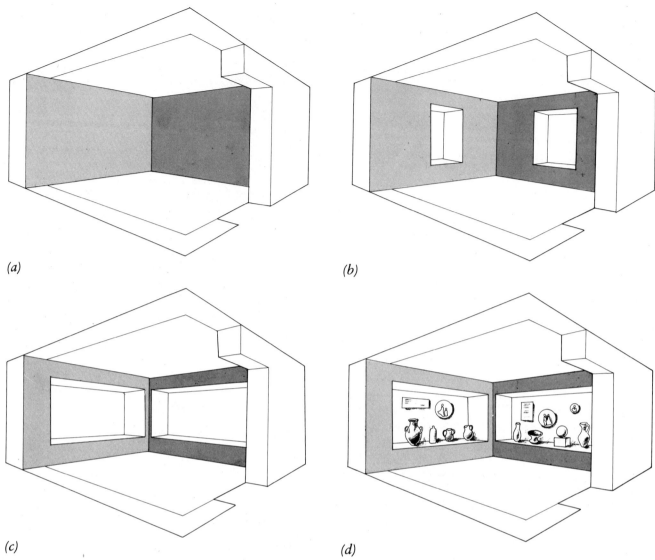

(a)

(b)

(c)

(d)

Figure 8-7. Proportional penetration of interior volume.

fills with perceptual stimuli. Although still tightly enclosed, Figure 8-7b begins to break the confinement of 8-7a by penetration of the walls with what might be exhibits or commercial display cases. A notable change toward spaciousness occurs in Figure 8-7c, where the original spatial envelope is now penetrated in greater proportion. Figure 8-7d has the same proportion of penetration as 8-7c, but represents a further stage of spatial articulation resulting from the introduction of forms in subspaces. In the last example the observer finds mental engagement in a room more visually spacious than the actual floor area, which remained unchanged as the space was sequenced.

A difference in the perception of spaciousness occurs when penetration of the boundaries are windows, doorways, or other openings in the spatial envelope, providing mental engagement for the eye by connecting the space of the observer with outside activities. Ne'eman and Hopkinson (1970) used a model office with adjustable window sizes and found that the main determinant for people's preference for window openings was the amount of visual information provided by the outside view.

In another study of windows, E. C. Keighley (1973a) studied people's reactions to various sizes and shapes of apertures. The most frequently preferred opening was a central, horizontally shaped window that provides a view to the skyline. As a backup study, Keighley (1973b) also studied the proportional amount of window openings, and found most people preferred a large horizontal aperture, and one that occupied 25% to 30% of the wall into which the window was cut. Twenty-five percent penetration is a significantly large proportion of a single spatial boundary, especially when other planes of the

Figure 8-8. Animation of space by rhythmic patterns of light and shade. [The Psalette, St. Gatien Cathedral, Tours, France]

total envelope are likely to be opened as doorways and other apertures.

There are two interrelated aspects of penetrating the spatial envelope that are exceptionally effective for the articulation and animation of architectural space. One is the *proportion of the envelope that is penetrated,* and the other is the *brightness ratios* established by the luminance on the envelope and the average luminance of whatever is seen through the openings. That combination has long appeared in historical design, and in principle is easily adapted to the architecture of today. Figure 8-8 shows the medieval cloister (*The Psalette*) of St. Gatien Cathedral in Tours, France. The surfaces shaping the arcade and the interesting stair tower in the corner form the spatial envelope, and the proportionally large openings in the elevations create a dominating rhythm of shadows under the arches that pauses as it turns the corner, but is not interrupted by the tower. The generous openings and the sculpted surface detailing above the arches reduce the massiveness of the stone. Gestalt good continuation of the repetitive openings and arcade details connect the two elevations as the corner is turned. Continuity of the two sides is reinforced by the linearism of the small balustrade along the top of the arches, which is repeated as a nice touch around the top of the stair tower helping to articulate the total envelope.

The proportional penetration of a spatial envelope strongly influences the total building mass and the re-

sulting sense of enclosure where building facades shape urban space. For centuries the loggia has been a prominent design feature for buildings, and when related to interior courts or integrated with urban squares, its arcade or colonnade is the pattern of openings that serves to articulate the space. To observe how proportion of penetration influences the total building mass and the perception of urban space, once more we turn to historical examples, comparing the elevations shaping the Place des Vosges in Paris (Figure 8-9) and the Foundling Hospital in the Piazza della Santissima Annunziata in Florence, Italy (Figure 8-10). Both public squares provide ready models for analyzing the effect of loggia openings on the entire spatial envelope and the feeling of enclosure. In the Place des Vosges, the loggia opening is only about 18% of the major elevations that surround the square, but in Florence it is approximately 45% of the total facade as measured from street level. Both elevations are approximately the same height, which may surprise some readers who are familiar with both sites, but the visual effect of the ratio of loggia opening to elevation is enormous for how the open spaces are comprehended.

On location, the Piazza della Santissima Annunziata does not convey a feeling of being bounded by tall buildings, but the opposite occurs in the Place des Vosges from a comparable viewing distance to any of the elevations. In Paris, the mass of the buildings dominates. In

Figure 8-9. Surface mass dominating the spatial envelope. [Place des Vosges, Paris]

Florence, the loggias dominate. A critical factor controlling the visual penetration through the arcades of both sites is the thickness of the structural supports. In Florence, the broader dimensions of the unit bays and the comparatively thin diameters of columns create an airy, open character for the loggia that belongs to the space of the piazza as much as it does to the building. In Paris, the more narrow bays and thick stone piers reduce visual penetration of the total building mass, and the facade plane dominates the spacial enclosure from a comparable viewing angle as Florence.

The principles that apply to articulation of urban

Figure 8-10. Penetration dominating the spatial envelope. [Foundling Hospital, Piazza della Santissima Annunziata, Florence, Italy]

Analysis of Architectural Space

Articulation with Subspaces

One of the most reliable design devices for generating visual interest and creating a stimulating quality of architectural space is the controlled use of subspaces working in harmony with a primary spatial envelope. Subspacing has been a prominent design feature in many of the great masterpieces of architecture, and its practical application and flexibility make it an efficient means for meeting certain program requirements in contemporary design. By definition, a *subspace* is one of only partial enclosure, identified by its own spatial envelope, but opening freely to join with the primary space to which it clearly relates. It can be a spatial inset or an element protruding from the boundaries of its parent space.

A historical example of articulation with subspaces is shown in the plan of the Baroque church S. Andrea al Quirinale in Rome (Figure 8-12), typical of a number of ecclesiastical buildings of the period in which a number of small, partially enclosed chapels surround or flank a central nave. The keynote for the design is set by the concave wall in front of the church, which forms a partial spatial envelope and introduces the theme of subspacing to be found in the interior. The visitor steps inside the church *through* one of the subspaces, and straight ahead lies another that contains the high altar. On each side

Figure 8-11. Articulation of space by pattern and luminance ratios. [Indiana State Office Building South, Indianapolis. Architects: HNTB. Photograph: Balthazar Korab]

spatial envelopes also apply to interiors of buildings. Through good articulation, spatial boundaries can be composed and detailed to animate space without sacrificing order and clarity of the envelope. The atrium shown in Figure 8-11 is articulated by pattern composition of openings in the vertical boundaries, coordinated with the detailing of skylight and floor. The shapes, proportions, and composition of the openings animate the space by the rhythms of visual movement around the atrium. In the view shown, the largest rectangular openings at ground level set a "slow" perspective movement to the other end, contrasted with the quickened tempo of the repeating smaller rectangles around the upper floors. The spacing of the piers regulates the openings in harmonic composition, adagio below, allegro above.

Penetrations of the spatial envelope open the atrium space laterally and upward. The wider spacing of the lower piers expands the space horizontally at eye level on the ground floor. The design effectiveness of the penetrations in the atrium's envelope depends on the brightness ratios created by light. Like the historical examples shown earlier, the principle of brightness contrast created by the difference in luminance on the primary envelope compared with the darker luminances seen through the openings enhances both the articulation of the total space and its visual animation.

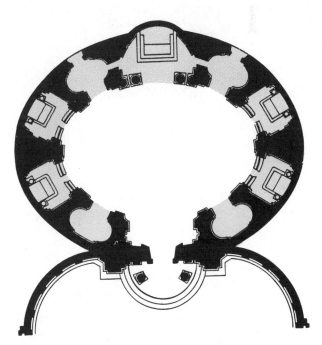

Figure 8-12. Spatial articulation with subspaces. [Architect: Gian Lorenzo Bernini]

are four more subspaces that join in a visual movement of spatial accents that wrap around the nave. Illuminated by a hidden window above, the daylighted space of the main altar appears brighter than the others, and whereas it may have attracted the scanning eye of the visitor when first entering the building, it is the nature of human vision that the eye does not stay fixed on one target very long. That's when the periodic subspaces come into play in the overall spatial composition. Instead of the visitor physically walking through a sequence of spaces, the effect here is one of *visually moving spaces around the observer.*

Among its many qualities of design excellence, the Paris Opera House contains a rich variety of spaces. One of its outstanding features is the grand vertical space where balcony levels overlook one of the finest staircases in the history of architecture. Figure 8-13 is a lateral view showing a portion of that renowned architectural space. The envelope is articulated by the stair itself and by balconies between the double-columned arcade. Protruding subspaces are formed by the balustrades of first level balconies. Standing in the one in the foreground, the visitor sees its same volumetric shape repeated directly across the way, which continues around three sides of

the space. Visitors standing in the balconies become both audience and performers. They look down on other theatergoers ascending and descending the stairs, while they stand on their own stage of a magnificently articulated architectural space.

Because subspaces bring into view additional sets of visual stimuli in the form of architectural details and human activities in the secondary areas, the designer must control those surfaces of the primary envelope that visually frame the subspaces. Overdetailing of those surfaces visually competes with the designs of the subspaces, and can create confusion for the overall spatial experience. Remember the foremost principle of spatial design: *No matter how a space is articulated—by pattern, penetration or protruding elements—the primary spatial envelope must remain intact, and maintain its own identity and clarity.* If the subspaces contain high visual stimuli, as do shops and their window displays in a shopping mall, the design emphasis should be on the stores. They are subspaces, related to the greater space of the mall. The segments of the mall's envelope that frame the shops should be perceptually simplified so they do not compete as a visual distraction, and they should be clear enough to visually order and sequence the major spaces of the entire mall to provide good orientation for the shoppers.

From the given camera angle, the sequential spaces of the mall shown in Figure 8-14 flow in two directions: horizontally and downward. Horizontally, the expanse of space moves straight ahead, angles to the left, and then again straight ahead. Open views provide spatial interconnections among all three floors. The greater en-

Figure 8-13. Interaction among subspaces.

Figure 8-14. Contrast between subspaces and parent space. [Galleria, Dallas. Architects: HOK]

velope is best defined by the vaulted skylight because of its regular pattern and continuous flow of surface, and by the linear banding of the fascias, which gives continuity to the second and third floors. Colorful shops animate the outermost spatial boundaries at all levels, and the linear circulation routes in front of them become intermediate subspaces between the greater mall and the shop interiors. The stores are filled with the customary activity (stimuli) of color, specialized lighting, display of goods, and shoppers. By contrast, the partial boundaries of the greater envelope are neutral in color and surface, avoiding visual competition. Their perceptual simplicity provides the clarity that holds the whole mall together in its own identity. Application of color to the articulation of space versus subspaces is a major design consideration. The more the color of the boundaries (skylight, fascias, and carpeting) of the primary envelope approaches the average hue exhibited by the subspaces (shops), the more the subspaces will blend with the parent space, and articulation by subspacing is weakened.

Subspaces can be longitudinal in shape, such as those formed by open circulation routes that are integrated with a larger parent space. The movement path in front of the stores (Figure 8-14) is a linear, intermediate subspace between the row of shops and the greater central

Figure 8-15. Intermediate linear subspacing. [Galleria, Dallas. Architects: HOK]

space of the mall. A closer view is shown in Figure 8-15 where the longitudinal envelope of the intermediate subspace is formed by the floor, ceiling, railing to the left, and the row of shops, which creates periodic subspaces that interact with the circulation route. The directional path of the space is emphasized by the two rows of indirect lighting and recessed down lights on the stepped ceiling, paralleling the spatial enclosure of the barrel vaulted skylight. As an intermediate subspace, it makes a transition between the bright skylight and the individualized lighting of the shop interiors. It also assists in retinal adaptation for people moving about among the various levels of lighted space, and thereby contributes to the ergonomics of the architecture.

Using subspaces to design interiors has numerous applications to contemporary workplaces. It is a practical means for organizing open-plan workstations in large office rooms or other situations where proximity of similar functions and semiprivacy are beneficial for work performance. Office system cubicles (Figure C-30) provide that semiprivacy, and their partial openness facilitates oral and visual communication as well as supervision. In their setting they are subspaces of the larger room, but their individual spatial envelopes shape the immediate environment of the workers. The inside surfaces of the partitions form minor spatial boundaries and, if permitted, workers may individualize their quarters with posters, paintings, or plants. The color and brightness of the cubicle's interior surfaces need to be controlled for how they serve as background for VDT screens, and for overall visual comfort probability (VCP), which lighting designers use to predict the relative freedom from discomfort glare created by surface reflections.

Spatial Banding

The nature of multistory building design calls for the composition and detailing of the structural members that define atria or interior courts in large public buildings. The designer may take advantage of the process of floor above floor building construction by using the structural framework to create linear patterns on the spatial envelope (Figures 8-16a and b). The fascias of floors that shape a central space form a series of horizontal bands that define and articulate the envelope. Those linear strips alternate with the voids of spaces above and below them, and create the design pattern of *spatial banding*. The thickness of those bands—in proportion to the voids—contributes to the design character of the space. If the fascias are narrow in width compared with their length, they create lines in space. Banding can also be vertical, formed by the surfaces that relate to structural

(a)

(b)

Figure 8-16a and b. Spatial banding as pattern and background. [Capital Square, Des Moines, Iowa]

piers and columns. Spatial banding is an effective pictorial device that by itself can animate a large, open space without adding more costs for surface decoration of the envelope.

Figure 8-16a shows the atrium of a large commercial building characterized by spatial banding. Two design details should be observed. First is the height of the linear openings of offices between the fascias. On the upper floors those openings are significantly less than the surface areas of the fascias. The second floor space is more open due to the detailing of the balcony railing, whose open pattern exposes more architecture behind it. That second floor balcony combines with the greater openness of the ground floor, and the two serve as a base for the vertical ascent of alternating fascias and voids that culminates with the skylight above. A second detail, so slight but ever so effective, is the thin dark line given to each fascia. The darkness of the lines makes them appear as fine strips of penetration into the fascias, which visually reduces the thickness of each floor. Those thin lines add to the visual movement horizontally around the atrium, and they further articulate the space by participating in the alternating light and dark lines upward. Darkness communicates void. Whether it is fascia surface or boundary penetration, the *proportion* of each band—bright or dark—is important for the role each will play in articulating the spatial envelope.

Spatial banding serves another design function as backdrop for other architectural features. Figure 8-16b takes a different view from 8-16a to show how the cumulative fascias comprise a patterned visual "ground" against which the "figures" of freestanding objects are seen. The circular planters and seating areas and the natural forms and textures of the trees spring to life as seen against the formality of the geometric pattern behind.

As these illustrations show, the power of banding as artistic line can be put to work for defining and animating architectural space. "The handling of line is full of adventure," Rudolf Arnheim tells us (1969, 168), and that adventure begins with the instinctive nature of the eye to follow the path of movement that line initiates. Flutes on classical columns, the linear pattern of Gothic cathedral interiors, and the vertical detailing on modern highrise buildings remind us of that basic relationship between linear design and human vision. Line goes somewhere, in both directions from any point along its length, and the eye will follow its course. It is therefore important to be aware of exactly what happens at the ends of line. In Figure 8-17, the two fascias create major lines of force, generated by their perspective angles and their brightness. They carry the eye into perspective depth, and form logical conclusions as they join at the pedestrian crossovers, partially closing off that segment of the mall, and giving it an identity for shopper orientation.

When skillfully handled, spatial banding is a design strategy for integrating spatial composition with the structural and mechanical systems of a building. Banding can be used horizontally, vertically, on curved planes, or diagonally to change levels. During design development, a structural system may suggest a banding pattern,

Figure 8-17. Banding as visual lines of force.
[Galleria, Dallas. Architects: HOK]

which can be refined as part of the articulation of a spatial envelope. When banding is well composed with perceptually simplified surfaces, it functions to stabilize a primary space and simultaneously enhances the overall spatial experience by framing views to subspaces. This was done in the atrium design shown in Figure C-31. Flanking the large central space are circulation routes and upper floor offices that appear as subspaces. Semicircular balconies project from the primary plane of the envelope, enriching the atrium by adding variety of subspace design without sacrificing the overall spatial clarity. Spatial banding articulates the entire spatial envelope of the atrium by the coordination of surfaces of vertical piers and horizontal fascias, and the union between the two as expressed by the simple rectangular bosses where piers and fascias intersect. The design and coordination of the components of the envelope give the atrium its spatial clarity, and its neutral color yields to the expressive features of wall hangings, the receptionist station, and the amenities of seating and plants that greet visitors to the building.

Curvature and Level Change

Curved spaces and those that involve changing from one level to another provide the opportunity for creating

Figure 8-18. Ramps and stepped terraces create sequential interaction. [Temple of Queen Hatshepsut, Deir el-Bahari, Egypt. Courtesy: Aramco World]

Articulation of the Spatial Envelope

dynamic architectural space due to the continuously unfolding views for people walking through them. Good articulation of the spatial envelope is especially important for those environments because design continuity is required along the path of movement.

Without changing levels, curvature alone can generate interesting spatial design. Animation of space resulted from the curvilinear composition of subspaces in Figure C-32. The view shows the dining area of a corporate building, where spatially interconnected eating areas mutually interact with each other and the circulation path. Shaping the floor plan was not an abstract decision just to create a curved space, but came about because that part of the building follows exactly the curved section of a race track outside, and the individual dining areas have window views of racing activities. The curvature of the plan and the rectangular openings in the partitions form interesting spatial relations for people sitting in the dining areas and for those moving along the aisle. The

partition openings set up the flow of alternating plants and piers, and those repeating harmonic relationships are what successfully articulates and animates the total space.

Interspatial relationships formed by the connections of changing levels have contributed to the design excellence of many of the great monuments from the past. They can be used as models for how the articulation of one space is coordinated with that of contiguous spaces. Good examples reach back as far as the ancient world. The terraces of Queen Hatshepsut's Temple (Figure 8-18) in ancient Egypt are joined by ramps that connect and interact with the broader spaces of the terraces. In the crisp African sunlight, patterns of alternating shadows and piers of the colonnades harmonize the terrace facades, and aesthetically "fit" the natural texturing of highlights and shadow in the background cliffs. The stepping of the terraces enables the colonnades to visually interplay as seen from viewing angles beginning on the

Figure 8-19. Coordinated subspaces in changing levels. [Spanish Stairs, Rome. Architect: Francesco de Sanctis. Photograph: Alinari/Art Resource, NY]

Analysis of Architectural Space

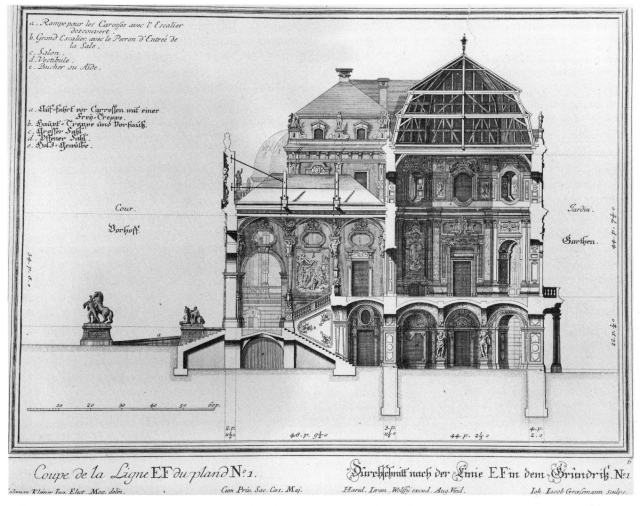

Figure 8-20. Integration of stair design and sight lines. [Section through Upper Palace, Belvedere Palace, Vienna. Architect: Johann Lucas von Hildebrandt. Photograph Österreichische Nationalbibliothek, Vienna]

site floor and continuing in sequence as the observer walks up the gently sloped ramps.

In Rome the historic Spanish Stairs (Figure 8-19) is an outstanding example of level change and design coordination. Connecting a lower piazza with a street in front of the church at the top of the hill, the stair design is articulated by units of steps, balustrades, and landings. People walk through a sequence of subspaces. Circulation paths join, divide, then join again, one flowing into another in melodic movement. As the walker is forced off axis on the ascent, the obelisk and church towers can be seen to shift in visual relationships and interplay in spatial dynamics. On the descent, from anywhere along the way the walker is presented with panoramic views to the piazza below. The Stairs also provides the amenity of places for people to sit. It is little wonder that it has been one of the most successful urban spaces in the history of architecture, and still today continues

to serve as a popular rendezvous point in the city for tourists and citizens of Rome alike.

In Vienna, the staircase in the Baroque Upper Belvedere Palace (Figure 8-20) is excellently proportioned and composed into the totality of the building and its site. It integrates change of level with dramatic visual sight lines through the major interior spaces and into the gardens outside. Approaching from the lower palace and formal gardens, the visitor enters through the low vaulted Hall of the Atlantids, and proceeds up the stairs to the midlanding. There, where the stair changes direction, is a single station point where the visitor can look down through the entrance hall below, and also up into the Great Marble Hall. From that same station point are views outside to the palatial gardens in one direction and the reflecting pool court in the other. Walking from the lower hall entrance to the Marble Hall is an exceptional experience of sequential space. As the section

---

Articulation of the Spatial Envelope   137

drawing shows, the three principal spaces progressively increase in size, sculptural decor is in harmony from space to space, and color crescendoes from the white lower hall to the rich browns and gilding of the Marble Hall. Strategically controlled door heights and window placements bring daylight into the total spatial composition, and make possible the connecting views to both interior and exterior spaces.

In Würzburg, Germany, is the grand ceremonial staircase of the Residenz (Figure 8-21), where in typical Baroque fashion the space is articulated by architectural detailing, sculpture, and mural painting, all integrated in a union of the arts. The ornateness of these Baroque interiors was cultural, and may be overdone in the opinion of some modern visitors. But mentally removing the decor reveals the basic spatial envelope, excellently composed with well-proportioned subspaces working in harmony with the greater parent space. Landings break the flight of stairs as pauses in visual composition and ergonomically offer physical relief while ascending and descending. Daylight enters through first and second floor

Figure 8-21. Unification of the arts in spatial composition. [Stairs toward south, Residenz, Würzburg, Germany. Architect: Johann Balthasar Neumann. Photograph: Foto Marburg/Art Resource, NY S0032933 606106]

windows just out of sight on the right side of the photograph. People traversing the stairs pass through modulations of reflected light, and the stairway sculptures and other architectural elements set up innumerable brightness-contrast relationships, seen from the moving point of view. Looking down, levels and subspaces rhythmically alternate in shade and light. Looking up, Tiepolo's paintings crown the whole spatial experience with color. In these historical examples, spatial articulation became an art.

As components of circulation systems, stairs, escalators, and ramps are nodes that can become exceptional design features as spaces are sequenced. But the task is not easy. A change of levels usually sets up an interaction among two or more partial spatial envelopes, and the fundamental problem facing the designer is that both spaces have their own envelope, and one is seen from the partial enclosure of the other. When ascending, the ceilings and vertical surfaces of the lower envelope are forced into design relationships with those emerging in the upper space, and will be either compatible or in conflict. Each level, as a partially open spatial envelope, has its own identity, and when passing from one to another a visual transition takes place by one set of dominant boundaries giving way to the next set.

The sculptural quality of the spiral stair in Figure 8-22 makes it an attractive focal center connecting the main lobby of the Arizona State Courts Building and the law library on the lower level. Answering to the curvature of the stair is a concave wall that forms a background subspace. Explicit articulation was carried out intentionally for both the stair and its surrounding envelope. Radial joints in the ceiling and floor are perfectly aligned with the edges of the steps, and the last tread is aligned with the doors of the law library that face the stairs. Set into the concave wall behind are delicate thin lines of polished bronze, coordinated in number with the polished bronze lines of the railing. Curved surfaces set up a fluid movement for the eye and, as we saw earlier with the nature of line, that movement requires good beginnings and endings for continuity in the flow of space. The spiraling rise of the black structural steel of the stair takes origin in the black granite outline of the raised disk on the floor, and concludes with the black fascia of the circular opening into which the stair ascends. The white underside of the stair blends with the white ceiling above, and provides the contrast that visually accelerates the linear movement upward.

Frank Lloyd Wright's Solomon R. Guggenheim Museum (Figure 8-23) can be used as a definitive example of a totally curved spatial boundary. The continuous balcony fascia sets into motion the spiral flow of spatial banding from ground floor to the uppermost balcony ramp. The sweep of monochromatic curved surfaces is unimpeded by texture, bright color, or decoration; those

Figure 8-22. Sculptural stair as a focal center. [Arizona State Courts Building, Phoenix. Architects; HNTB. Photograph: © Fred Licht]

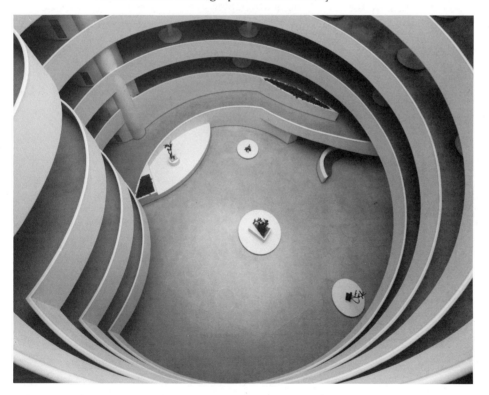

Figure 8-23. Spatial banding and the flow of space. [Architect: Frank Lloyd Wright. Exhibition: Picasso and the Age of Iron, *March 19–May 16, 1993. Photograph: David Heald. ©The Solomon R. Guggenheim Foundation, New York. Exh 545]*

design qualities are reserved for the art on display. Spatial interest is created by the alternating fascias and the subspaces of the spiraling circulation route, and by the interplay of convex and concave surfaces illuminated by the abundant daylight entering from the central skylight high above.

The challenge of designing a multistoried circular staircase around an open cylinder of space lies in the fact that two spatial envelopes are involved, an outer one that encases the total stair system and opens to ancillary spaces, and an inner one formed by the stair structure facing the central open space. The interaction between the two offers the potential for exciting interspatial views. By well-planned placement in a building, and through good spatial articulation, a circular staircase becomes a special feature in the building and animates connections of space. The central staircase in Figure C-33 joins two wings of Harvard's Kennedy School of Government, and shapes a rotunda as it connects the lower entrances to the building with a faculty dining room on the top floor. The stairs interconnect with lobbies on the intermediate floors, and the openness of the spatial envelopes makes interesting visual connections with different levels of the building and with the exterior courtyard (below in the photograph). The inner envelope of the stair is stabilized by the structural piers, which correspond with the outer piers and mullions of the exterior wall. That coordination integrates the inner and outer envelopes of the space. Set against the stability of those piers, the stair fascias and railings interplay in countermovement. The structural members and the detailing make possible the rich spatial activity. The piers and stair fascias *frame* the views; the railings *screen* the views. At the landings, spatial interaction invites social interaction by the provision of seating areas in subspaces along the outer wall.

Successful architectural design finds solutions to the requirements of program and circulation. Equally important is proper control of the total building environment through HVAC and other mechanical and electrical elements that must be woven through the structural system. They are as vital to a building as bones, tissue, organs, and arteries are to the human body. Structure is the vital framework that holds all together, and integrates exterior form and the interior spaces. Structure makes possible the harmonious union of outside and inside, by daylight playing over its exterior form, and entering through openings in the building to join with electric illumination in bringing the interior to life. Interior spaces are shaped directly or are influenced by the structural system. The relationship between structure and interior space requires a special analysis, the topic of the next chapter.

CHAPTER 9

Role of the Structural System

Pots are formed from clay,
but the empty space within it is the
essence of the pot.

Walls with windows and doors form the house,
but the empty space within it is the
essence of the house.

—*Lao-tzu*

No other component of construction is as determinative of the major spatial configurations in a building as its basic structural system. The shapes and locations of a number of permanent spatial boundaries are fixed once the structure is engineered and set in place. At that time bearing walls begin to define horizontal limits of interior spaces, and major floors and ceilings demarcate vertical dimensions. Supporting piers and columns become termination points or planes for walls or other segments of spatial envelopes, and often become physical and visual obstacles in interior space. At the larger scale of megastructures where more internal flexibility exists, some structural members serve as carriers to which dependent floors and ceilings are hung, breaking down interior space into smaller units. For our purposes here, most consequential of all is how the structural system determines locations of openings for incoming daylight. Moreover, structure positions the major surfaces on which manufactured support lighting will be located.

Prominence of Building Form

In Chapter 7 we saw how natural spaces have been shaped by canyon walls in Arches National Park in east-

ern Utah. Nature also offers dramatic examples of spaces shaped by structure. Figure 9-1 shows the result of those natural forces and illustrates design theory of structure alone shaping form and space. The arches were formed out of the harder upper layers of sandstone whose greater strength dominated when moving water eroded the softer layers underneath. Like the ribs of a space frame, the arches shape exterior form and interior space simultaneously, and direct the downward penetration of sunlight.

In modern architecture we find the same principle of structure concurrently shaping form and space. Built in the 1950s, Eero Saarinen's Kresge Auditorium (Figure 9-2a) is a domical thin-shell resting on three points, and is an instantaneous visual statement of a building form derived from its structural design. Architects and critics praised that kind of technological originality that was bringing in new architectural imagery characterized by the dynamics of structural action. When structural form is preconceived to dominate a building design, the major interior spaces are affected both in layout and shape. The interior spaces of the Kresge Auditorium relate directly to its basic structural system, which also directs the entry of daylight. In the auditorium itself, the span of the domical structure permits unobstructed viewing of a per-

Figure 9-1. Natural structure shaping form and space. [Arches National Park, Utah]

formance or speaker, but major circulation and lobby spaces (Figure 9-2b) result from the space of the auditorium subtracted from the overall building form. The spatial envelopes of those "remainder" spaces are thus shaped as a consequence of the dominance of a structural form. The dynamics of dome meeting floor at a point is dramatized, a feature made popular in architectural media shortly after the building was completed. The lobby seems to give top billing to the structure more than to the spatial experience of visitors moving in sequence from outside the building to an auditorium seat. Further, the shortened head clearance near the structural point is not as objectionable when the lobby is empty as it is when it is crowded before or after an event. The steadily reduced clearance as the dome descends is perhaps why the announcement stand is placed in front of the point as shown in the photograph of Figure 9-2b.

Dynamic structural schemes offer the potential for interior spatial excitement, and should be used to achieve such a goal as long as practical demands are not ignored. The building type and schematic design need to suggest that interior spaces would benefit from the undersides of shells, folded plates, or some other system. Notwithstanding what some critics have had to say about its

structural bravura, the exterior form and interior space of Eero Saarinen's Trans World Airways terminal at Kennedy Airport in New York intentionally and appropriately fit its purpose (Figure 9-3). The building was designed to express the feeling of flight. Its flowing interior surfaces, elevated walkways gliding through space, and views out to arriving and departing aircraft are visual chords of the prelude to flying for awaiting passengers.

In their time, the media featured the new structure-dominated designs and their designees. They were soon trailed by camp followers who sometimes applied the new construction shapes and techniques to projects where they did not belong or had little meaning. Interior spaces were forced into or ill-fitted to a building's exterior form, dictated by one of the new "visually exciting" structural systems. In some internal parts of a building human living was encased in distorted spatial envelopes. A room might be shaped by a straight wall on one side and angled with another to form a wedge-shaped corner, all capped by a curved ceiling overhead where a portion of a structural shell made its unwelcomed appearance. Internal spaces suffered from curvilinear or folded interior ceilings meeting illogically with interior walls and floors. Awkward and dead spaces often resulted. The

Analysis of Architectural Space

(a)

(b)

Figure 9-2. Dominance of structural form. a. Exterior and b. interior space.
[Kresge Auditorium, MIT, Cambridge, Massachusetts. Architect: Eero Saarinen]

Figure 9-3. Liberation of interior space. [Trans World Airways terminal, Kennedy Airport, New York. Architect: Eero Saarinen]

camp followers, as followers often do, failed to understand the conceptual relationship between structure, form, and space for human living. They began putting houses, banks, and shops beneath the popular structural forms or spherical roofs they saw in journals or magazines. Sometimes it worked. Often it did not. Interior spaces were deformed or distorted as their envelopes broke down in the wake of forced application of a structural concept. Homes and small public buildings were not the only victims. One need only remember the acoustical, constructional, and financial fiasco of Australia's Sydney Opera House, designed so that the "sails" of its auditoria could "float" on the shore of Sydney Harbor. Music, in this opera house no less, quite literally played second fiddle to the visual dramatics of exterior form.

On the other side of the coin are the modular assemblies of post-and-beam construction where structural columns or piers support beams generally crossing at right angles. The engineering of these systems locates many of the permanent boundaries for interior spatial envelopes, where normally offices and apartments are cubic and regular. Peripheral rooms on each floor receive daylight from windows conforming to exterior elevation design, and interior rooms usually receive electric support lighting distributed by uniform ceiling plans.

Modular grid construction is economical, which accounts for much of its continued appearance in contemporary architecture, but its use does not presuppose that interiors will be little more than a composition of side-by-side, cell-like spaces without relief. Greater structural spans allow for internal spatial variations from otherwise cubic monotony. As is often found in large public buildings, portions of floors are simply omitted from modular assemblies to open a vertical atrium or other central space, or to create spatial relations between floors. When that is done, advantage can be taken of the structural design to be integrated with the detailing for spatial articulation. This can be seen in the Computer Center of Brown University (Figure C-34), where geometric relationships were created between structural members and the detailing of floors, walls, and ceiling. Surrounding the lobby on the ground floor are large computer auditoria and computer clusters. Walls were set back to make the piers stand out, creating a subspace circulation route around the central space. On the second floor, the circulation route connects computer training rooms, and its balcony areas open the space upward as seen from the ground floor. Piers and beams locate the basic dimensions of space; the detailing of the space by second-floor railings and patterning of floor and ceiling articulate the space—all in accord with the structural system.

A word is in order concerning the prominence of building form as it relates to the random exterior spaces of the city, those that are most often accidental happenings in the ongoing piecemeal process of urbanization. An outer wall of a building is a boundary that shapes space on *both* sides, interior and exterior. When two neighboring buildings are contrasted in form, they consequently shape a distorted urban space between them. What is being said here should not be misconstrued as an altogether negative critique of form-centered building designs. It is not their existence that is being questioned, only their location. Form-oriented buildings do have their place in the city, but as monuments or edifices held in high regard by the majority or major segments of the citizenry. They should be well designed, and given open space around them, which diminishes the effect of their exterior walls shaping urban space. It is only when neighboring buildings contribute to a collective tapestry of disassociated architectural imagery that potentially beautiful urban spaces are miscarried.

Structure Patterning the Spatial Envelope

The more that design elements or surface decoration can be brought into architecture by way of construction process, the less that will have to be done by adding finishing surfaces. Building construction is the putting together of structural units, and some can be assembled as design patterns to embellish the spatial envelope. There are many fine precedents for this. Islamic architects gave to the world exceptional examples of structure and decoration being one and the same process, particularly in the brickwork construction of medieval Persia through the seventeenth century (Figure 9-4). Bricks were woven into intricate design patterns as they were mortared into walls, vaults, and domes. Historian and critic Arthur Upham Pope (1965) called it "structure as beauty," and English architect Sir Edwin Lutyens said "Do not speak of Persian brickwork but rather of Persian brick magic." Islamic brickwork laid in creative and delicate patterns was labor intensive, but was also craftsmanship intensive, as the construction process was taken into the area of aesthetics. A brick is a unit, and units can be assembled into patterns. This applies to modern construction methods, and when done well, structural design shaping the boundaries of space follows in the footsteps of "structure as beauty." In schematic design, initial structural thoughts may spawn aesthetic ideas for engineering refinement as the structure is developed. This is the common ground where the talents of architect and engineer meet to create high-quality design.

Space frames are made-to-order structural systems for articulation of the spatial envelope. That is because by nature they form design patterns, a feature that most likely contributed to the acceptance and popularity of geodesic domes and other space frames. Like the combination of structure and visual effects of Islamic brickwork, the structure and pattern of space frames are one (Figure 9-5).

Figure 9-4. Brick construction as decoration. [Madrasa, Poi-Kolyon Complex, Bukhara. Photograph courtesy of Aramco World]

Figure 9-5. Geodesic construction as structural pattern. [Mitchell Park Horticultural Conservatory, Milwaukee, Wisconsin]

The architect needs to consider exactly what a space frame does for spatial design. Foremost, it allows for the passage of light, and therefore two important design aspects need to be addressed. First, as we saw in the botanical garden photograph, the space frame is vivid against the background sky where its pattern is crisply defined, and therefore requires good structural design in its own right. Second, and most important for spatial design, is the theme of Chapter 3, "the effects of light." A space frame casts its shadows on the surfaces below (Figure 9-6), and uses the sun to articulate the spatial envelope through the course of the day. What then, is the pattern of shadow that the space frame creates? Where will those shadows fall as the sun moves? Will they pass along a plain wall, animating its surface by the changing effects of daylight? Will they pattern the floor for spatial interest? Or will the shadows be detrimental by falling on walls or floors already highly patterned as rich visual stimuli, thus deteriorating spatial clarity, and wasting the animating effects of light?

As is often found in contemporary architecture, a space frame or other structural system merely covers a space, resting on top of a peripheral wall organization, and there is little or no harmony between its design and that of the supporting walls. To achieve spatial aesthetics, *the design of the space frame should be coordinated with the design of the overall spatial envelope.* An excel-lent example is the skylight of the Guggenheim Museum (Figure 9-7), which is articulated by structural members that emerge from the uppermost walls. Thin concrete partitions that form subspaces along the outer wall change role as they rise overhead where their hairpin turns are integrated with the patterns of steel and glass. There is no sharp division between wall and ceiling. In typical Frank Lloyd Wright design philosophy, the skylight is an "organic" conclusion for the spiraling flow of vertical space as seen from ground level. On the upper-most floor, the inclined ramp is seen against the stable composition of the skylight, where its curved sweep ener-getically begins its descent to the galleries below.

We move from one master designer to another. Pier Luigi Nervi demonstrated that the decorative effects of patterned structures need not be lost when light is not permitted to permeate the surface like it does with geode-sic and other transparent space frames. The design prin-ciple of structural pattern applies to systems where the cells between the framing members are opaque, but in-stead of the presence of brightness-contrast, textural ef-fects are formed by reflected light and shadow. Figure 9-8 shows the interior of the Palazzo dello Sport in Rome, which Nervi designed with Marcello Piacentini in the 1950s. This building is an excellent lesson for architects and architectural engineers, illustrating how visible structure itself can contribute to a well-designed environ-

Figure 9-6. Space frame shadows animating interior space. [IBM Office Building, Purchase, New York. Architects: Pei Cobb Freed & Partners. Photograph: © Steve Rosenthal]

Figure 9-7. Structure and spatial aesthetics. [Architect: Frank Lloyd Wright. Photograph: David Heald. © The Solomon R. Guggenheim Foundation, New York]

Figure 9-8. Mastery of structural organization. [Palazzo dello Sport, Rome. Architects: Pier Luigi Nervi with Marcello Piacentini. Photograph: Scala/Art Resource, NY]

ment. The roof is a ferro-cemento dome measuring 328 feet in diameter, and its radial pattern of static forces is a marvelous display of skillful design. More than just a structural roof, the dome adds to the spatial aesthetics of the entire interior. Three dominant elements create the spatial envelope: dome, supporting ribs, and seating, all coordinated in clarity and decorative character—by structural pattern. In the hands of Nervi, structural organization became "structure as beauty."

Knowledgeable readers may interject here that Nervi's concrete work was labor intensive, and not economical for advanced industrial societies. Ferro-cemento construction required skilled laborers, who worked the layers of mortar and mesh into molds by hand. But each of Nervi's commissions was won against other competitive bids submitted under the prevailing economic conditions in Italy. What should not be lost in such debates is the principle we are exploring here: *A dominant boundary of space can be designed with structural members orga-*

nized as aesthetic pattern. Nervi was more than an architectural engineer. He was a master whose designs transcended the mere act of structural support. His accomplishments, leadership, and direction for achieving architectural and structural beauty are summarized in the words of his fellow countryman Mario Salvadori,[1] who said:

If I were asked why Nervi's structures are so keenly admired the world over by architects, engineers, and laymen, my immediate answer would be: "Because they are so true." Nervi combines two opposite frames of mind in one person: the synthetic, intuitive, artistic approach together with the analytic, mathematical, scientific outlook. These two divergent

[1] Salvadori is quoted from his "Foreword" to Pier Luigi Nervi's book, *Structures* (1956, vi).

viewpoints do not oppose but complement each other in him, and their expression is characterized by such unswerving adherence to physical reality and to beauty as to suggest the word truth.

The Sources of Light

When the structural system is designed, engineered, and erected on site, and when the last exterior surfaces of the building are in place, the principal locations of light sources are set. The orientation of the building then determines how its design will take advantage of the sun's "93,000,000 miles of effect." Openings in exterior walls and roofs are shaped and proportioned for the introduction of daylight, which will enter some rooms, and be shut out of others. It will stretch into some corridors and down stairwells, but not others. The design of the structural system will also establish the generalized locations of electric lighting for those spaces where daylight will not reach, and of support illumination in all spaces for overcast days and for nighttime.

Buildings under construction show this structure-to-light relationship exceptionally well. It is an invaluable exercise to stand inside the skeletal framework and contemplate the role of the structural system for how light eventually will reach the major spatial boundaries once they are completed. How will they be surfaced, and exactly from where will they receive light? What is the ceiling height? What distance will illumination have to travel to provide task lighting or special features of lighting design? What will the light sources themselves look like once they are in place, either as windows admitting daylight or manufactured luminaires supplying electric light? For buildings under construction, most of those questions were already answered during the stages of design, but they need to be reviewed over and over again, because their answers underscore the importance of the design and engineering of a building's structural system for the interaction of space and light.

In the case of curved shells, there are important perceptual considerations. The brightness of the openings and direction of the light admitted must be carefully studied for how the light openings themselves are perceived against the curvilinear surface of the shell. If too bright, an aperture creates simultaneous contrast in its immediate vicinity, which darkens the area of shell around it and modifies the appearance of its curvature. Contrast effects, or lack thereof, depends on exactly how light is reaching the surface of the shell.

Figure 9-9 shows the helical form of the dome over the sanctuary of The Temple of RLDS at Independence, Missouri. The form emanates from a floor plan in shape of the chambered nautilus and was intentional to sym-

Figure 9-9. Curvature of form and space. [The Temple of RLDS, Independence, Missouri. Architects: HOK]

bolize life. Natural light enters the interior through a continuous clerestory, which begins as a horizontal strip at the base of the dome and is gradually transformed into a conical helix. How the clerestory relates to the interior surface of the dome prevents simultaneous contrast, because the flow of the inner shell is never at true right angles to the entering daylight. The result is a continuous blending of middle values of reflected light along the spiraling surface. The line of clerestory alternates with a strip of incandescent downlights, and the two combined bring together a union of space and light in upward movement. The middle values of reflected light on the dome's surface behave for the electric lights as they do for daylight, preventing simultaneous contrast. Day and night, the two strips of light activate the dome, and define spatial action winding its way upward.

Integration of structure with the sources of light belongs to the art of spatial design. In the main office space (Figure 9-10) of the S. C. Johnson Wax Administration Building at Racine, Wisconsin, Frank Lloyd Wright created hollow dendriform columns that simultaneously structure the ceiling and articulate the space. Their thin proportions (only 9 inches at the base) allow the forms to accent rather than divide the working space. Technically, the columns support little more than their $18\frac{1}{2}$-ft-diameter capitals, whose spreading undersides form the upper spatial boundary of the room. Both daylight and electric illumination permeate Pyrex glass tubing, which diffuses the light flooding downward among the circular

Figure 9-10. Structure as spatial composition. [Photograph courtesy of the Johnson Wax Company]

patterns. The overall quality of light in the entire room is one of evenness and softness and is free of shadows. Reflected light illuminates the underside of the capitals (receiving assistance from "Johnson Waxed" floors), reducing the harshness of brightness-contrast that otherwise would appear where capitals frame illumination. The overall feeling of the room is one of spaciousness even though penetrated by structural members. The openness was intentional. The company considered workers as family, and Frank Lloyd Wright brought them together in this spacious room, joined with its companion mezzanine. Structure, space, light, and social interaction became one. In his autobiography Mr. Wright (1943, 472) referred to its design as "socio-architectural," and personally considered the building "to be as inspiring a place to work in as any cathedral ever was to worship in."

Through the last half of the twenty-first century, the awakened need for energy conservation stimulated architectural and technological developments aimed at bringing greater amounts of daylight into interiors. Shapes of building forms and interior spaces required structural systems that would accomplish that goal. The atrium in Figure 9-11 is a light-gathering design whose purpose is to bring sunlight into the central and adjacent spaces of the Blue Cross and Blue Shield Building at North Haven, Connecticut. The building's structural system was inte-

grated with the energy-saving design concept that shaped the atrium and its related spaces. The central space is oriented east-west, with a south-facing clerestory running its length. A section of roof over the atrium is angled to reflect light downward into the central space and its neighboring work places, all of which are generously opened by the broad spacing of the structural piers. The openness of the floors permits flexibility for changing of workstations, and the abundance of daylight reflected into the interior benefits all employees.

The structural system of a building is important for how it influences aperture sizes and locations for entering daylight, but not to be overlooked is how it positions slabs for floors that can be penetrated to create interesting vertical relationships of space by the interplay of direct and reflected light. The main shopping space of the mall shown in Figure 9-12 is covered by a skylight that brings abundant daylight into the interior. As skylights normally do, it spreads an expanse of patterned steel and glass overhead, and in this case chiefly benefits the uppermost floors. Advantage was taken of the brightness of the skylight pattern as it relates to the lower floors and ceilings. Spatial interest is created by brightness relationships that result from *framing* the upper spaces. Framing sets up brightness ratios and color relationships that can enliven spatial design. That is what is happening with the changing levels of floors in this

Figure 9-11. Coordination of structure, daylight, and space. [Blue Cross and Blue Shield of Connecticut Office Building, North Haven, Connecticut. Architects: Ellenzweig Associates, Inc. Photograph: © Steve Rosenthal]

Figure 9-12. Layering of space and light. [Westridge Mall, Topeka, Kansas. Architects: Law Kingdon, Inc.]

mall. Each floor is penetrated by circular or angled openings that successively frame brighter areas above, culminating with the skylight from where in daytime the majority of the light originates. In this and similar examples, the design of the structural system determines where, how much, and what shape of penetrations can be made. When structural design and building design are coordinated, the outcome makes possible engaging dialogue between architectural space and light.

Structural Synthesis for Architectural Beauty

In recent times the selection of a structural system for a building often has been made in step with changing trends in construction popularized by architectural and engineering media. Sometimes technological faddism governs the derivation of a building's form, and relationships of space and light are forced to conform to a preconceived structural system. In addition, humanism and the basic functions of the building often become secondary considerations. Architectural design excels when a building's functions are unified with its structural system, coordinated in exterior form and interior space. Separation or unnecessary interruption of functional relationships of human living for the sake of structural expression alone is a denial of architectural integrity. In the waning decades of the twentieth century criticism has been levied against much of our architecture for lacking integrity and architectural beauty, contrasting it with exemplar historical examples that show a harmonious relationship among form, living spaces, and a building's structural system.

In 1860 the American Transcendentalist Ralph Waldo Emerson wrote an enlightening essay entitled "Beauty." In that essay, he makes a point of how structure is integral with the aesthetics of form in nature and offered parallels for the literary arts and visual design. Although he directed his views primarily to poetry and literature, again and again Emerson looked to nature as the paragon, searching for a tasteful union between the role of structure and the derivation of form. "We ascribe beauty," he wrote, "to that which is simple; which has no superfluous parts; which exactly answers its end; which stands related to all things; which is the mean of many extremes." Emerson's advice is sound for application to architecture. Structure is one of beauty's qualities, he thought, and is not something that just stands alone. Nor is it merely to be taken for granted as something that just happens in the random process of assembling or composing constituent parts. Emerson (1860, 177) was precise about this:

Beyond their sensuous delight, the forms and colors of Nature have a new charm for us in our perception that not one ornament was added for ornament, but each is a sign of some better health or more excellent action. Elegance of form in bird or beast, or in the human figure, marks some excellence of structure: or, beauty is only an invitation from what belongs to us. 'Tis a law of botany that in plants the same virtues follow the same forms. It is a rule of largest application, true in a plant, true in a loaf of bread, that in the construction of any fabric or organism any real increase of fitness to its end is an increase of beauty.

Emerson's phrase "excellence of structure" can be misleading when applied to contemporary architecture. It could be taken to include a certain method of construction, like a high-tech space-frame, and simply designing and building it exceptionally well, which would give it "excellence of structure." That is, it has excellence for that type of structure. Emerson, however, took the meaning of structural excellence a step further. As a quality for beauty, the structure of something written or designed must fulfill, as he says, a "fitness to its end." In architecture it could be argued that the *end* is the dramatic expression of a structural system itself, for novel effects or out of popularity of a construction technique. But when the *end* is the humanization of architecture,

structure is consigned to a role of integrating building form and living space for human needs and comfort, and not just to accomplish a technological demonstration. A structural system conceived out of faddism or showmanship is not necessarily an increase in architectural beauty. *Structure contributes to beauty when it synthesizes form and space in an artistic coherency for quality human living.*

Let's look at that principle in theory. In its synthesizing role of harboring life's functions, structural beauty is elegantly stated in the "architecture" of living nature. A premier example is the chambered nautilus (Figure 9-13), a mollusk inhabitant of the deep Pacific Ocean. The form of its structural shell is a thin membrane shaped by its periodic development. As the mollusk grows, natural secretions form a new chamber every few weeks. With the accumulation of as many as 38 chambers, the shell continually enlarges with mathematical consistency, creating its appealing spiral form. The series of chambers is connected internally by a thin tube, the *siphuncle*, which is used to regulate the ratio of air to liquid contained in all the chambers, controlling buoyancy for ascending and descending in the ocean's depth. It is the same principle as the airtight ballast tanks of the submarine. The mollusk lives in its most recent chamber, but functionally uses the spaces of its former "rooms" for locomotion. The structure of the nautilus thus shapes both exterior form and internal space to sustain its living activities. The morphological laws of growth are vividly expressed in this natural example of structure as synthesis, protecting life and expressing the continuation of life as the mollusk grows. The life-relatedness of the structural system is in perfect harmony with living functions, and in principle (not shape or style) the mollusk provides a theoretical model for integrating the components of architectural design for the well-being of human living. In Nature's shells, nothing is forced or artificial. There is natural beauty, a beauty that subscribes to the Emersonian definition by its "excellence of structure" and "fitness to its end."

Our focus of attention here is only on structure in its role as synthesis. Not structure as shape. The functional and visual harmony among livable spaces in architecture depends on efficient coordination with structure. Different from the nautilus where one life is chambered in its most recent room, architecture serves multiple inhabitants in an organization of programmed spaces of various functions. Interior rooms are the "chambers" of the greater dwelling, and corridors, stairs, and elevators are the connecting *siphuncles* as interior circulation routes. As the nautilus shell serves the mollusk, the life-relatedness of a building's structural system plays a major role in determining the quality for human living. In high-quality architectural design, structure derives the exterior form as a natural consequence of the arrange-

Figure 9-13. Structure as synthesis in living nature.

ment of interior functional relationships, and is a key for achieving beauty in the design of the human environment.

There are ample historical precedents to demonstrate structure as synthesis for the well-planned organization of a building's functions. Aside from the sheer enjoyment of experiencing architectural masterpieces, the search for and verification of valid design principles are the true reasons for present-day study of the history of architecture. The great historical monuments establish standards according to which architectural design from any period can be compared. Sometimes buildings from certain historical periods are discounted by designers who dislike the regimentation of classical design or the ornateness of Byzantine, late Gothic, or Baroque designs. This is precisely the danger in looking at style rather than principles of design. To reject totally an ornate architecture because of its decorativeness is to throw out the baby with the bath water. Byzantine or Baroque decor can be mentally stripped away as cultural upholstery to discover the intrinsic elements of design lying beneath.

In Istanbul, Turkey, stands the great sixth-century Byzantine church of Hagia Sophia (Figure 9-14). Today's visitors can see the basic structural system when viewing the building from inside or outside, despite the assorted appendages that have been added to its original design. Later service additions, and interior surface overlays confuse the architecture it once was, but what is still visible today is a clear expression of structure shaping form and space and directing the entry of daylight. Its floor plan shows how massive interior piers play double duty by supporting the dome and pendentives while separating the main central space from the side aisles. The four semicircular exedras form subspaces that articulate the interior and sensitively expand the central space to merge with side aisles. The section drawing shows how the dome and half-domes conduct a fluid visual movement of surfaces over the central space as they work in transferring structural forces from high above down to the ground. Lower floor and upper level arcades provide interior support, and at the same time further articulate the central space by screening views to ambulatories

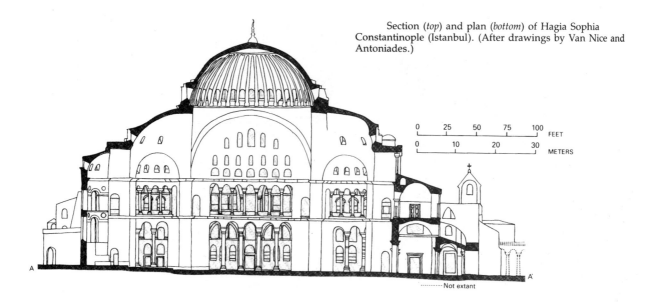

Section (*top*) and plan (*bottom*) of Hagia Sophia
Constantinople (Istanbul). (After drawings by Van Nice and
Antoniades.)

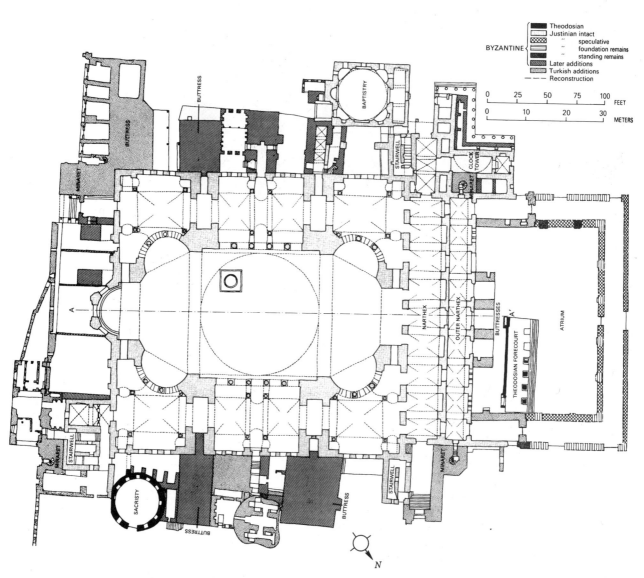

Figure 9-14. Structure as synthesis in architecture. [Hagia Sophia, Istanbul, Turkey, A.D. 532–537. *From
Gardner's Art Through the Ages by Horst de la Croix, Richard G. Tansey, and Diane Kirkpatrick, copyright
© 1991 by Harcourt Brace & Company, reproduced by permission of the publisher. Plan and section.*]

and galleries like a structural veil. Structure and space harmoniously work together. Forty windows arched into the base of the dome and those in the half-domes and outer gallery walls create the mystical light of the interior, a phenomenon that archives reveal has been marveled at by visitors ever since the original building was finished. The drama of light and space owes its debt to a magnificently coordinated structural system.

Gothic builders erected masonry structures epitomizing dynamic relationships of form, space, and colored light (see Figure 7-18). Sunlight reaching into the interiors was transformed into chromatic effects as it passed through stained glass windows. Processions moved through an array of colored light alternating with shadows cast by the vertical members of the structural system. Stone vaulting overhead covered the grand interior, and spaces became articulated in linear design by ribs and piers expressing structural compression. Structure became the synthesizing agent creating architectural beauty and provided the "fitness to its end" for liturgical ceremony. Emotional spaces of light and color were created using essentially only two building materials: stone and stained glass.

In recent times, the emotional quality of screened space produced by the structural system has been master-fully achieved in the works of E. Fay Jones. Standing in a grove of trees, his Thorncrown Chapel (Figures 9-15 and C-35) surrounds worshipers with delicate structural elements of wood. Exquisite structural detailing aligns a row of diamond-shaped openings formed by steel truss connectors, forming a central spine of scintillating light directing vision to the sanctuary—and beyond to the peace of nature. Clear glass walls open to the woods where oaks and dogwoods abound, and the structural system screens the views to trees, plants, rocks, birds, and butterflies. The design of the building's structure is in accord with design in nature, as vertical supports and overhead trusses reply to the trunks of trees and overhead branches growing immediately outside. From dawn to dusk, luminance effects in the interior of the chapel are as one with the surrounding natural setting. Flickering light filters through the branches of overhanging deciduous trees, and enters the chapel through a companion network of open-patterned trusses. As evening approaches, the gradual reduction of sunlight inside the chapel replicates the arrival of nighttime in the forest. For observers experiencing a sunrise at Thorncrown when early morning shafts of light break through trees behind the sanctuary, they witness a virtual moment of Genesis (Figure C-35). Here again structure becomes one

Figure 9-15. Structure screening light for interior mood. [Thorncrown Chapel, Eureka Springs, Arkansas. Architect: Fay Jones & Associates]

with spatial sensation. During breakfast one morning at an architecture conference, this author and the architect of Thorncrown discussed at length the relationship between structure, space, and architectural beauty. Mr. Jones stressed the importance of devoted and disciplined effort that is required throughout the development and refinement stages of design, without losing sight of the initial creative intent. "Most designers," he said, "give up too early." They declare a work finished before it is refined, and do not take that extra step across the threshold where genuine architectural beauty can be reached.

In Thorncrown the relationship between structure, form, and space is obvious, but some high-quality building designs have structural systems that are just as direct in forming that relationship, but not as immediately self-evident. Take for example the Robie House (Figure 9-16) in Chicago by Frank Lloyd Wright. A critic looking for structural expression *per se* will point out units of bearing walls and cantilevered roofs. But its design expresses just as much the totality of its exterior form, just as much the union between its interior and exterior spaces, and just as much its fenestration, integrally participating in the play of light and shade inside and out. Vertical and horizontal structural members partake in a unified function of support, and together seem to grow from within, allowing the whole to come together in harmony. Walking through the house, the spaces flow in league with one another and yet maintain their own

integrity. That's because the structure has integrity, beautifully expressed in its role as synthesis, not dominance.

In summary, this principle can be stated as follows: *The appropriateness and correctness of the structural system fitting the concept and program requirements of a building is a standard for the achievement of quality architectural design.* In the closing decades of the twentieth century, structural integrity sometimes has been compromised for the sake of design novelty, personal freedom of the designer or engineer, or the creation of a building as a visual attraction for tenant identity. At times exposed structure is needlessly dramatized for no meaningful reason other than technological theatrics. Those buildings have succumbed to fashion design, and have been stripped of their candidacy to be considered architecturally beautiful. While modern society's fads and fashions have gone in and out of popularity in brief periods of a decade or less, the Robie House by contrast has drawn attention generation after generation for a century now. Like other exemplary monuments, it transcends time like a rock ledge standing firm against the pounding ocean surf, while momentary styles and fashions break up as easily as that surf. But as rocks of civilization the Robie Houses of history remain, demonstrating the principle of structural integrity in a unity with form and space. In quality architecture, there is indeed a correctness of structure, and a correctness in the way it contributes to shaping the spaces people inhabit. It

Figure 9-16. Structure's role for design excellence. [Chicago Historical Society. Photograph: Richard Nickel ICHi-21070]

Analysis of Architectural Space

is not a structural aesthetic that is to be sought, but an architectural aesthetic of which a proper structural system is a part. Mario Salvadori (1963, 5) said "It is undeniable that a 'correct' structure satisfies the eye of even the most unknowledgeable layman, and that a 'wrong' structure is often offensively ugly." His advice centers on the relationship between structure and architectural beauty, and cautions against the overstatement of the role of structure in building design. He makes this point by saying "it would be hard to prove that esthetics are essentially dependent on structure. It is easy to show, instead, that some 'incorrect' structures are lovely, while some 'correct' ones are esthetically unsatisfying. It may perhaps be wiser to say that correctness of structure is, most of the time, a necessary condition of beauty, but is not sufficient to guarantee beauty." The idea of synthesis returns in these thoughts. In a quality-designed building, structure, form, space, and light are interdependent, and their harmonious integration makes evident the presence of beauty.

CHAPTER 10

Movement through Space

An architecture must be walked through and traversed. It is by no means that entirely graphic illusion certain schools of thought would like us to believe in, organized around some abstract point that pretends to be a man, a chimerical man with the eye of a fly and vision simultaneously circular. . . . Instead, our own man has two eyes set in the front of his head, and he stands six feet above the ground and looks ahead.

—Le Corbusier
*Talks with Students**

Other than for freestanding sculpture, architecture differs from the other visual arts mostly because it is experienced by physically moving through and around it. In the course of day-to-day living, people encounter environments ranging from the simple and familiar to the complex and unknown. Robert Bechtel (1967) studied human movement in architecture and described familiar territory as that through which visitors move in a *habitual* manner and are scarcely aware of their architectural environment. But when a building is unfamiliar, he said, they move through it in an *exploratory* manner, looking in all directions, hesitating, and sometimes retracing steps. It is in the unknown or less familiar places that the spatial perception of architecture is highly significant. The task of the designer is to minimize the confusion while people are finding their way, yet still insert and integrate visual interest and design excitement along the paths of sequential space.

* Le Corbusier, 1961. *Le Corbusier Talks with Students*. Translated by Pierre Chase. New York: The Orion Press, pp. 44–45.

Le Corbusier was absolutely correct in saying people have two eyes mounted in front of the head at a fixed distance above the floor, and move forward in space. He was not stating the obvious but making note of the quintessential. True, people move as governed by their motivation at the time, but they also move according to how they see, hear, and experience their total environment, as we saw in Part 1 of this book. Spatial organization and the lighting of certain features of the built environment prompt people's movement patterns, and those features can be manipulated to make architectural design more comprehendible and meaningful.

Stimulus for Movement

In Chapter 4 we explained how the human eye is attracted to or distracted by *focal accents*, which were analyzed to demonstrate their power for assuming dominance over less noticeable objects or surfaces in a visual scene. Focal accents are helpful for creating nodes of special interest in a building, especially when the intention is to attract people to certain locations. A center of attention is stronger when it is carefully integrated with the design of the spatial envelope(s) through which pedestrian circulation is routed. Therefore, focal accents should not be placed about in spatial composition indiscriminately. When an environment is overdone by focal accenting, visual attraction to just one or two centers breaks down in the scanning process of human vision. As people move about the environment, what exactly is it that they see, and from where? What is prominent in their field of view, and what specific design attributes attract their attention?

Figure 10-1 shows the entrance to a small shopping center in Arizona, beyond which lies a court surrounded by stores and supporting services. From this point of entry, an arched opening connects two spaces and frames an interest area lying straight ahead. The tree and landscaping in the court are a focal center, which is enhanced by the perceptually simplified design of the small spatial envelope in the foreground. The clarity of the foreground envelope benefits from two design features: restrained surfacing and minimal articulation. The stucco surfaces

Figure 10-1. Focal accent as a lead through space.
[Tlaquepaque, Sedona, Arizona]

and stone pavement are in keeping with the architecture of America's Southwest. It is precisely the relative simplicity of the foreground spatial envelope that emphasizes the tree and urns leading into the court. The shapes of nature draw shoppers through the small entry space, because their partial visibility communicates that something more is to come on the other side of the arch. Upon advancing, people find the shops, arranged around the perimeter of a rectangular court.

An important consideration for stimulating movement of the walker is how much and what kind of focal accenting is visible when a second space is framed by openings in the observer's spatial envelope. In the museum gallery of Figure 10-2, glimpses into two neighboring galleries stimulate movement for the art aficionado by offering more art to come. The visual draw of the partially exposed paintings in the two adjacent galleries tempts movement to the right and left. The principle is the same as that shown in the shopping court of Figure 10-1, where the size and lean of the tree trunks suggest more space opens to the left. In these examples, the feature of seeing only a fragment of an interesting object or a continuous surface pattern creates a temporary state of incompleteness, which prompts movement by the observer to complete the image. There is satisfaction in doing so. A partial view of something interesting and appealing becomes temptation to see the whole. The design of the initial spatial envelope and the quality of the focal accent lying ahead combine to stimulate movement.

A spatial connection can be effective by using pattern detailing that is coordinated in spatial composition. Figure 10-3 shows a curved wall detailed with a simple geometric pattern of glass squares that diffuse the light and images on the other side of the wall. It gains in visual attraction as it differs from the other perceptually simplified surfaces in the visual field. The same detailing of squares appears again on the far distant wall that marks a connecting node at the end of the corridor. The grid of squares there suggests the presence of something more significant than the intermediate subspaces along the way, and attracts visual and physical movement in its direction.

Centers for visual attraction can be used to integrate horizontal and vertical spaces. This can be seen in Figure 10-4a, where the vertical space of an atrium interacts with surrounding horizontal spaces. On the upper three floors, paths of movement toward the atrium feature views to similar spaces across the vertical space, framed by openings in the atrium walls. The atrium openings attract attention from any of the floors, and as visual references, provide orientation at all levels. The lobby below and the openings in the atrium become visual centers that relate to the movement of people in the building, and are spatially interrelated horizontally and vertically. As seen from the upper floors, a mosaic on the

Figure 10-2. Partial views stimulating movement. [Kimbell Art Museum, Fort Worth, Texas. Architect: Louis I. Kahn]

Figure 10-3. Pattern design as a spatial draw. [Touche Ross, United Missouri Bank, Kansas City, Missouri. Architects: Abend Singleton Associates. Photograph: © Paul Kivett]

(a)   (b)

Figure 10-4. Horizontal (a) and vertical (b) interaction by focal accenting. [Morgan Hall, Harvard Business School, Boston. Architect: Moshe Safdie and Associates. Photograph: © Steve Rosenthal]

lobby floor (Figure 10-4b) gradually attracts attention as it comes into view when people approach the railings. The mosaic is seen close-up upon first entering the lobby, and then reappears from various angles as people move through the building at the upper levels.

Using the perceptual strength of *focal accents* (see Chapter 4, p. 62) to attract human vision offers the designer a wealth of opportunity for articulating paths of movement by effectively distributing the accents as visual leads through a sequence of spaces. The series of photographs of Figure 10-5 illustrates a major circulation route through a small public park that connects a cultural center with a prominent hotel. In a walk through the sequence, focal accents accompany and stimulate pedestrian movement. At one end is a small cafe (Figure 10-5a) where people sit leisurely under a canopy of colorful canvas strips providing protective shade from the summer sun. The linear pattern and vivid colors of the awning strips are directional accents that create a strong perspective depth cue paralleling the physical movement through the full length of the space. The canopy's strong shadows on the pavement amplify the visual thrust forward.

Midway down the space (Figure 10-5b) the visual movement forward is accented even more dramatically by the shadows of the canvas strips, and the spatial envelope becomes more open laterally. New focal accents are introduced, which by distraction begin to "slow down" the forceful linear perspective of the canopy. A sidewalk lined by street lamps approaches diagonally from the left. Like a beacon guiding the forward direction (and at night it certainly does), one of the street lamps is framed by the open end of the canopy. Also, a line of fountain spouts makes its presence known by introducing a combination of focal accents: brightness, movement (of the water), a new strong visual pattern, and contrast as seen against the backdrop of the hotel across the street. These new focal accents take over as the transition from one space to another takes place with each step forward.

As people walk through the last patterns of shadow cast by the canopy (Figure 10-5c), the street lamp strikes a momentary note of emphasis, giving way to both the sight and sounds of the fountain, which announce a change in the direction of movement. The activity of the fountain introduces a new kind of animation to the total sequence: sound. With each step the observer takes, the sounds of people's voices at the tables behind gradually diminish as those of the fountain rise in volume.

In the last phase (Figure 10-5d), the fountain joins

Figure 10-5 a–d. Spatial sequencing with focal accents. [Barney Allis Plaza, Kansas City, Missouri. Architects: The SWA Group]

with a row of trees and planters to form one side of a new space. Tables for people are reintroduced along the base of another row of trees and planters to form the other side of this next spatial envelope. In time the trees will grow to arch their branches over the walkway, creating a canopy of nature. The sequence finishes as it began at the other end, as an amenity offering people a place to sit while shaded from the sun.

Focal accents stimulate the movement of people through directional spaces such as the public park and also are highly effective in environments composed in various spatial configurations. Figure 10-6 shows the Guggenheim Museum in New York, where a variety of focal accents sets up attractions in a number of different directions, drawing people from place to place. Contrasting shapes and colors of sculpture and paintings

Figure 10-6. Movement, focal accenting, and the transformation of space. [Guggenheim Museum, New York City. Architect: Frank Lloyd Wright. Photographer: © Balthazar Korab]

are contrasted in strong figure-ground. As people move about, the works of art are integrated into rich spatial relations. Curiosity is established by partial views into nearby or distant subspaces that open as people move toward them. The curious mind is also drawn to accents and spatial views that have attracted other people. The arch at the top of the photograph frames the brightness and activities of another space that has captured the interest of those standing at the railing.

People Move Toward Light

Essential as it is for the growth and development of living organisms, light also conditions orientation in the plant and animal kingdoms. Human beings are no exception. From the ancient Greeks comes the word *phototropic* ("to seek light"), with its meaning possibly de-

rived from recognition of the behavior of plants bending in the direction of sunlight as they grow. By the nineteenth century, botanists and physiologists were using the term *phototropism* to scientifically designate the movement of plants and animals toward light, and research has now supported this fundamental behavioral trait found in people. The entry of light into the retina causes extreme physiological change as it stimulates the photoreceptor cells, and any bright surface or light source in the visual world attracts the focus selector. This is the reason for high brightness, particularly brightness-contrast, being listed as an exceptionally strong focal accent, which arrests the saccadic movement of the eye as it scans the environment. Having two eyes in lateral position, human beings instantly respond to light or high-luminance brightness when the source first appears in the peripheral vision of one eye. This causes the head to move, enabling the focus selector of the other eye to fixate on the same attracting source, neurologically correcting the asymmetrical imbalance. As the head turns toward the bright light source, it influences movement of the body. In this regard visual perception is an orienting system. There is, of course, the input of people's desire or need to move, but even when a person is walking in a certain direction by personal volition, a sudden appearance of light or brightness-contrast coming from any direction in the field of view will cause the head to move and potentially the body.

Psychologists have observed the natural response to light and brightness in infant vision. Even before a child is physically developed enough for creeping or walking, its vision has already been responding to the attraction of light. The observations of Piaget (1954, 210) and others have traced this early development of phototropic reflex behavior:

> These considerations, applied to the perception and execution of movements, make clear how the formation of space is outlined from the time the apparatus of sight or of balance begins to function. From the sixth day of life, Preyer's child turns his head toward the window as he is carried away from it, and does so in order to recover the agreeable sensation of light; this single act of seeking an aliment that is functional to his looking constitutes, independently of any precise coordination, a group of displacements immanent in reflex activity.

The awareness of reflex behavior has led scientists to investigate the phototropic effects of light in a number of human activities. LaGuisa and Perney (1973) studied schoolchildren to observe attention they paid to visual aid display cards in classroom conditions, comparing the brightness level of the cards with other luminances in the room. When the cards were brighter than all other surrounding surfaces, the researchers found that the display was effective in attracting—and holding—student attention to the cards, regardless of the presence or absence of verbal instruction. In this classroom situation, movement was by eye and head only, but the findings of the study lend further support to the theory that brightness in the architectural environment is important for how it attracts human vision.

Of particular interest to architects and interior designers is whether or not the natural effect of phototropism influences the movement of people from one place to another. Will light or bright surfaces and objects actually stimulate a person to move toward them when there are alternative choices to move in directions where light is not a dominant feature? This is the question Taylor and Socov (1974) sought to answer in an experimental study of the influence of light on pedestrian traffic patterns. The layout of their study is shown in Figure 10-7. Subjects entered a room through a curtained entrance way,

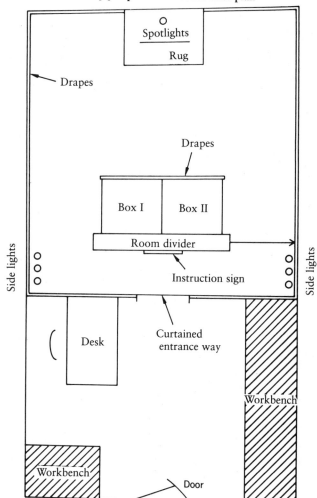

Figure 10-7. Taylor and Sucov experimental room [Lighting Design & Application. January 1974, p. 54. Published by the Illuminating Engineering Society of North America, 120 Wall Street, New York, NY 10005]

and immediately in front of them found a room divider on which a panel of instructions explained that they were participating in a study of lighting arrangements for consumer products, but no clue was given that they were being observed for their choice of movement in optional directions. On the other side of the room divider was where the subjects expected to find the lighting arrangements and consumer goods. To proceed to that room, they faced perpendicular walls which were variably illuminated. When one of the end walls was illuminated more brightly than the other, people tended to choose the brighter way. The higher the ratio of brightness between the two end walls, the higher the percentage of subjects who proceeded in the direction of the brighter wall. Because of its obvious relationship to architectural space planning, more research of this kind is needed to further our knowledge of the phototropic nature of human behavior, but current evidence supports the fact that people do indeed move toward light.

The phototropic effects of light aid the designer by combining a functional and aesthetic approach to building design and spatial composition. On the functional side, a bright area or object can be located to attract human vision and influence the movement of people. Figure C-36 shows the attracting power of light leading the way for entry into the building, contributing to aesthetics. The interior lobby is the brightest, brought out by the darkened screen of the two piers separating the three entrance openings in the facade. The sequence is a composition of brightness levels, first with intermediate zones (colonnade), then dark (entrance piers), then the climax of the bright lobby. The end result is an artful shaping of lighted spaces inviting people into the building, moving toward light, as different brightness levels are sensitively composed around them as they walk.

For designing sequences of lighted spaces, the LBR Scale of brightness zones presented in Chapter 5 is exceptionally helpful (Figure 5-3). Combinations of selected zones can be visualized in different sequential orders. Anticipating how brightness levels will compose with the arrival of illumination, the architect positions the major surfaces and selects the building materials for how they will respond to light. The architect also penetrates a major plane or screens a space behind, and the spatial interplay of brightness levels goes to work. The surface luminance creating a certain brightness at a certain place can be calculated by the lighting engineer to derive a composition of surface brightness that makes possible interesting spatial relationships like those shown in Figure C-36.

The composition of brightness levels to influence people's movements is also important for interior spatial sequencing, again combining the functional with the artistic. The hotel lobby and lounge area of Figure C-37 shows a circulation path leading through a series of spaces to the receptionist station. The color values of carpeting and brick partitions are of intermediate brightness levels, raising the brightness of two recessed ceilings of indirect illumination. In the view shown, the shapes of indirect lighting alternate in contrasting luminance with the lower ceilings in a linear perspective into depth. The brightness of the wall behind the receptionist is heightened by the framing effect of the comparatively darker surfaces of the last brick partitions. That furthermost wall is not the brightest surface in the spatial sequence, but bright enough to attract attention in its direction. In the overall visual field, the brightness levels are composed in a way that they are spatially interesting, and attract movement straight ahead to the receptionist station, assisted by the behavioral factor that people move toward light.

The Zone of Transition

Earlier we learned that the human retina undergoes light or dark adaptation when human vision is subjected to changes of brightness levels surrounding the eye. Movement through the architectural environment strongly influences that adaptation, particularly between two adjacent spaces of significant brightness-contrast. An abrupt change from bright daylight into a darkened first entry space of a building causes severe retinal reaction, as does the sudden departure from a bright interior into the darkness of night. The retina needs time to adjust during the move from one extreme of lighted environment to another, and to promote the humanization of architecture, a spatial *zone of transition* is needed, just like airlocks relieve extreme shifts in temperature. How convenient it is that airlocks can be designed to act also as visual zones of transition for retinal adjustment.

Exterior entrance portals and interior foyers make effective zones of transition when moving from the bright light of day into building interiors, or the reverse at night. These transitional areas provide the necessary time for the photoreceptors in the retina to adjust from one condition of brightness to the next. This was achieved by the entrance space shown in Figure 10-8. The two smaller subspaces at the sides are reduced in size, making prominent the center space and the axial line of entry. The center envelope containing the revolving door begins spatial enclosure and reduces brightness of daylight in preparation for the further reduction of light in the interior. As a transitional zone, the recessed portal assists the retina by avoiding a quick change from bright daylight to interior illumination. White soffits over the doors help the transition to the bright out-of-doors when leaving the building.

Entrance portals are as important for retinal adjustment at night as they are in daytime. Figure C-38 illustrates how an entrance design provides a good transition to a bright commercial interior at evening and nighttime. The white surfacing material inside the portal structure is effective for reflecting light and brightening its spatial envelope, illuminated by the strip lighting along the upper walls. After the last of daylight, the bright portal surfaces begin retinal light adaptation for evening shoppers entering the building. The overall building design and its lighting are aesthetically designed. The broad horizontal panels above step downward and inward from the primary facade plane, countering the portal structure that projects forward like a spatial welcome. The illuminated logo, the strip lighting washing the horizontal panels, and the lighting inside the portal are all coordinated in a composition of building form, space, and light.

It is hardly coincidental that as a transitional space the loggia has appeared throughout the history of archi-

Figure 10-8. Entrance portal as transitional zone. [7400 Lighton Plaza, Overland Park, Kansas]

tecture. The design of the arcade or colonnade of a loggia and its distance out from the wall present the opportunity for creating spatial aesthetics. Inside the loggia, light becomes an effective instrument for animating space and generating a high degree of human appeal—by the design of shadows. How interesting that can become, beautifying the space in which people walk, and letting the sun do the work. The interior court of the Renaissance Foundling Hospital (Figure C-39) is a vivid example. Its designer Filippo Brunelleschi knew full well how to create pictorial effects of light by manipulating the shape and proportions of the colonnade, to screen the sunlight, and cast patterns of shadow on the floor and wall under the loggia. No decoration (nor added expense) is required on the surfaces of the wall. Shadows are the decoration. Interposing the slender columns and lyrical curves of the arches at the vertical plane of the central spatial envelope, Brunelleschi let the sun draw photograms of patterned light and shade in musical rhythms on the pavement. In his day and ours, visitors to the building walk through harmonic intervals of lines and curves. As the sun moves during the day so do the shadow patterns, changing from one side of the court to the other, creating variations of the same melodious theme that animates the entire space. Brunelleschi was a skilled composer,

versed in the aesthetics of form, space, and light. From examples like this the lesson for today's designers is clearly stated: *Do not design with light; design with the effects of light.*

There are numerable occasions when outdoor circulation routes pass through and interact with part of a building, allowing the designer to create rhythms of brightness in spatial sequence. Figure 10-9 shows the connection between a public walkway and park (behind the camera location) and an open-air courtyard and the cafes of a hotel. The steps were designed in short segments that make the ascent comfortable for the human stride, and are visually attractive by the rhythmic shadow patterns of the risers. Both sides of the passage are stepped, adding their own subtle rhythm. The walking distance through this zone of transition to the bright beginning of the courtyard is relatively short, so the space is shadowed in ambient light that pleasantly dims but does not darken the passage, and the retina is not forced to undergo significant dark adaptation as people pass through. Overhead lighting brightens this zone of transition at night, and in daytime the shadowed passage brings up the brightness of the court beyond, attracting pedestrian movement to the shops and cafe tables in the next sequential space.

Analysis of Architectural Space

Figure 10-9. Zone of transition in outdoor spatial sequence. [Charles Square Hotel, Cambridge, Massachusetts. Architects: Cambridge Seven Associates. Photographer: © Steve Rosenthal]

Brightness Changes as a Function of Movement

As they are seen while walking through architecture, the brightnesses on surfaces do not stay fixed as they appear when observing them from a stationary point of view, nor as they appear in still photographs published in books and journals. Except for changing daylight effects resulting from sky conditions and gradual movement of the sun, surfaces stay in a relatively constant state of luminance. But to the eye, the colors and textures of surfacing materials change in brightness as seen by a person walking through the architectural environment.

A common occurrence of surfaces changing in brightness as seen by people moving through space is caused by light and dark adaptation of the eye (Figure 10-10). The eye adapts to the lighted space it is in or passing through, and as a result, the color and brightness of surfaces in an upcoming space will not look the same once the viewer enters it. The adaptation level of the eye varies according to the luminances of the dominant surfaces surrounding the observer at the time. When light adapted, the eye is less sensitive to weak stimuli

(which applies to subtle design detailing) that may appear in contrasting dark areas and shadows in the scene. The concept of the spatial envelope is effective for observing and analyzing the influence of the dominant spatial boundaries surrounding the vision of a person walking through successive spaces of alternating luminance contrasts. In principle it can be applied to a covered passage between two buildings, a pergola, a pedestrian tunnel, or any of a number of alternating light contrasts in spaces inside or outside a building. When passing through the covered space shown in the drawing, the eye of the walker is momentarily adapting to the relative dimness of the prevailing ambient light. Moving further ahead, the eye encounters the brighter surfaces of the next space, at which time the iris constricts, forcing light adaptation. When the person enters the immediate area where the two spatial envelopes are merging, the activity of the photoreceptors in the retina will be most pronounced, caused by the last edges of the darker spatial boundaries successively uncovering the brighter surfaces in the oncoming space.

Illustrating the principle in the real architectural environment, Figure 10-11a and b show a small exterior court in a corporation complex as seen from a connecting

Figure 10-10. Retinal adaptation and spatial brightness.

passageway. In the location of Figure 10-11a, the eye has adjusted to the comparative shade of the passageway as it looks straight ahead toward the brighter surfaces in the court. Note the brightness of the structural beam overhead, the side wall, and facade straight ahead. The photograph was taken far enough back in the passageway to show a station point just before the eye begins adapting to the brightness of the court. The brightnesses of the surface areas (labeled in zones of the LBR Scale) are different from how they appear in 10-11b, which was photographed at the exact point where the relative dimness of the passageway loses its dominant influence. The surfaces have darkened by one gray zone, which means they have darkened in color value. The photographs are intended to simulate how the retina responds to changing conditions of brightness.[1] In similar situa-

[1] Due to the reciprocity of film, which does not behave in the same physiological manner as the photoreceptors in the retina, it is virtually impossible to photographically reproduce the exact brightness of surfaces as they appear at the actual site. Some of the gray surfaces in Figure 10-11b were adjusted in the darkroom to approximate as closely as possible the real brightness changes that result from retinal adaptation for a person walking toward the court shown. For further explanation, see "Photography and the Human Retina" in the Appendix.

tions of passing from a dimly lit space into bright daylight, a white ceiling or soffit will appear near totally dark when seen against the sky just before stepping into the daylight.

The preceding analyses show the importance of the designer's decisions regarding shapes, dimensions, and connections of spatial envelopes, and choosing the building materials that will surface the dominant spatial boundaries. Spaces need to be connected in such a way as to facilitate a pleasant transition between them, which depends on the brightness levels of what precedes and what follows. The designer should be aware of the effects of light/dark adaptation, keeping in mind that important aspect of visual perception while taking mental walks through floor plans and sections of a building during design development. Surfaces need to be considered for how they will appear in the overall composition as seen while walking along major circulation routes, and how they can contribute to an ergonomic transition from one space to the next.

Part 2 has presented an analysis of architectural space for design application based on perception by the human visual system. The spatial envelope was developed as a

(a)

(b)

Figure 10-11 a and b. Brightness change as a function of movement. [Solana, Westlake, Texas. Architects: Maguire Thomas Partners]

working concept to encourage and facilitate a common dialogue across various professional fields dealing with the design and lighting of the architectural environment. Architect, interior designer, engineer, and lighting designer all contribute to the shaping and surfacing of the envelope. We showed that the assembly of major boundaries in orderly composition results in perceptual ease for comprehending space, and the surface design of the envelope is important for creating the basic character of space. We also learned how articulation of the envelope is achieved by adding pattern and color, and by penetrating the boundaries with subspaces—all of which are methods for animating space. The structural system of a building was analyzed for its essential role of space organization, as well as for its functions of allowing the entry of daylight, and determining the major areas requiring electric support lighting. We then investigated how people move through the architectural environment, how they respond to the stimulation of light and focal accents, how the continual process of walking from place to place visually transforms the basic spatial envelope, and how surfaces change in appearance as seen while passing through a sequence of differentially illuminated spaces.

Where this section focused on design theory related to the composition of the boundaries of space, Part 3 takes in hand the challenging and difficult task of illuminating the spatial constructs. It will explore the mutual interaction of space and light and its relevance to the professions related to architecture, explaining methods of designing with light to take advantage of its potent and stimulating nature.

Figure C-6. **Vivid color as focal accents.** *[Union Station, Washington, D.C. Architects: Ben Thompson & Associates. Photograph: © Steve Rosenthal]*

Figure C-7. **The brightness of wood species in composition.** *[UTILICORP, Kansas City, Missouri. Architects: HNTB]*

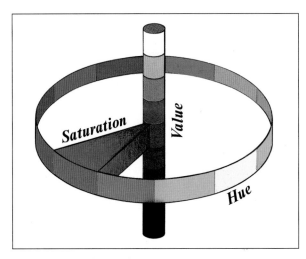

Figure C-8. **Color attributes.**

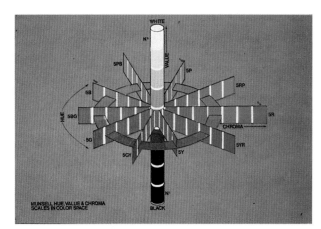

Figure C-9. **The Munsell system for color notation and specification.** *[Courtesy: Munsell Color Co., c/o Macbeth Corp., New Windsor, New York]*

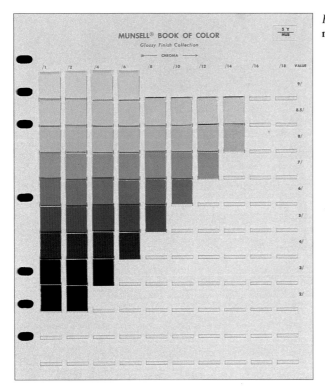

Figure C-10. **Munsell notations for color measurement.** *[Munsell Book of Color]*

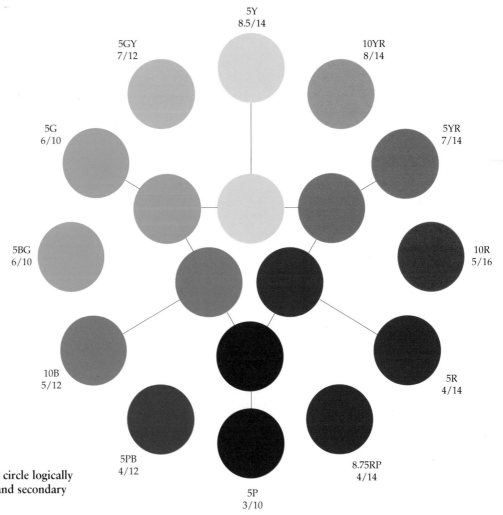

Figure C-11. **A 12-step color circle logically developed from the primary and secondary hues.**

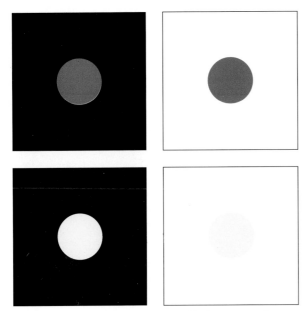

Figure C-12. Contrast by dark and light surrounding fields.

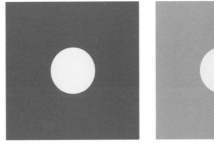

Figure C-13. Complementary contrast for purity of hue.

Figure C-14. Retinal tint as response to complementary hue.

Figure C-15. Color rendering for commercial attraction. [Daffy's, Wayne Towne Center Mall, Wayne, New Jersey. Courtesy: Philips Lighting Co.]

Figure C-16. Radical color change under different illumination. [Courtesy: OSRAM SYLVANIA INC.]

Figure C-17. Color change by different fluorescent sources. [Courtesy: OSRAM SYLVANIA INC.]

Figure C-18. **Color change of reflected light.** *[CIGNA Corp. Architects: The Architects Collaborative. Photograph: © Steve Rosenthal]*

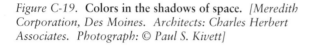

Figure C-19. **Colors in the shadows of space.** *[Meredith Corporation, Des Moines. Architects: Charles Herbert Associates. Photograph: © Paul S. Kivett]*

Figure C-20. **Retinal adaptation to colored space.** *[IBM Marketing and Technical Support Center, Westlake, Texas. Architect: Ricardo Legorreta. Photograph courtesy of Maguire Thomas Partners. Photography: Jim Hedrich, Hedrich-Blessing]*

Figure C-21. **Lighting influencing color value and saturation.** *[Harvard Station, Massachusetts Bay Transportation Authority, Boston. Photograph: © Steve Rosenthal]*

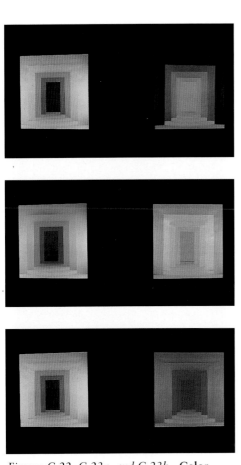

Figure C-24. Behavioral and perceptual effects of spatial color. *[Shore Country Day School, Beverly, Massachusetts. Architects: Perry Dean Rogers and Partners. Photograph: © Steve Rosenthal]*

Figures C-22, C-23a, and C-23b. **Color brightness and spatial depth cues.**

Figure C-25. Perceptual clarity over discordance. *[75 State Street, Boston. Architects: Graham Gund and SOM/Boston. Photograph: © Steve Rosenthal]*

Figure C-26. **Polychromatic urban space.** *[Burano, Italy]*

Figure C-27. **Polychromatic interior space.** *[Methuen School, Methuen, Massachusetts. Architect: HMFH Architects, Inc., Cambridge. Photograph: © Steve Rosenthal]*

Figure C-28. **Spatial articulation by pattern organization.** *[Rowes Wharf, Boston. Architects: SOM/Chicago. Photograph: © Steve Rosenthal]*

Figure C-29. **Articulation animating interior space.** *[Missouri Court of Appeals, Kansas City, Missouri. Architects: Abend Singleton Associates. Photograph: © Paul S. Kivett]*

Figure C-30. **Modular workstations as subspaces.** *[Central States Pension Fund, Chicago. Architects: HNTB]*

Figure C-31. **Integration of spatial banding and subspacing.** *[The TJX Companies, Inc., Framingham, Massachusetts. Architects: The Architects Collaborative. Photograph: © Warren Jagger]*

Figure C-32. **Curvature and spatial interaction of subspaces.** *[Meditech, Canton, Massachusetts. Architects: Koetter, Kim and Associates, Inc. Photograph: © Steve Rosenthal]*

Figure C-33. **Animation of space by staircase design.** *[Kennedy School of Government, Harvard University, Cambridge, Massachusetts. Architects: The Architects Collaborative. Photograph: © Steve Rosenthal]*

Figure C-34. **Structure and spatial articulation.** *[Brown University Computer Center. Architects: Cambridge Seven Associates. Photograph: © Steve Rosenthal]*

Figure C-35. **A moment of Genesis by filtered light.** *[Thorncrown Chapel, Eureka Springs, Arkansas. Architect: Fay Jones & Associates]*

Figure C-36. **Composing a sequence of brightness levels.** *[Becton Dickinson and Co., corporate headquarters, Franklin Lakes, New Jersey. Architects: Kallmann, McKinnell & Wood. Photograph: © Steve Rosenthal]*

Figure C-37. **Brightness sequence in interior design.** *[Charles Square Hotel, Cambridge, Massachusetts. Architects: Cambridge Seven Associates. Photograph: © Steve Rosenthal]*

Figure C-38. **Lighting a transitional zone.** *[Saks Fifth Avenue, Palm Beach Mall, Palm Beach, Florida. Architect: James P. Ryan. Photograph: © Balthazar Korab]*

Figure C-39. **Poetics of light and shadows.** *[Foundling Hospital, Florence, Italy. Architect: Filippo Brunelleschi]*

Figure C-40. **Integration of spatial and lighting design.** *[KTMG Peat Marwick & Co., Detroit. Design: Quantum Design Group, Inc. Photo: © Glen Calvin Moon]*

Figure C-41. **Indirect lighting from visible fixtures.** *[Eliel Saarinen Studio, Bloomfield Hills, Michigan. Photograph: © Balthazar Korab]*

Figure C-42. **Indirect lighting for large public spaces.** *[Mill Woods Town Centre, Edmonton, Alberta, Canada. Architects: Designcorp Ltd., Wensley Webster Fry Architects, Ltd. Lighting Design: Sylvan R. Shemitz Associates, Inc. Photograph: Merle Prosofsky. Photograph courtesy of elliptipar, inc.]*

Figure C-43. **Lighting accents in spatial composition.** *[Bozell, Inc., Southfield, Michigan. Designer: Quantum Design Group, Inc. Photograph: © Glen Calvin Moon]*

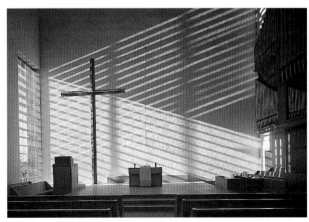

Figure C-44. **Sunlight animating the spatial envelope.** *[Sweeney Chapel, Christian Theological Seminary, Indianapolis. Architect: Edward Larrabee Barnes. Window Design: James Carpenter. Photograph: © Balthazar Korab]*

Figure C-45. **Ever-changing color patterns by sunlight.** *[Harvard Business School Chapel, Boston. Architect: Moshe Safdie and Associates. Photograph: © Steve Rosenthal]*

Figure C-46. **Accenting a zone of transition.** *[Hood Museum, Dartmouth College, Hanover, New Hampshire. Architects: Charles Moore with Chad Floyd of Centerbrook Architects. Photograph: © Steve Rosenthal]*

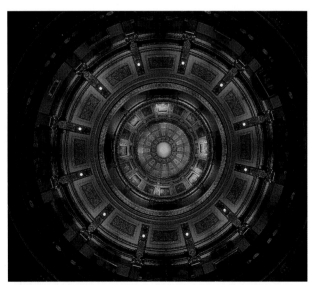

Figure C-47. **Lighting historical preservation.** *[Michigan State Capitol, Lansing. Restoration Architect: Richard Frank. Lighting Designer: Gary Steffy. Photograph: © Balthazar Korab]*

Figure C-48. **Tenebrism in interior design.** *[C. & H. Rauch Jewelers, Turfland Mall, Lexington, Kentucky. Architect: Kenneth J. Parr. Photographer: Doug Hedrich]*

Figure C-49. **Lighted forms in animated space.** *[Styling Dome, Chrysler Technical Center, Auburn Hills, Michigan. Architects: C.R.S.S. Lighting Designer: Stefan Graf. Photograph: © Balthazar Korab]*

Figure C-50. **Objects of light shaping subspaces.** *[Williams College Museum of Art, Williamstown, Massachusetts. Architects: Charles Moore and Robert L. Harper of Centerbrook Architects. Photograph: © Steve Rosenthal]*

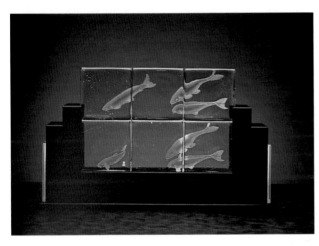

Figure C-51. **Edge lighting forms in space.** *[Peter David Studio, Seattle, Washington. Photographer: Steven Wall, Seattle, Washington. Photograph: Courtesy of Pittsburgh Corning Corporation]*

Figure C-52. **Apparent luminance in spatial connections.** *[Hood Museum, Dartmouth College, Hanover, New Hampshire. Architects: Charles Moore with Chad Floyd of Centerbrook Architects. Photograph: © Steve Rosenthal]*

Figure C-53. **Facade of low luminance heightening interior displays.** *[C. & H. Rauch Jewelers, Turfland Mall, Lexington, Kentucky. Architect: Kenneth J. Parr. Photographer: © Doug Hedrich]*

Figure C-54. **Alternating brightness levels to set up a visual objective.** *[Meditech, Canton, Massachusetts. Architects: Koetter, Kim and Associates, Inc. Photograph: © Steve Rosenthal]*

Figure C-55. **Art connection.** *[Detroit Institute of Arts. Designer: William Kessler. Photograph: © Balthazar Korab]*

Figure C-56. **Double connection.** *[Detroit Institute of Arts. Designer: William Kessler. Photograph: © Balthazar Korab]*

Figure C-57. Color screening color.

Figure C-58. Color dependency on size of opening of the screen.

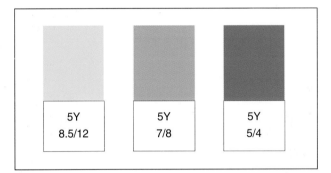

| 5Y 8.5/12 | 5Y 7/8 | 5Y 5/4 |

Figure C-59. Color change related to grille brightness. *Munsell color system.*

Figure C-60. Color testing fabrics under variable light.

Figure C-61. **Screening with patterns of brightness and color.** *[AT&T Town Pavilion, Kansas City, Missouri. Architects: HNTB Photographer: Bob Shimer, © Hedrich-Blessing]*

Figure C-62. **Layering of screened spaces.** *[Meditech, Canton, Massachusetts. Architects: Koetter, Kim and Associates, Inc. Photograph: © Steve Rosenthal]*

Figure C-63. **Design for specialized concept.** *[IBM, Purchase, New York. Architect: I. M. Pei and Partners. Photograph: © Steve Rosenthal]*

Figure C-64. **Visual centers created by focal accents.** *[Medical Building, Rochester, New York. Courtesy: Lithonia Lighting, Conyers, Georgia. Photograph: Rion Rizzo, Creative Sources Photography, Inc., Atlanta, Georgia]*

Figure C-65. **Composition of brightness and color in subdued spatial light.** *[BP America, Inc., corporate headquarters, Cleveland. Architects: HOK Photograph: Bill Mathis]*

Figure C-66. **Focal center of images suspended in space.** ["Fisherman's Memorial," proposal model for Port of Seattle, Peter David Studio, Seattle. Photographer: Steven Wall, Seattle]

Figure C-67. **Bright focal center as spatial transition.** [The Temple of RLDS, Independence, Missouri. Architects: HOK Photograph: © Balthazar Korab]

Figures C-68 and C-69. **Programming mood by colored light.** [Private residence. Architects: McLarand, Vasquez & Partners, Inc. Neon Designer: Eric Zimmerman. Photograph: Eric Figge. Courtesy: Pittsburgh Corning Corporation]

Figure C-70. **Silhouetting forms in colored space.** [*Private residence. Architects: McLarand, Vasquez & Partners, Inc. Neon Designer: Eric Zimmerman. Photograph: Eric Figge. Courtesy: Pittsburgh Corning Corporation*]

Figure C-71. **Color extension for spaciousness.** [*Chestnut Place, Worcester, Massachusetts. Architects: Perry Dean Rogers and Partners. Photograph: © Steve Rosenthal*]

Figure C-72. **Framing a visual sequence.** [*"Treasure Houses of Britain," National Gallery of Art, Washington, D.C. Architect: National Gallery of Art, Design Department. Photographer: William Schaeffer. Photograph: Cooper Lighting*]

Figure C-73. **Distributing focal centers in sequence.** [*"Treasure Houses of Britain," National Gallery of Art, Washington, D.C. Photographer: William Schaeffer. Photograph: National Gallery of Art*]

Part 3: Designing with Space and Light

CHAPTER 11

Lighting the Spatial Envelope

The starlight was so full that I distinctly saw not only the bay with its multitude of glittering bergs, but most of the lower portions of the glaciers, lying pale and spirit-like amid the huge silent mountains. The nearest glacier in particular was so distinct that it seemed to be glowing with light that came from within itself. Not even in dark nights have I ever found any difficulty in seeing large glaciers; but on this mountain-top, amid so much ice, in the heart of so clear and frosty a night, everything was luminous, and I seemed to be poised in a vast hollow between two skies of equal brightness.

—*John Muir*
"The Discovery of Glacier Bay"
*Wilderness Essays**

A room is given volume by structural members and interior partitions, and is colored and textured by surfacing materials. It receives daylight through windows, skylights, or openings to adjacent spaces, and electric support lighting from manufactured sources. The occupant then moves in with an assortment of interior furnishings. Architect, engineer, interior designer, lighting designer, and owner all play their hand to influence the final outcome. Each profession influences and sometimes counterinfluences the work of one or more of the others.

As it was analyzed in Part 2, the spatial envelope is a primary tool for spatial design. It also provides an operative framework for analyzing and controlling the lighting of space. As a basic frame of reference, the spatial envelope gives all design-related professionals a common denominator for the development and refinement of the architectural environment. Its dominant boundaries become essential control planes, because their relatively large surface areas are those on which the major action of reflected light occurs. After the installation of lighting and finish surfacing materials, the consequent color and brightness values are composed, and the interaction of space and light takes place. Once constructed and illuminated, the visual array of the surrounding major boundaries then becomes the backdrop for freestanding objects and other decorative furnishings, creating new spatial relationships of color and brightness.

It is easiest to understand the interaction of architectural space and light by first working with the volume of a simple room. Beginning thoughts for lighting its space should focus on *how the dominant boundaries will receive light*. Most of the time the boundaries are prominent in the field of view, and as they convey the

---

* Muir, John. 1980. The Discovery of Glacier Bay. In *Wilderness Essays*. Salt Lake City: Peregrine Smith, Inc., pp. 23–24.

effects of light, their colors and textures will be rendered on a scale of brightness from dim to very bright, and are therefore consequential to the overall appearance of a room and its mood. Therefore, decision making should focus on how the surfaces of the dominant boundaries of space are to appear in color and brightness, and the illumination quantity, quality, and locations of the light sources should be selected to achieve design goals.

The Entry of Daylight

For all architectural spaces whose envelopes are penetrated by any opening to the exterior environment, lighting design begins with recognition of the entry of daylight.[1] It is a first consideration because the presence of daylight in an interior strongly influences spatial perception and also changes the color of surfacing materials in terms of how they appear elsewhere in the room under a number of different kinds of electric illumination.

Lighting the spatial envelope of an interior space that receives both natural and electric light is complex and challenging. The immediate problems stem from the mix of different qualities of illumination, and from the fact that wherever sizable openings of windows or glass walls penetrate the spatial boundaries, there is often the dilemma of preventing light from reaching surfaces where it is not wanted. If daylight is to penetrate any of the spatial boundaries, the designers involved can resort to one or more of four basic measures for handling its appearance at the openings:

1. It can be blocked out completely (in the case of remodeling an existing structure).

2. It can be redirected by intentionally placed reflecting panels or other major surfaces.

3. It can be diffused by the type of glass or plastic through which it passes.

4. It can be screened with decorative architectural grilles.

The amount of sunlight reflected about an interior is determined by the size and shape of apertures in the spatial envelope—*as they relate to the proportions of a room.* Direct daylight will penetrate deeper into a room the higher the top of the window is above the floor. Tests made at the Texas Engineering Experiment Station demonstrated the distribution of daylight that enters

rooms of varying lengths and ceiling heights under an overcast sky. Figure 11-1 shows diagrams of that study, adapted from drawings published by Benjamin Evans (1981, 59). The left row of graphs shows daylight entering a long, rectangular room having windows only at one end and their top located at the height of the ceiling. Evans determined that when the ceiling height is dropped from 14 to 12 feet, the reduction in the vertical size of window opening decreases the illumination entering the back of the room by 19%. When the ceiling was lowered to 8 feet, illumination at the back of the room was reduced by 63%. The row of graphs at the right shows changes that occur when the window opening and ceiling height stay constant, but the room varies in length. An 18% reduction of daylight occurs when the depth of the room is increased from 24 to 28 feet, and 28% when the room is increased to 32 feet. As the sun moves, the total spatial envelope undergoes gradual transformation. The singular boundaries change in brightness relationships, depending on the proportions of the space, the reflectance (color and texture) of the boundaries, their respective angle of slant to the incoming light, and the quantity of sunlight. *How each wall, ceiling, and floor appears in interrelated brightness comprises the starting conditions for creating lighted space when daylight is a part of the total illumination.*

Spurred by the energy conservation movement of the past half century, architects, engineers, and lighting consultants have adapted building design to direct sunlight into today's interiors. An opaque ceiling of relatively high reflectance can serve as an indirect light source when it receives ample quantities of sunlight. This can be achieved by exterior and interior lightshelves, and by prism panels that can send daylight into interior space at specific angles. Unless the ceiling is covered with a mirror or other specular surface that sometimes appears in contemporary interior design, sunlight reflected off a bright, matte ceiling is usually glare-free, and spreads a soft, ambient light about the room. Numerous schemes for the design of exterior walls to bring daylight into the interior await the architect's imagination and application.[2]

Exterior elevations can be designed to reflect daylight into the interior and shade wall glazing at the same time. This was done in the energy-saving design of the Blue Cross and Blue Shield of Connecticut Building (Figures 11-2 and 11-3). This is the same atrium discussed earlier (see Figure 9-11). A long south elevation of the building is oriented toward the sun, and projecting floors step outward to reduce solar heat gain during the summer

---

[1] For excellent texts of general principles and application of daylighting related to architectural design, see J. A. Lynes (1968), Benjamin Evans (1981), M. David Egan (1983), Fuller Moore (1985), and William M. C. Lam (1986).

[2] For principles and guidelines to bring sunlight into the interior, see William M. C. Lam (1986), Chapter 6: "Sidelighting: Strategies, Techniques, Devices, and Forms," particularly the section "Using the Ceiling as the Principal Source of Reflected Light."

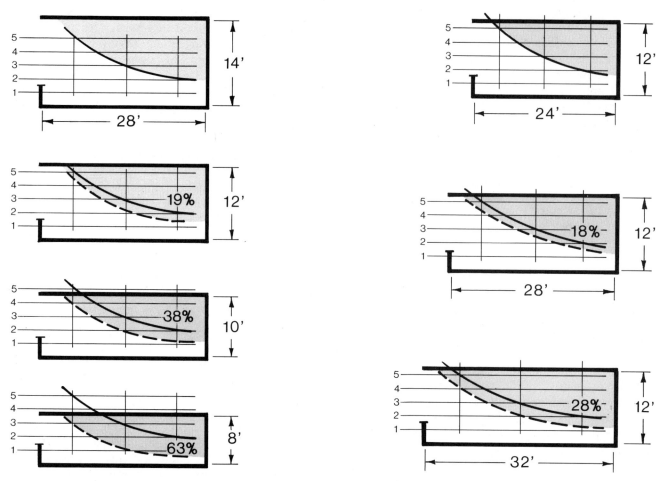

Figure 11-1. Daylight reaching into interior space. The extent to which daylight will penetrate into a room depends on the height and size of the window in relation to the proportions of the room. [After Evans, Benjamin. 1981. Daylight in Architecture. Architectural Record, *pp. 57, 59. © McGraw-Hill, Inc. All rights reserved. Reproduced with the permission of the publisher.]*

months by shading the windows below. The structure of the south elevation incorporates horizontal light-shelves at each floor to reflect sunlight into the peripheral spaces after it reflects a second time off interior ceilings. Lightshelves were also placed in the interior along the length of the atrium to reflect sunlight arriving from the clerestory. The atrium's angled roof functions in the same way as the perimeter office ceilings, first receiving sunlight reflected off horizontal surfaces outside, then redirecting it into the central open space below.

The fundamental problem of illuminating interiors with light from a moving sun while the building remains in a stationary position continues to bring about technological solutions. The ground floor of the atrium of Morgan Hall at the Harvard Business School (Figure 11-4) receives reflected light throughout the day and year. The atrium is four stories tall and only 12 feet wide. A computerized daylighting and mechanical system takes photo-

metric readings of the floor, tracks the path of the sun, and rotates four reflector panels above the skylight at angles to direct daylight down into the atrium. Available daylight always reaches the floor, even in winter when the sun is low. In the heat of summer, the panels are programmed to shade the sun. Between the structural piers and above the fascias of the lower floors are interior reflecting panels at the sides of the atrium. They are designed to return reflected daylight upward to illuminate the soffits and ceilings of the offices around the space.

Perhaps the most difficult task for the lighting and interior designer is that of adding manufactured light to spaces pronouncedly illuminated by daylight. Even where large work spaces are bounded by exterior glass walls, supplemental task lighting is still needed to augment the incoming daylight. Mixing natural and electric light means mixing color of light, which changes the surface color values of interior walls, floor, and ceiling.

Figure 11-2. Daylighting for energy conservation. [Blue Cross and Blue Shield of Connecticut Building, North Haven, Connecticut. Architects: Ellenzweig Associates, Inc., Cambridge, Massachusetts. Photograph: © Steve Rosenthal]

In cases like the examples analyzed by Benjamin Evans (Figure 11-1), where long rooms receive natural light from windows only at one end (the front, for example), the side walls will be illuminated by natural light in the front of the room and electric light at the back. If incandescent lighting is used as the supplementary illumination, the portions of wall in the middle and back of the room will appear yellowish compared with areas in front illuminated by the whiter daylight. But thanks to *color constancy* in visual perception, the mind will compensate for colors that the eye sees, and the surfaces under the yellow-reflected light will be perceived as white. Depending on their color-rendering properties, fluorescent lamps can approximate the appearance of

natural light, eliminating the tints from incandescent light. If the windows are glazed with tinted glass, further modifications of color are introduced in the room. In conditions where major sectors of a room are illuminated by different colored lights, architectural articulation of the spatial envelope is an option for creating demarcation corners or steps where the meeting of natural and electric light generally takes place. Selections of interior surfacing materials and location of furnishings and wall hangings must take into account these factors of mixing daylight and manufactured illumination. It is for these reasons that lighting the spatial envelope begins with considerations of whether or not natural light will be present.

Section

1. Atrium
2. Light monitor
3. Office area
4. Mechanical equipment room

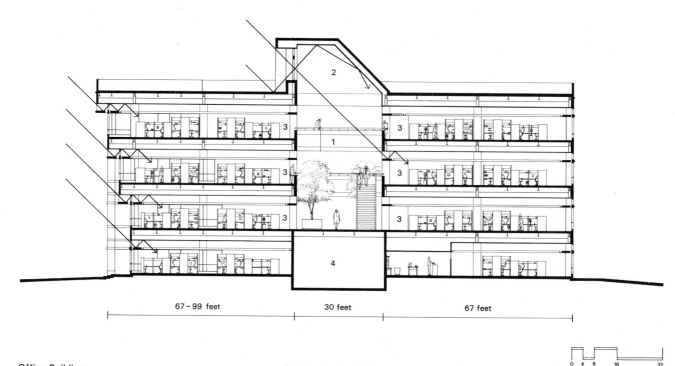

67 – 99 feet   30 feet   67 feet

Office Building   Section Looking West
Blue Cross and Blue Shield of Connecticut

0   4   8   16   32

Figure 11-3. Reflected daylight for interior illumination. [Blue Cross and Blue Shield of Connecticut Building, North Haven, Connecticut. Architects: Ellenzweig Associates, Inc., Cambridge, Massachusetts. Drawing: Ellenzweig Associates, Inc.]

Figure 11-5 on page 178 shows a gallery of the Kimbell Art Museum. A cycloid roof system and reflector panel over the galleries were developed to admit natural light, as requested by the museum director. A 2½-ft-wide skylight strip penetrates the length of the cycloid. Direct sunlight enters through that opening and strikes a linear reflector, which returns some of the light to the underside of the concrete vault, where bright daylight is converted to soft ambient light that spreads throughout the space below. The impact of reflected light on the cycloid curves is enormous, as revealed by photographs of the space before and after installation of the reflector.[3] Figure 11-5 illustrates the harmonious luminances of the total spatial envelope, with each boundary rendered in similar zones of brightness as measured on the LBR Scale. Balanced

light, however, especially on the works of art in the center of the gallery, was not easy to achieve. Daily and seasonal changes in the angles that daylight enters the space required a sophisticated design for the reflector, which was developed through a series of mock-up model tests and on-site experiments. The reflector had to be transparent. If not, very little sunlight would have reached its underside, making it appear as a dark strip as contrasted against the cycloid surface (compare the darker linear frame in its center). Furthermore, it would have blocked daylight from reaching exhibits directly underneath. The reflector was made from thin aluminum sheeting punctured by closely spaced 0.050-inch holes on 3/32-inch staggered centers. That allowed a greater proportion of the light entering through the skylight to be reflected back up on the vault's surface, while a portion of it sifts downward through the perforations in the reflector to illuminate the center of the space. Reflected

[3] Photographs of a Kimbell gallery before and after installation of the reflector are published in Marshall Meyers (1979, 62).

Figure 11-4. Tracking the sun. [Morgan Hall, Harvard Business School, Boston. Architect: Moshe Safdie and Associates. Photograph: © Steve Rosenthal]

daylight also enters the linear subspace seen to the right in the photograph, which is supplemented by electric light from canisters on the overhead ceiling. Electric support lighting is also located down the length of the reflector to add supplemental lighting for the exhibits, and to enhance the center of the gallery at night and on overcast days.

Lighting the Walls

Because of their customary role in shaping major sections of the spatial envelope, walls require special attention for the way they receive light. Their overall appearance is important for spatial clarity, and, as we will see, their brightness contributes to feelings of enclosure and spaciousness. As the dominant vertical boundaries of space, they are also the visual surround for furnishings and activities in a room, so their color and brightness are the background against which luminance ratios are measured for any elements considered to be in a figure-ground relationship with the walls. In the general practice of architectural and lighting design, illumination of

the walls usually results from a few basic categories of lighting techniques.

Walls often receive their light from a long-standing conventional method for illuminating interiors known as *general lighting*. In large public environments with ceilings under 14 feet high, general lighting usually calls for rows or other patterns of regularly spaced fluorescent lamps behind glass or plastic diffusers, either suspended from or inset flush with the ceiling. HID sources, particularly metal halide lamps, are better suited for spaces having ceiling heights significantly higher than 14 feet. The number of luminaires and their locations are calculated to spread uniform lighting throughout the space. The IESNA handbook (Rea, 1993, 460ff) publishes "Illuminance Categories and Illuminance Values for Generic Types of Activities in Interiors," which provides ranges of illuminances for a variety of residential, commercial, institutional, and public assembly interiors. Using the method of general lighting, walls of the spatial envelope receive approximately even amounts of light, so brightness differences result from choices of color, texture, and reflectance of the surfaces.

When illumination strikes a surface, the luminance that results depends on the reflectance of the furnishing materials. For general room lighting, the IESNA advises that walls be surfaced with materials of 50% to 70% reflectance, and other interior vertical partitions should reflect between 40% and 70%. How do those reflecting surfaces appear in brightness? Using the LBR Scale as a guide, materials within those reflectance ranges will appear brighter than middle gray, zone V (Munsell N6), which is 30% reflectance. Partitions enclosing workstations should be surfaced with materials that are matte in surface finish to avoid discomforting glare in the immediate vicinity of the workers. Because general room lighting sends illumination to *all* surfaces in a room, reflectances of materials become important for how they contribute to color and brightness composition. That is acceptable for many kinds of architectural spaces, but keep in mind such even distribution of lighting may not have the greatest aesthetic appeal. Control of brightness on the walls is critical to the success of lighting design for architectural space, especially as it relates to human comfort. When overlighted and large in surface area, bright walls of working interiors can cause discomfort for the workers. R. L. Oetting (1971) described a 1945 study, which demonstrated how walls of high reflectance and under full illumination created serious visual problems when workers looked up from office tasks and bright walls entered the field of view. In such situations the retina fills with additional high levels of reflected light, increasing eye fatigue already initiated by prolonged staring at paperwork and other bright objects on desks and tables.

Figure 11-5. Spatial definition by reflected light. [Kimbell Art Museum, Fort Worth, Texas. Architect: Louis I. Kahn]

Instead of illuminating the entire room with general room lighting, which affects almost all surfaces of the spatial envelope, *wall-washing* (Figure 11-6) is a method of lighting the vertical spatial boundaries by bathing them with light cast downward from shielded or diffused sources at the ceiling plane. The IESNA defines wall-washing as illumination that "provides greater luminance of the wall than of the ceiling." Wall-washing should not be confused with *accent lighting,* which directs light to selected targets, or features shapes of light composed in the overall space. Linear illumination is normal for wall washing, but when fluorescent light is used, eight to nine feet of vertical surface is a maximum height for effective application of this technique. This is due to the inverse square law, as luminance falls off with distance from the light source, gradually reducing brightness downward on the wall. The upper two feet receives 80% of the light from a source near the ceiling, the middle to lower wall 50%, and the area near the floor only around 20%. This fading off of light is acceptable in most cases. Interior furnishings usually occlude visibility of the lower wall where that 20% of reflected light is located. The brightest areas are the middle to upper walls, and those less obstructed surfaces are the ones that mostly influence perception of the spatial envelope.

In situations where the lower walls generally will remain exposed, fluorescent wall-washing is not recommended for vertical surfaces higher than nine feet, which would leave too much proportional lower wall area relegated to lifelessness.

There are guidelines to be considered when designing with wall-washing. For ceilings of 9 feet high, the luminaires need to be located $2\frac{1}{2}$ to 3 feet out from the wall to prevent hot spots from appearing on the wall immediately below them. The lamps should be screened with diffusing panels, especially when the wall will be seen most often at angles where the light sources are visible. Wall-washing is recommended for matte surfaces only. It can create problems when used on surfaces of specular reflection, such as plastic laminates, polished stone, metals, or other glossy materials, all of which are prone to reflect the image of the light source or its diffusing panel. Note the effects on the walls of Figure 11-6.

Wall-washing is a good application for commercial interiors. Higher brightness of the peripheral walls adds to the spaciousness of a store. It also attracts shoppers to the outer display walls by heightening the presence of merchandise, which can be seen over the lower sales counters in the central areas of the store. Illumination on the outer walls will also emphasize manufacturer's

Figure 11-6. Washing walls with light. [Apple Market Center, Infomart, Dallas]

or merchandise signage, which serves as orientation for shoppers. When wall-washing is used on peripheral or interior sales walls, once again the distance of the luminaires out from the wall is critical. If the light sources are too close to the wall, they are ineffective for some retail sales purposes. Many products are large, such as large equipment or mannequins displaying clothing, and parts of them can fall outside the descending illumination. Moreover, shoppers remove articles from shelves for close examination and to read labels, and the product then might be seen outside the illumination washing the wall. In most commercial settings, wall-washing requires support lighting in the interior of the room.

Professional articles have been written on the merits of wall-washing, and some writers contend such surfaces are visually uninteresting, lacking the dramatics that accent lighting can provide. The designer must be cautious of that kind of reasoning. A monotone wall of evenly balanced wall-washing does indeed lack interest, but that can be its greatest advantage. An evenly washed wall rarely is left as a singular surface to be seen for its own sake. The balanced spread of illumination by wall-washing is an excellent method of creating a visual ground at a controlled brightness level for walls that are intended to feature photographs, graphics, or other

decorative elements. The wall itself therefore should be visually uninteresting, as a noncompeting architectural surface. The even illumination that wall-washing provides allows for wall hangings and other decor to be changed from time to time, without having to conform to a fixed lighting pattern like permanently recessed scallop downlighting. Wall-washing is appropriate for walls surfaced with high-quality woods, elegant fabrics, or other overall embellishment, to feature those decorative qualities without the interference of accent lighting.

Related to wall-washing is *wall-grazing* (Figure 11-7), a technique that emphasizes the textural qualities of stone, wood, brick, fabrics, and vinyls. Falling on the wall directly from above, illumination animates the surface with highlights and shadows. Wall-grazing is best achieved with point light sources, but is possible with linear sources as well. Most frequently used is incandescent, HID, or fluorescent light. Fluorescent luminaires need to have top reflectors, specifically designed for downlighting. Incandescent sources need to be spaced close enough to each other to illuminate the wall evenly. It is recommended that the luminaires mounted in or at the ceiling be within 12 inches of the wall, where their light can be directed straight down. Because of that downward direction of light, wall-grazing is *not* recommended for plain walls that suffer from flaws of poor

Figure 11-7. Wall-grazing in spatial composition. [Worshipers Path, The Temple of RLDS, Independence, Missouri. Architects: HOK]

craftsmanship, such as unevenness of faulty gypboard finishing.

Wall-grazing to bring out the qualities of a wall's texture was done effectively in the "Worshipers Path" (Figure 11-7) in The Temple of RLDS in Independence, Missouri. Light scintillates over the textured stone wall and brings out its natural beauty in a way that no other decor on its surface is necessary. The design shows how wall-grazing can be composed with other support lighting in the same space. The decorative luminance of the grazing and the graceful curvature of the stone wall are spatially balanced by the subspace on the left, illuminated to feature the wooden cross and cast its shadow through which worshipers walk. The animated surface of the textured wall is answered by the gravel and rock in the alcove and by the rough-hewn surface of the cross. The rhythmic composition of light and shadows makes the corridor spatially interesting and inspirational. The shape of the spatial envelope and the distribution of luminances mutually interact to create a pleasant flow of objects and surfaces in spatial balance.

Lighting walls of large public spaces involves many of the same principles of lighting small spaces, but the difference is size of the volume normally calls for greater architectural articulation of the spatial envelope due to the proportionally larger areas of visible boundaries. Figure 11-8a and b show the atrium of a hotel where contin-

uous wrap-around balconies articulate the vertical surfaces, and contain the horizontal circulation paths to and from the elevators (left). The two photographs illustrate the different effects of day and night lighting. At both times, the vertical boundaries benefit from the cantilevered balcony floors and ceilings, which are principal light-reflecting surfaces that contribute to the basic character of the space. A skylight illuminates the atrium in daytime hours (Figure 11-8a), and the ground floor is illuminated like a patio out-of-doors. The projecting floors and ceilings of the balconies reflect daylight in linear patterns that sweep around the entire space. The alternating horizontal strips of highlight and shadow animate the vertical boundaries, and randomly placed planter boxes provide further articulation of the envelope. The balconies also shade the windows and doors of the rooms beneath them during daytime hours.

Figure 11-8b shows the same atrium illuminated at night, when a significant difference is made by the electric lighting. As they did in daylight, the ceilings and floors of the balconies again reflect light, but at night the door lamps of the rooms create rhythms of pointillistic highlights around the space. The lamps and their reflections on the ceilings above activate the entire spatial envelope in a visual dance of light. Collectively the door lamps give the atrium an appearance of a small village illuminated by street lights. Here again, light and space inter-

(a)

(b)

Figure 11-8. Daylight versus electric lighting in an atrium. (a) Day and (b) night. [Embassy Suites, Overland Park, Kansas]

act. The envelope is animated by light composed on spatial boundaries already structurally articulated. The vertical boundaries of the space create a pleasant and attractive setting for the enjoyment of people relaxing in the lounge. At night, the darkened sky outside is replicated by the black atrium ceiling, against which the brightness contrast of the uppermost balcony roof appears like a framing cornice for the wrap-around facade.

The two photographs also make an interesting study of daylight versus electric light reflections. In the day view, the door lamps are turned on just as they are in the night view, but their reflections on the balcony walls and ceilings are washed out by the powerful reflected sunlight. Yet the door lamps remain as points of light, set back from the lines of reflected daylight on the over-hanging balcony edges.

Ceilings of Light

Like walls of a room, the ceiling is a major boundary of the spatial envelope, but its design brings about a different set of issues to be faced and problems to be solved. Its importance for spatial design lies in the fact that it is unobstructed by interior furnishings that normally occlude the lower sections of the envelope as seen from most viewing angles. Because of its prominent visibility, it needs to be coordinated with the overall architectural and lighting design.

The upper portions of the spatial envelope most often are the locations of the light sources. If they are visible and exceptionally bright, they attract or distract human vision and draw attention to the ceiling. A major decision of consequence is that of determining *to what extent the ceiling should become a visually active—or perhaps the most active—boundary of the spatial envelope*. Architectural and lighting designers need to stay in control of the composition of brightness relationships that are created for this all important boundary of interior space, including the appearance of the light sources and the surfaces they illuminate.

It has become standard practice to use general room lighting for many architectural environments, and in the 1950s and 1960s, *luminous ceilings* often characterized offices, retail stores, and other public spaces. That term refers to the lighting practice of placing a number of luminaires behind a continuous ceiling of light-diffusing material, collectively spreading a vast "sea of light" over the entire space. In such cases, many surfaces received light where it was unnecessary, and unnecessarily high operating and maintenance costs prevailed. Throughout the last half century, many work and other public spaces have been covered by ceilings dominated by rows or patterns of fluorescent fixtures, which in many cases also flood the total environment with light.

Frequently found in contemporary interiors are ceilings dominated by visible light soures. An analysis of lighting the ceiling plane begins with the reminder that *any exposed source of illumination will be an extremely prominent element in a visual field*. Excluding views to bright daylight, the lenses of electric light sources are most often the brightest elements in a room, and are potential sources of glare. Remember, brightness, contrast, and rich pattern are three of the highest stimuli in the hierarchy of focal accents that attract or distract human vision (see Chapter 4, p. 62), and patterns of fluorescent or incandescent lights embrace all three of those accents simultaneously. Any lighting system whose overall layout is a preponderance of exposed light sources surrounded by contrasting opaque surfaces will render the ceiling as an eye-attracting array of light.

How many ways can types and locations of lighting be composed at the ceiling plane? The reader is directed to an article on the aesthetics of ceiling lighting by Der Scutt (1972), who provided a feast of photographic illustrations showing a variety of illuminated architectural spaces and patterns of light sources in public work areas. Der Scutt discusses those examples in terms of visual boredom, eye fatigue, glare reduction, linear effects, scale, and other design fundamentals. Some of the illustrations show distributions of light sources that draw attention to the ceiling plane; other arrangements do not, but still provide good task lighting.

Indirect lighting is a method for reflecting illumination off the ceiling or other surface. When painted or surfaced with a relatively bright material (high on the LBR Scale) and washed with indirect illumination, the ceiling of a room appears to glow, and the room below fills with soft ambient light. In rooms illuminated only by indirect lighting, there are no bright light sources in any field of view, and there are no harsh shadows. This method of reflected ceiling illumination is more applicable to small rooms, and in many such spaces, no other illumination is necessary. In context of lighting the total spatial envelope, it is important to control the luminances of the walls and floor as they receive overhead indirect lighting. The soft ambient light created by indirect lighting is preferred for some offices and other small work rooms. The softer and uniform wall luminances provide good background for VDTs, as long as the surfaces are neutral in color.

The overhead cove in the main lobby of an accounting firm (Figure C-40) is indirectly illuminated by linear sources, and its luminance is worked into the lighting composition of the total space. Supplemental lighting is provided by the recessed downlights that accent the walls with broad-beam scallops. The two sconces brighten the piers separating the windows, and send uplighting to brighten the underside of the beams. Light reflected off the floor returns to illuminate the ceiling surfaces framing the cove, reducing luminance contrast that would overemphasize the brightness of the curved surface. The fabric wall covering and painted ceiling components are all of similar color value. It is the articulated shape of the spatial envelope and the locations of the light sources that integrate space and light in the scene.

Figure C-41 shows another indirectly illuminated coved ceiling, but the row of suspended visible fixtures adds supplemental lighting that accents the spatial sequence. The cove receives uplighting from the suspended fixtures, and its curvature returns reflected light downward to softly wash the walls. The spatial envelope is architecturally more simplified than Figure C-40, but is articulated by the lighting fixtures, carpeting, and furniture. The effects of light differ significantly from the previous example due to the presence of the carpet, which prevents specular reflections on the floor.

A lighting technique normally associated with walls and specialized installations is *track lighting,* but such systems introduce design problems related to the ceiling. Unless camouflaged, the track itself and its visible fixtures increase visual stimuli at the ceiling plane, often adding to an overload array that also includes vents, sprinkler systems, audio speakers, and other mechanical and structural elements. Manufacturers have produced numerous track systems and visible fixtures designed to serve as decorative elements in their own right, but

Figure 11-9. Concealing light sources in the field of view. [*Courtesy: ALKCO Lighting*]

"look-at-me" exposed fixtures draw attention to themselves, and consequently become prominent features attracting attention to the ceiling. They either contribute to or deteriorate the total spatial aesthetic. In many installations, a flock of luminaires seems to hang from the ceiling like bats in a nesting haven; their contrasting shapes and contours seen in front of the ceiling plane make them more prominent than the display they are illuminating. All too often an error in the choice of track luminaire is a result of the perennial problem of "decision making in the abstract," i.e., by selecting luminaires as pictured in advertising literature, without regard for how they will be perceived as collective elements in spatial design, not just as visible fixture design.

As an alternative to exposed track lighting, the development of *recessed track systems* (Figure 11-9) has made it possible to conceal the actual luminaires and their supporting track inside a thin linear opening at the ceiling plane. Hidden behind the dark opening, luminaires on the recessed track can be fitted with a variety of lamps and lenses to cast different beam spreads of light into the environment below. They can shape scallops or other light patterns on the vertical surfaces, wall-wash part or all of the spatial envelope, or spotlight objects in the interior of space—all of this can be achieved with the entire lighting system appearing as little more than a dark linear strip at the ceiling. The intense brightness or glare of the light sources is nearly all removed from the visual field. Recessed track systems make it possible to treat all environmental service systems as design ele-

ments. The lines of recessed tracks can be harmonized with other linear elements of both ceiling and walls, such as structural edges, moldings, other strip openings for HVAC, etc., to bring into harmony the meeting of wall and ceiling by coordinating surface detailing, and at the same time articulate the boundaries of space. Pinhole downlighting is the same principle, created by specially designed luminaires recessed in the ceiling behind an aperture only about 2 inches in diameter. The light source is nearly hidden from view, and a series of downlights can be composed in illuminated ceiling patterns.

Chapter 9 discussed how the structural system of a building can be designed to articulate the overhead enclosure of the spatial envelope. Lighting the patterns created by a structural system further animates the ceiling plane, and can be done inexpensively when economical illumination is combined with good architectural design. This was achieved in the central space of the Priory Chapel Abbey of St. Mary and St. Louis (Figure 11-10). At night, the design of the dome is economically enhanced by fluorescent lighting mounted at the base of the upper level windows. The soft reflected light spreads over the entire worship area below. A synthesis of the pattern of light and the structural pattern of the dome creates a spiritual canopy hovering over the heads of worshipers.

The overhead cover of malls and other large public spaces is often a configuration of structural patterns. Lighting needs to coordinated with the structural system and the overall spatial composition. Over the central space of the mall shown in Figure C-42, a barrel vault

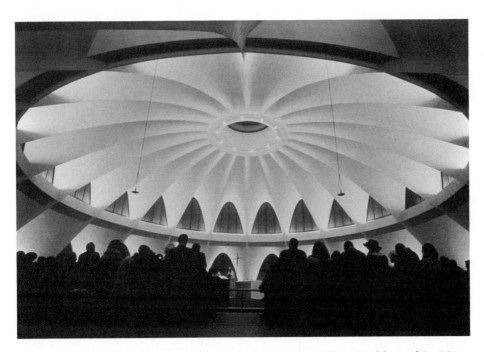

Figure 11-10. Lighting structural articulation. [Priory Chapel Abbey of St. Mary and St. Louis, St. Louis, Missouri. Architects: HOK. Photograph: George Silk]

is the major space-defining boundary and is illuminated by 400-W metal-halide lamps mounted in sconces on the upper fascias paralleling the base of the vault. The luminaires are designed to spread broad beams of illumination, which reflect on the structural units above. The geometric patterns of truss work and roof panels are bright enough to provide spatial definition, but their luminances do not take precedence over the independently illuminated and brightly colored shops below.

Because the ceiling is a vital area for controlling the mood of space, the conceptual purpose (see Chapter 14) for which a room is created is the basis for all design decisions related to that uppermost boundary. Consider a court of law, which requires serenity and dignity. Figure 11-11 shows a state judicial center, and the formal design of the room states its purpose and seriousness. Finished in fine woods and illuminated by fluorescent rim lighting from above, stepped walnut panels draw attention to and serve as background for the seats of honor. Mercury vapor downlighting is concentrated on the tasks of attorneys and those they represent, and also highlights the seating of the justices, which prevents them from appearing in silhouette against the reflected fluorescent light on the background vertical panels. It is lighting above the spectators' seating that warrants special analysis. Overhead fluorescent light is screened by small delicate cells of closely spaced walnut wood blocks joined by thin aluminum webs. The walnut used for this section of ceiling harmonizes with the wooden vertical

panels below, and the illumination filtering through the cells softly reflects off the dark wood as seen from anywhere in the room. The porous ceiling also helps absorb spectator noises, and its screened light serves as an *impassive supplement* to the overall lighting design of the room. There is no forceful brightness attracting attention to the ceiling. Judges and attorneys receive the attention. The sensitive control of light distributed about the total spatial envelope has produced an environment appropriate to the functions of the room, a room illuminated not for dramatics, but for solemnity.

Lighting Accents on the Spatial Envelope

When the walls of space are evenly illuminated by general room lighting or wall-washing, decorative articulation of the spatial envelope normally is done by graphics, paintings, wall hangings, or overall decorative surfacing. Another means for accenting the spatial envelope is by *patterns of light,* composed in space as independent design accents or in combination with architectural articulation of the boundaries.

For special lighting effects, decorative patterns of brightness can be formed by beam spreads creating *scallops* or other shapes of light. Figure C-43 shows the main presentation room of an advertising firm, where accent lighting was coordinated with that of the entire room. On the walls are scallops that are both functional and decorative. They are separated enough—spatially—from images on the projection screen on the far wall, while accenting the side walls in a balanced composition of brightnesses. Luminance of the two linear strips of indirect lighting makes a good transition in brightness for the merger of walls and ceiling. Overhead, a pattern of recessed downlights provides task lighting for the conference table. The wall scallops are functional, illuminating the table-height presentation shelves along the sides. The narrow wooden strips on the walls are secondary presentation shelves, which when needed, fold down to accommodate additional display materials. The secondary shelves partake in the linearity of the room, creating perspective lines that converge on the slide screen. In this well-designed space, lighting accents contribute to the articulation of the spatial envelope.

A series of scallops as accent lighting adds pattern to a space, and each pattern added increases visual complexity of the scene. When a certain point is reached, multiple patterns compete and spatial clarity is jeopardized. Accent lighting, therefore, is to be used judiciously. If the wall to be illuminated is already architecturally detailed, decorative lighting needs to be

Figure 11-11. Ceiling light as impassive supplement. [Supreme Court Room, Kansas Judicial Center, Topeka. Architects: Kiene and Bradley Design Group]

Designing with Space and Light

coordinated with that detailing. *The composition of scallops or any other light patterns should conform to the design elements of the spatial boundaries.*

The scallop shape is created by a point light source casting a conical beam of light by a luminaire normally housed at or recessed in the ceiling or some other overhead horizontal plane. Some luminaires are adjustable to change the angle and shape of the scallop cast on the wall. The edge of the beam spread is called the *cutoff.* The cutoff can be sharp, creating a crisp parabolic shape, or its edge can be softened by PAR lamps or a diffusing lens in the luminaire. When multiple relecting (MR) lamps are used, a variegated pattern of reflections appears near the vertex and the cutoff creating a more decorative scallop.

Manufacturers produce a variety of luminaires designed to cast different angular dimensions of scallop beam spreads, from narrow to broad. Their catalog descriptions, beam spread diagrams, and mounting instructions should be consulted. When used to feature a piece of artwork on the wall, the size of the scallop must be greater than the size of the object or image it illuminates, so that corners or other edges of the piece are not cut off by the darker surround.

It should be remembered that scallops or other lighting accents on the walls add light to a major component of the spatial envelope, and the designer must be cognizant of the difference between animating the walls with decorative hangings or doing so with light—or both. By themselves, scallops are a viable means for articulating the total spatial envelope, as long as it is kept in mind that a pattern of light is a decoration. It is a "painting" on the wall as a composition of light images, as well as being a technique to illuminate objects appendant to the walls.

When scallops are used as design accents, the question arises of how bright they will appear as images of light on a given surface. The LBR System provides guidance for determining a scallop's contrast with whatever color and brightness of the surfacing material on which the image is cast. It may at first seem that a lighting accent will look brighter on a dark surface than it will on a lighter one, but the opposite is true. A demonstration was constructed in the lighting laboratory to cast an identical beam spread and illumination intensity on the nine Munsell surfaces of the LBR Scale (Figure 11-12). The effectiveness of brightness-contrast of the scallop is plain to see for each respective zone. The entire scale was illuminated with the laboratory room lights to give the scallop of zone V (middle gray) a luminance close to 10.00 cd/ft² on which the brightness of the LBR Scale is based (see Chapter 5, Table 5-2). The luminance ratios of scallop to background is about 3:1 for each zone as Table 11-1 shows.

Table 11-1 and Figure 11-12 illustrate the difference between measured luminance and subjective brightness. All the scallops created approximately the same 3:1 luminance ratio[4] with their respective background, yet the observer in the laboratory sees the scallop brightening as it proceeds across the LBR Scale from black to white. The visual images of Figure 11-12 show how the brightness of the scallops can be used for reference in lighting design refinement. When the reflectance of a surfacing material is known, visualize it within the borders of the appropriate zone on the LBR Scale (see p. 76), and the brightness of the scallop can be visualized according to the respective image in Figure 11-12. Intense scallops on dark-colored surfacing materials require more energy and more operating costs. If bright accents are desired, the logical conclusion is to select surfacing materials from the middle to higher zones of the LBR Scale. Energy costs are thereby reduced. Bright scallops and other lighting accents readily appear on white walls (Figure

---

[4] Luminance measurements of the Munsell surfaces were taken individually under the same luminaire in a special scallop demonstration model, to avoid output variations in different lamps common to the manufacturing process. The slight differences in the luminance ratio column of Table 11-1 was due to minor power fluctuations and rounding off ratio fractions.

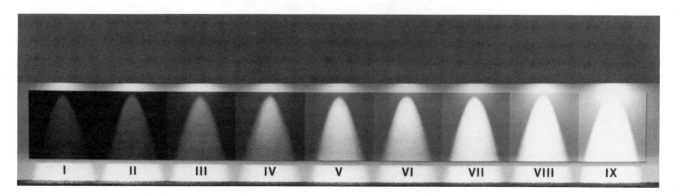

Figure 11-12. Luminance ratios for scallops.

Table 11-1. Photometric readings of scallop laboratory demonstration

		Munsell Notation	Munsell Reflectance	Scallop (cd/ft^2)	Background (cd/ft^2)	Luminance Ratio Scallop to Background
(black)	Zone I	N2	3.1%	1.01	0.35	2.89 : 1
	Zone II	N3	6.6%	2.17	0.75	2.89 : 1
	Zone III	N4	12.0%	3.94	1.36	2.90 : 1
	Zone IV	N5	19.8%	6.52	2.24	2.91 : 1
(middle gray)	Zone V	N6	30.0%	9.87	3.40	2.90 : 1
	Zone VI	N6.75	39.5%	13.08	4.49	2.91 : 1
	Zone VII	N7.5	50.7%	16.69	5.74	2.91 : 1
	Zone VIII	N8.5	68.4%	22.51	7.76	2.90 : 1
(white)	Zone IX	N9.5	90.0%	29.60	10.17	2.91 : 1

11-13). The key is the room illumination in the immediate area where the accents are located.

Ideally, choosing scalloped or any other accent lighting is one and the same decision as detailing the architecture of the wall to receive the illumination. The exhibition display in Figure 11-13 shows how lighting design is coordinated with architectural articulation. The spatial envelope is a curved alcove with a strong high-contrast pattern of recessed squares in which video screens deliver a corporation's message. Absence of direct illumination on the ceiling provides a soft, ambient light for the alcove, which brings out the scallops. Contrast for the videos is preserved by their being recessed from the primary plane of the curved wall, preventing interference from the scalloped downlights. Strategically located above each of the divisional piers, the downlighting creates a pattern that is integrated with the pattern of dark recesses, giving the alcove an attractive identity. Combining the focal accents of brightness, high contrast, and strong pattern, the vivid scallops attract visitors from

Figure 11-13. Harmony of lighting and architectural design. [Cybertek Corp., Infomart, Dallas]

Designing with Space and Light

farther down the hall, and articulate the shape of this small subspace that invites entry. Once in the alcove, the colorful attracting power of the video screens takes over.

There are problems related to accenting downlights that are fixed permanently into the ceiling. Lamps burn out and may not be replaced due to inefficient maintenance, and the rhythmic effect of repeating scallops is broken. A common misuse of permanently installed scallop lighting occurs when owners or managers change the decor but not the lighting, as illustrated by Figure 11-14. The number and placement of the three decorative prints are obviously out of step with the three existing scallops of light. Moreover, if luminaires are adjustable for beam direction or have movable lamp shields, maintenance people replacing lamps may fail to realign the light beam properly, producing different shapes of scalloped light, probably not what the interior or lighting designer had in mind.

Sometimes the lack of coordination between lighting and the objects being lighted creates social commentary and even humor. Figure 11-15 suggests this leading hotel corporation clearly places a higher priority on the potential emergency of fire than it does on art. An applause is in order praising the management's concern for the safety of their guests. Yet remembering that human inefficiency is often the cause of misdirected lighting accents as a result of changing lamps or decor, the photograph prompts a grin. A closer look at exactly where the two

scallops are concentrated might please the manufacturer of the wall fabric, knowing the display of their product was given precedence over both fire control and art.

Moving sunlight offers the designer an unlimited range of possibilities for accent lighting on the envelopes of space, and the history of architecture is filled with demonstrations of how the natural "effects of light" can be converted into fascinating points of interest with no energy costs. Visitors to the Alhambra in Granada, Spain, are treated to many such examples as they walk through space after space in that masterpiece of architecture. Figure 11-16 shows a small alcove along the east side of the Court of the Myrtles (Figure 3-15). In the summer afternoon, patterns of sunlight are shaped by two delicately carved window grilles, whose images are projected onto the wall below, extending the decoration of the outside facade into the alcove. Gradually the window patterns of light move across the shadowed alcove, like a sundial, for visitors today as they did for the former inhabitants of the palace.

In modern times, technological advances in prisms, prism panels, and specialized glass make available similar means of activating the spatial envelope with sunlight, waiting only the imagination of the designer. The religious interior shown in Figure C-44 is a simplified volume of space, but it is brought to life by the dramatic beams of sunlight cast on the chancel wall. The rays emanate from egg crate patterns of dichroic glass

Figure 11-14. Accent lighting and wall hangings out of step.

Figure 11-15. Misfit of lighting accents.

tween the levels being connected. The staircase in Figure C-46 is broken into sections, coordinated with the stepped pattern of windows and hand railings. Torch-like decorative luminaires are correlated with the stepped rhythm of those architectural features. They are placed in front of wall surfaces that reflect their colorful glow, animating the overall articulation of space.

The designer does not have total freedom to compose accent lighting when dealing with historical restoration projects, because the luminaries and their light need to conform to the period architecture. The refurbishing of the rotunda of the 1879 Michigan State Capitol is an excellent example of lighting an historical spatial envelope. Figure C-47 shows the view up into the dome through the upper floors, where a series of concentric surfaces brighten as they ascend. The sequence begins by soft luminance on the ceiling of the first level, created by uplight passing through a glass floor below. On the second floor, new visible fixtures were mounted in existing architectural brackets, making a ring of accenting points of light around the space. At the highest level, light is directed through the circular balustrade to illuminate

mounted against a southwest-facing window. Responding to the moving sun, the double course of reflected rays slowly changes in angular direction, and their brilliant pattern animates the scene and forcefully attracts attention to the sanctuary. The lighting gives an emotional quality to the room that fits the spirit of inspired communal worship, and in afterhours transcends the prevailing quietude, preserving that spirit of worship for individual visitation and contemplation.

Daylight transformed into colorful rainbow effects by a prism is an ingeneous means for creating moving lighting accents on the spatial envelope. In the small chapel of Figure C-45, concave sections articulate the walls of a generally cylindrical spatial envelope. Mounted under a sloped skylight around a portion of the perimeter is a prism system that sends transitory polychromatic images across the boundaries of space. A computer system tracks the sun, and directs refracted light from the prisms into the interior throughout the course of the year. The effect is an impressionistic light painting, and the moving images in space become a spiritually moving experience for visitors to the chapel.

As we saw in Chapter 8, one of the principal means of articulating architectural space is by changing levels, and often the opportunity presents itself for accent lighting to be designed as part of the zone of transition be-

Figure 11-16. Cost-free accent lighting. [Alhambra, Court of the Myrtles, Granada, Spain]

Designing with Space and Light

paintings between pilasters, further increasing the brightness over the floor immediately below. The oculus in the center of the dome is a brightness climax, illuminated by a ring of blue-filtered metal-halide fixtures. Here, accent lighting coordinated with architectural articulation preserves the historical character of the building, which first received electric light in 1901.

Enclosure, Light, and Spaciousness

When working with the concept of a spatial envelope, a distinction should be made between *enveloping* space for analysis and design and *confining* space in the context of human behavior. If the space is relatively small, dimly illuminated, and has no views to the outside, the prevailing feeling is one of confinement. Even in moderately sized or large rooms, some people experience claustrophobia when deprived of brightness and views to an adjoining scene. Regardless of its actual physical size, a bright room will be perceived as more spacious than when it is dimmed.

In a classic study by a team of researchers headed by John Flynn (1973), a rectangular conference room was set up at General Electric's Nela Park and modified by six different lighting combinations including wall-washing, downlighting, and combinations of the two. This often quoted and republished study revealed significant find-

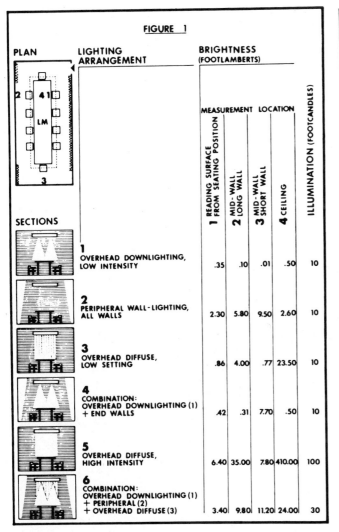

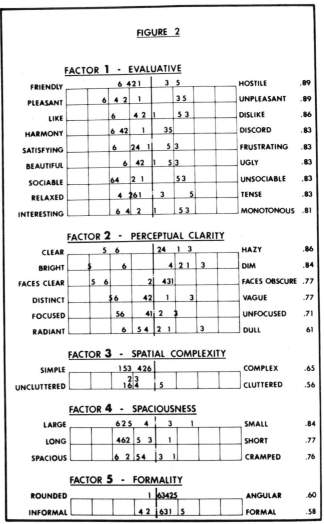

Figure 11-17. Impressions of room lighting arrangements. [Flynn, John E., Terry J. Spencer, Osyp Martyniuk, and Clyde Hendrick. 1973. "Interim study of procedures for investigating the effect of light on impression and behavior." Journal of the Illuminating Engineering Society, 3:87–94. Published by the Illuminating Engineering Society, 120 Wall St., 17th Floor, NY, NY 10005.]

ings related to the brightness-spaciousness relationship, and is valuable for its application to lighting the spatial envelope. Figure 11-17 provides the floor plan of the test room, schematic diagrams of lighting layouts, and response ratings from the study. Subjects' impressions of the various lighting conditions were measured by factor analysis using semantic differential (SD) rating scales. Using interpretations of "spaciousness" (factor 4), it will be noted that most participants judged the room highest in that category when the *walls* of the spatial envelope were prominently illuminated (arrangements 2, 4, and 6). This is confirmed by examining the luminance ("brightness") measurements provided for the "mid-wall, long wall" in arrangement 1 compared with arrangement 2. Reviewing other analysis factors of "Evaluative," "Perceptual Clarity," and "Spatial Complexity," it can be noted the arrangements that *included peripheral wall lighting* (direct or reflected) were given positive responses by the participants, including specific qualities of "pleasantness," "harmonious," "sociable," and "interesting." In a later study designed to test the practical applications for their Nela Park experiment, Flynn (1975)[5] used three different conference rooms of different dimensions, and included an auditorium. The findings added support for the fact that rooms look more spacious under peripheral wall illumination. Citing these studies is not to be misconstrued as a recommendation that "a brighter spatial envelope is better." They are provided here to underscore the importance of understanding the nature of light levels on the spatial envelope itself, and for how the illuminated envelope influences human perception of architectural space.

There are a number of practical applications of brightness related to spaciousness, especially for people who occupy a tightly enclosed space for an extended period of time. Such is the case when traveling by aircraft. Figure 11-18 shows the interior of a Boeing 737, whose ceiling and outer walls are illuminated by indirect lighting, brightening approximately half of the spatial envelope. The brightness of those surfaces contributes to the feeling

[5] For further information on the work of Flynn and other research on the subject of spaciousness, see Boyce (1978).

Figure 11-18. Brightness and spaciousness for air travel. [Courtesy: Boeing]

Designing with Space and Light

of spaciousness, particularly important for some passengers when first boarding and taking their seats for departure. In flight, wall-washing on the curved walls above the windows reduces brightness-contrast when looking out at bright sky and clouds. The windows are also splayed, providing further contrast reduction between the surface around the window and the outside view.

There are other applications. Harry Weese & Associates teamed up with William Lam (1977, 293) to design the underground Washington Metropolitan Area Transit Authority Stations, where the need for spaciousness was essential to reduce claustrophobia as experienced by many people in underground tunnels. For the Washington subways, tubular vaults were designed with coffered structural surfaces, which were well illuminated to characterize the space as a bright activity center and to minimize cloistered feelings of being beneath the street.

Spaciousness has its place in the design of the architectural environment, and should be considered only for environments where it is appropriate. Some settings require privacy and intimacy, and the immediate surroundings need to be surfaced with dark materials and/or given low illumination to create the appropriate mood. A secluded, candle-lit table for two in a restaurant calls for visual emphasis on the people dining and the food, not necessarily on the extended surroundings around them. It is the conceptual purpose architectural space is to serve that determines where the feeling of spaciousness is required and where it is not, and then decisions should be made of how to light and color the spatial envelope.

In this chapter attention is focused on lighting only the spatial envelope, intentionally avoiding the issues of how its illuminated appearance affects any freestanding objects it encloses, and how any one lighted envelope interacts with adjacent spaces. Those matters are the subjects of following chapters. The envelope has been isolated for analysis because it is the basic configuration of major surfaces for spatial definition and generally is the most permanent element in the life of an individual space. It provides a working frame of reference to control the eventual composition of all colors and reflected light as the total environment is assembled. When the infill of furnishings is added, or when a large room is divided by semi-enclosures like modular workstations in a large office, the visual perception of the overall environment remains strongly influenced by the primary outer boundaries.

The creation of a clear, well-designed, and well-illuminated spatial envelope is vital for aesthetic spatial design. The envelope must have integrity. Integrity is achieved by the ordered and balanced composition of the boundaries that define the space, and the elimination of discordant parts. Above all, the envelope must not be distorted in any way that psychologically impairs the well-being of people. The designer must stay in control of the envelope, working and reworking its dimensions and surfaces to shape the light that will bring the space to life. It must be known when to emphasize the envelope itself, or when to minimize its role as a supporting background for the furnishings it will eventually harbor. "Integrity" is an important word. It issues forth in discussions of great art. When it is achieved in the design of the spaces of architecture, they in turn advance the quality of the overall building design. Each envelope is a component of a system of connected spaces, and therefore each must be of good design to contribute to the integrity of the total building.

CHAPTER 12

Lighting Forms in Space

Wake! For the Sun, who scattered into flight
The Stars before him from the Field of Night,
*   Drives Night along with them from Heav'n,*
*   and strikes*
The Sultán's Turret with a Shaft of Light.
                                —Omar Khayyám
                                *"The Rubáiyát"**

An architectural space can be animated by surface articulation and specialized lighting on the spatial envelope, but a number of problems and design considerations arise when supplemental lighting is added to feature freestanding objects. As we saw in the preceding chapter, lighting the spatial envelope establishes the brightness levels on the major boundaries of space, and contributes to the ambient light in the room. Objects *in the space* receive that ambient light, and acquire a given brightness by their color and texture as compared with their background. Any additional, specialized light cast on them alters their luminance, and changes their brightness relationships as perceived against the spatial envelope and among their compositional relationships with other objects nearby. That is what makes the overall design and lighting of the spatial envelope crucial. The illuminated envelope is a controlled reference for brightness perception and for calculating luminance ratios for the interior furnishings. Adding light to feature specific forms in space is a delicate procedure that requires special guidelines for creating a quality illuminated environment.

* Khayyám, Omar. "The Rubáiyát." Translated by Edward Fitzgerald, in *The Norton Anthology of Poetry,* revised 1975, p. 327. With permission of and © Walter J. Black, Roslyn, NY.

Objects of Light

Tenebrism, as we learn from the art of painting, is the method of spotlighting a figure to dramatize its presence against darker surroundings. It has been a highly effective compositional device for painters and stage designers for centuries and its use in those fields provides good analytic study for illuminating objects in the architectural environment. Brightly contrasting forms in a dim environment is a most expressive means for attracting visual attention. Objects so illuminated often appear as the sources of light themselves rather than as the recipients of light. Tenebrism was popularly used in seventeenth-century Baroque art for its ability to supercharge a painting's content with emotionalism, drama, or spirituality. The Italian painter Michelangelo (Merisi) Caravaggio (1571–1610) executed it par excellence, and its analysis in painting offers invaluable artistic theory applicable to lighting design.

Caravaggio's *Martyrdom of St. Matthew* (Figure 12-1) illustrates the use of tenebrism to isolate and emphasize key features composed in pictorial space. The figures are illuminated to make them objects of light, arranged in a sophisticated composition. He used the contrasting effects of tenebrism to render details at levels of brightness fitting to their roles in the overall composi-

Figure 12-1. Composition of light in painting. [Caravaggio, Martyrdom of St. Matthew, *1599, S. Luigi dei Francesi, Contarelli Chapel, Rome. Photograph: Art Resource, NY]*

tion. Attention is first drawn to the brightest images in the scene: the executioner and the victim. The distribution of brightness-contrast about the scene was not just a simple matter of highlighting the center and letting less bright details fade away outward in the composition. The faces, arms, and hands of the surrounding figures are near equal in brightness compared with that of the executioner and victim, but those details are lesser in surface area. Because of the smaller size of those units, they do not immediately attract attention, but lie back in wait for the eye of the viewer scanning the painting. Here in this two-dimensional visual field, the coordination of elements in varying brightness effectively weaves together the parts of the story in animated suspense. Illumination descends on the scene and key features respond, brought to life in the void of darkness. Objects materialize in light.

The application of tenebrism to lighting design in architecture follows the same theory found in Caravaggio's painting: the distibution of light to emphasize selected freestanding objects as accents in a room, and the controlled brightness relationships for all other surfaces. The technique of tenebrism should be reserved for only those lighting design situations that require high contrast of selected objects in subdued surroundings, such as can be found in some sculpture galleries, specialized commercial or other exhibitions, religious settings, intimate restaurants and cocktail lounges, and the theatrical stage. The brightly illuminated objects serve as beacons attracting and guiding people through the space. In a number of situations, however, precautions must be taken. In public spaces, enough luminance must exist on the spatial envelope and all freestanding objects for the safety of people moving about. In stores, enough ambient light must be provided for merchandise security.

Figure 12-2 shows a Rodin sculpture exhibition in the National Gallery of Art in Washington, D.C. The greater spatial envelope of the distant architecture is subdued in luminance, as are the trees that create subspaces within the gallery. That subdued background and localized illumination dramatize the forms of the white marble sculptures, which become "objects of light." An

Figure 12-2. Lighting forms as focal centers. [Rodin Exhibit. Courtesy: National Gallery of Art, Washington, DC. Photographer: William Schaeffer]

atmosphere was created for the repose and dignity of the works of art and for contemplation by the observer. Quiet and tranquility prevail. The specialized downlighting was carefully maintained to emphasize highlights and shadow, to manifest the aesthetic qualities of the sculptures, and to make visible the descriptive information subtlely inscribed on the pedestals. The brightness-contrast of the sculptures and their purity of form attract attention and guide visitor circulation through the exhibition.

Figure C-48 shows the principle of tenebrism at work in a jewelry store, where interior and lighting design were brought together in harmonious relationships. The arriving shopper is first attracted to the displays of jewelry in the foreground showcases, which are the brightest elements in the store. Incandescent downlighting is appropriate for rendering the precious metals and minerals in the dazzling brilliance they require. To avoid glare, the architect experimented with beam spread, fixture spacing, and the direction of overhead light emanating from MR 16 downlights, which rendered the jewelry in sparkling attraction.

For design aesthetics of the total environment of the jewelry store, the designer artfully composed the lighting and the lighted objects. The walls and ceiling were painted a dark, hunter green color (darker in the photograph than at the site), which raised to prominence the showcases and perimeter displays. Milled red oak wood was used for detailing walls, ceiling, and showcases, bringing into harmony the forms in space with the detailing on the spatial envelope. All luminaires set into the darkened ceiling create an organized pattern of the light sources. They are small enough in size not to overpower or draw attention away from the displayed merchandise, and they appear as an array of points of light that is communal with the scintillating reflections on the jewelry below. The perceptual clarity of the space was achieved by holding the number and color of the permanent building materials to a minimum, avoiding excessive architectural detailing, and composing the brightness levels of all surfaces in the total space.

For commercial displays and exhibitions, lighting a group of objects is as important as the illumination of any one constituent. Figure C-49 shows the Styling Dome of the Chrysler Technical Center, featuring three new automobiles by spotlighting. Overlapping disks of light on the walls join multiple shafts of light from luminaires recessed in the dome, combining to animate the spatial envelope and to create a festive atmosphere for the scene. The relatively darkened floor heightens the spotlighting of the cars. Each is a focal center, and the three are composed as a group, coordinated by light. There is a delicate interplay between the visual strength of their image and their animated background. The fluid contours of the cars occlude the patterns of light on the walls and disks of light on the floor, and their color is emphasized against the neutrality of the entire spatial envelope. The abstracted light image of the corporation's logo appears like a signature for the products on display.

Objects of light that draw attention to themselves at the same time can become the principal means for shaping architectural interspaces (see Chapter 4, p. 55ff).

Needless to say, good lighting design for a display is only as effective as the quality of design for the layout receiving the light. The museum gallery of Figure C-50 is a composition of vertical exhibit panels that establishes interspaces and directs the flow of circulation around the works of art. The paintings stand out in colorful "figure" against the neutral "ground" of the display panels. Ambient light is added by indirect illumination on the ceiling. The paintings attract visitors by their subject matter and by the aura of soft light, which gives each its focus of attention.

Multiple Levels of Light and Brightness Enhancement

The painter has an enviable advantage over the architectural lighting designer. The brush can apply highlights to any element anywhere on a canvas, and the painter needs to be aware of only the logical direction of light, not the kind of light source that is needed to create a precise effect. Caravaggio did not have to be concerned about installing small luminaires here and there to cast the desired amount of light on a hand or garment. He did not have to contend with the realities of working with the quantity and quality of electric light, nor with

its inverse square law that often foils or frustrates intentions for sophisticated lighting design.

Due to the inverse square law, the farther an object lies from the light source, the greater it drops off in luminance. Therefore, when the primary luminaire must be located far from the subject, an intermediate support source may be needed at a level closer to the subject in order to achieve a desired brightness or to highlight details. This is illustrated by Figure 12-3. The accenting downlight from above loses intensity at the level of the showcase due to the distance from the ceiling. Moreover, the farther the light source is from its target, the more its beam size increases as it approaches its objective. If the luminaire is not one that is equipped with adapter panels, framing shutters, or a specialized lamp for specific beam definition, spill light may unintentionally illuminate unwanted elements outside the center of interest. Those encroaching details enter the target's sphere of light, detracting from its isolation as a design accent.

Sometimes architectural articulation of the spatial envelope provides solutions for bringing the light source down to a lower level where it can efficiently highlight a target without adding excessive ambient light into the space. This is shown in Figure 12-4, where the spatial boundaries are illuminated primarily by indirect lighting. The projecting strip articulating the ceiling near the wall made possible a lower level for locating the recessed downlighting over the painting. The niche cut into the

Figure 12-3. Multiple levels of light.

Figure 12-4. Subtle placement of light in composition. [Private residence, Barrington, Illinois. Photo: Courtesy of Halo Lighting—brand of Cooper Lighting]

wall provided a still lower level for housing the luminaire that illuminates the figurine. The entire spatial envelope is softly illuminated, while the freestanding plant and works of art are emphasized by contrast.

Lighting does not always have to come from above. Edge-lighting of glass and Plexiglas effectively highlights any image etched into the material's surface. The luminaires can be totally hidden, illuminating artwork or graphics as if they were suspended in air. Images cast into glass blocks respond to light transmitted through the otherwise clear medium. Figure C-51 shows how attractive this means of lighting images in space can be. Using a Japanese process of etching the print of an actual fish onto glass, artist and craftsman Peter David created this display where the etched images are illuminated by light sources hidden from view. Using the technique of edge lighting, an infinite range of image color and brightness is possible by passing light through transparent material and modifying it by colored filters and/or colored lamps in the luminaires. Because the medium is transparent, the background luminance for the display is crucial for the creation of good figure-ground relationships, and to emphasize the brilliance of the edge-lighted images. This example again shows the importance of controlling the brightness of the spatial envelope, or any other background surface, for lighting this kind of form in space.

Contrasting Brightness for Visual Accents

When freestanding objects are to be highlighted as visual accents in architectural space, luminance ratios serve as a guide for brightness-contrast, but remember there is a difference between *measured* luminance and *perceived* brightness.[1] Further, it is well known to lighting designers that doubling the amount of light on an object will not make it appear twice as bright. The question arises of just how much contrast is required for visual accenting, and published literature reveals that different viewpoints persist among designers, lighting engineers, and psychologists regarding exactly how much luminance separation is enough for brightness-contrast effectiveness.

To address this issue, a laboratory exercise was set up to study the theory of perceived brightness related to the problem of illuminating a form in space. Figure 12-5

---

[1] A 1965 study at the Pratt Institute showed that people do not perceive brightness in architecture according to the way surfaces are actually measured in luminance. See William M. C. Lam (1977, 47), Chapter 3, "The Perception of Brightness."

Designing with Space and Light

(a)

(b)

(c)

Figure 12-5 a–c. Brightness lighting for focal accent.

shows three photographs taken in a laboratory research/ demonstration model, where a minstrel figurine was subjected to variable illumination for observing changing brightness ratios related to figure-ground prominence. The background was given minimal illumination to provide some sense of environmental depth as opposed to

having observers feel they were looking at an object suspended in a limitless black void of space. The figurine was illuminated by an overhead diaphragm-controlled incandescent downlight, which was modulated by a dimmer. Forty-three architecture and interior design students participated in the study. They were told to consider the setting as a public sculpture exhibit in a museum. Using their subjective sense of design, they were told to raise and lower the light level on the figure until three stages were reached:

(a) Maximum brightness of the figurine. No additional light is necessary to create prominent figure-ground in an isolated museum setting.

(b) Prominence of figure, while creating appropriate mood for the minstrel.

(c) Minimum brightness of the figurine. Less illumination would render the figure unacceptable for appropriate mood and detail recognition.

The luminance of the minstrel was measured in ratio with its background as it appeared at the average setting by all observers in the study. Luminance readings were taken at generalized areas from the minstrel's shoulder to knees, including the cape. The average setting for each of the three conditions was then photographed (Figure 12-5 a, b, and c). The measured luminance ratios are as follows:

Setting (a) 4.17:1

Setting (b) 3.24:1

Setting (c) 2.61:1

Returning to the luminance ratios discussed in Chapter 3, a surface 3 times brighter than its surround was said to appear as visually prominent in its environment, and settings (a) and (b) support that brightness relationship. As it appeared in setting (c), the figurine was only 2.61 times the luminance of its background; its surface texture was highlighted, but the figure itself did not stand out prominently against the background as it did in the other two settings. It was also said in Chapter 3 that a contrast of 10:1 would make a surface stand out as a dominant visual force as seen in its environment, a ratio sometimes given as a guideline in lighting publications. In this study, setting (a) shows the figurine as exceptionally prominent in the scene, but it was only 4.17 times brighter than its surround. No student in the study wished to raise the lighting on the figurine to even half of the 10:1 ratio, where it would indeed appear as a visual force in the field of view.

Students reported a number of pertinent observations while performing this exercise. One was surface glare on the minstrel's face, cape, and bagpipe that appeared when the illumination was raised to higher levels. Aside from the increase in brightness needed for the figurine to contrast its background, for many students the appearance of glare signaled a stopping point for continuing to add more light on the figurine. One student commented on using the meaning of the figure for determining the appropriate illumination for the mood of setting (b) and as a result selected a brightness slightly higher than the average participant. She said, "I set the illumination rather brightly to create a mood of liveliness and energy, since bagpipers bring to mind a joyous lively occasion." But even with that added spirit given to the figure, she selected a luminance ratio of only 4:1 for setting (b), still below the average of all participants for setting (a), the setting considered as a maximum contrast that would make the figure stand out prominently against its background.

The figurine would become even more prominent if imagined in bright, colorful oranges or yellows as contrasted with the same neutral gray background used in the study, and under the same illumination. What color was the figurine? Mostly tans and weakly saturated earthy greens. Selection of a brightly colored figurine was intentionally avoided for better study of the influence of light alone. For practical applications that prominently feature forms in space, the designer simply must keep in mind that bright hues and the pastels will create greater luminance than darker colors under the same light.

These laboratory studies provide helpful design theory for application of luminance ratios to actual architectural conditions. Taking advantage of the phototropic nature of human vision, architectural and lighting design can effectively combine to create strong figure-ground relationships in brightness-contrast that attract attention to a designated object or locality. Figure 12-6 shows how controlled contrasts feature lighted forms in space. Downlighting highlights the chair on exhibit; its brightness is enhanced not by excessive illumination, but by the dark background of the walls. Like Robert Frost credited darkness for bringing out the light of a star, the darkened spatial envelope of the foreground room brings out the brightness of the chair, which becomes a focal center by brightness-contrast. The three spaces shown in the photograph brighten in sequence as they recede, with the brightest wall inviting movement into the distant room. The plant and table are accented by their own downlight, making that node a focal accent midway in the sequence. The success of the lighting design resulted from controlling the brightness levels in all three rooms, and localizing specialized illumination for the objects on display.

Lighting of forms in the central areas of space often means that the light sources are going to be located near or directly overhead of the object being illuminated.

Figure 12-6. Focal accents in spatial sequencing. [AllSteel exhibit in Pacific Design Center. Design: Gensler and Associates/Architects. Photo: Toshi Yoshimi]

Therefore, another issue needs to be addressed: the design of the luminaires themselves. When tenebrism is used, it means the ambient light of the room is dim. Ceilings above are normally dark or screened, and aside from the lamp or diffusing lens, the light fixtures can be visually hidden. But when the ceiling is raised in brightness to appreciable visibility or is softly illuminated, visible fixtures such as track lighting or special effect luminaires become more prominent. In the visual field of the observer, they too become forms in space, just like the objects they illuminate below. The best way to select luminaire design is to consider exactly what figure-ground relationships the lighting fixtures themselves will make with the ceiling or upper walls as seen from normal viewing angles. Suspended luminaires may compete with mechanical equipment, sprinkler systems, structural components, or high-tech structural detailing. The design of the fixture (so prominently portrayed by close-up photography in advertising media) can be lost amid adverse visual clutter. Being aware of the ceiling area while walking through contemporary public and private buildings reveals this often violated territory of architectural space. The ceiling *is* a major spatial boundary, highly visible in the panoptic view of space. It is a key component of the entire spatial envelope. It contributes to the character of the space, in either visual simplicity or clutter, or somewhere between the two. When the ceiling characteristics are already determined at the time specialized lighting is to be added, selection of the luminaire design must take into consideration what kind of figure-ground relations will take place as the fixture is seen against the ceiling. Choosing the design of a suspened luminaire is a delicate decision for both designer and client. Choices range from the highly ornate to simplicity of design. The design of the luminaire is going to fall somewhere along the continuum between the figure attracting attention to itself and that of a low profile image left unpretentious in the field of view. The final consideration, however, is the fact that it gives off light. That light goes somewhere, reflects off something, and intentionally or not, goes to work shaping the space of which the exposed luminaire is a notable part.

Lighting for Tasks

Other than specialists practicing in exhibition design or other similar interior architecture, few designers have the opportunity for creating the dramatic effects of spotlighting forms or displays in dimmed spatial surroundings. In the daily world of urban living, most people's activities require adequate performance illumination known as *task lighting*. It is a common sense method of putting sufficient light precisely where it is needed.[2] In most public environments like large offices, stores, classrooms, and industrial shops, tasks of similar kind predominate in the room, so task lighting is provided by general room lighting directed to desks, tables, or work stations where tasks are performed. Often originating from rows of luminaires at or near the ceiling, light floods downward and outward and simultaneously illuminates the spatial envelope of the room and its freestanding contents. Therefore, the brightness ratios of the room's furnishings will be determined largely as a result of the color and other surface qualities of the interior furniture as seen against the color and texture of the middle to upper walls (depending on the density of wall hangings or pin-ups). Zones of the LBR System are a guide for comparing the brightness of interior furnishings as seen against the walls. Aesthetic qualities of space are determined almost solely by architectural and furniture design, not specialized lighting design. Most interior workplaces and many public spaces are illuminated by either

generalized room lighting or by an integrated system, which combines some level of uniform ambient lighting with localized supplementary light at certain stations where higher illumination is required.

Figure 12-7 shows controlled, localized task lighting fitted to a small demonstration classroom of a corporation's marketing center. The room is semicircular in plan and equipped with permanently fixed seating and electronic instructional devices. The front of the room contains a projection screen and VDT activated at a computer station, which also serves as a speaker's lectern. Like any other classroom where audiovisual demonstrations are the most common method of instruction, varying brightness levels had to be distributed about the room to make the VDT and other projection facilities easy to see, while supplemental task lighting is required for the seating area. The graduated, stepped ceiling is the location for both direct and indirect illumination. At the rear of the space, wall sconces bounce light off the lowest ceiling section, brightening the primary circulation route from the entrance door (behind the camera). Recessed canisters provide balanced downlighting for the seating, made evident by the location of shadows directly under each of the seats. Task lighting therefore serves the needs of each person attending a demonstration. Note how the brightness of the walls and ceiling gradually decreases from back to front of the room, easily observed along the stepped ceiling. That lighting scenario provides relative dimness in the front, which allows the instructional station to be raised to prominence by spotlighting and

Figure 12-7. Task lighting for room shape and function. [Apple Marketing Center, Infomart, Dallas]

---

[2] For a brief history of the development of performance-based standards throughout the 1970s, see C. Cuttle (1978), *The New Photometry*. Also see Yonemura, G. T., "Light and vision," in Lynes (1978).

heightens the presence of the VDT. This makes the instructors and demonstrations the center of attention for the audience.

When adding supplementary illumination, the fundamental question is "how much light is needed to achieve the desired design objectives?" It is sometimes heard that "more light means better seeing." That adage is true to some degree, but only where light is poor and visual acuity is weak. Once the luminance level for a given task is raised above 6 to 10 cd/ft^2, the law of diminishing returns comes into play. Within that range of luminance, a further increase in illumination will increase visibility only slightly. People older than 50 years of age may have difficulty with task performances below 6 cd/ft^2, but when the luminance is raised higher than 10 cd/ft^2, they too will not experience substantially greater acuity from the addition of more light (see pp. 10–11). This should be considered when adding supplementary light to objects or specialized areas in an environment. Enough illumination should be supplied for good visibility of surface details when they are important, but overlighting is inefficient and a waste of energy.

Acuity can be increased by means other than the addition of more light. In an environment of low illumination levels such as a dimly lit restaurant, acuity for reading a menu can be improved by increasing print size, increasing color contrast between print and page, and avoiding a common mistake of imprinting text over graphics to the extent that the printed word appears in a poor figure-ground relationship. These guidelines should be remembered when considering adding supplemental light for restaurant settings, museum exhibits, commercial displays, or anyplace where ease of reading print materials and seeing fine details are essential.

Lighting Forms at the Periphery of Space

Contrasts of color and brightness set up focal centers in interior space and on the surfaces of the spatial envelope. The addition of supplementary lighting to emphasize freestanding objects along the periphery of space means a change in brightness centers in the overall spatial composition. In cases where the spatial envelope itself is a primary focus for lighting design (e.g., wall-washing, wall-grazing, indirect cove lighting, etc.), to some extent a share of that light finds its way to the interior of the space, adding luminance to the surfaces on which it falls. By a reverse process, when supplemental lighting is introduced to create focal centers in the interior of space, unless rigidly controlled by lamp placement or fixture design, some of that light may reflect on portions of the spatial envelope.

Known to sculptors, exhibit and theater designers, and photographers, the direction of light is significantly important. At the slightest angular change in directional light, new highlights appear on an object while other surface areas fall into shadow. Fine gradations and modulations of brightness shift across protrusions and hollows of three-dimensional forms as the direction of light is changed or as the object is rotated at its location. Light coming from directly below casts mysterious shadows on people and sculptures of humans and animals, particularly on faces. Cuttle (1973) reminds us of the effects of light related to form perception, noting that under different lighting conditions, objects can assume attractive, neutral, or even aggressive characteristics. In aesthetic terms, the interplay of light and shadow on the surface of an object is as important as the interplay of illuminated forms in space. For this reason the education of the lighting designer and all fields related to illuminating objects in space should include a thorough study of the history of the sculptural arts. As the Kreitlers (1972)[3] tell us about the play of light on a work of art:

A small protrusion may be made to appear large when more brightly lighted than neighboring surfaces; a sunk-in form may appear set-off; and a convexity may seem to recede. Light effects may also transform the apparent quality of the statue's material, i.e., airy lightness may be imparted to the most heavy and intractable masses, an effect favored by many Renaissance sculptors, while transparent surfaces may appear to dissolve into space, an impression sometimes produced in Naum Gabo's Plexiglas sculptures. . . .

The play of light on objects positioned around the periphery of a room requires special attention, because brightness relationships there influence one's perception of the entire room in a manner different from viewing illuminated objects in the central regions of space. Spotlighting objects located near walls consequently involves the spatial envelope directly, which is the immediate background for the pieces as seen from most viewing angles. Unless the luminaire is equipped with internal beam control or external hinged shutters, illumination spills beyond the object and casts shapes of light on the wall (albeit sometimes done for intended design effects). The simultaneous illumination of object and spatial envelope influences the *spaciousness of the room.*

---

[3] See the Kreitlers' Chapter 10, "Surface, Material, and Motion in Sculpture," especially the section "Material, Movement, and Activation." The earlier and standard work of Arnheim (1969) should also be consulted.

Designing with Space and Light

Figure 12-8. Lighted forms against a bright spatial envelope. [Kimbell Art Museum, Fort Worth, Texas. Architect: Louis I. Kahn]

Contrasting luminances of lighted objects at the periphery of space needs special attention. Let us begin by using an example of forms illuminated against a relatively bright spatial envelope. Figure 12-8 shows a row of sculptural figures set against a wall of travertine, a characteristically bright material as visually located on the LBR Scale. By contrast, the comparatively dark sculptures stand out in prominent figure-ground. However, their dark stone necessitated the addition of supplemental lighting to enhance their surface details of incised lines and contour modeling. The luminaires suspended overhead are teamed to illuminate the front and sides of the figures, as museum exhibiting usually requires. Scallop images appear on the travertine wall, but they are not prominent enough to compete with the sculpture. Yet even after supplemental lighting was added to the sculptures, their luminance in ratio to the travertine is still contrasted enough to create good figure-ground separation to make the exhibit as clear and attractive as it is, and to draw museum visitors from the center of the gallery to this boundary of space.

Different conditions of brightness-contrast exist when lighting peripherally located objects that are seen against a darkened spatial envelope. Figure 12-9 shows another sculpture exhibit, this time combinations of dark and light stone figures, all set against a dark blue wall of a hotel. The exhibit provides a good opportunity for observing the comparative visibility of light and dark figures when all are subjected to the same illumination and background. Note, however, that some of the objects along the entire length of the wall receive more light than others, resulting from the fluorescent panels down the center of the ceiling, observed by referencing their locations to the greater areas of brightness on the carpeting below. The sculpture panels receive supplementary light from the recessed luminaires directly overhead. It is the quality of the stone, *not quantity of light*, that makes some pieces on the same panel appear brighter than others. The middle group is the most prominent of the three, because it receives illumination from both the fluorescent panel and the recessed downlighting (note the scallops above them), but even so, it is the surface luminance of the lighter color value of their stone that contributes mostly to their prominence. In the far right group, the darker stone figures are dim by comparison, because they have less luminance-contrast with their background, not because they are receiving less light.

Now let us take up lighting forms along the periphery of space, as it relates to the *spaciousness of the room*. In the preceding chapter we explained how a room will appear larger with a bright spatial envelope. That is happening in the museum gallery shown in Figure 12-8. The light-colored travertine wall and floor are brightened by the ambient light in the gallery and the supplemental downlighting for the sculpture (again note the scallops appearing down the length of the wall, and the brightness of the perpendicular wall at the far end). The significance of brightness is appreciated by imagining the dark wall of Figure 12-9 inserted in place of the travertine wall of Figure 12-8. As seen from the center of the room, the apparent spaciousness of the gallery would subside.

As a related exercise, visualize the walls and exhibit panels of Figure 12-9 resurfaced with a material comparable in brightness to the travertine in Figure 12-8. The hall would appear more spacious laterally than it actually is, and the darker sculptures would heighten in figure-ground prominence instead of those of the light-colored stone. The mood of the space would shift from one of artistic intimacy to one of more public openness. These analyses are not intended to assess either one of the exhibitions as "better" than the other. They are given here only for the study of perceptual luminance-contrast, not spatial aesthetics.

From the examples in this chapter it is apparent that lighting forms in space is not a simple task of just adding supplementary sources of illumination. When interior

Figure 12-9. Lighted forms against a darkened spatial envelope. [Loews Anatole Hotel, Dallas]

furnishings or objects are given emphasis by specialized lighting, their form is enhanced, color is intensified, and surface details become more prominent. That changes their luminance relationships with the boundaries of space, and restructures the brightness areas throughout an environment. Visual perception of the total room changes. The designer should *think spatially* when coordinating or contrasting the color and brightness of illuminated forms in space. This is the reason it is important to maintain control over the surfacing and lighting of the surrounding spatial envelope. It goes without saying that good architectural design of that envelope is essential prior to the arrival of light. Good proportions, good surfacing, and good color selections are prerequisites for the creation of a quality illuminated space. Designers must know when and where to emphasize any part of the spatial envelope, and when to showcase selected forms with light.

CHAPTER 13

Connecting Spaces with Light

Where is the way to the dwelling of light,
and where is the place of darkness . . .
                                    Job, 38:18

It is important to devote attention to the design and lighting of singular rooms in order to focus on the specialized problems that need to be solved, but such spatial quarantine suggests a myopic approach to the total building design, and often neglects the art of spatial sequencing. The visual interplay of illuminated surfaces as seen from one room into another can bring about sheer design excitement. When looking through an opening into another space, a glimpse of something appealing arouses human interest. Spatial connections provide the designer with opportunities for stimulating curiosity or satisfying expectations, and for creating a flow of architectural features that give harmony to the total architectural experience.

Looking from one space into another, however, involves different perceptual phenomena than scanning the environment of a single room, and to the human eye, the connected space does not always look like it does in photographs or as it was intended by design. To solve design problems associated with visual connections of illuminated spaces, we must now introduce a different set of factors for analysis.

Interspatial Adaptive Brightness

The luminance on the surface of an object remains constant as long as that surface does not change in position related to the distance and direction of the light source. However, its brightness and color appear to change when the ambient light around the viewer changes. This is due to light or dark adaptation of the retina and is easy to demonstrate on a surface that is visible through a door, window, or from between two large, freestanding partitions. *Interspatial brightness-contrast* is the appearance of a contiguous space when it is illuminated significantly higher or lower than the viewer's space. It is a frequent occurrence in the architectural world, indoors and out, day or night, wherever there is a prominent visual connection between two spaces and one contrasts the other. The eye adapts to the space it is in, and that makes surfaces that are visible in the adjacent space change in brightness from the way their actual luminances are measured. Color values also change. To deal with these problems, the spatial envelope becomes an expedient device for analyzing and designing connections of contrasting light. It is the major lighted surfaces of the envelope surrounding the observer that normally are the primary fields of reflected light to which the retina adapts, and the luminance on those surfaces will determine how bright the adjacent space will appear.

Before proceeding with an analysis of interspatial lighting, a clarification of terms is in order. The change in the brightness of surfaces in a neighboring space, caused by light or dark adaptation of the eye to the space it is in, is called *adaptive brightness*. In lighting design and related literature, the term *apparent brightness* is frequently used, sometimes creating semantic misinterpretations of this all important perceptual phenomenon of human vision. By the definition introduced in Chapter 2 and used throughout this book, brightness is the luminance appearance of a surface when compared with another that is lighter or darker. The term *apparent brightness* carries the connotation that the appearance of a surface is something of an illusion from what the eye is actually seeing. This is not the case. There is nothing "apparent" about brightness at all. Regardless of the conditions to which the eye is adapted at the time, a surface will nevertheless take on its brightness depending on how it compares with other surfaces in the vicinity. It is not apparent *brightness,* but apparent *luminance* that the eye sees. *Adaptive brightness,* therefore, is intended to describe the perceived visual sensation of a surface that changes in situations where its physical luminance stays constant, but its brightness is modified due to light or dark adaptation of the eye. The phenomenon of adaptive brightness is easily observed by standing some distance back from an open doorway of a room while looking into another room of middle illumination (neither high nor low). Having someone switch the lights on and off in your room will make the surfaces in the adjoining room shift to brighter or darker appearances. That is, the surfaces in the adjacent room undergo adaptive brightness resulting from your eyes responding to the changing light conditions of the space in which you are standing.

To learn more about the theory of interspatial adaptive brightness, a laboratory exercise was created to observe how the luminances of two illuminated spaces change in brightness relationships as a result of retinal adaptation. A spatial figure-ground condition (Figure 13-1) was set up in an Interspace Model (see the Appendix), where upper level and graduate students of architec-

ture, interior design, and lighting design studied adaptive brightness in connected spaces. A rectangular block (figure) was placed spatially in front of the rear wall (ground) of Space B in the model, and was proportionally sized to provide adequate surface area for brightness comparisons with the wall behind. A foreground "room" (Space A) was established by inserting a framing wall with an opening simulating a doorway. All surfaces were covered with the same material to maintain common reflectance.

The task of the exercise was to observe brightness changes for the block, the distant wall, and the surface of the framing wall as a result of increasing illumination in Space A. To facilitate this, Space B was held constant at a series of regular intervals, while Space A was used as the light-inducing variable space for retinal adaptation. The block was illuminated by a source mounted on an optical bench and was also held constant. Only the block, the rear wall, and floor were visible in Space B, but that was enough to provide the appearance of a full room. Both spaces were independently illuminated by luminous ceilings, with the intensity varied by dimmers in the research model's control panel.

The exercise began in a darkened laboratory with Space A also darkened, and Space B set in mood to create what was called a "softly lit room" (Figure 13-2), which was recorded at 1.2 units of illumination. Subjective as it was, students were asked to memorize the appearance of Space B by comparing the brightness of the block with the wall behind it. Their academic background in design was especially helpful for this task. Next, Space B was raised to a 1.3-unit setting (Figure 13-3a). Subjects

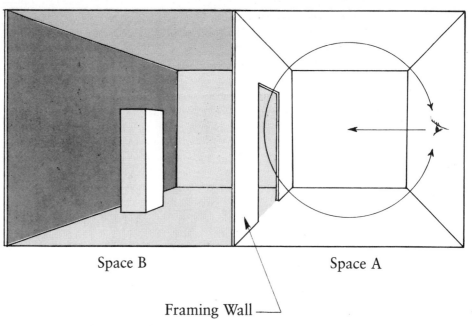

Space B   Space A

Framing Wall

Figure 13-1. Adaptive brightness for spatial figure-ground.

Figure 13-2. Control Space B: the "softly lit room."

then introduced illumination to Space A until the distant wall behind the block appeared to return to its original setting of the "softly lit room." This was the experience of interspatial adaptive brightness. It occurred because the retina had adapted to the light-inducing Space A, and caused Space B to look slightly darker even though its illumination did not change. Each observer performed this step six times. The process was repeated for five more settings of Space B, arithmetically raising its illumination in increments of 0.1 unit. At each increased setting for Space B, subjects restored its initial "softly lit" appearance by raising the illumination in Space A, darkening what was visible through the doorway.

Figure 13-3 shows a series of photographs[1] documenting the exercise and showing how Space A was steadily brightened and how Space B darkened as a consequence, in spite of the fact that the distant space was increased in luminance.

How did those participating in this laboratory exercise respond to the changing conditions of interspatial brightness? Among 83 students reporting their observa-

tions, there was remarkable consistency in their selections of illumination for Space A, but only up to the level of 1.5 units for Space B (Figure 13-3c), i.e., only for the first three of the six incremental increases of light required to restore Space B to its original appearance as a "softly lit room." There was widespread disagreement when Space B was set at its last three settings. Only 48% of the students continued to raise the illumination of Space A at approximately the same proportional increases for the highest three settings of Space B. Their data is given in Table 13-1.

Mention should be made of the increasing luminance on the block, as a result of rising ambient light in Spaces A and B. Of significance is the fact that it actually tripled in luminance over the six settings, yet it appeared to lose brightness as the framing wall gained in brightness, all caused by the retina adapting to the increasing light on the spatial envelope of Space A.

The graph of Figure 13-4 plots the luminance readings from Table 13-1 against the increases in illumination of Space B. Increases of luminance on the rear wall (RW) are compared with those on the surface of the framing wall (FW). The line RW shows the relatively consistent increases in luminance on the rear wall as the illumination for Space B was increased at regular intervals of 0.1 unit. It is line FW that calls striking attention to the nature of interspatial adaptive brightness. It shows that once Space B was raised in illumination above the first

---

[1] The photographs are vivid reminders of the difference between the chemistry of film and the activity of photoreceptors in the retina of the human eye (see the Appendix). Some surfaces vary slightly from what might be expected from the luminance measurements given later in Tables 13-1 and 13-2. Darkroom adjustments of the illustrations were made to approximate the brightness relationships.

(a)

(b)

(c)

Figure 13-3. Laboratory study of interspatial adaptive brightness. a. Space B: 1.3 units; b. Space B: 1.4 units; c. Space B: 1.5 units; d. Space B: 1.6 units.

Designing with Space and Light

(d)

Figure 13-3. (Continued)

three steps (i.e., above 1.5 units), much greater increases of light surrounding the observer's eyes were required to visually reduce the brightness of Space B to approximate its original appearance as a softly lit room. The graph tells us something else. The difference in luminance between the framing wall and the rear wall is relatively close for the first three settings of Space B (up to 1.5 units), and it was at those lower levels of illumination that nearly all students could perform the task with ease. But when the lighting of Space B was raised to and above 1.6 units, half of the total group (made up of advanced design students) had difficulty looking through the brightness surrounding their eyes to establish what they remembered to be the original appearance of the softly lit room.

The results of this exercise give further insights into the all important relationship between luminance ratios and acceptable brightness-contrast for human vision in architectural space. That is, what is the limit for contrast that—when exceeded—is perceptually detrimental to human comfort? In Chapter 3 it is stated that a surface that is 3 times that of its background will create a prominent focal area in its environment, and one 10 times its background will appear as a dominant visual force. The exercise for lighting a figure in space presented in Chapter 12 in the section on contrasting brightness for visual accents, p. 197 confirmed that a luminance ratio of 3 : 1

is necessary to establish a visual accent in space, but a ratio of 5 : 1 is an upper limit beyond which it is unnecessary to add further contrast to give a figure visual prominence. Now let us consider the results of the present exercise, which investigated figure-ground relationships in interspatial conditions based on adaptive brightness. Luminance ratios for the doorway, block, and rear wall are listed in Table 13-2: At the highest setting for Space B (1.8 units), the contrast of the surface around the doorway was 4.38 times the rear wall, much greater than how it appears in the photograph of Figure 13-3d. When looking into the research model at that setting, Space B looks near totally dark. Even when the doorway was raised to that highest level of luminance, the *measured* difference in actual luminance never reached a 5 : 1 ratio.

The appearance of the block went the reverse direction from that of the surface around the doorway. At the lowest setting for Space B (Figure 13-3a), the block was 20.73 times the luminance of the back wall, appearing brilliantly in space. At 1.4 units (Figure 13-3b) the block fell quickly to a 9.27 : 1 luminance ratio with the rear

Table 13-1. Surface luminances (cd/ft²)

Space B Settings	Rear Wall	Block	Framing Wall
1.3 units	0.0477	0.9899	0.0732
1.4	0.1178	1.0918	0.2355
1.5	0.2642	1.2859	0.6971
1.6	0.5156	1.7061	1.8016
1.7	0.8912	2.3554	3.6605
1.8	1.4578	3.4695	6.3883

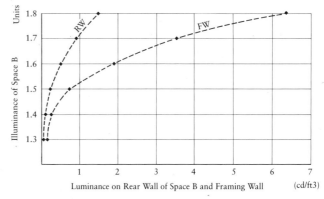

Figure 13-4. Luminance relationships for interspatial adaptive brightness.

Table 13-2. Luminance ratios

Space B Settings	Luminance Ratio Doorway to Rear Wall	Luminance Ratio Block to Rear Wall
1.3 units	1.53 : 1	20.73 : 1
1.4	2.00 : 1	9.27 : 1
1.5	2.64 : 1	4.87 : 1
1.6	3.49 : 1	3.31 : 1
1.7	4.11 : 1	2.64 : 1
1.8	4.38 : 1	2.38 : 1

wall, and at 1.5 units (Figure 13-3c), it was reduced to 4.87 : 1. Note at 1.6 units (Figure 13-3d), the block has lost brightness dominance in an interspatial relationship with the doorway, although it maintains dominance as figure to ground in its own space. The important lesson to be learned is that the diminished figural brightness of the block and the space it occupies was caused *by the light in the space of the viewer,* not by its own surrounding illumination, nor its own luminance.

This study was an attempt to improve on guidelines for the designer trying to steer between the troublesome Scylla and Charybdis, between the *measurement* and the *appearance* of luminance ratios to achieve desired interspatial brightness relationships. The difficulty of performing the task after the framing doorway was raised to 3.5 times the luminance of the back wall (the 1.6 units setting in Table 13-2)—as experienced by half of the participants—showed that there are upper limits for the amount of luminance contrast in creating good spatial connections. Further, when the contrast between two spaces is too high, and in the absence of a transitional zone between the two, the movement from one to another violates good practice for humanistic design due to the abrupt change for the retina. When connecting adjoining spaces of different lighting levels, these principles need to be remembered:

- Any increase of illumination in the room of the observer will darken the appearance of an adjacent space as seen through an opening in a common wall.

- Conversely, any decrease of illumination in the room of the observer will brighten the appearance of surfaces in an adjoining room.

Application of Adaptive Brightness to Architectural Space

Measuring after-the-fact installations of lighting is obviously quite different from making before-the-fact calculations of illumination to achieve what the designer wants for a desired effect. When a design situation calls for a certain space to appear brighter or darker as seen from an adjacent room, steps can be taken to give its dominant surfaces a luminance level necessary to counteract retinal adaptation and create the desired apparent luminance.

Hopkinson and Collins (1970, 186ff) published the adaptation level curves of Figures 13-5 and 13-6 to be used for deriving the actual luminances required to make distant surfaces appear at a brightness desired by the designer, when it is known that contrasting lighting in the observer's immediate environment will consequently change the brightenss of the distant surfaces as a result of retinal adaptation.[2] Their methodical series of design steps is so logical and easy to follow it is paraphrased here. The graphs originally were drawn to the older luminance units of footlamberts, and to preserve the accuracy of the curves, the footlambert unit was used in Figures 13-5 and 13-6 and in the example to follow, instead of the now accepted unit of candela.

Hopkinson and Collins give the problem of an exhibition hall, in which an exhibit is to appear at a brightness contrast of 10 : 1 to make it stand out in its environment. If the background for the display is at 10, the exhibit

[2] The reader may also wish to consult J. M. Waldram (1954, 1978), Hopkinson and Kay (1969), and Dietz and Lam (1976, 34).

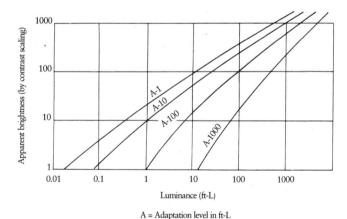

A = Adaptation level in ft-L

Figure 13-5. Adaptation level curves for proposed apparent luminance. [From Hopkinson and Collins, 1970]

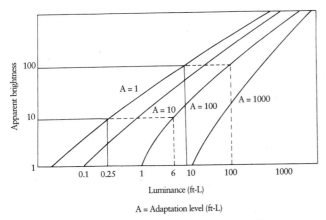

Figure 13-6. Working example for proposed apparent luminance. [From Hopkinson and Collins, 1970]

will have to appear at 100. That is, the exhibit must have a luminance to make it *appear* 10 times greater than its background. To achieve this, Hopkinson and Collins suggest the following method:

1. By choice, the designer selects a desired average luminance for the exhibit that will make its details easy to see and graphics easy to read. The first decision is to prescribe the average illuminance for the exhibit to meet that visibility task, which is to be not less than about 50 fc. Assume the surfaces of the exhibit have an average reflectance of 20%. The average luminance of the exhibit must therefore be $0.2 \times 50 = 10$ fL.

2. Select the adaptation level curve (A) from those of Figure 13-5, which will convert the average exhibit luminance of 10 fL to the *apparent* luminance (their "apparent brightness") of 100 to create the 10 : 1 ratio initially prescribed. This adaptation level curve is found to be approximately 1 fL.

3. Now find the luminance for the surface area surrounding the exhibit, using the 1-fL adaptation level curve taken from step 2. Following the 1-fL curve of Figure 13-6, it can be seen from the graph that an "apparent brightness" of 10 will require an actual luminance of 0.25 fL. That is the required luminance of the background for the exhibit to have the 10 : 1 contrast dictated by the design problem.

4. The last step is to provide the illumination for the background, i.e., to give a luminance of 0.25 fL. If the reflectance of the surfacing material is 10%, the required luminance would be achieved by a value of illumination of 2.5 fc.

Hopkinson and Collins' adaptation level curves (Figure 13-5) lend themselves to the analysis of interspatial adaptive brightness when connecting two spaces. Instead of asking how much brighter an exhibit should appear against its background, the question becomes how much

brighter or darker should the spatial envelope or other major surface of an adjoining space appear in ratio to the framing wall of the observer's space like Figure 13-1. This assumes that the connecting wall is similar in luminance to the other major surfaces surrounding the observer.

Figure C-52 illustrates conditions of interspatial adaptive brightness in a museum setting. The spatial envelope of the foreground gallery is dimly illuminated, which brings out the prominence of the exhibits. As we saw with the laboratory study of Figure 13-3, the apparent luminance of the bright panel exhibiting the painting in the next gallery can be manipulated in brightness ratios by the framing doorway. Increasing the overall illumination in the foreground gallery would reduce contrast with the distant wall and painting (and also reduce its appeal as a visual draw into the next gallery). The surfacing materials of the two spatial envelopes (foreground and adjacent gallery) are also influential for how their luminances communicate brightness. Two systems can now be brought together for creating spatial aesthetics in sequencing two connected rooms similar to the galleries shown in Figure C-52. First, the brightness comparison or contrast between the major surfaces involved in the spatial connection can be studied using the brightness zones of the LBR Scale. The Munsell notations of those zones are of known reflectance (Chapter 5, p. 73), the necessary factor for calculating luminances. Second, using those reflectance values along with Hopkinson's adaptation level curves and method for calculating apparent luminances, the designer has guidelines for the ultimate selection of surfacing materials and illumination levels to achieve aesthetic spatial connections. An adjoining space intended to entice entry must be given apparent luminance at a brightness ratio that will draw people toward it, and at the same time provide appropriate illumination for the function of the room once the observer has moved into it.

Consider the importance of visual draw as it applies to stores in a shopping mall, where the independent merchants compete for potential buyers. In most cases, the lighting of the mall proper is a given condition of illumination before the designer of any individual shop begins to work. Therefore, the general lighting in the area of the mall directly in front of a shop creates the luminance of whatever building material frames the shop's entry. That framed entrance influences the apparent luminance on the walls and furnishings inside.

Figure C-53 shows a jeweler's shop in a mall, illustrating the theory of interspatial adaptive brightness. The wood around the entrance is the surface for brightness comparison with the interior of the shop. The subdued interior envelope would darken considerably more if the framing entrance was brightened significantly. Looking along the centerline directly into the left entrance of the store is the same visual field seen in the last chapter (Figure C-48). The sensitive, tenebristic lighting of the floor display cases maintains the store's appeal from outside the store, primarily due to the lower luminance of the wood on the exterior shop front.

The Shape of Things to Come: The Visual Objective

In the experiences of life, what are the things that build anticipation? For some it can be the approach of a weekend, holiday, or vacation. Or it could be the concluding chapter of a good mystery, or the crescendo finale of Ravel's "Boléro" or Tchaikovsky's "1812 Overture." Each of these is an "objective" involving a thought or activity along a time line, and is imbued with qualities of curiosity, suspense, climax, or a sense of completion. The same is true for the visual world, like walking in a forest and sighting a distant snow-covered mountain peak framed by tall ponderosa pines; or stepping into a street at night and seeing the full moon framed between two buildings. Throughout the architectural environment there are many such visual encounters.

Fixation on an object or graphic strategically placed for visual prominence from specific viewing angles focuses attention on that element. It becomes a *visual objective*, attracting and momentarily holding attention for a person moving through a connecting space. The concept is an outstanding planning tool for spatial sequencing. When well done, a glimpse of something interesting through an architectural frame arouses curiosity and stimulates interest by giving hints of the shape of things to come.

We saw in Chapter 10 how seeing but a fragment of an alluring image can arouse curiosity and entice movement in its direction. As the observer advances, the partially visible form gradually unfolds. This quality is what has made the streets of Old Europe interesting to tourists. Figure 13-7 shows the south transept of Chartres Cathedral in France, framed by a narrow street. The cathedral's magnificent rose window and sculptured portal create a powerful visual draw through the space. The building's effectiveness as a visual objective is amplified by the fact the spatial envelope of the framing street is perceptually more simplified in detail than the cathedral. The photograph was taken in the morning sun, when lighting contrast adds to the effectiveness of the cathedral's transept as a visual objective. The perpendicular street in front of the facade and the steps leading to the portal catch direct sunlight and are framed by the shadowed street. The experience of walking to the end of the street is sheer spatial excitement. Gradual expansion of space

Figure 13-7. Curiosity and exploration. [Chartres Cathedral, France]

accompanies the line of travel, while the cathedral looms larger and larger with each forward step. Upon approach, the full transept comes into view, and details of the richly sculptured portal enlarge to become the next area of focal interest.

In Baroque Rome the great master Bernini clearly understood how to focus attention on a work of art. His Scala Regia in the Vatican (Figures 13-8 and 13-9) should be etched in the memory of every architect and interior designer. At the end of an axial line from the narthex of the basilica, he placed a monumental equestrian sculpture of the Early Christian Emperor Constantine (right in Figure 13-9), a powerful visual image framed by the narthex entry. Its focal prominence invites approach. Arriving at its base, the observer then discovers another visual objective, which in turn attracts attention up the stairs of the Scala Regia. To achieve this, Bernini covered (and darkened) the entire stair with a barrel vault, but broke the excessive length of the ascent by inserting a window and landing at midpoint where light interrupts the darkness. Under the vault of the second stage, the stair dims again. At the end of the space,

Designing with Space and Light

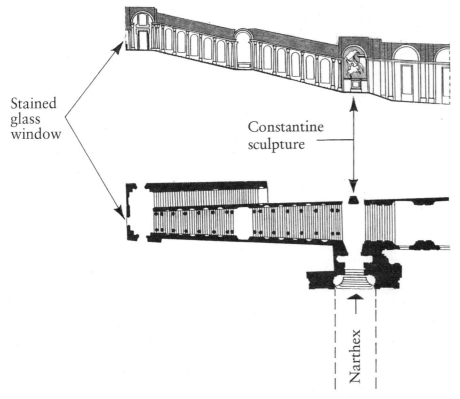

Stained glass window

Constantine sculpture

Narthex

Figure 13-8. Plan and section of the Scala Regia. [Vatican, Rome]

a stained glass window breaks the darkness like a beacon of colored light. The Constantine sculpture, the mid-landing, and the window are each dominated by light. They forcefully and rhythmically draw the eye to those pivotal locations in space.

Aristide Maillol's reclining nude *L'Air* (Figure 13-10) in the court of the Kimbell Art Museum takes prominence essentially because of its sculptural form. The fact that its image is a human figure places it at the top of the hierarchy of perceptual focal accents (Chapter 4, p. 62). Its fluid contours contrast the surrounding architectural geometry, adding to its conspicuousness. Placed in its setting it is a strong visual objective, connecting the spaces of interior gallery and exterior court. It would be stronger yet without the competing intense brightness under the vault, and without the glaring reflections on the floor.

Carefully placed visual objectives can enrich the walk through a building and make it more enjoyable. Numerous opportunities present themselves when designing spatial sequences, and these interest centers can be created without lavish expenditures to exhibit them. Figure C-54 shows how perceptually simplified but spatially attractive the design for a visual objective can be. The ceiling and all vertical surfaces of the small connecting space are monochromatic, and the compatible colors of carpeting and wood detailing of the handrails enhance

the definition of the path of movement. Framed at the end of the space is a small painting, whose image is heightened by a single downlight emphasizing its presence.

Framing the Visual Objective

Placing a frame between the walker and a visual objective makes the objective more effective by blocking out any distracting influence of neighboring visual activity (Figure 13-11). An important part of framing a visual objective is the role of light. Due to luminance variations of all surfaces in the environment, it is helpful for the designer to remember two working principles for the brightness relationships that will develop between the frame and what is framed. These are shown in Figure 13-12: the *contrasting frame* and the *connecting frame*. The distinction between the two is determined by the average luminance on the frame compared with the visual field beyond. The contrasting frame can be either a dark-to-light or light-to-dark condition, both of which create an emphatic separation of the space. If what is behind the frame are multiple surfaces, the average luminance of major surfaces is used.

the contrasting frame principle in the light-to-dark mode at the entry of an office building. The luminance of the brick surface creates a comparatively bright frame for the arched opening leading to the entrance doors. Three sidewalks converge in a small space just in front of the doors. That space is cast in shadow, contrasting the outer arched frame. The shadowed space is a zone of transition, helping the eye of the entering visitor to adapt to the darker interior of the building. Contrasting brightness of the circular opening above adds spatial interest.

The Light at the End of the Tunnel

Spatial framing is not limited to simply cutting holes, slits, or doorways into a plane separating two adjacent spaces. The shape and lighting of a circulation space can be exceptionally effective in setting up a visual objective and enriching the path of movement. The directional shapes of corridors, stairways, ramps, and escalators,

Figure 13-9. Art as visual leads through space. [Scala Regia, Vatican Palace, Vatican State, Rome. Architect: Gian Lorenzo Bernini. Photograph: Alinari/ Art Resource, NY S0031186 AL11831]

The connecting frame applies to a condition in which the luminance on the surface of the frame is close to the average luminance behind it. Contrast between the frame and the field beyond is weak, and the space of the viewer and the space framed are more connected than separated. The situation can be light-to-light or dark-to-dark. In either case the reduced luminance-contrast mitigates the impact of the frame as a dramatic perceptual stimulus. When passing through a connecting frame, the sense of lighting change tends to be only subliminal.

An example of the connecting frame is shown in Figure 13-13, showing an arched entrance to a corridor space that follows. A bright red, backlit corporation logo is set into a pure white, gently concaved wall, and presents a vivid visual objective as seen from a distant approach (right of the camera). The sweep of the arch frames and clearly invites entry into the next space of similar luminances in sequence.

The contrasting frame accentuates the edge of the opening as a perceptual stimulus. Figure 13-14 shows

Figure 13-10. Form-dominant visual objective. [Kimbell Art Museum, Fort Worth, Texas. Architect: Louis I. Kahn. Sculptor: Aristide Maillol]

Designing with Space and Light

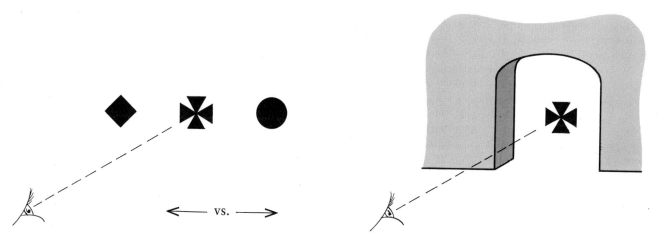

Figure 13-11. Theory of spatial framing for increased emphasis.

make natural frames for "the shape of things to come." Their elongated spatial envelopes telescope the observer's view toward surface areas or spatial intersections that lie ahead. Those surfaces and intersections are premier locations for a visual objective. Contrast between the framing space and the objective gives greater emphasis to the oncoming scene—like the proverbial "light at the end of the tunnel."

Figure 13-15 shows the principle of a visual objective framed by the natural directional space of a loggia in the landscaped court of the Seattle Science Center (also see Figure 13-23). The loggia shades its interior space at a luminance level comfortable for human vision. At the end of the loggia, landscape elements become the visual objective, framed and screened by two arches. The walker's attention is naturally drawn to trees, a bench that invites sitting, and a strategically placed fountain, whose sound, movement, and glittering brightness are high on the hierarchical list of focal accents for percep-

tual attraction. The brightness and interest of the court lead the visitor through space.

Figure C-55 shows a circulation tunnel that was designed to connect new galleries at the Detroit Institute of Arts. The walls of the tunnel are dark, and on its ceiling was painted a rainbow of stripes, which appears to glow under the influence of linear fluorescent lighting in recessed coves. The tunnel focuses on a sculpture by Jean Arp, which serves as a visual lead into one of the galleries. The vivid, colorful stripes create a powerful perspective thrust toward the sculpture. The visual draw is heightened further by the contrasting bright field behind the sculpture. Surface modulations on the figure were enhanced by support lighting mounted overhead. The illuminated sculpture and its bright backdrop effectively serve as the "light at the end of the tunnel" that leads museum visitors to the next gallery. Space, light, color, and art are integrated into a unified visual experience.

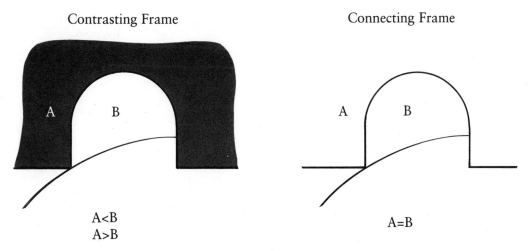

Contrasting Frame

Connecting Frame

Figure 13-12. Contrasting versus connecting frame.

Figure 13-13. Connecting frames in sequence. [3M, Infomart, Dallas]

Figure 13-14. Contrasting frame, light to dark.

Figure 13-15. Directional space framing a visual objective. [Seattle Science Center. Architect: Minoru Yamasaki]

Figure 13-16 shows the intersection of two corridors, looking into a technology demonstration area. The visitor is attracted to a first visual objective, then a second. The graphic logo is the first visual lead for people approaching from the right, and arrival at the intersection brings into view a second graphic feature. Framed by the two angled walls is a large illuminated map that is only partly visible. With all other spatial boundaries designed in perceptual simplicity, the map becomes the prominent visual objective. Its partial visibility announces a change of direction in the distant space. Spatial connection via light is reinforced by architectural detailing. The curved end of the logo points to the map, and the vivid dark inset strips add linear action to the directional quality of the space.

Creating and illuminating a spatial connection with a visual objective was beautifully—and quite simply—done by Eero Saarinen in his design for the MIT Chapel. Visitors enter the building through a small entry space bounded by walls of translucent glass (Figure 13-17a). Even on bright, sunny days, the general light level in the entrance space is soft, as is the brick interior of the chapel (Figure 13-17b). The low ambient light pervading both spaces heightens the bright marble altar table and the sculptural hanging behind it. Serving as more than just a visual lead into the chapel, the design

of the sculpture is fitting and refined for its immediate setting. Set against the austere spatial envelope of the cylinder that shapes the chapel's space, it appears as a stop-action fall of shimmering light. It is fashioned out of glazed metal chips suspended on wires, and their spacing gradually decreases downward. The effect is one of inspirational light descending from above, and also lifts vision upward toward the source of light, a covered oculus above the altar. The portion of greater density of the chips is what is framed by the doorway of the entry. Joining the gleaming brightness of the altar table, the array of glittering light beckons the visitor to enter the chapel.

It is clear from these examples that good use of visual objectives is not just a matter of plugging in a form or graphic at locations that more or less simply came about in the routine of design. *Quality architectural design using a visual objective depends on the mutual interaction between the featured object and the character of the focusing architectural space,* each working in reciprocation, each depending on the other for the interchange of surface luminances in brightness composition. The clarity and integrity of the directional spatial envelope must be maintained, and the visual objective must be protected from any surrounding visual disturbance such as unnecessary or ill-placed detailing. As the design pro-

Figure 13-16. Visual objectives inducing movement. [Mission Network Technology Center, Southwestern Bell Telephone Company, Mission, Kansas. Photograph: © John Brewer]

(a)   (b)

Figure 13-17. Visual invitation to enter. [Kresge Chapel, Massachusetts Institute of Technology, Cambridge. Architect: Eero Saarinen. Altar hanging sculpture: Harry Bertoia]

cess moves from stages of development to refinement, detailing should be introduced to support the visual objective, and never intrude on its sphere of work as a focal accent.

Visual Objective Planning

Setting up visual objectives to connect spaces is a potent device for adding human interest to the mainstream movement patterns through a building or city. It is executed most successfully when made part of the initial schematic design of a building, or when coordinating building-space relationships in the larger context of the city. The hypothetical plan shown in Figure 13-18 conveys the theory of visual objective planning in a variety of connected nodes of interest, coordinated with major circulation routes. The diagram suggests rhythms of space and light sequences, changing levels, and intermittent expansion and contraction of varying spatial envelopes. The objective nodes can be visualized as sculptures, kiosks, murals, exits or entries, receptionist stations, intersections of underground concourses, a chil-

dren's play area in a park, or a highrise seen in the distance signaling a change in direction of the street. Visual objectives not only direct paths of movement, but relay significant distance clues for awareness of walking or driving times.

It was a visual objective that made the connection shown in Figure C-55 successful. We explained earlier how that connection came about as a result of new additions to the original building of the Detroit Institute of Arts. Figure C-56 shows the Jean Arp sculpture from another vantage point. Its placement on axis of the tunnel connects it with another piece of sculpture framed by the other end of the tunnel, leading to another exhibition space. The Arp was positioned in a lobby for an auditorium and set against a semicircular, floor-to-ceiling glass cove. Through that glass wall, the double spatial connection of the sculptures is visible. Architectural planning made possible this interplay of major works of art, all enhanced by the control of spatial light.

Visual objectives have been consciously planned into the layout of architectural and urban design for more than 300 years. Baroque architects skillfully created architectural form-space relationships by intentionally placing focal accents as leads along pedestrian and vehic-

Designing with Space and Light

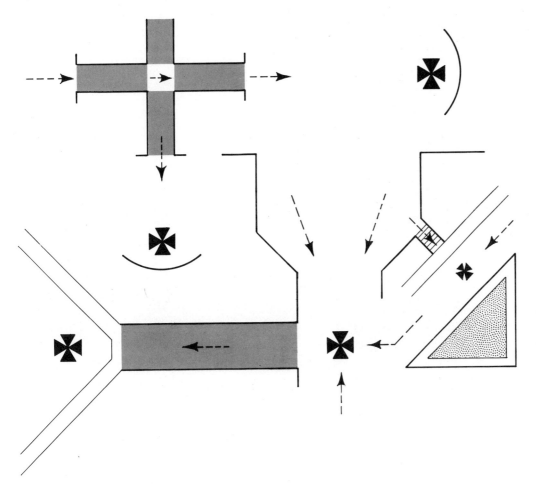

Figure 13-18. Visual objective planning.

ular traffic routes. In Baroque Rome obelisks marked important urban sites, linked by major streets. People today still benefit from those decisions. From the base of the Spanish Stairs, the obelisk in the center of the Piazza del Popolo (nine city blocks away) is clearly visible, framed by the connecting street. The same obelisk is a focal center for two other streets entering the piazza.

Paris is the benefactor of the planning imagination of Georges-Eugène Haussmann and others, where strong focal accents have long provided orientation for Parisians and visitors alike, as well as providing clues for travel distance. Standing in the court of the Louvre, the distant obelisk in the Place de la Concorde is framed through the arches of the Arc de Triomphe du Carrousel. Looking north from that obelisk, the church of La Madeleine is framed by the Rue Royale. The famed boulevard of the Champs Élysées rises gently to focus on the Arc de Triomphe, which in turn serves as a visual objective for 10 more major streets that enter its spatial sphere. Seen from the northwest, the Eiffel Tower is framed by the Palais de Chaillot and the Trocadero Gardens, and straddles a shaft of space that culminates at the École

Militaire. The Paris Opera House and the Church of the Invalides are also masterful architectural climaxes for major spatial thoroughfares in the city. Those architectural landmarks take on meaning beyond their value as historical monuments. Seen from distances, people know whether to walk or take a taxi. Visitors find their way around more comfortably. Directions are given more easily.

In interior architecture, visual objective planning is instrumental for coordinating major functional spaces and their connecting circulation routes. This is especially applicable to highrise design, to connect a space on one floor with others at different levels. Elevator stations require visual prominence, particularly in spacious entry lobbies of hotels or other buildings where the ground floor contains a number of diversified activities. The interior of the elevator itself becomes a spatial intermezzo between the building's entry floor and the floor of destination. The architect may not always enjoy the liberty of creating spacious elevator lobbies at each floor, but visual objective planning can be helpful for continuing visitor orientation even where space limitations pre-

Connecting Spaces with Light

Figure 13-19. Food for thought. [American Republic Insurance Company, Des Moines, Iowa]

Figure 13-20. Night illumination for spatial interaction.

(a)

(b)

(c)

Figure 13-21. Visual draw from street to interior. [UMB Financial Corp., Kansas City, Missouri. Architects: Abend Singleton Associates.]

vail. As an example, Figure 13-19 shows a small upper floor hall of a multistoried building, where elevators give egress to an insurance company's cafeteria. Employees and visitors alike know exactly which way to proceed immediately after stepping out of the elevator. Two sculpted apples provide a delightful—or perhaps delicious—visual objective. They say: "The cafeteria is this

way." Note the role of light. The framing spatial envelope of the hall is softly illuminated. The apples (one yellow and one red) provide the only color in the field of view, and stand out in vivid figure-ground against a white partition, which directs the flow of people left and right into the cafeteria. No signage is needed. Visitors to the building asking for directions to a luncheon meeting can be told quite simply: "Go to the sixth floor, and you'll see where to go from there."

Visual objective planning at the schematic stage of building design can establish interaction points for circulation between the exterior city and interior architecture. With night lighting, the interior springs to life, attracting the notice of passersby. Figure 13-20 shows the entrance of a bank framing interior visual objectives in the lobby. On the axis of entry, a piece of sculpture creates a visual draw. Trees inside and a graphic on the second floor all attract attention. Seen from the street, the effectiveness of these visual objectives becomes more interesting architecturally by the *screening* of the glass entrance wall, a topic we take up next.

The sequence of photographs of Figure 13-21 shows how a fountain and sculpture set up the experience of entering an exterior court of a bank building, as seen from the outer urban environment. Beginning at a street intersection (Figure 13-21a), an avenue of pedestrian space leads into the court, from where access to interior offices is found. The fountain, sculpture, and trees are framed by the columns, steps, and ramp for the handicapped. Midway along the entrance path (Figure 13-21b), the far elevation of the bank has blocked out the neighboring buildings, and openings in the flanking columns begin to reveal the spatial envelope shaping the court. The brightness of the court is heightened by the framing effect of the contrasting black and dark brown granite sheathing of the columns. Once the observer arrives at the fountain (Figure 13-21c), the narrow, vertical spatial envelope of the approach has given way to the broad, horizontal envelope surrounding the court. From there, stairs and other entrances lead into the building. They become the next visual objectives, continuing the logical flow of movement from street to building interior.

The planning of space and the planning of light can set up conditions for emphasizing selected nodes in interior and exterior architecture. Throughout the public environment, carefully designed visual objectives make them more easily remembered and thus useful for orientation and way finding. At the same time they bring spatial excitement to the visual environment. Outdoors in Paris, directions may be given for finding the Place de la Concorde by pointing out its obelisk several blocks away. In the lobby of a Des Moines insurance company building, directions may be given for finding the cafeteria by saying: "Push the elevator button for the sixth floor, and then look for the apples."

Figure 13-22. Screened space as architectural beauty. [Court of the Lions, Alhambra, Granada, Spain]

Screened Light in Space

One of the richest features of design aesthetics that has persisted through architectural history and across cultural lines is the screening of space and light. Its consistent appearance has doubtless been due to its basic human appeal. In the ancient world, its use for prominent buildings surely stemmed from early discovery of its sensuous and mystical effects. The sacred axis of Egyptian temples is veiled by screened light in the hypostyle hall, filtered through stone grilles in a clerestory high above. The Parthenon on Athens' Acropolis is first seen through the screening columns of the entrance Propylaea. Examples of screened space in Islamic mosques and palaces provide encyclopedic lessons worthy of study and restudy. In the Alhambra's Court of the Lions (Figure 13-22), the loggia surrounding the court humanizes the environment and articulates the space in design excellence. Small pavilions at each end of the court step into the space accompanying the visitor's forward path of movement, and hold in focus the fountain of the lions in the center of the space. Slender columns of the pavilions screen the surrounding arcade, and create alternating light and shade in poetic rhythm. Subspaces of the loggia and pavilions gracefully merge with that of the court in a unified spatial experience, each supporting the other. All is activated by only one light source: the sun. The Alhambra provides a textbook definition of architectural beauty.

The popularity of the loggia throughout the history of architecture stems from its practicality of offering protection from the sun and from how it contributes to design aesthetics. The screening effect of its structural supports creates patterns of interspatial brightness relationships that effectively articulate architectural space. Like those of the Alhambra, the structural members of the loggia at Seattle's Science Center (Figure 13-23) appear in near silhouette as seen from inside the loggia, in contrast to the brighter concrete and water in the court bathed in sunlight. In design harmony the arches forming the screen repeat as detailing on the buildings across the court. As the visitor walks along, the fountains and trees are seen shifting in and out of the arched openings. The camera location for the photograph is the same as that seen previously in Figure 13-15; both illustrations show how carefully planned screens effectively animate the architectural environment as seen from a variety of viewing angles.

Screened lighting effects have become increasingly popular for spatial connections in contemporary interior architecture. They define subspaces within a larger parent room, create intimacy for the subspaces while merging them with the greater room, and increase air flow compared with solid partitions. Screens are available in a variety of materials, but basically fall into two categories: *transparent plane* (tinted or textured glass, glass block, etc.) and *openwork grilles*. Nonperforated, transparent materials do not permit air and heat flow, but they do

Figure 13-23. Screening the sun.

visually connect two adjacent spaces by communicating a presence on the other side when there is higher illumination behind the surface than in front. The use of grilles, however, involves a number of complications for designers, because their physical openings and surface finishes introduce different perceptual phenomena.

There are four fundamental considerations for choosing from the wide variety of designs available from grille manufacturers: (1) pattern style, (2) the amount of penetration through the grille, known in the trade as percent of opening, (3) thickness of the grille, and (4) type of surface reflectance including its color value. These considerations influence visual perception through the grille, and determine the quality of connection of illuminated spaces. The percent of opening influences visibility and object recognition through the screen. Some grilles have a very small percent of opening to provide minimal visual screening while avoiding complete opacity. The proportional amount of openings in the grille is critical to the success of connecting spaces with light and the quality of mood that results. The thickness of grille design comes into play when seen from different viewing angles. Seen at a slant, thick grilles with small openings tend to close off an adjoining space visually. Thick grilles with a small percent of openings does not mean the grille is a poor design. Their internal and outer surfaces become visually active under the influence of surface reflectance. Re-

flected light on the interior walls and on the outer surfaces of thick grilles can be used to create wonderful mood effects when the screen is angled away from the observer.

For analysis of screened space related to grille design, there are two categories of spatial relationship to be considered: *space merger* and *space separation.* Two spaces *merge* when the percent of opening is large enough and the visual scene behind the grille is of ample illumination to make the observer fully aware of the content and character of the environment on the other side of the screen (Figure 13-24, left). Spaces visually *separate* when a presence behind the screen is more implied than comprehended (Figure 13-24, right).

Under certain conditions of illumination, instead of two spaces merging through the screen, they can appear to separate visually depending on how the grille surface compares in brightness with the general luminances in the space behind the screen. If the space of the observer is much brighter than the space behind the grille, visual merger diminishes or does not take place at all. Conversely, when the screened space is brighter than the space of the observer, visual connection takes place as expected.

From Figure 13-24, it is tempting to formulate a simply stated design guideline: To increase spatial connection, increase the percent of opening of the grille. But it

Figure 13-24. Greater percent of opening tends toward spatial merger. When ample illumination exists on surfaces behind a screen, percent of opening in the design of the grille influences spatial connection or separation. The space of the observer tends to close off from a screened space the more the percent of opening is reduced.

is not that simple. An analysis of screened space in its role of merging or separating two adjacent spaces must also take into consideration the effects of *reflected light on the surface of the grille*. When the grille has a modeled or faceted surface (Figure 13-25), reflections occur at various angles. As a result, multiple brightness ratios are introduced at the plane of the screen, which will then interplay with patches of brightness behind the grille. That interplay influences spatial perception. Therefore, when choosing grille design, more than just style and percent of opening must be considered; it is necessary to anticipate expected modeled arays of brightness that

will take place on the grille surface once it is installed in an illuminated environment.

The theory of the relationship between grille surface reflectance and size of opening is demonstrated in the Interspace Model. In Figure 13-26a, both figurines behind the screens are of equal luminance, and both rear chambers are equal in illumination to that of the foreground space. The grille on the left (Lincane) has 44% of opening, compared with 48% of opening for the grille on the right (Cloverleaf). Both grilles are manufactured perforated sheets of aluminum, and both have nearly the same specular finish. However, they differ in surface

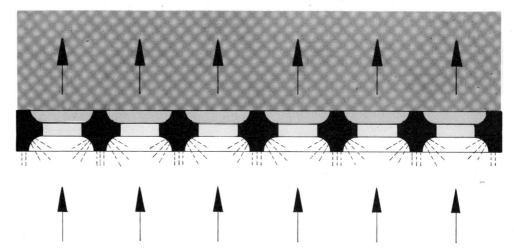

Figure 13-25. Grille surface reflectance inducing perceptual interference. Scattered reflected light on the surface of a dimensional grille creates multiple brightness ratios at the grille plane, which then interact with patterns of brightness behind the screen, significantly influencing interspatial perception.

Designing with Space and Light

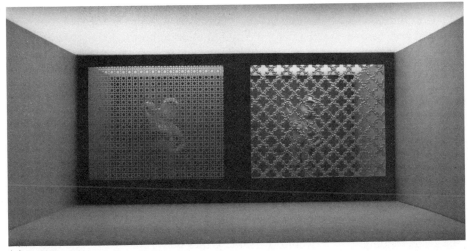

(a)

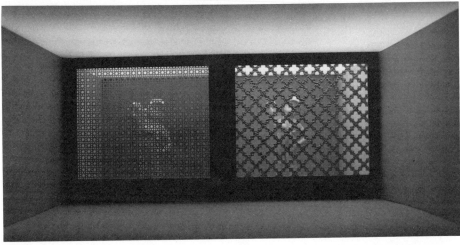

(b)

Figure 13-26. Grille surface reflectance versus percent of opening. a. Two identical figurines are equally illuminated. The one on the left is seen through a flat grille plane with smaller percent of opening, but is more clear than the one on the right seen through a dimensional grille. Multiple surface reflectance on the surface of the dimensional grille blends with patches of brightness and shadow on the figurine behind, camouflaging its form. b. Brightness of the screened space was raised, which increased spatial connection.

texture, and that means they behave differently under the influence of light. The Lincane pattern is totally flat, having a uniform level of brightness across its surface. By contrast, the Cloverleaf is embossed. Its modeled surface has highlighted protrusions, and indentations that trap shadow. Its textured surface thus produces a variegated pattern of brightness. Therefore, numerous patches along the edges of the grille openings blend in value with surface patches on the figurine in the same brightness zones of the LBR Scale. That blending diminishes the effect of edge perception at the grille plane, breaking down its spatial contrast with the figurine behind. A kind of luminance camouflage is taking place.

The Lincane grille offers much less screen surface interference because its surface is flat, and the figurine in that space is actually easier to see despite the fact the percent of opening is *less* than the Cloverleaf. The image of the figure is being rendered not unlike the rows of pixels on a VDT.

How can spatial merger be increased while using either one of the screens? As would be expected, it can be done by increasing brightness in the screened space, which was done in Figure 13-26b. This had the effect of darkening the surfaces of the grilles, and increasing the feeling of spatial connection as the brighter screened space merges with the foreground space. The figurine behind the Lincane gained in prominence along its outer contour, but not at its surface details due to the smaller sizes of perforations in the grille. The figurine behind the larger openings of the Cloverleaf does present greater visibility of its surface details, but it remains somewhat incognito. That is because even with less luminance on the Cloverleaf screen, there is still visual interference because highlights and shadows on the grille and the figurine continue to blend together, but now they are just in different zones on the LBR Scale. Under the higher illumination of the rear chambers, both grilles tend to merge foreground and background spaces, but not to the same degree. The greater percent of opening of the Cloverleaf tends to heighten the feeling of connection, but the smaller openings and flat surface of the Lincane weaken the flow of vision through the grille, tending to close off the space in front.

Because of the visual overlay of a grille pattern on whatever is seen behind it, the perceptual phenomenon of simultaneous contrast changes the appearance of brightness of surfaces behind the screen. Figure 13-27 shows a laboratory study of three white pine wooden grilles of identical design pattern and percent of opening. Two were stained to create variations in surface brightness. Both the room of the observer and the room behind

Figure 13-27. Grille surface modifying brightness in the screened space.

the grilles were painted identical gray. A student is shown testing the brightness relationships of the two rooms by changing the illumination in both. The photograph was taken when both rooms were of equal illumination. Comparing a horizontal row of square openings across all three grilles shows how the brightness of the grilles modifies the appearance of the distant wall behind the screen, caused by simultaneous contrast. The dark walnut grille brightens the space behind; the bright unstained grille darkens the space.

How does color behave when screened by grilles? It changes. And under certain conditions of interspatial lighting, the change is severe. This was tested in the Space and Light Laboratory (Figure C-57). Three broad bands of the primary colors were applied to the screened wall, behind the same grilles of Figure 13-27. The unstained white pine grille (left) appears brighter in front of the red and blue, but slightly darker in front of the yellow. Having a red tone as part of its basic chemistry, the maple stained grille in the center tends to merge with the red strip, but contrasts the yellow and blue. The dark walnut stained grille contrasts all three hues. Again, the effects of simultaneous contrast are readily observed by following one row of each by the three colors all the way across the same row of openings in the grille. Each of three hues darkens under the influence of the unstained white pine, but brighten and appear to glow behind the dark walnut.

Special tests were made to study the influence of percent of opening on color (Figure C-58). A number of different sizes of openings were used to observe the influence of simultaneous contrast on surfaces behind the screen. Three full-scale grilles were then constructed based on those tests, each of a different size of opening. A five-inch square (the grille on the right) was found to be the maximum size of opening through which the color behind the square was totally affected by simultaneous contrast. Seen through an opening larger than that size, the effect weakens.

When differences in illumination of the two rooms take place, however, hues behind the differentially colored grilles of the same percent of opening (Figure C-57) undergo significant change, sometimes drastically. In the lab demonstration of interspatial adaptive brightness discussed earlier, we saw that raising the illumination in the observer's space darkens the appearance of a connected space. To observe the behavior of color in a screened space, the illumination of the two rooms was adjusted so that the grille plane was measured at five times that of the distant wall. All of the color bands dropped in value and saturation under the influence of the brighter screens. Figure C-59 shows the change in color that took place. The yellow band on the laboratory wall is Munsell 5Y 8.5/12. Behind the bright unstained white pine grille (left in C-57), the yellow band dropped

1.5 steps in value, and 4 steps in saturation (chroma), to Munsell 5Y 7/8. What in reality was a bright, pure yellow in the screened space dropped in appearance to a yellowish light brown, when seen through the grille. When the grille plane was increased to just over the 5 : 1 ratio, the yellow dropped further, appearing as a murky olive color (Munsell 5Y 5/4). The red and blue went through similar changes. All three hues, however, change only slightly as they appear in the photograph caused mostly by two-dimensional simultaneous contrast. The colors as seen in the photographs are *not* what is seen by the human eye when looking at the actual screened space. As changes in illumination of the observer's space take place, another perceptual phenomenon occurs: light or dark adaptation. Adaptation combines with simultaneous contrast. This does not happen with the camera, which has no retina. Visitors experiencing these phenomena in the Space and Light Laboratory quickly become convinced of the difference between what is seen in reality and what is seen in photographs.

The designer needs to anticipate perceptual reactions to screened space, and realize that viewing such environments in pictures and advertising literature is far different from how colors and patterns of fabrics will appear in the real world of illuminated architecture. Paint samples and fabric and vinyl swatches can be tested in studio conditions (Figure C-60). Tests of this kind in the Space and Light Laboratory led to the creation of the Color Modulator (see the Appendix) to study and measure color shifts under the influence of simultaneous contrast and retinal light/dark adaptation. Such visual testing of color and luminance ratios will help prevent disappointments about how a surfacing material will look in a permanent screened space installation.

When screening spaces of contrasting illumination, the illusionary flares of the Hermann grid effect will appear (Chapter 2, p. 17). They are easily seen in Figures 13-27 and C-57. Bright flares appear on the walnut grille; dark flares appear on the unstained grille. They are very evident when standing in the real space. Once aware of them, it is difficult not to keep looking at them. Concern for this surface activity does not imply that the designer should avoid using screen styles that tend to generate these illusions. Only under extreme conditions of brightness-contrast can Hermann grid effects contribute to dazzle or visual discomfort. In most cases where the Hermann grid phenomenon is present, the illusions work to animate the surface of the grille itself, and can add visual interest to the total screening effect.

Laboratory theory comes to the aid of the designer when making decisions about screen pattern, color, and lighting. The small waiting room shown in Figure C-61 successfully merges with the lobby in the foreground in a pleasing connection of color, space, and light. The hue of the distant wall is compatible with the wood of the screen; this means that if contrasts occur they will be created more by light than by color. Downlights raise in brightness the two sides of the far wall, which contrast the darker appearance of the grille, but only at the three bays of the grille on each side of the door. Seen through the outer two bays, the brightness values of the interior room blend with those on the surface of the grille, creating similar camouflage effects observed in the laboratory demonstrations (the right chamber of Figure 13-26a). Just like the visual perception of figure-ground, the more the color and brightness of the grille's surface approach the color and brightness of the surfaces behind it, the less pronounced the screening effect. This is observed in the laboratory demonstration of Figure C-57, which compared the unstained grille against the yellow strip, the maple against the red, and the walnut against the blue.

Screened space is especially effective for creating intimate settings in restaurants and other public buildings. Figure 13-28 shows how the design characteristics of the grille influence the spatial perception and mood of a dining area. The percent of opening is moderate (44%), permitting reasonable object recognition through the grille. The surface of the grille is painted black, intensifying the contrast with the screened space. The brightness behind the grille tends to merge the two spaces. When seen at a slant, as is the grille at the distant right in the photograph, the thickness of the grille closes off more of the space behind it, causing its screened space to separate.

Screened space has a wide variety of applications to both interior and exterior architecture. The combination of screen pattern and luminance-contrasts between two spaces enliven the spatial experience. Figure 13-29 shows an entrance lobby where the framework of the doors and windows screen the out-of-doors and their patterns of highlights and shadows move across the floor in response to the moving sun. Interior walls are brightened by reflected light from the sconces around the room, preventing excessive contrast with the outside view that otherwise would be caused by stronger dark adaptation of the retina.

In the center of a corporation building is a large garden court (Figure C-62), designed as an amenity. The architect's intent was to bring a tropical setting into a New England climate, and to bring as much natural light as possible into the building's interior. A hipped glass roof admits abundant daylight into the garden. In the court is an open-framed wooden pavilion, with a bench for sitting. Skylight roof, pavilion, and large floor-to-ceiling glass windows around the spatial envelope of the garden create a variety of experiences of screened light. The framework of the skylight high above casts patterns of light and shadow downward, where they penetrate and intermingle with similar patterns inside the pavilion cre-

Figure 13-28. Grilles subdividing the greater space. [Doubletree at Corporate Woods, Overland Park, Kansas]

Figure 13-29. Screening daylight and spatial animation. [Unity School of Christianity, Unity Village, Missouri. Architects: HNTB]

Designing with Space and Light

ated by its own structure. Visitors to the building enter a reception room, where their view into the garden looks across a lily pond and is screened by the panes of the court windows. A layering of spatial planes—from the window-wall to and through the pavilion, to the distant visual boundary of the garden—enriches spatial depth, all activated by light and shadows.

The "Art of Transition"

Assembling the spaces of a building into functional order while creating aesthetic appeal is integral to the architecture of excellence. Walking through a building can be an uneventful pass through a series of rooms in spatial repetition or an exhilarating experience created by variations that behavioral scientists remind us are basic to the well-being of the human organism. Good transitions therefore become important to avoid monotony along a sequence of spaces, and they are generic to the creation of spatial aesthetics.

Masters of literature, poetry, and music have given ample models of how to connect major themes or passages. Nineteenth-century composer Richard Wagner did it skillfully by what he called "the art of transition." His was a wrestling with connections of sound rather than architectural spaces and light, but the problem is much the same. Wagner's concern was how to create harmonic flow from one verse to another. In a letter he once mentioned his compositional technique for constructing musical bridges to connect one melodious passage with another of contrasting mood:

I now realize that the special fabric of my music (always, of course, most precisely related to the poetic conception) . . . owes its construction above all to the highly sensitive feeling which directs me to interlink and interrelate every element of transition between the most extreme moods. I should now like to call my deepest and most subtle art the art of transition, for the whole fabric of my art is built up on such transitions: sharp and sudden changes I have come to dislike . . .[3]

Wagner's advice is to be well taken. Good transitions contribute to harmonic relationships, whether in great music, novels, or the sequencing of architectural spaces. They are important for accommodating changes of mood, for building up and letting down. The introduction of transitions in architecture does not mean an additional, intermediate space needs to be added where a

[3] Richard Wagner, quoted in Barth, Mack, and Voss (1975, 189).

(a)

(b)

Figure 13-30. Sequencing rhythmic light. a. Entrance, b. Inside transition zone. [Talaquepaque, Sedona, Arizona]

Figure 13-31. Natural visual objective as transition. [Gilman Village, Issaquah, Washington]

where additional shops are found. The interior arches are stuccoed like the exterior of the building, and the repeating arches and surfacing set up an alternating rhythm of reflected light. From outside, the diminution of light in the passageway is framed by the brighter entrance arch, then from inside, the arches frame and contrast the brighter fountain and court. Figure 13-30b was taken midway in the shadowed transitional zone. Luminances on the stuccoed arches glow softly in poetic cadence. Small tastefully designed shop logos identify the stores, whose interior lights (just out of sight) make their presence known as the shopper passes through the space. Vision has adapted to the reduction of light in the passageway, and gradually will readapt to daylight as the walker continues forward into the court or to electric light of the adjacent shops. This transitional area is not just an added space. It is an outgrowth of careful planning. The court lying ahead expands in both space and light with each advancing step through the zone of transition. Subtle sounds of the fountain's cascading water add a musical accord to the visual rhythm of arches, which picks up again with the arch behind the fountain, giving continuity to the total architectural experience.

The pergola shown in Figure 13-31 connects independent buildings of an open air marketplace in west central Washington. Overhead, a wooden trellis work creates horizontal patterns of light and shades the circulation route on the deck below. The longitudinal space frames the next building in sequence. A small court opens to the right, just as a transition is taking place along the path of the pergola. At that point the height of the trellis work was dropped, contracting the space in the next phase leading to the stair in the distant view. But that break in vertical section accomplishes more than just a variation in spatial size along the path of movement. It creates a rectangular "window" framing a mountain peak miles away from the site. That natural visual objective is part of the transition between the two different heights of the pergola and the contraction of space. Becoming visible only briefly in the visitor's walk, the mountain participates in a momentary transition from space to space, bringing the beauty of nature into the architectural experience.

doorway connects two rooms. Nor does it necessarily mean more lighting is to be added (to the building and the budget) just to enhance spatial sequencing. During design development, some spaces may be intentionally planned to satisfy functional requirements and at the same time serve as transitions. Figure 13-30a shows the entrance of a small commercial center, where shops surround a landscaped court. A series of arches defines a zone of transition from entrance to court, shaping a small, dim circulation space in which shoppers find access to interior shops right and left of the line of movement. The last arch frames a small fountain, a visual objective drawing visitors further into the complex

CHAPTER 14

Creating Lighted Space

"Who needs sight when we got vision!"
—Herb Gardner
I'm Not Rappaport*

The preceding chapters formulated a body of space and light theory for analysis and design of the human environment. We saw how complications arise in professional practice from having to choose from the profusion of available building products and lighting systems, and then assemble them to shape and illuminate architectural space. Moreover, it was noted how reaching design goals gets sidetracked when designers and engineers operate independently and significantly alter the interaction of space and light contrary to the input of either profession. Therefore, it is a well-formulated *concept* that holds in focus the intentions of the varied professions, and out of their unified effort a successful spatial design emerges.

Designing from Concept to Space

In the artistic professions we sometimes hear the expression, "I have a good concept for this project." Quite often, *concept* in that sense is meant to refer to a visual image, a style, or even a color scheme, applied to either the exterior form of a building or as a decorative treatment of an interior. What is lacking in that use of *concept* is the direct and all important association with the meaning of the building and functions it is to serve, and accordingly how it is to be programmed. Concept is the raison d'être of a building, the purposes for which it is to be built, including any symbolic content it is to contain.

Conceptually, a school is a place for the interchange of learning and teaching; a manufacturing plant for the management and production of products; a hospital for the treatment and care of the injured and the sick. When a building undergoes adaptive use, it changes in concept, which governs the reorganization and design of its new physical environment. A building's exterior form and interior design should emanate from a well-developed and clear concept as naturally as a plant takes origin in its seed. The form and spaces of a building are to be directly related to that concept throughout the stages of design development and refinement.

Conceptual design for space organization does not mean starting with an abstract form for a building and inserting its functions into it. Many eighteenth-century architects did that, forcing living quarters into floor plans shaped by a square, circle, or letter of the alphabet. In the Age of Romanticism that followed, eclectic architects practiced a similar design method, forcing "modern" functional requirements into historical forms from the past. Scrutiny of that kind of design method frequently will reveal distorted interior living areas that became spatial leftovers after a few principal interior spaces were located within a predetermined form. Eclectic designers gave precedence to covering interior surfaces with stylistic finery instead of solving the perceptual problems of interior and lighting design that the 20th century has come to know.

Taking the spatial view of environmental design does not mean there is no place for form-dominated architecture, a building design conceived primarily to emphasize its overall exterior image. There are times when the con-

* Gardner, Herb. 1986. *I'm Not Rappaport.* New York: Grove Press, p. 16.

cept of a building calls for the dominance of its exterior form. This applies to public buildings of civic importance, monuments, and memorials. An excellent example from the eighteenth century is Etienne Louis Boullée's proposal for a Cenotaph for Newton (Figure 14-1). Although it can be criticized as a design based on abstract geometry, conceptually it was a great spherical building to honor the scientific achievements of Isaac Newton. It was also to symbolize the cosmos, and in Boullée's own description, was to be an "abode of immortality." The domical structure encloses a spacious interior, intentionally left as an empty void except for the tomb in the center, which also served as an entrance. From there visitors would view the vast heavenly sphere overhead portraying the infinity of the universe and a symbolic image of the supreme Creator. Form and space became one and the same, shaped by the spherical shell. From outside and inside the monumental design is conceptually correct for a monument to Newton, the scientist on whose thought almost all modern science is based. The concept for the building is not its spherical shape, but the memorializing of Newton's contributions to science.

A true meaning of concept is necessary for architecture, to distinguish between buildings that warrant dominance of exterior form and those that do not, those that should become a prominent visual node in the city and those that should be relegated to a lesser role. The manifestation of concept in the form of a building is what artist Ben Shahn called *content*, being the inherent meaning in the work of art. Content should be apparent to someone viewing the work. Shahn (1957, 81) left us these guidelines for the inseparable union between artistic form and the ideas it represents:

For form is not just the intention of content; it is the embodiment of content. Form is based, first, upon a supposition, a theme. Form is, second, a marshaling of materials, the inert matter in which the theme is to be cast. Form is, third, a setting of boundaries, of limits, the whole extent of idea, but no more, an outer shape of idea. Form is, next, the relating of inner shapes to the outer limits, the initial establishing of harmonies. Form is, further, the abolishing of excessive content, of content that falls outside the true limits of the theme. It is the abolishing of excessive materials, whatever material is extraneous to inner harmony, to the order of shapes now established. Form is thus a discipline, an ordering, according to the needs of content.

Shahn applied those principles to his paintings and they fit the practice of architecture. The form and consequently the spaces of a building should visibly embody its content, expressing the concept from which they took birth. Concept directs the development of architectural

form and governs the programming and organization of interior spaces in a direct and logical way, or as Shahn said, "the relating of inner shapes to the outer limits, the initial establishing of harmonies."

Bringing a building's form and interior spaces into harmony is the architect's challenge. In Chapter 9 we saw the importance of the structural system for integrating exterior and interior. This was masterfully done by Frank Lloyd Wright in his design of the Robie House (Figure 9-16). In his autobiography (1943, 142), he said what was on the "*outside* of the house" was "all there, chiefly because of what had happened *inside*." The spaces he organized on the inside are harmoniously interconnected for human living and expressed on the exterior in a state of compositional balance.

As the principal theme of this book, people reside, walk, work, shop, worship, and recreate in architectural space. For this reason the emphasis has been on the analysis and design of space, how it is perceived, and how those perceptions influence daily living. How does lighting fit into all of this? It too should respond to the conceptual basis on which architectural space is conceived and shaped.

Culture engenders the concepts for the design and lighting of the built environment. Take for example the relationship of noise to the amount of illumination. People have become accustomed to lowering their voices in dimly lit environments, such as religious settings, candle-lit dinners, theaters, and intimate cocktail lounges. Some of this may be in evolutionary change in recent times, as evidenced by the loud music and voices associated with "rock culture" of the modern world, but nevertheless, people still seem to lower their conversational voices in response to lowering the levels of light. This was measured in a study at the University of California at Northridge in the 1970s (Sanders, Gustanski, and Lawton, 1974). The exercise was conducted in a hallway of a classroom building where students gathered while awaiting dismissal of classes. The hall was illuminated by overhead fluorescent light of 15 to 24 fc, which was varied over a period of time by turning off up to two-thirds of the light panels. Under low illumination, voice level measurements were recorded at 50.3 decibels. Under high illumination, the voice levels rose to 61.1 decibels. Two different environments—one intended for intimacy or solitude and the other for festive public gathering—differ in concept and require dissimilar levels of illumination.

When a clear concept is crystallized for design development, dialogue for achieving design goals is more easily communicated along interdisciplinary lines. Figure 14-2 shows a lobby and transitional space between visitor parking and an educational performance theater in a college building. It is the concept of theater that here is separated from the other academic activities in the

Designing with Space and Light

(a)

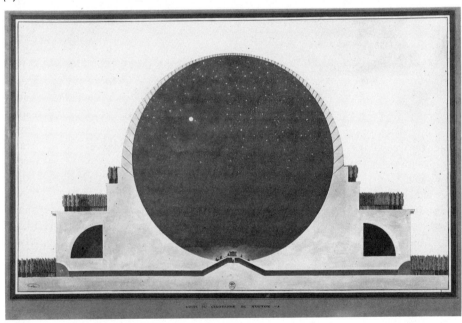

(b)

Figure 14-1. Concept shaping form and space. a. Exterior form. b. section. [Design for Newton's cenotaph. Architect: Etienne Louis Boullée. © cliché Bibliothèque Nationale de France, Paris]

remainder of the building. After entering the lobby, the direction toward the theater leaves no doubt. The spatial envelope is joined with that of the auditorium by a stepped subspace making a zone of transition. In that zone are Donna Dobberfuhl's brick sculptures that conceptually say "theater." Seven-feet-tall bas-relief figures represent the performing arts, and change the mood of the spatial flow from parking garage to performance in the auditorium to come. Moreover, the sculptures are continual promotional images of theatrical productions for passersby at times other than scheduled performances. Architecturally, the space of the raised level of the transitional zone contracts from the greater space of the lobby. As it does, light dims. Against the lower luminance of the walls, downlighting raises the presence of the sculptures in dramatic highlights and shadows like

---

Figure 14-2. Concept for interdisciplinary professional dialogue. [Cultural Education Center, Johnson County Community College, Overland Park, Kansas. Architects: Peckham Guyton Albers Viets. Sculptor: Donna Dobberfuhl]

those that will appear on the theater stage. An easy to understand concept—a transitional space between parking and theater seat—guided all of the design decisions by architect, sculptor, and lighting specialist.

Figure C-63 shows a cafeteria, but it was managerial concept refinement that accounts for the layout shown here. Known in the food service industry as the "food court system," entrées are grouped by specialty, and people follow signage to the unit offering their food of choice rather than going through the traditional long cafeteria line that includes all selections. That concept difference shaped the space. Architecturally, the stepped units divide the traffic flow by isolating the speciality foods, each identified by clear, easy-to-read signage. The units create a rhythm of form relationships, moving in design as do the people, toward a visual objective of a freestanding unit at the end of the space. Lighting design is integral with architectural design. In each unit, lighting emphasis is placed on the food offerings as it should be. Overhead neon stripes parallel the path of the tray slide on both sides of the space, turn at the corners of the units, and as a linear design culminate with the same striping over the unit at the end of the court. Concept holds together forms in space and lighting.

Application of Selection in the Visual World

In Chapter 4, *scanning* was explained as a natural process of human seeing by which the eye explores the environment. We saw that fixations are determined by "selection in the visual world," by which in either a voluntary or involuntary way, the eye selects momentary targets as it scans the environment. Those attracting stimuli were presented as focal accents (p. 62) to integrate the design of the human environment with the natural process of seeing. That can be done by inserting them into spatial composition for positive effects, and by avoiding misuse of them when they would add too much visual stimuli to a scene or have a negative influence on humanizing the built environment. Presented in hierarchical order, we saw how people and movement generally top the list of focal accents because of their strong attracting power to arrest the scanning eye. The architect and interior designer influence those two accents when organizing spatial relationships and locating the kinds of activities that people perform. The remainder of the list is especially useful for both aesthetic and ergonomic designs of architectural space. That is, the focal accents lend themselves as basic design elements for spatial composition, while aligning with the natural physiological process of drawing the attention of the human eye.

One of the reasons brightness is high on the hierarchical list of focal accents is the phototropic nature of human vision, as the eye is attracted toward light and exceptionally bright surfaces in the field of view. The designer needs to be aware of this, using acceptable levels of brightness where they are an advantage for design, and knowing when a high level of brightness is detrimental to human visual comfort.

By definition focal accents draw attention, and those farther down the hierarchical list from people, movement, and brightness may be lesser in perceptual attraction, but are exceptional tactics for design. The focal accent of high contrast heightens the appearance of color and pattern, and emphasizes figure-ground relationships, as applied to select architectural detailing and lighting accents on the spatial envelope, and to freestanding objects as seen against their backgrounds. Vivid color, particularly when contrasted in its setting, also draws the scanning eye to elements in the visual field.

In Chapter 8 we saw how the very nature of assembling architecture in its manufacture and construction presents innumerable opportunities to create pattern as a means of articulating space. The reason pattern is a focal accent is because it is embedded in Gestalt psychology, following the Gestalt laws of similarity, proximity, and good continuation (see p. 19). The designer benefits from those laws when organizing and detailing the design of architectural space. When pattern is strong—contrasted by color or the effects of light—it is greater in its attraction power and contributes significantly to design character.

Repetitive elements in a linear pattern set up a line of direction and create visual rhythm. By Gestalt perception, linear pattern entices the eye to follow it, stimulating curiosity and search. Linear pattern includes patterns of light cast on plain walls, floor, or ceiling, which becomes an effective method for lighting and decorating space simultaneously. A row of light scallops is a good example of a rhythmic line of movement. If not overdone, light patterns on flat, undecorated surfaces is a good lighting design technique for a connection space like a corridor, animating it somewhat without detracting from the design of the spaces preceding and following.

Design patterns made by architectural surfacing and lighting are exceptionally valuable as focal accents for creating *interspatial relationships*. Figure 14-3 shows a row of circles in octagons that pattern the floor, forming a directonal flow from a lobby to an elevator space. The

Figure 14-3. Focal accents in interspatial relations. [75 State Street, Boston. Architects: Graham Gund and SOM/Boston. Photograph: © Steve Rosenthal]

flow is a rhythm of pattern. Rhythms, as we have seen, go somewhere and if stopped abruptly, can create a visual collision. Here, they lead to the plant, which attracts the eye and terminates the flow of floor pattern. There is also a rectilinear pattern of darker marble frames around the elevators, which are coordinated with the dark frame of the entry doorway and the two vertical piers in the foreground of the photograph. The plants—as forms in space—make a triangular pattern composition of their own and participate in the sequence. They provide variety of texture that contrasts the surrounding, smooth marble surfaces; similar foliage is repeated in the strip planter above. Like the framing role of the darker doorway connecting the elevator space, the two foreground plants spatially frame the entry. The location of the lighting effects makes this a good example of focal accenting in space and light design. There are two corridors that intersect. In the ceiling over the perpendicular path just behind the foreground plants are three recessed downlights. Light from the outer two canisters casts glowing scallops on the segments of wall behind each plant, heightening their figure-ground relationship. The middle canister ties in with the row of downlights down the middle of the elevator space, and light from the last one brightens the wall behind the distant plant. A triangular pattern of scallops and plants is formed, and is spatially integrated with the forward "movement" of the inlaid floor patterns. The plant at the end is a framed visual objective, a lead into the elevator space. It is modest in size, but made prominent by its brightness-contrast with the accent lighting on the wall behind it.

It stands to reason that if focal accents attract the scanning eye, the visual centers they create can be used to balance design relationships in spatial composition. The principle is illustrated by Figure C-64, which shows a sectional seating area forming a subspace in the greater room, and made prominent as a visual center by the vivid color of red, contrasted against the dark carpet below and the brighter wall and floor behind. On the wall is another visual center, an abstract landscape sculpture. There is no intense brightness of light sources in the field of view, and the walls and background floor are neutral in color. That allows the abstract patterns and colors in the artwork to become a visual center on the wall, spatially composing with the vivid red seating area.

In Chapter 13 the design principle of framing a visual objective was analyzed to show how effective that technique can be as a visual draw from one space to another. The focal accents lend their drawing power for use in those situations, as illustrated by the spatial connection in Figure 14-4. As we saw in the Yarbus scanning studies (Figure 4-10), the presence of other people in the visual world attracts the scanning eye more so than any other visual feature in the environment. Even in the spaciousness of a large public building, a solitary human figure draws attention. The man sitting at the receptionist station is small in the field of view, but perceptually prominent. In addition, other focal accents are present that influence the visual draw into the second space. Spatial framing makes the receptionist station more conspicuous yet, heightened still further by the brightness of the wall behind the man, against which he is contrasted. In the foreground lobby, the inlaid floor patterns "point" to the receptionist. The bright circle of marble around the darker square follows the Gestalt law of similarity in union with the circular dome above, which hovers overhead in soft indirect lighting. Downlights in the dome raise the luminance of the floor pattern. The bright circle on the floor gives the appearance of a circle of light cast from the circular dome above. In the straight-ahead view, the brightness of the recessed dome and floor circle spatially compose with the brightness at the receptionist station. It is the union of spatial design and lighting design that brings these two spaces together.

A misuse of focal accents is an overabundance of different kinds in any one environment. Assembling a multiplicity of them destroys perceptual simplicity (see p. 23). The human visual system can not easily process a perceptually complex array of stimuli in a field of view,

Figure 14-4. Composition of focal accents for visual draw. [75 State Street, Boston. Architects: Graham Gund and SOM/Boston. Photograph: © Steve Rosenthal]

created by excessive detailing of multiple patterns, color values, textures, contrasts, reflections, distorted shapes, and obscure figure-ground conditions. Clear visual centers need perceptual breathing room, an absence of prominent perceptual stimuli between them. Positioning visual centers is not just an act of putting something here and there, but should be the result of consciously applying focal accents to attract the natural saccadic movements of the eye and to create good spatial composition. In that way, spatial design correlates the work of the designer with the natural seeing process of people.

Distribution of Light, Color, and Brightness

We saw how initial thoughts on spatial design take origin in the concept of the space. From concept comes the vision for spatial design. That vision formulates the design character and mood the space is to have. This is where thoughts regarding the brightness of a space enter the design process. The question to be asked, quite simply, is this: Is this space to be bright and colorful, or subdued or neutral in color values? Conceptually, the answer lies in what will go on in that room, what tasks will be performed. Should the room be bright overall? It is like lighting designer William Lam (1977, 77) said: "A generally high illumination level throughout a space makes sense only when the special tasks which demand those levels are also distributed throughout the space." In that statement is the recognition of concept preceding design. Some retail stores, manufacturing spaces, open office pools, and other workplaces conceptually warrant a spread of higher illumination throughout the space. Let us begin the analysis of composing color in space by first applying it to overall bright environments.

Related to the decision of choosing appropriate brightness for an environment is that brighter rooms appear more spacious. That perceptual phenomenon should underlie decisions of color values and light for a room's design. Some rooms may need to appear more spacious than others, justifying selection of surfacing materials that will appear brighter by color value and illumination.

Surfaces of higher reflectance are more energy efficient. Using the LBR Scale, zone V (Munsell value N6) is middle brightness between black and white, but reflects only 30% light, not 50%. Just one step down in zone, a Munsell value of 5 reflects only 20% of the light that strikes its surface. The guidelines for color and reflectance published by IESNA (Rea, 1993, 121ff) need to be followed. IESNA specifies materials of 50% to 70% reflectance to be used for walls, and cautions designers that "unless all the colors in the color scheme of a room layout are very light, well over 50% of the light is absorbed." If colors of Munsell value 5 are used (LBR zone IV and below), 80% or more of the incident light in a room is absorbed. Only the last three zones of the LBR Scale reflect 50% or more. Therefore, colors of high value used for walls and ceilings are much more efficient in light distribution than colors of low value.

A bright and generally monotoned spatial envelope provides the opportunity for introducing color contrast, to make more prominent the focal centers spatially distributed throughout an environment. This was done in Figure C-64, where the seating area, wall sculpture, and plants are made vivid by the contrasting neutrality of the floor and walls. The lighting brightened the spatial envelope; as background, it intensified the accenting colors.

When concept requires a space to be characterized by low luminances, such as those needed for spiritual, intimate, or relaxed moods, control of brightness distribution becomes more critical. These too can be energy-saving environments because of the smaller amount of illumination required, but by reducing the amount of lighting, colors of higher value are necessary to prevent a space from becoming too dark. Of first concern is providing adequate luminance on the spatial envelope and the interior furnishings for public and private safety, particularly for the elderly and people with defective vision.

Many public spaces become low-luminance environments at night, and when controlled specialized lighting is coordinated with spatial design, the subdued spatial envelope provides contrasting background to feature high interest areas. This is shown in Figure C-65. With business activity having subsided with the arrival of evening, the dimming of light in the atrium of a corporation's headquarters building brings out the intensities of the landscape architecture of the plaza on the main floor. High-wattage, low-voltage point light sources mounted high above on the atrium walls focus on the landscaped area. Support lighting below adds highlights to the fountains and plantings. The success of the plaza design comes from coordination of lighting with the architectural and natural shapes on which it falls. The foliage of the trees and plants glows in soft luminance. In vivid contrast to the plantings and to the dark floor are the low retaining walls that shape the landscape units. Because the foliage absorbs much of the arriving light, the greater reflectance of the harder surface creates bright lyrical lines that animate the space. Set within the planted units are nodes of red flowers, which by their contrast, are "points" of color in the overall composition.

With color scarcely present or even eliminated entirely, brightness-contrast combined with pattern makes an exceptional design vocabulary for creating strong visual centers. Earlier we saw how edge lighting picks up surface etching or images cast within the medium of glass (Figure C-51). Glass artist and designer Peter David has demonstrated how that technique can be used to virtually suspend lighted images in space, and form a prominent visual center that can be placed in a greater environment. Figure C-66 shows his scale model for a 28-foot-long "Fisherman's Memorial" proposed for the Port of Seattle. Using the same technique described for Figure C-51, the images of fish and casting net convey the sea world of the deep in this public art project. At full scale, lighting for the work would be installed in the base, and travel through the glass to illuminate the etched images. The architecture forms a gently curved subspace, in which the suspended images of the fish and the illuminated memorial plaque in the center are all brightly contrasted against a glowing background. Numerous spatial effects of light can be created by projects like this, by varying the illumination in the base to pass upward through the glass, and by controlling the light in front of and behind the display. Add the imagination of a gifted artist to the technique of suspending images in space, and a diaphanous veil of crafted glass becomes an alluring and dynamic work of art.

A significant part of composing brightness areas in space is the distribution of surfaces illuminated by ambient versus direct light. Normally, surfaces illuminated by ambient light appear soft, and are comfortable for human vision. In rooms predominantly illuminated by ambient lighting, some surfaces can be illuminated directly to make them appear brighter. Direct light is used to feature certain surfaces and to create lighting accents like scallops or other patterns. In spaces where the dominant surfaces are similar in reflectance, the composition of all direct and ambient light becomes very important with regard to where the luminance brightnesses are distributed about the environment. This can be seen in Figure 14-5, which shows a museum gallery illuminated by ambient light, and the exhibit cases and artifacts by direct lighting. The surfaces illuminated by ambient light appear softer, and reflect only faintly on the varnished floor. Contrasted with the lower luminances of the overall room, the brighter areas draw attention and feature the exhibits. Note how the brighter areas are coordinated with circulation, as if always drawing the visitor to the exhibits. The sculpture in the outer hall is a strong visual objective, framed by the ambient light on the doorway and contrasted against the bright wall behind it. Its size fits the framed view and attracts attention to the next museum space. When the museum visitor advances to view that work of art, another major sculpture appears:

the great Buddha (Figure 3-4), positioned on a lower landing of a flight of stairs. All of this was set up as part of the distribution of brightness areas in the gallery of Figure 14-5. The subdued ambient light in the room and around the doorway is responsible for the attraction of spaces to come.

Distributing brightness areas as focal centers in one space always needs to include how any one center will function in a spatial connection. A bright focal center can serve as a visual lead, and also create visual interest when a transition is made from a space of one brightness level to another of significant contrast. Figure C-67 shows the sweeping curvature of the primary interior circulation route around the dome of Figure 9-9. The walker's vision has adapted to the luminance level of the circular hall when encountering the attractive doorway surrounded by glass etched in a forest scene. Downlighting just behind the doorway animates the glass by highlighting the fine craftsmanship of the engraver's art. That highlighting brightens the doorway plane, making a focal center of light and art as a transition to the next space. Its effectiveness becomes apparent by mentally removing the illuminated etched glass, and visualizing the entrance surrounded only by the opaque wall, and noting how it would frame the wall of similar luminance that shows through the opening. What a difference is created by the illuminated etched glass. It is very bright compared with

Figure 14-5. Brightness by direct and ambient light. [The Nelson-Atkins Museum of Art, Kansas City, Missouri. Photograph: © Paul Kivett]

Designing with Space and Light

the opaque wall around it and the next space in sequence. As a transition between two spaces, it is brief, but brilliant as a focal center and point of interest. By comparison, the next space that it frames could be dull and uneventful. But it isn't. The combination of interesting design and the sequential distribution of brightness levels continues as the visitor enters that next space: the one shown in Figure 11-7.

It is now commonplace in public buildings and private residences to have facilities for reducing and raising illumination to suit different task requirements or simply to modify the environment for mood. Dimmers, light sensors, and combinations of different lighting systems make it possible to change the intensity and color of the light sources. The customary way of distributing color about a space is through selection of the surfacing materials for the spatial envelope and the color of the interior furnishings. Whereas dimmers clearly modify color value and saturation of the materials, interesting color changes take place by changing the color of light, either by means of color filters internal or external to the luminaires or by the color of the light source.

Figures C-68 and C-69 show the dining room of a private residence with a color-variable glass block wall that enlivens a room that receives no natural light, because that section of the house is built into a hillside. The glass block is illuminated by four neon tubes of red, yellow, purple, and turquoise light. A control panel allows color mixing and a variety of light intensities for the various hues. Colors can be changed from extremely slow to very fast by a variable-speed programmer. The changes of color and intensity provide a variety of moods for different occasions, and for the occupants who use the same environment on a regular basis. The major differences between a colored wall of opaque material like paint or other wall covering and this wall of glass is the luminosity of the color. As an example, light passing through the red stained glass of a cathedral window is very intense compared with "white" light illuminating a wall painted red. When transmitted through glass block, light is diffused by internal glass reflections, but the colored light of that segment of the spatial envelope makes a totally different experience from the opaque surface color seen in the rest of the room. Neon reflections are seen on foreground surfaces, on the front of the wooden cabinet next to the glass wall, and as color tone washed across the ceiling. Those reflections change according to whatever color neon is activated at the time, but they are always compatible with the glass wall. Note the other lighting in the room as it relates to the total spatial envelope. The support lighting prevents the glass block wall from appearing overly intense as would happen by simultaneous contrast if the surrounding wall were considerably darker.

The illuminated glass block wall goes beyond what at first might be seen as an isolated decorative feature. In a spatial context, we noted how it is a source for distributing and changing colored reflections about the room. It also builds interesting relationships with other artwork, picked out especially for the room by the owner, a professional interior designer. The colors in the abstract painting compose with whatever illumination colors are activated by the glass block wall. Further, the luminescence of the glass wall provides a striking background for the room's furnishings in spatial figure-ground relationships (Figure C-70). The chairs and profiles of the two sculpted heads stand out in stark silhouette against the illuminated glass. The illuminated wall and the room's furnishings create a colorful spatial composition in response to the effects of light.

Procedural Check for Space and Light Design

A series of checks on the design process is helpful for decision making from the initial formation of the spatial envelope and its furnishings to their final organization when illuminated in the architectural world. The following stages are guidelines for that decision making:

1. *Shaping the spatial envelope.* In response to concept, the function(s) of a space and program requirements direct the shaping and proportioning of the spatial envelope and determine how it conforms to the overall organization of a building, or to a sector of the city if it is an outdoor space. Is the overall shape of the envelope free from visual distortions that are psychologically upsetting to human comfort and well-being as perceived by the visual system?

If the envelope forms the partial enclosure of a subspace does it clearly relate to a larger parent space?

As a check on its shape and proportions, visualize the basic envelope as a pure white model—free of color, surface patterns, textures, and any suggestion of accent lighting.

2. *Penetrations of the spatial envelope.* Openings for views to adjacent spaces affect the perception of the spatial envelope of the observer.

Are there windows, skylights, or any other opening through which daylight will enter? How is the space oriented to movement of the sun?

What visual connections will openings in the envelope make with contiguous spaces? Is it a space that is intended to flow in a direct spatial sequence?

How much of the basic spatial envelope remains after all major penetrations are made in the dominant boundaries? The size and location of openings in the spatial envelope will influence eventual interspatial color relationships and brightness ratios.

3. *Projections from the spatial envelope.* This refers to any prominent elements that are attached to the basic envelope planes, including structural members like ceiling beams and wall pilasters; balconies and boxes in a theater; raised floor levels; and stepped ceilings. This also refers to elements on elevations that shape outdoor spaces, such as solar lightshelves and apartment balconies.

How will those projections articulate the spatial envelope? How will they create dominant patterns of highlights and shadows that will "texture" the spatial envelope?

Are design rhythms created by the projections?

Significant projections into the void of space will influence locations of major electric light sources and support lighting.

Note: Stages 2 and 3 determine the final physical configuration of the spatial envelope.

4. *Visualize the required interior furnishings.* Like the spatial envelope, types of furnishings are largely determined by the concept of space. They include permanent and movable furniture, modular workstations, semipermanent partitions, display counters, and the like. Anticipate inevitable additions, deletions, and change of location by the users of the space.

Furnishings in space create internal circulation patterns. They become forms in space (Chapter 4). As such, they establish design form-space relationships, and perceptual figure-ground relationships. Furnishings often require specialized task lighting. The relatively permanent furnishings will influence overall lighting design.

5. *Previsualize color, texture, and brightness on the spatial envelope and furnishings.* This is the conversion of the pure white model into color. Space begins to take on design character and mood. Does its concept require it to be bright and colorful, or subdued for a specialized purpose? Will the room appear spacious due to overall brightness of the envelope? Should apparent spaciousness be minimized, calling for darker color values on the dominant spatial boundaries?

This stage generates initial schematic thoughts on the distribution of colors and brightnesses in spatial composition. They set up preliminary color relationships and brightness ratios.

Surface characteristics of materials are to be contemplated for reflectance and reflections: "the surface action of light" (Chapter 3). How will texture influence color value and saturation? How will surface color change

by angle of slant as seen from predominant circulation paths? Which surface planes have the potential for causing glare? How will the major planes respond to the presence of daylight?

Where are focal centers to be set up and featured as interior design nodes? How will they attract human visual scanning by the hierarchical list of focal accents (Chapter 4)? What surfaces should be subdued so they do not compete with intended focal centers? Are visual objectives to be located as visual leads from other spaces, and how are they to be framed by color and brightness?

Where—if at all—will significant light or dark adaptation take place at the most common viewing stations, and in circulation spaces? How will this influence selection of color values (from dark to light)?

6. *Previsualize pattern design.* Pattern is an effective means of articulating space (Chapter 8). By Gestalt principles, pattern contributes to the visual organization of the spatial envelope and its interior furnishings. Pattern is created by regularized units of architectural construction (modular beams, coffers, etc.), surface patterns (wall coverings and furniture fabrics, carpeting, inlays in floors and walls), and organized groups of freestanding objects (a seating area, display cases, planted urns).

Do repeating units create a linear pattern (related to a given direction)? Does the pattern conform to the shape of the space? Does the pattern create rhythm? If so, to where does it lead the eye, and does it have a logical and pleasing conclusion?

Anticipate light patterns on the major spatial boundaries, created by lighting accents (scallops, disks on floor). Will they be cast on other surface patterns, creating design conflict? Will the light sources (recessed luminaires, visible fixtures) create organized pattern?

7. *Previsualize the arrival of light.* Light quality and quantity will modify all of the above stages. *Strive for creating an energy-efficient environment.*

If present, the entry of daylight and its movement become a first consideration for light distribution. Capitalize on the dynamic effects that daylight can bring to an interior. If bright daylight is disturbing, filter it, or screen it into a decorative pattern for spatial articulation and aesthetics.

Is the spatial envelope to be illuminated by general room lighting? Or will the major spatial boundaries be illuminated by specialized technique, and lighting forms in space by separate and controlled supplementary lighting?

Identify those surfaces to which electric light needs to be added either directly or indirectly by ambient light. Select an appropriate electric illumination system(s) to achieve what was previsualized in Stages 5 and 6. To derive color and brightness of the major surfaces, select illumination *quality* for the desired color of the building materials, and illumination *quantity* for desired luminance levels. Use the LBR Scale as a guide for brightnesses, and creating brightness ratios (Chapter 5).

Determine locations of the electric light sources to achieve the desired "effects of light." Consider textures and shadows that will result. How will the angle of arriving light and the distance of the light sources influence the color value of the materials? Which of the spatial boundaries are suitable for wall-washing or wall-grazing? All task lighting requirements are to be met.

Will reflections take place, as seen from where? Do they work to the advantage or disadvantage of reaching design goals? How can disturbances of glare be eliminated?

8. *Selection of the finishing materials.* Color and other surface characteristics of a building material will undergo change when subjected to the realities of illuminated architectural space.

Selections of finishing materials are *not* to be made under light quality that is different from that which will illuminate the materials when installed at the site.

Actual samples of paints, wood species, wall coverings, and carpeting should be tested in studio mockups simulating the predominant lighting and viewing angles of the major spatial boundaries, under the quality and quantity of illumination that will be installed at the site. Computer imaging does not take the place of this important step.

At the finished job site, color and brightness of materials will be seen as *apparent* luminance—not *calculated* luminance—when under the influence of simultaneous contrast and light or dark adaptation of the observer. Adjustments of color values may be necessary.

9. *Refinement of the lighting process.* When it is desired that a specific finishing material take on a certain appearance for a project, its surface color and texture may require refinement of the previsualized lighting conditions in Stage 7.

In the studio or at the site, the actual building materials can be subjected to numerous lighting tests using different qualities of light, filtering materials, and dimming devices to refine the luminance appearance of the materials.

There is an enormous range of colors and textures of building materials on the market. Given the state of the art of lighting technology, a seemingly infinite variety of quality and quantity of illumination can be cast on those materials. This is the give and take between spatial design and lighting design. It is how a building material responds to light *in a spatial context* that is important. It is only the interaction of space and light that people see in the environment.

In the organization of Part 3 of this book, it may be implied from Chapter 11 that lighting architectural space *begins* with lighting the spatial envelope. It is not that the spatial envelope should be lighted first, but that it is to be *controlled.* Architectural space is experienced as a total environment, which means the interior furnishings are perceived against the luminances that exist on the spatial envelope. Chapter 11 focuses on lighting the envelope only for analyzing that lighting task. Freestanding objects or furnishings may be choice features as focal centers apart from the spatial envelope. Illuminating those interior centers with specialized lighting may also require toning down the spatial envelope by reducing its illumination, by lowering the color value of its surfacing materials, or both.

Sometimes the choice of a specific color or surface covering style becomes a first step in the design of a room. That is a designer's prerogative. But a review of the first seven stages just listed reveals what will happen to the appearance of a certain material by the time it is finally installed and the lighting is turned on. Wanting a "blue room" from the start is all right, but that doesn't take into account the shape of the spatial envelope, whose surfaces angled to the light sources will determine the value of the blue as it eventually will appear in the room. Moreover, different qualities of lighting may turn the "blue" to some other chromatic appearance.

Spatial design is not just a simple process of shaping a pure white model of a space and distributing about it the effects of color and light. When working from schematics to design development and refinement, the practicalities of bringing architecture into existence also have to be included. In what they call "working with constraints," Kellogg Smith and Bertolone remind the architectural and lighting designer of four major factors for every lighting design: meeting schedules, confronting the complexities of construction, meeting codes for public health and safety, and budget. "Creativity alone," they aptly say (1986, 51), "will not create a successful lighting design; it must be coupled with a high regard for what is practical and economical." Included in the integration of spatial and lighting design is the challenge of solving the problems of practicalities with economic efficiency.

Three-point Coordination for Design Continuity

The value of the spatial envelope as a design tool is its use for spatial sequencing. For a person moving through space, openings in the envelope extend the range of vision that often includes another set of boundaries coming into view as another spatial envelope. Insofar as the visual framework of a single envelope is expedient for analyzing spatial design, it may be misguiding in one respect by overplaying the design of one space without regard to how it relates to neighboring spaces.

Preoccupation with the design of a single space may be rooted in how we visually communicate "models for design" as they appear in the frozen view of still photography. Published views of exterior forms and interior spaces may look architecturally good, dynamic, or exciting, but too often only from a token point of view—the one framed by the photograph. Professional photographers strive to find "the best possible view" or a novel view, and those images are the ones that most likely will appear in the media. It is well known that published photographs are often cropped to conform to page layout or to eliminate a discordant part of the design, and those measures further restrict communicating the real conditions at the actual site. On rare occasions two photographs are shown in sequence, illustrating how the spaces relate to each other, and how the design of each reflects the relationship between the two.

Quite often teaching and public lectures also are done that way. Color slides are shown of project after project with a few supporting details thrown in, and people in attendance are bombarded with a mirage of images, most of which fall on the wayside of memory. In many academic and design office slide collections, there are very few spatial sequences illustrating how one space gives way to another. There is good reason for this. Sequential photography is not easy to do, because of the added time it takes, extra costs for film and processing, and encountering extremes of changing light, caused by different sun angles or uncooperative weather, or by high brightness-contrast in interiors or night lighting. But even the professional photographer often is restrained from taking good spatial sequences because quite simply there is not a good sequence there to photograph, or the full view into an adjacent space may include discordant parts that would bring negative criticism to the project. This is not true at many renowned historical sites, a number of which have been mentioned in the earlier chapters. A short list includes the Alhambra, the Paris Opera House, Gothic cathedral interiors, The Gardens of the Villa d'Este in Italy, the Spanish Stairs in Rome, the Belvedere Palace in Vienna, the piazzas of Venice, New York's Rockefeller Center, and Fallingwater and other works of Frank Lloyd Wright. In those spaces, the photographer easily finds a good architectural space, can walk ahead, set the tripod down again, and find another well-designed space in continuity. That means there is good spatial flow. Each singular space meaningfully relates to the next, and gives integrity to the total building or urban square.

In Chapter 2, a distinction was made between the visual world, which is the totality of an environment as perceived by the moving eye and body, and the visual field, which is a theoretical single stop-action image in that visual world. The stopped visual field provides the apparatus for perceptual and design analysis. That is the positive side of still photography. It is an exceptional means for allowing the critical eye to pour over details and to evaluate how they assemble into the greater composition of architectural space. But what is lacking is enough visual information for the analysis of interspatial connections, unless critical sequential photography is provided. With sequential views, the successive change from one spatial envelope to another can be assessed, and what is seen from one space can be evaluated for how it influences the design of one that follows.

Color in spatial sequencing influences feelings of spaciousness. Mahnke and Mahnke (1987, 27) tell us that "Visual spaciousness increases when similar colors are carried from one room to another." So color plays an important part of connecting spatial units in that it enlarges the experience of any one space when another of equal or similar color is seen in the view lying immediately ahead. An example is the lobby of the office building shown in Figure C-71. The security desk and two structural columns are detailed in cherry wood and black Italian marble, coordinated with detailing on the curved wall. The remainder of the walls is a yellow ochre color, which is carried forward into two connecting spaces beginning behind the security desk. One leads to service facilities for the building, the other to a retail space. The extension of the same ochre color into the smaller connecting spaces not only gives continuity to the sequential paths of movement, but adds to the spaciousness of the lobby by experiencing a walk through one of the service spaces.

A good evaluation check on sequential design is a method of three-point coordination, applied to major circulation routes and to locating station points for analyzing interspatial connections. The method is illustrated by the computer-generated graphics of Figure 14-6, which show a spatial sequence from a reception lobby, into an elevator hall, and then into an office work room. Each viewing station was selected according to how the general view of each space would be seen from a natural vantage point by a visitor to the building, proceeding along a principal path of movement. Upon arrival in the lobby (Figure 14-6b), the visitor finds an information desk. Major elements in the connected spaces are seen from Station Point #1. In the foreground are stairs to a second floor, in the second space are elevators to other levels, and in the distance is the business space. At the very end of the sequence is a sculpture, which as a visual objective makes direction and distance clearly perceptible. The perspective views from that first station point provide references for design coordination. The modular

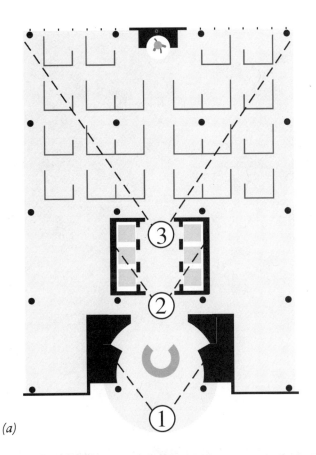

(a)

beams of the building's structural system hover over the lobby. In structural harmony, they continue as perspective lines through the space on the second floor, are repeated in kind in the lower elevator hall (Figure 14-6c), and continue overhead into the work space (Figure 14-6d). Station Point #2 shows the elevator hall. Indirect lighting articulates the ceiling, and repeats the pattern of luminaires on the second floor as seen from Station Point #1. The receding perspective lines of the beams and rhythm of the luminaires are answered by the visual climax of the sculpture at the end of the sequence (Station Point #3). As focal accents, nodes of brightness in all three spaces fit into the spatial sequence. Task lighting brightens the top of the information desk, which is flanked by accent lighting on the urns at the two sides. In the second space, brightness centers continue with the ceiling luminaires and downlights over the elevator doors. At the end of the third space, the bright cove behind the sculpture concludes the sequence of brightness nodes, and makes prominent the sculpture by brightness contrast.

What the graphics of Figure 14-6 show is the conversion of the visual fields into a simulation of the visual world, the world in which people walk. The three-point coordination method of spatial design permits quick shifting in viewpoint, back a space, or ahead to the next,

(b)

Figure 14-6. Three-point coordination for design continuity. a. Floor plan. b. Lobby and receptionist station. c. Elevator hall. d. Office work space. [Computer Graphics: Brent Anderson]

(c)

(d)

Figure 14-6. (Continued)

Designing with Space and Light

to study design relationships for merging the three spaces. Using this method, the first of three station points can be anywhere in or outside a building. It can begin with the environment out-of-doors before entering a building, followed by a second view at an entrance portal, and the third inside the lobby.

Why are *three* spaces to be used? Three spaces are easy to work with, and some significant portion of a third space often is visible when looking from one space through a second one. It's like the old method of connecting a locus of points with a French curve. Three successive points are used along the curve, but the part of the curve drawn only extends a little beyond the second point. The third point provides the direction. In spatial design, the character, surfacing, and lighting of a third space gives valuable information for refining the design of a first and second space. The third space gives direction for design decisions, serving as a control for developing continuity.

Figure C-72 shows the entry to a temporary exhibition "Treasure Houses of Britain" once displayed at the National Gallery of Art in Washington, D.C. The doorway in this first space is soft in luminance and neutral in color. Spot lighting heightens the relief sculpture in the pediment, announcing the passage taking place into a gallery of art. Proceeding through the door the visitor steps into a second space, the exhibition gallery shown in Figure C-73. Nearly concealed luminaires focus their light on the spacial envelope of the gallery, and neutrality of color tones gives prominence to the masterpieces of art. Architectural articulation is integrated with the electric light sources, all woven into a unified network that patterns the ceiling without pulling attention away from the colors and imagery of the paintings below. From this second station point, the repeating rhythms of light on both sides of the ceiling direct a perspective view to the end of the space. The moderate brightness of the row of lighted units on the right side of the ceiling concludes with the large bright figures in the painting below on the end wall. The row of lighted units on the left side terminates with another doorway, through which the exhibit activity of color and brightness picks up again as the sequence continues into the third space. The design of the door repeats the one through which the visitor had just passed. As focal centers of colors and brightness, the works of art are the carriers of attention as they are distributed throughout the sequence. Framed by the first doorway, they create a strong visual draw into the exhibition space. Within that gallery, they are composed about the room awaiting the visitor's perusal. Those in the next gallery create another visual draw, leading visitors into the next room in sequence. In all the spaces, the locations of the luminaires for the tasks they perform are so well integrated into this harmonic sequence of space and light that their presence is scarcely realized.

We have seen how CAD programs are especially helpful for the three-point coordination method of design development and refinement. So are the conventional means of three-dimensional models, as well as the simultaneous coalescing of floor plan and sections that some designers can do easily in their minds. Whatever the means, the focus of attention is on creating harmonic continuity from space to space, not just creating a "cover shot" room that makes a good photograph but has little relationship to adjacent spaces.

By publishing spatial sequences, the media could play a vital role in promoting awareness of harmonic relationships in the design of connected spaces. Plans and sections regularly appear in the architectural journals, and for the most part camera angles of the related photographs are easily located or explained by the written word. But many photographic illustrations show only a partial view into a connected space, leaving the serious reader with questions of what exactly comes next, and how the connection is made. Those questions could be answered by sequential views not only to help the reader experience the actual conditions of the building or site, but to provide a visual study of the problems and solutions associated with the task of connecting spaces along important circulation routes. The publication of photographs taken from three carefully selected station points, with camera locations keyed on floor plans and sections (as was done in Figure 14-6), will demonstrate to designers (particularly student designers) the art of continuity in spatial sequencing. This also would foster a "criticism mentality" directed toward what architecture really is: the design of the built environment as experienced by people moving through it. The station points selected to illustrate spatial connections need not be just at doorways or stair landings to show perspective views. They can be at mid-points, showing how transitions are made, how design elements are carried forward along a path of movement, and how one focal center relates to another. The spatial sequencing should be so well done, with such design harmony in the spatial connections, that it should frustrate photographers as they decide where—*exactly*—is the best place to position the tripod for the next shot. That often is the case when photographing or just experiencing the great architecture of the past, and needs to become an integral part of the architecture of the future.

Creating Spaces for a Humanized Architecture

Architectural creativity is often looked on as a process of one person doing *all* the design work—the architecture, the spatial surfacing, and the lighting—but in most cases, a variety of related professions are involved from the inception of design to the final illuminated environment that is built. Considering the enormous turnover of materials and lighting systems on the markets, today's architects face innumerable problems of creating good compositions of reflected light and colors without inadvertently impairing visual comfort for the users of space. The concern is that humanism does not get lost in the process of architectural creativity, and for this reason the ergonomics of architecture and lighting were made integral to the principles of design put forth in this book. In today's world, available building materials and technology are in a continual state of change. By contrast, and to the advantage of the designer, the principles governing space and light design remain stable in their focus on creating environments that nurture the comfort and well-being of people in their physical surroundings, while at the same time working toward order and beautification of the architectural environment.

The major thrust of this book has been seeing space and light in mutual interaction, not architectural design or lighting design as independent professional practice. Lighting design suggests light is "veneered" on the shells of architectural space. To an extent it is, but, we have seen how the architecture of space is perceived differently under modifications by light. The success of high-quality architecture, therefore, depends on the union of good architectural design and good lighting design—not one independent of the other. As they work, the architect and interior designer need to anticipate the quality and quantity of illumination, and the locations of the light sources. The lighting designer and engineer bring to the project an understanding of light and lighting that fast-moving technological change has pushed far out of reach of most practicing architectural and interior designers. The lighting designer should not be reduced to a role like the old adage of hiring a good landscape architect to cover up the architect's mistakes. The lighting designer should enhance space, not sidetrack a start toward aesthetics that the architectural designers made at the time spaces and their connections took shape.

To channel the designer's attention on how people respond to their architectural surroundings, the initial working content of this book included selected principles of visual perception, featuring those that are integral to the fields of psychology and art. In the 1920s Gestalt psychologists put together laws according to which the environment is perceived by human vision. Fifty years later and still today, those laws are well seated in the critical apparatus used to explain order as perceived in the visual arts. Acclaimed for his contributions to the design and criticism of art and architecture, psychologist Rudolf Arnheim explained perceptual order as the organization of parts related to a greater whole. "The sim-

plest among the rules that govern these relations," Arnheim says (1971, 55), "is the rule of similarity, which does indeed confirm one of the oldest assertions of the theory of association: things that resemble each other are tied together in vision." In the restaurant shown by Figure C-74 design animation is created by the interaction of light in interspatial relationships. In an environment that at first glance might seem complex or bordering on the complex, similarity of the parts gives it a sense of order without creating a static spatial design. Squares and rectangles repeat in glass blocks, steps, and the carpet pattern. Similar curves repeat in shapes of walls, ceiling articulation, and furniture. This composition of similar parts related to a greater whole holds in check an interior design that easily could have become a perceptually complex environment if given further variety of detailing.

In another publication, Arnheim (1966, 123–124) explains the eternal battle between what is visual order and what is complex:

Order and complexity are antagonistic, in that order tends to reduce complexity while complexity tends to reduce order. To create order requires not only rearrangement but in most cases also the elimination of what does not fit the principles determining the order. On the other hand, when one increases the complexity of an object, order will be harder to achieve.

In the restaurant interior of Figure C-74, the complexity of the whole is reduced by the similarity of pattern in the parts and by elimination of elements that would not fit the design scheme. So in this case the pendulum swings toward order, away from the antagonist complex. Further, Arnheim (1966, 123) defined order as:

. . . the degree and kind of lawfulness governing the relations among the parts of an entity. Such lawfulness, or obedience to controlling principles, derives from the over-all theme or structure, to which the behavior of all parts must conform.

The spatial design of the restaurant is one of visual movement played out by curves and contours, but is not one of unbridled license. There is a limited number of patterns and colors, and when they were brought into spatial composition, they were made to conform to the greater whole like what Arnheim would call the lawfulness derived from the overall theme or structure. Now observe the role of lighting in all of this. Lighting easily could have added to the complexity, by increasing the number of visual parts and patterns instead of just enhancing the architecture that is there. In itself, the lighting is unpretentious, bringing out the patterns and contours of materials composed in space. Lighting animates some of the surfaces, but its diminution in subspaces creates areas of more intimate surroundings for private gatherings. The luminous walls of glass block unite the connected upper level, but screen it with translucence to add spatial interest. Colors from the space behind reflect internally in the glass walls and become part of the coloring of the spatial envelope of the foreground space.

In spatial design, composition is the organization of elements into a comprehensible whole, but it needs to be comprehensible to average people, not just to a group of artists or critics who understand it in an arcane language of design or technology. Eugene Raskin (1966, 101ff) explained architectural composition as "the putting together of things *in certain ways* [italics are his] rather than in other ways." He added that "order and relationship in a building must be made apparent to the observer not only to convey meaning but also to impress upon him that the building is a planned entity. . . ." Even in a person's first encounter with a public building, architectural spaces should be so composed to communicate their role in that planned entity, conveying a sense of place and orientation, and be made interesting as well. The shape and proportion of the corridor shown in Figure C-75 are determined by its function as a directional space intersecting with other pathways of the building's circulation system. Lighting design is correlated with architectural design to clearly communicate the circulation paths to visitors in the building. Recessed elevator doors on one side and the stepped wall on the other break up the vertical planes, and together with the decorative scallop lighting animate the lower spatial envelope. In counter action, the linear indirect lighting above gives a strong visual thrust to the spatial flow and changes of direction. Moderate luminance values on all major surfaces prevent excesses of bright or dark areas. The lower envelope is further animated by the composition of patterns and colors of the building materials and plants, making the walk through architectural space an enjoyable and interesting experience.

A sculptor models form, working and reworking smoothness and textures that respond to light and transform raw mass into art. Each nuance of protrusion and indentation, each rub and rasp, and each glaze and acid bath modulates the surface in gradations of reflection and shadow. The sculptor distributes the effects of light over the contours and facets of form. Painters blend pigments into highlights and shadows across the picture plane in the development of composition. On the design palette of the architectural designer is a host of colors and brightnesses from which to choose, all emanating from the vast storehouse of available surfacing materials and lighting techniques, and all awaiting their location assignment in a certain way, as Raskin said, and not in some other way, or in a way that "just happens" when lights are turned on in a room.

Also on the architectural designer's palette is the potential for harmful glare and disturbing reflections, but they too can be transformed into luminances compatible with human vision, and converted into artistic components of spatial composition. Figure C-76 shows a private pool and entertainment facility, the nature of which includes still water and hard surfaces that normally could reflect mirror images of light sources and other high-brightness centers. By bouncing light off surfaces before it proceeds elsewhere, and by using light-diffusing luminaires as the visible fixtures suspended over the pool, intensely bright light is moderated into the calm reflected images that are part of the distribution of brightnesses in the overall environment. In the case of a large reflecting area like the pool's surface, good composition of the real space is even more important because of its being doubled on the surface of the water. That applies to the connected space as well. In the adjacent room, illumination is directed toward the ceiling, which pleasantly glows in that space and in the reflected image as seen from across the surface of the pool.

In shaping and lighting good architectural spaces, the designer arranges illuminated surfaces in skillful ways like the composer at the keyboard. At the time the photograph was taken, the tones of color and brightness in Figure C-76 impart a quietude, like a musical passage scored in *adagio*. In the lobby of Figure C-77, tonal rhythms of reflected light animate the space, yet are scored in a different melodic composition. Compared with the former example, it is just slightly up tempo, from adagio to *andante*. At the floor, slender columns begin a vertical ascent, merge into stepped rectangular shapes that spatially interplay from negative to positive, alternating in brightness as they do, in concert with geometric rhythms that visually move full circle around the room. The design atmosphere fits the kind of public space that it is: a lobby for a museum, like a prelude for the exhibitions to come. The space is reserved in chroma, holding back experiences of full color that will be found in the galleries that follow in sequence. A good transition is made from abundance of light of the out-of-doors, to the controlled composition of light on the interior surfaces of the architecture.

The best evaluation of spatial design, is taken from the panoptic viewpoint natural to human vision. In the final stages of design, a *360° check* is necessary for refinement, horizontally and vertically, because people see their environment in all directions. Floor plans, elevations, and one-point perspectives are invaluable communication devices for designers and all involved with a project, but the visual experience of the architectural environment comes from the eye scanning its surroundings in the totality of space. The 360° check seeks answers to questions such as where are the major luminance areas, and do they convey a dominant hue or a polychromatic ambiance? How do the interior furnishings compose in color and brightness with the spatial envelope and in spatial connections? Are there discordant parts that are eroding spatial order and harmony? Are there distortions of the spatial envelope or glare that are detrimental to human comfort? Are focal centers balanced about a room in good spatial composition, and if one or more are visual objectives, to where will they lead the curious eye?

A mainstream of this book is the *humanization of architecture,* which looks to uphold those aspects of design and construction that directly relate to promoting the comfort and well-being of people. A companion theme in the book is the promotion of design principles that bring visual order and harmony to the human habitat and contribute to architectural aesthetics. Application of those principles needs to focus on how people respond to the light and colors that are shaped around them as they experience the architectural environment (Figure C-80).

Where does design *style* fit into all of this? In the application of space and light theory, it is not necessary to think in stylistic design imagery such as classical, Art Nouveau, Art Deco, Modern, Post Modern, or Next Modern. The problem with designing by style, fads, and fashions is that the fundamental design elements of form, space, color, texture, and light are subordinated to preconceived imagery, instead of being used directly to create a new design environment out of concept, site, and program requirements. Designing by style sometimes involves plugging into a composition visual elements that just don't fit in order to conform to conventions of stylistic figuration.

It can be argued that people *want* style and fashion in their surroundings, and that is part of their comfort. That line of reasoning is acceptable, as long as the stylistic elements do not violate ergonomic design for human living. Too often they do, as attested to by projects appearing in architecture publications and the mass media in the past few decades. This includes distorted shapes of forms and spaces that are upsetting to the visual system and impair the physiological and psychological balance that human beings require. Not to be overlooked are the use of glitzy surfacing materials that spawn annoying reflections; high brightness-contrast on surfaces angled to predominant sight lines; dark glass used for exterior pattern design but creating a gloomy interior or the need for adding unnecessary electric light; overload of visual perception stimuli in an immediate environment; abrupt changes from dark to light or light to dark without adequate transition for retinal adaptation; exposed light sources of excessive contrast; and glare (often filtered out of photographs for publication). These dehumanizing architectural transgressions on the human living condition unnecessarily tax the human nervous system. When they exist for stylistic reasons, or only to raise eyebrows and draw grins from compatriots in the architectural community, or simply just out of insensitivity to the biological needs of people, then harmful mistakes have been made. In the late 1920s architect Richard Neutra (1954, 86) advanced his "bio-realism" philosophy, directly linking the human physiology with architectural design:

> It has become imperative that in designing our physical environment we should consciously raise the fundamental question of survival, in the broadest sense of this term. Any design that impairs and imposes excessive strain on the natural human equipment should be eliminated, or modified in accordance with the requirements of our nervous and, more generally, our total physiological functioning.

Why is it then, that what seems so basic to the professional practice of architecture—the creation of a built environment that best serves the physical and psychological needs of people—is at times cast aside in favor of designing buildings that work against those fundamental biological needs? Responding to the urge for change that is embedded in contemporary culture, some designers customarily seek guidance from the fashion worlds of New York, Paris, and Tokyo. What they find through the media or personal travel are projects that look like architectural game playing, some of which have been featured on the covers of professional journals. The creation of humanized architecture remains the ultimate goal. The spaces of the built environment belong far more to the masses of society than to the individual creators and critics that vie for magazine and journal space. Many recent projects have been little more than pseudo-monuments created to bring attention to the designers themselves, rather than exemplar works that are satisfying to the human spirit and add beauty to the architectural world. In league with those designers is another group whose understanding of creativity means only "to make something look different" and in the process casts aside basic human values.

In view of the complexities of the changing world that surely will continue into the twenty-first century, the opportunities already exist for directing the creative impulse to a much larger scope of architectural problem solving. That scope includes increasing specialized concepts for building types and urban spaces, the complexities of their program requirements generated by an ever-changing social and technological world, increasingly new technologies for constructing and servicing buildings, the inevitable challenges of meeting code and budget restrictions, and the varying influences of site adaptations. As those problems are addressed, the solutions need to include two essentials: the humanization of architecture through ergonomic design and surrounding people with architectural beauty through disciplined design composition. Interesting enough is the fact that to some degree each of these has been evident in the human-centered masterpieces that regularly have appeared in the history of architecture.

The architecture of the future, therefore, comes right down to a fundamental decision regarding the direction in which designers expend the intellectual and intuitional energies that we have come to know as creativity. There certainly is the role of the client in that choice of direction. But for the designer, there is also the choice of building monuments to themselves, or of shaping, coloring, and texturing architectural spaces and furnishings in ways that will celebrate the arrival of light and also safeguard human comfort and well-being. As part of the same decision to create a humanized architecture, is the designer's choice to create genuine architectural beauty for the surroundings of human living.

This book has been about seeing and perceiving, but when it comes to influencing direction for the future of architecture, there is an abyss of significant magnitude between sight and vision. Those responsible for creating the world of architecture, especially those in positions of leadership, need a very special kind of seeing . . .

There is a scene in playwright Herb Gardner's *I'm Not Rappaport,* in which Nat and Midge, both virtually blind, are sitting on a park bench discussing living in a world they cannot see. They are talking about facing personal dilemmas, and discover their friendship is bonded by that very special kind of seeing.

Nat turns and puts his arm around Midge, and says:

"Who needs sight when we got vision!"

APPENDIX

Photography and the Human Retina

References were made in the text regarding how a photographic image of an environmental scene compares with what is perceived by human vision. The eye resembles the camera in some ways, but not in others. Both receive light from the visible surfaces of the world through a lens that inverts the images passing through it. Whereas the film and consequently the photographic print can be righted for viewing, the images received by the eye are inverted to their "correct" position by a complex neurological process between the retina and the brain. The lens of the camera and the human eye are controlled by an adjustable iris that admits the quantity of incoming light. As light reflected on physical surfaces passes through the camera lens and then is focused on the film plane, the shape of the lens stays fixed. The lens of the human eye changes shape as it focuses on objects, and as we saw in Chapters 2 and 6, that physiological change influences depth and color perception.

As is well known by professional photographers and competent amateurs, different camera lenses change the appearance of spatial dimensions. Wide-angle lenses are used to bring into view more of the peripheral subject, but they distort distance in the view straight ahead. Long-range telephoto lenses are able to bring distant subjects closer to the camera, but the distance between distant objects is shortened. When photographed with a very long lens, two highrise buildings may appear as if they are side-by-side neighbors when in fact they are separated by several city blocks. Distortions of the real sites by camera lenses are critically important for analyzing buildings and architectural space as seen in photographs. Teachers who regularly repeat courses as part of their profession

and individuals who are familiar with architectural sites easily recognize photographic spatial distortions. It takes a well-trained or professional photographer to capture accurately the true spatial impressions that appear at the actual site. The selection of photographs for this book avoided exaggerated spatial views.

For the perception of spatial depth as seen by the human organism, a most important difference from the camera is *binocular vision*. The retinal images from both eyes are transmitted to the brain, which combines the two into one visual experience. Binocular vision is a very important depth cue, easily demonstrated by opening and closing one eye. A bush or tree about 30 or 40 yards away and viewed against others of similar color and texture will look flattened out and nearly camouflaged to the single eye.

The perceptual depth cue of *motion parallax* is especially important for the analysis of architectural space. Parallax conditions are created by movement of the head. In Chapter 2 an example was given holding up a finger at arm's length, moving your head back and forth, and observing spatial relations between the finger and the scene behind. A still photograph, as well as movie, television, and computer screens, are all *flat* images. This is realized by watching a stopped or near-still scene on television, moving your head laterally and noting that spatial relationships do not change next to the edges of foreground objects, like they do when performing the same movement while looking about in the real room. In the same way, photographs and pictures in books convey spatial depth, but lack the depth cue of motion parallax, and it is absent on computer monitors. Although spatial relations are changing on the computer monitor as objects or perspective views are rotated or changed in viewing angle, the spatial perception is different from what would be seen as a result of the head of the observer moving, especially when combined with binocular vision. This is not to deny nor lessen the value of CAD as a design tool, but only to distinguish between the electronic images on a monitor and the images perceived by direct human vision.

The significance of eye movement for visual perception is also important as related to the *size* of a visual field and its distance from the viewer. The eye moves when scanning the details of a flat painting or graphic, but unless the picture is relatively large in size, the eyes may be all that is moving during the time the subject is being studied. When watching movies and television, the continually changing images are brought to the viewer through camera lenses, rather than requiring movement of the rest of the body other than the eyes. For this reason movies showing magnificent landscapes suffer immeasurably when shown on television, because the size of the screen, like most photographs, narrows the viewing angle. People are remote from the television screen, sitting away in a chair. Peripheral vision takes in the surrounding room, and the great panorama of landscape in a movie is condensed by the television screen to mere picture image. Even in the large, panoramic views of the movie theater, people in the rear move mainly their eyes to watch the unfolding scenery, but people down front move their heads, not unlike watching a tennis match from the sidelines at midcourt. In all, the imagery projected on film is incomparable to experiencing Nature's grand landscapes first-hand while walking in the great natural environments of mountain, canyon, or forest. The visual experience of architectural space is similar, even in the case of just a small room, which is far more spacious when perceiving it by turning the head than by seeing pictures of it taken by the camera.

A most important difference between looking at pictures—whether photographs or video screens—is the light/dark adaptation of the eye of the viewer. The camera has no retina, and records what it sees according to the lens used and the chemistry of the film. The eye of the viewer is light or dark adapted to the illumination level of the room in which the printed photograph or computer image is being viewed. Light or dark adaptation creates perceptual differences when looking at a picture printed in this or any other book when the viewer is in a well-lighted environment, compared with looking at a photographic slide in a darkened room. Looking at pictures in books or views on a VDT, the eye of the viewer cannot enter—*and adapt to*—the first space shown on the computer monitor or in a picture in a book, and that is the one which would modify the brightness levels and color values of all spaces seen beyond or adjacent to that first space. Further, when looking at a video screen, remember that the eye is looking at images of electronic light, not the luminances created by light interacting with actual building materials as is the case when those materials become illuminated surfaces in the real-world environment. It was out of consideration of the important visual perception phenomenon of retinal light or dark adaptation that explanations were often given in the text of this book regarding the author's understanding of how an architectural space in an illustration would be experienced in reality.

Another significant aspect of color and black and white photography relates to the chemistry of the photographic process. Some films are more sensitive to certain hues than others, and how they are exposed for accuracy of color on the finished photographic print usually separates the amateur from the professional photographer. Even professional photographers struggle with the problem of rendering color, and each has favorites of film quality for certain conditions of illumination quality in natural and architectural settings. Manufacturers in various industries are very concerned about how their products are rendered in color as they will be seen in the media, especially in advertising. One of the major lighting companies recently stopped photographing comparative lighting setups of the same subject under different light displays, at least for the time being, because they could not accurately capture on film the colors of displays that are seen by the human eye. When looking at a photographic print of a showroom illuminated by a certain light quality (e.g., cool-white fluorescent vs. incandescent) some manufacturers would be satisfied by the color appearance of their products, but other manufacturers would not. Some products look better on one film than on another.

Although strides are being made to improve the quality of film and photographic paper, an antagonist of picture making long has been *reciprocity,* which strongly influences the appearance of luminance levels at both ends of the photographic gray scale, where there are high contrasts of light or dark. This creates difficulties when photographing scenes that include extremely dark shadows or extremely bright surfaces, such as the light sources themselves. In printed photographs, reciprocity may cause bright light sources to appear as flat white shapes, but at the site the eye would see details of diffusing panels of the luminaires. In like manner, details in dark shadow areas in a photograph may be eradicated by reciprocity, but are visible to the eye at the scene. In many photographs of interior rooms, details of a view outside a window nearly vanish, but the eye in the real space easily sees the exterior scene. All of this creates a virtual nightmare when using photographs to communicate space and light theory, realistic luminance levels, reflectances, glare, or light and dark retinal adaptation. In the case of the author's own photographs in this book (those not credited to someone else), darkroom adjustments were made on some of the black and white images. This was done for some of the black and white photographs taken in the Space and Light Laboratory, and sometimes the light levels in the demonstration models described later were adjusted to give better photographic representations of the actual conditions seen in the lab. When that was done and it was thought the photograph would be somewhat misleading, explanation was given in the text.

As this book demonstrates, a major component of architectural space and light theory is brightness. All the reflected light that we see in the natural or built environment falls somewhere in the range of what physicists call "visible light," but it is impossible to record on film the brightness range that the human eye can see. The ratio of highlight to shadow that the eye can handle in perceiving the visual world is about 10,000:1. When recorded on film, the ratio falls to about 1000:1 for a film transparency (photographic slide), and only about 80 or 100:1 for a reflective copy (printed photograph). Imagine, therefore, trying to communicate the actualities of architectural and lighting design by way of photographs printed in books or bright color slides that look so convincingly "real."

Some photographers practice "existing light" photography (sometimes called "available light"), which means they expose film under the actual lighting conditions at the site, with no fill-in lighting to adjust for the chemical shortcomings of film. Using high-speed film and fast lenses they are able to photograph subjects at existing light levels. The high-contrast conditions often found in architecture, however, still create reciprocity for film, which cannot be solved by "existing light" photography other than by the challenging and difficult method of making multiple exposures.

Contrast problems are countered by adding photographic support lighting on the scene, but unless in the hands of a highly skilled photographer, the result can look forced, theatrical, or contrived. A major problem occurs in the architectural community when designers see those photographs in the media, accept them as "pretty pictures" or lighting dramatics, and try to emulate them in the projects they are designing. They are then modeling off photographic images, not conditions at the real site, where the color of surfaces are much different under existing illumination. Sometimes the photographic support lighting contributes to distorting the appearance of architectural space. When photographing architectural interiors, some surfaces reflect light at brightness levels created by the photographic support lighting rather than the permanent architectural lighting. This can be detected by looking at photographic illustrations in books, journals, or manufacturers' catalogs, and looking for unnatural highlights and shadows, those that do not appear to be the result of the project's own architectural lighting. The quality of photographic support lighting was taken into consideration when se-lecting photographs for this book. Sometimes images were used even though modified by support lighting, because the photograph had value in communicating the particular points or design principles as explained in the text. In most cases the author discussed the particular image with the photographer or architect personally, to confer on actual color and brightness.

Competent professional photographers stay informed of new developments in the chemistry of photography, and have the knowledge and experience necessary for adding support lighting to the architectural scene while preserving the project's design integrity. Before ever setting up the camera, the top-line photographers make a thorough study of the setting to get a feeling for how a building or interior appears in its own existing light and at different times of day. Auxiliary lighting is then placed to counteract the behavior of film so that the finished photograph communicates the subject the way it really appears to the human eye. Most professional photographers are very good at this. Many of the photographs in this book were made by Steve Rosenthal, Balthazar Korab, and Paul Kivett, professional photographers who have learned how to *see* architecture through years of experience in successful careers, and whose works have often appeared in the professional and popular media. They are highly skilled architectural photographers who understand how to place auxiliary lighting with precision and discretion, to portray the scene exceptionally close to how it actually appears on site. In his studio, Steve Rosenthal devotes a considerable amount of time making photographic studies and recording data of the appearance of subjects and materials under different lighting quality that appears in architecture, using different film quality.

With the continuing advances being made in the technology of photography and computerized image production, modifications of an original photograph can be made at the discretion of the photographer and the technician to make changes in the scene for some specific purpose. Digital cropping can take out a building or some other detail from one photograph and transport it to another, or disturbing elements in the photograph can be removed electronically. When this is done, the photograph becomes a film graphic, but is no longer a document of the site. None of those appear in this book.

Space and Light Laboratory

A laboratory for studying the interrelationship between lighting and architectural space has been developed at the School of Architecture and Urban Design of The University of Kansas. The lab was conceived as a teaching and research support facility to study the appearance of the spaces of architecture under the influence of light as perceived by the human visual system. The laboratory research models described later were developed by the author to observe directly how the surface characteristics of building materials visually change in color and brightness under variable illumination. The models also serve as research "shells" in which simulated architectural designs can be tested for illumination and color effects in spatial and interspatial conditions under different lighting applications. Students use the lab's facilities to construct architectural models related to studio design projects (Figures A-1a and b) and to test brightness and color appearance of actual building material samples selected for the design. Some of the photographs appearing in the text were taken in those models. The lab also maintains collections of wood species, wall fabrics and vinyls, and other architectural surfacing materials contributed by industry; those materials are sized for testing in the research models.

The Space and Light Laboratory accompanies The Bob Foley Illumination Laboratory in the Department of Architectural Engineering, also at The University of Kansas. The combined facilities provide demonstration and research capabilities that serve faculty and students in architecture, architectural engineering, lighting design, interior design, and theater design.

The research/demonstration models described and illustrated next are normally used in a darkened laboratory so illumination of their spaces can be controlled. The photographs that illustrate them were obviously taken with the room lights on for better views of the models.

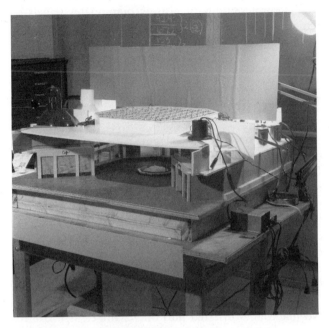

Figure A-1 (a) Student lighting study model.

Figure A-1 (b) Students with lighting study model.

Interspace Model

The Interspace Model (Figure A-2) was developed to demonstrate the interaction of two connected but independently illuminated spaces. It shows brightness and color changes in an adjacent space resulting from light or dark adaptation of the eye in the observer's space. Conversely, it reveals perceptual phenomena that appear in the space of the observer caused by brightness changes in the connected space. The model is adaptable for experiments that integrate the fields of architectural design and visual perception psychology.

The model is outfitted with incandescent and fluorescent light sources, controlled by dimmers. Changeable interior "ceilings" make possible observations of numerous lighting methods, direct or diffused, which can be modified in chroma by the use of color filters. Removable "wall" components allow specialized lighting to be cast into the interior from outside the model. In the foreground of the photograph is a physics optical bench illuminator showing how any desirable shape of light can be directed into the model's interior. A spot luminance meter takes measurements on interior surfaces.

Interchangeable partitions between the model's two interior spaces make possible a variety of design options for spatial connections, in the form of door openings, archways, partial openings, or windows. Scaled architectural grilles may be inserted for testing object recognition and color contrasts as seen through various grille designs, providing theoretical testing of screened space that later is tested at full scale in connected rooms of the Space and Light Laboratory (see Figures 13-27, C-57, and C-58).

The model has been used for studying simulated conditions of domestic spaces, restaurants, offices, and other architectural settings. It also accommodates panels of actual building materials, which can be tested for their appearance in interspatial lighting conditions.

Luminance Viewer

The Luminance Viewer (Figure A-3) was created especially for development of the LBR System explained in Chapter 5. The viewer was designed as a research apparatus for observing research participants' judgments of perceptual brightness of different architectural materials. It has two independently illuminated chambers that receive samples of surfacing materials, like wood, wall coverings, slate, marble, painted surfaces, or any other material, whose brightness can be varied by changing lighting levels.

When used for the LBR System, a panel of Munsell N6 material is inserted into one chamber as a control standard. A sample of a building material to be tested

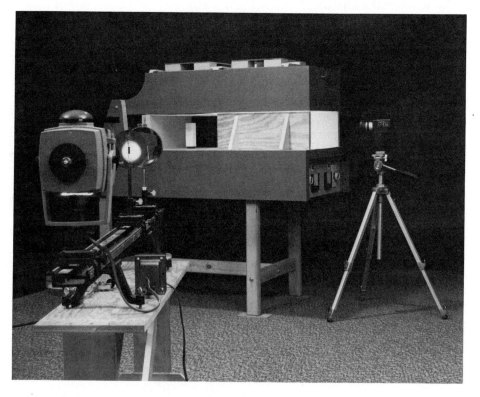

Figure A-2. Interspace Model.

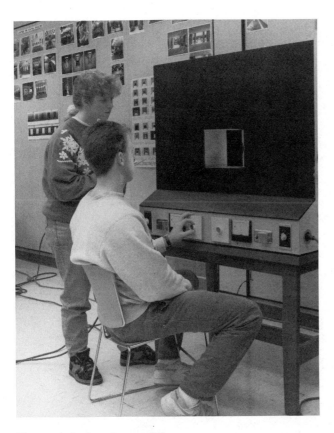

Figure A-3. Luminance Viewer.

is inserted into the adjacent chamber. Both chambers are separated by a narrow dividing partition of two mirrors, which help distribute uniform luminance over both surfaces from lighting inside the model. Dimmers allow the observer to set any one material at a selected brightness level, and increase or decrease the illumination on a panel in the adjacent chamber to acheive a brightness match or some other condition of brightness comparison or contrast. The viewing aperture in front allows taking luminance measurements with a photometer from outside the model.

The Luminance Viewer has ample internal illumination to raise in luminance a dark material for comparison with another material of high reflective value. The model is internally insulated and vented to handle the few occasions where high incandescent illumination is required. Automatic timers shut off the illumination in the event the model is left unattended.

Multiluminator

This model belongs in every architectural design office and stores that sell interior surfacing materials. The Multiluminator (Figure A-4) provides the observation of

four independently lighted viewing chambers for making comparative studies of color, texture, and other surface characteristics of architectural materials when subjected to changes in quality and quantity of light. The chambers are angled to a central viewing area in front of the model to provide the observer with simultaneous views of the four demonstrations, and to facilitate taking photometric luminance measurements of each chamber from a single station point.

All light sources are located behind the upper vertical panels, out of sight from observer positions in the front of the model. Light levels in each chamber can be varied by dimmers. The most common light sources available on the market can be inserted with relative ease, a different kind in each chamber. When identical samples of surfacing materials are placed in the chambers, at a glance the designer (or customer in a store) is able to see how the material appears in color under the influence of different qualities of light. If project requirements specify use of only a certain light quality, that light source can be put into all four chambers, and different product lines, styles, and colors can be placed in the viewing chambers to observe how each will appear under that light. Using the building material collections in the Space and Light Laboratory, panels of wall coverings, carpeting, and wood species are inserted in the Multiluminator for making visual judgments of color value for a project's walls, floors, or furniture.

First-time observers of these demonstrations often express surprise and disbelief when seeing how the same material appears under different light quality. The demonstrations are equally surprising when showing how human flesh appears under different illumination, particularly when seen under incandescent versus cool-white fluorescent light.

The Multiluminator serves a dual purpose. The viewing chambers into which the surfacing materials are inserted are removable, and can be replaced by scale models of architectural and interior designs to make comparative studies of their appearance under varying illumination quality and quantity. Student projects have converted the entire apparatus into a shopping mall complete with illuminated logos over entrances. Studies were made to determine appropriate lighting quality and overall brightness levels for the type and design of the individual shops as they would be seen from the greater central space of the mall.

Directional Space Model

One of the common spaces in architecture is a corridor or a space that is similarly proportioned, and that kind of space requires special considerations of lighting and interior design. Such corridor spaces usually have a com-

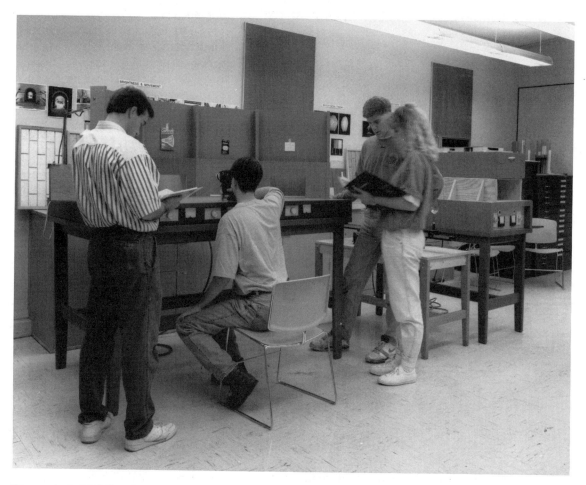

Figure A-4. Multiluminator.

mon design for their total length. For people walking through them, normally the retina has adapted to a general lighting level for the corridor, while the eyes look toward a spatial connection that often is different in brightness. The Directional Space Model (Figure A-5) was developed to test lighting schemes and perceptual phenomena associated with conditions such as Figure 13-15. This model too is a basic architectural shell, and has removable components with built-in variable illumination that accommodates surfaces that simulate floors, walls, ceilings, and a variety of lighting designs.

A corridor visually frames the observer's view toward some feature lying at the end of the space, like the wall of a perpendicular space, or a sculpture, mural, or some other special element. The model provides variable lighting at three places: the corridor proper, the intersection at the end, and another space on the other side of the intersection simulating spatial sequencing. This allows the observer to make studies of color and brightness of those sequential spaces based on retinal light and dark adaptation to the corridor.

When the model is used to simulate a directional space that is terminated by another perpendicular corridor, a blank wall or some design feature of the perpendicular corridor lies dominant in the viewer's line of sight. At the far end, a "wall" panel can be back-lighted to study color and brightness relationships of both spaces, one influencing the other.

The model demonstrates a number of visual perception phenomena, such as gamma movement (brightness advances) of the distant wall, and aspects of depth perception applied to architecture. A variety of corridor designs can be created to emphasize or minimize the apparent length of the space. Variable illumination of the spatial components also can be used to influence depth perception.

This model converts to architectural design environments other than a corridor. With its interchangeable parts, on different occasions it has become an elongated restaurant dining area, and a church interior with a sanctuary at the end and architectural grilles screening side aisles.

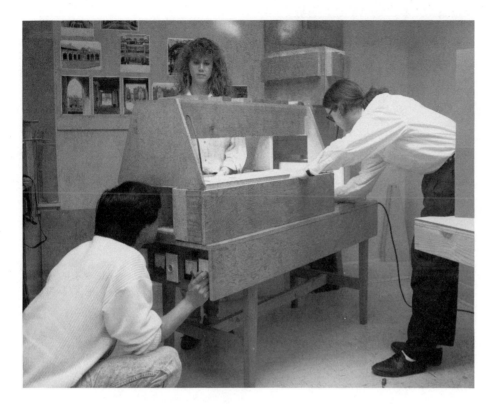

Figure A-5. Directional Space Model.

Lighting Accent Demonstrator

This demonstration model (Figure A-6) casts nine identical illumination scallops or other lighting accents on the Munsell neutral value panels of the LBR Scale of brightness. It was built to demonstrate brightness-contrast of accent lighting on surfaces of varying reflectance, from black to white. Internal cells above each panel house the lamps and changeable diaphragms that control the shape of the lighting accent. Like the other research/demonstration models in the Space and Light Laboratory, this one also accommodates samples of actual building materials to observe how two or more would compare in their capability for reflecting lighting accents. When the model is used for that purpose, a protective shield is placed over the Munsell papers to protect them from surface damage.

This was the model used for the photograph of Figure 11-12 that appears in Chapter 11. However, due to variations of illumination output that is normal to lamp manufacturing, a single-chamber version of this model was used for taking the photometric luminance ratios that appear in Table 11-1. Munsell notation papers for each zone of the LBR Scale were inserted in the single chamber apparatus to eliminate inconsistencies of output that may appear over the nine zones of the Lighting Accent Demonstrator.

Color Modulator

The Color Modulator (Figure A-7) was developed to test the appearance of color, texture, and brightness of actual building materials in a variety of applications to lighting interior space. It has two viewing chambers, each with a front and back compartment to demonstrate the interaction of various hues by simultaneous contrast under different illumination intensities. The two chambers provide side-by-side comparisons of the same or different surfacing materials, one serving as a control standard. Each compartment is equipped with dimmer-controlled compact fluorescent and incandescent lamps, providing observation of illumination quality and quantity, and mixtures of both.

In both chambers, samples of building materials can be rotated to change their angle to the observer's line of sight from in front of the model. In the left chamber, the luminaires stay fixed to reveal how the surface changes in color value, texture, and brightness as it is angled toward

Figure A-6. Lighting Accent Demonstrator.

Figure A-7. Color Modulator.

or away from the light source. In the right chamber, the light sources move with the test surface, simulating how the material changes appearance as it would be angled in slant to the observer as seen from different locations in a room.

Demonstrations reveal how the pattern and texture of fabric weaves and wall vinyls change when angled in slant to the observer or light source (see Figures 5-11 and 5-12), and how glare is introduced on specular surfaces at various angles to the observer or light source.

The front and back compartments on both sides provide comparative testing of color change created by simultaneous contrast of an intermediate hue under variable illumination. Luminance qualities and size of opening are studied for application to lighting spaces with architectural grilles.

Bibliography

Abercrombie, Stanley, *Architecture as Art,* Harper & Row Icon Editions, New York, 1984.

Acking, C. A., and R. Küller, "The perception of an interior as a function of its colour," *Ergonomics,* Vol. 15, No. 6, 1972, pp. 645–654.

Albers, Josef, *The Interaction of Color,* Yale University Press, New Haven, Connecticut, 1963.

Alexander, Christopher, *The Timeless Way of Building,* Oxford University Press, New York, 1979.

Alexander, Christopher, *Notes on the Synthesis of Form,* Harvard University Press, Cambridge, 1967.

Allen, E. C., and J. P. Guilford, "Factors determining the affective values of color combinations," *American Journal of Psychology,* Vol. 48, 1936, pp. 643–648.

Anstis, Stuart M., "Interactions between simultaneous contrast and adaptation to gradual change of luninance," *Perception,* Vol. 8, No. 5, 1979, pp. 487–495.

Appel, John, and James J. MacKenzie, "How much light do we really need?" *Building Systems Design,* February 1975, pp. 27–31.

Appleyard, Donald, "Motion, sequence and the city," in *The Nature of Art of Motion,* edited by Gyorgy Kepes, George Braziller, New York, 1965.

Appleyard, Donald, "Why buildings are known: a predictive tool for architects and planners," *Environment and Behavior in the Built Environment,* edited by Geoffrey Broadbent, Richard Bunt, and Tomas Llorens, John Wiley & Sons, New York, 1980.

Arnheim, Rudolf, "Inside and outside in architecture,"*The Journal of Aesthetics and Art Criticism,* Vol. 21, No. 1, Fall 1966, pp. 3–7.

Arnheim, Rudolf, *Toward a Psychology of Art,* University of California Press, Berkeley, 1966.

Arnheim, Rudolf, *Art and Visual Perception,* University of California Press, Berkeley, 1969.

Arnheim, Rudolf, *Visual Thinking,* University of California Press, Berkeley, 1971.

Arnheim, Rudolf, *The Dynamics of Architectural Form,* University of California Press, Berkeley, 1977.

Ashihara, Yoshinobu, *Exterior Design in Architecture,* revised ed., Van Nostrand Reinhold, New York, 1981.

Ashihara, Yoshinobu, *The Aesthetic Townscape,* translated by Lynne E. Riggs, The MIT Press, Cambridge, 1983.

Attneave, F., "Symmetry, information, and memory for patterns," *American Journal of Psychology,* Vol. 68, 1955, pp. 209–222.

Avant, Lloyd L., "Vision in the Ganzfeld," *Psychological Bulletin,* Vol. 64, No. 4, 1965, pp. 246–258.

Bachelard, Gaston, *The Poetics of Space,* translated by Maria Jólas, Beacon Press, Boston, 1969.

Ball, R. J., and S. H. Bartley, "Changes in brightness index, saturation and hue produced by luminance—wavelength—temporal interactions," *Journal of the Optical Society of America,* Vol. 56, No. 5, 1966, pp. 695–698.

Barth, Herbert, Dietrich Mack, and Egon Voss, *Wagner, A Documentary Study,* Oxford University Press, New York, 1975.

Bartley, S. H., *Principles of Perception,* 2nd ed., Harper & Row, New York, 1969.

Bechtel, Robert B., "Human movement and architecture," *Transaction,* Washington University, St. Louis, May 1967.

Beck, Jacob, "Contrast and assimilation in lightness judgments," *Perception and Psychophysics,* Vol. 1, No. 10, 1966, pp. 342–344.

Beck, J., *Surface Color Perception,* Cornell University Press, Ithaca, 1972.

Bell, Paul A., Jeffrey D. Fisher, and Ross J. Loomis, *Environmental Psychology,* Saunders, Philadelphia, 1978.

Benedikt, M., "To take hold of space: isovists and isovist fields," *Environment and Planning,* Vol. B6, 1979, pp. 47–65.

Berkeley, George, *An Essay Towards a New Theory of Vision,* 1709.

Berlyne, D. E., *Conflict, Arousal and Curiosity,* McGraw Hill, New York, 1960.

Berlyne, D. E., "Experimental aesthetics," in *New Horizons in Psychology 2,* edited by P. C. Dodwell, Penguin, New York, 1972.

Bernecker, Craig A., "Designing for people: applying psychology of light research," *Architectural Lighting,* November 1987, pp. 36–40.

Beston, Henry, *The Outermost House,* Ballantine Books, New York, 1971.

Birren, Faber, *Light, Color and Environment,* Van Nostrand Reinhold, New York, 1969.

Birren, Faber, *Principles of Color,* Van Nostrand Reinhold, New York, 1969.

Birren, Faber, *Color and Human Response,* Van Nostrand Reinhold, New York, 1978.

Blackwell, H. R., *A Unified Framework of Methods for Evaluating Visual Performance Aspects of Lighting,* CIE Publication 19, Paris, 1972.

Blackwell, H. R., "A human factors approach to lighting recommendations and standards," *Proceedings of the Sixteenth Annual Meeting of the Human Factors Society,* Santa Monica, California, 1972.

Bortz, Jürgen, "Beiträge zur Anwendung der Psychologie auf dem Städtebau. II. Erkundungsexperiment zur Beziehung zwischen Fassadengestaltung und ihrer Wirkung auf den Betrachter," *Zeitschrift für Experimentelle und Angewandte Psychologie,* Vol. 19, 1972, pp. 226–281.

Botha, E., "Past experience and figure ground perception," *Perceptual and Motor Skills,* Vol. 16, 1963, pp. 283–288.

Boud, John, *Lighting Design in Buildings,* Billing & Sons Ltd., London, 1973.

Boyce, P. R., "Age, illuminance, visual performance, and preference," *Lighting Research Technology,* Vol. 5, 1973, pp. 125–144.

Boyce, P. R., "The luminous environment," *Environmental Interaction: Psychological Approaches to our Physical Surroundings,* edited by D. Canter and P. Stringer, International Universities Press, New York, 1975.

Boyce, P. R., "Investigations of the subjective balance between illuminance and lamp colour properties," *Lighting Research and Technology,* Vol. 9, No. 11, 1977, p. 11.

Boyce, P. R., "Under the influence of lighting," *Developments in Lighting—1,* edited by J. A. Lynes, Applied Science Publishers, London, 1978.

Boyce, P. R., *Human Factors in Lighting,* Applied Science Publishers, London, 1981.

Braunstein, Myron L., *Depth Perception Through Motion,* Academic Press, New York, 1976.

Brown, G. C., *Sun, Wind, and Light,* John Wiley & Sons, New York, 1985.

Bruce, Vicki, and Patrick R. Green, *Visual Perception, Physiology, Psychology and Ecology,* 2nd ed. Lawrence Erlbaum Associates, Hove and London, 1991.

Burnette, Charles, "The mental image and design," in *Designing for Human Behavior,* edited by Jon Lang *et al.,* Dowden, Hutchinson & Ross, Stroudsburg, 1974.

Bush-Brown, Albert, "The architectural polemic," *The Journal of Aesthetics and Art Criticism,* December 1959, pp. 143–158.

Camara, Dom Helder, *A Thousand Reasons for Living,* Fortress Press, Philadelphia, 1981.

Carruthers, Kenneth D. B., "Architecture is space, the space-positive tradition," *Journal of Architectural Education,* Vol. 39, No. 3, Spring 1986, pp. 17–23.

Carson, Daniel, Ed., *Man-Environment Interactions: Evaluations and Applications I–III,* Dowden, Hutchinson & Ross, Stroudsburg, 1975.

Chapnis, A., and D. A. Mankin, "The vertical-horizontal illusion in a visually rich environment," *Perception and Psychophysics,* Vol. 2, June 1967, pp. 249–255.

Ching, Francis D. K., *Architecture: Form, Space and Order,* Van Nostrand Reinhold, New York, 1979.

Chermayeff, Serge, and Christopher Alexander, *Community and Privacy: Toward a New Architecture of Humanism,* Doubleday and Company, Garden City, 1963.

Clark, W. C., A. H. Smith, and Ausma Rabe, "The interaction of surface texture, outline, gradient, and ground in the perception of slant," *Canadian Journal of Psychology,* Vol. 10, No. 1, March 1956, pp. 1–8.

Clark, W. C., A. H. Smith, and Ausma Rabe, "Retinal gradients of outline distortion and binocular disparity as stimuli for slant," *Canadian Journal of Psychology,* Vol. 10, No. 2, June 1956, pp. 77–81.

Clark, W. C., A. H. Smith, and Ausma Rabe, "Retinal gradient of outline as a stimulus for slant," *Canadian Journal of Psychology,* Vol. 9, No. 4, December 1956, pp. 247–253.

Clulow, Frederick W., *Color, Its Principles and Their Applications,* Morgan & Morgan, New York, 1972.

Cohen, W., "Spatial and textural characteristics of the ganzfeld," *American Journal of Psychology,* Vol. 70, 1957, pp. 403–410.

Coren, S., C. Porac, and L. Ward, *Sensation and Perception,* Academic Press, New York, 1979.

Coren, Stanley, "Brightness contrast as a function of figure ground relations," *Journal of Experimental Psychology,* Vol. 80, 1969, pp. 517–524.

Coyne, Robert K., and R. James Clack, *Environmental Assessment and Design,* Praeger, New York, 1981.

Craik, K. J. W., "The effect of adaptation on differential brightness discrimination," *Journal of Physiology,* Vol. 92, 1938, 406–420.

Craik, K. J. W., "The effect of adaptation on subjective brightness," *Proceedings of the Royal Society of London,* Vol. 128, 1940, pp. 232–247.

Crouch, C. L., and L. J. Buttolph, "Visual relationships in office tasks," *Lighting Design & Application,* May 1973, pp. 23–25.

Cullen, Gordon, *Townscape,* Reinhold Book Corp., New York, 1968.

Curtis, Charles P., Jr., and Ferris Greenslet, *The Practical Cogitator or the Thinker's Anthology,* Houghton Mufflin, Boston, 1962.

Cuttle, Christopher, "The sharpness and the flow of light," *Architectural Psychology: Proceedings of the Lund Conference,* edited by R. Küller, Dowden, Hutchinson & Ross, Stroudsburg, Germany, 1973.

Cuttle, Christopher, "The new photometry," *Developments in Lighting—1,* edited by J. A. Lynes, Applied Science Publishers, Ltd., London, 1978.

Cuttle, Clarence, "The sharpness and the flow of light," *Architectural Psychology: Proceedings of the Lund Conference,* edited by R. Küller, Dowden, Hutchinson & Ross, Stroudsburg, 1973.

Daugherty, Andrea, and Paulette Hebert, "Studying light and color," *Lighting Design & Application,* Vol. 17, No. 4, April 1987, pp. 12–15.

Davidson, Cynthia Chapin, "Cubic disturbances," *Architecture,* September 1990, pp. 80–85.

De Grandis, Luigina, *Theory and Use of Color,* Harry N. Abrams, New York, 1986.

De La Croix, Horst, Richard G. Tansy, and Diane Kirkpatrick, *Art through the Ages,* Harcourt Brace Jovanovich, San Diego, 1991.

Dember, W. N., *The Psychology of Perception,* Holt, Rinehart and Winston, New York, 1960.

Deregowski, Jan B., "Pictorial perception and culture," *Scientific American,* Vol. 227, No. 5, November 1972, pp. 82–88.

De Valois, Russel L., and Karen K. De Valois, *Spatial Vision,* Oxford Psychology Series No. 14, Oxford University Press, New York, 1988.

Dewey, John, *Art as Experience,* Capricorn Books, New York, 1958 (1934).

Dietz, Albert G. H., and William M. C. Lam, *An Approach to the Design of the Luminous Environment,* State University Construction Fund, Albany, 1976.

Downs, R. M., and D. Stea, *Maps in Minds: Reflections on Cognitive Mapping,* Harper & Row, New York, 1977.

Duncker, Karl, "The influence of past experience upon perceptual properties," *American Journal of Psychology,* Vol. 52, No. 2, April 1939, pp. 255–265.

Dunton, George, "Artificial lighting," *Architects' Year Book 5,* Elek Books Ltd., London, 1953.

Egan, M. David, *Concepts in Architectural Lighting,* McGraw-Hill, New York, 1983.

Egeth, Howard, "Selective attention," *Psychological Review,* Vol. 67, No. 1, 1967, pp. 41–57.

Egusa, Hiroyuki, "Effect of brightness of perceived distance as a figure-ground phenomenon," *Perception,* Vol. 11, No. 6, 1982, pp. 671–676.

Ehrenzweig, A., *Psychoanalysis of Artistic Vision and Hearing,* Julian Press, New York, 1953.

Eliot, T. S., "The music of poetry," in *The Partisan Review Anthology,* edited by William Phillips and Philip Rahv, Holt, Rinehart and Winston, New York, 1962.

Ellinger, Richard G., *Color Structure and Design,* Van Nostrand Reinhold, New York, 1980.

Emerson, Ralph Waldo, "Beauty," *The Conduct of Life,* published in *The American Transcendentalists, Their Prose and Poetry,* edited by Perry Miller, Doubleday, Garden City, 1957.

Epstein, William, and John Park, "Examination of Gibson's psychophysical hypothesis," *Psychological Bulletin,* Vol. 62, No. 3, 1964, pp. 180–196.

Erhardt, Louis, "Should we design by illumination, luminance, or adaptation level?" *Lighting Design & Application,* Vol. 19, No. 8, September 1989, pp. 8–12.

Evans, Benjamin H., *Daylight in Architecture,* McGraw-Hill, New York, 1981.

Evans, Gary W., John Fellows, Marion Zorn, and Kim Doty, "Cognitive mapping in architecture," *Journal of Applied Psychology,* Vol. 65, No. 4, 1980, pp. 474–478.

Fantz, Robert L., "The origin of form perception," *Scientific American,* Vol. 204, No. 5, 1961, pp. 66–72.

Farnè, Mario, "Brightness as an indicator to distance: relative brightness per se or contrast with the background," *Perception,* Vol. 6, No. 3, 1977, pp. 287–293.

Fechner, G. T., *Elemente der Psychophysik,* translated by H. E. Adler, edited by D. H. Howes and E. G. Boring, Holt, Rinehart and Winston, New York, 1966.

Fischer, D., "A luminance concept for working interiors," *Journal of the Illuminating Engineering Society,* Vol. 2, No. 2, 1973, pp. 92–98.

Fletcher, Colin, *The Man Who Walked Through Time,* 2nd ed., Vintage Books, New York, 1972.

Flynn, J. E., "A study of lighting as a system of spatial cues," EDRA-6 *Workshop on the Psychological Potential of Illumination,* The University of Kansas, April 1975, pp. 1–9.

Flynn, J. E., and T. J. Spencer, "The effect of light source color on user impression and satisfaction," *Journal of the Illuminating Engineering Society,* Vol. 6, No. 3, 1977, pp. 167–179.

Flynn, J. E., "A study of subjective responses to low energy and non-uniform lighting systems," *Lighting Design & Application,* February 1977, pp. 6–15.

Flynn, J. E., T. J. Spencer, O. Martyniuck, and C. Hendrick, "Interim study of procedures for investigating the effect of light on impression and behavior," *Journal of the Illuminating Engineering Society,* Vol. 3, 1973, pp. 87–94.

Flynn, J. E., T. J. Spencer, O. Martyniuck, and C. Hendrick, *Interim Report to Illuminating Engineering Research Institute,* New York, Project 92, 1975.

Forgus, Ronald H., and Lawrence E. Melamed, *Perception, A Cognitive Approach,* 2nd ed., McGraw-Hill, New York, 1976.

French, Jere Stuart, *Urban Space, A Brief History of the City Square,* Kindall/Hunt, Dubuque, Ia., 1978.

Frisby, John P., *Seeing, Illusion, Brain and Mind,* Oxford University Press, New York, 1980.

Frost, Robert, "Take Something Like a Star," *The Poetry of Robert Frost,* edited by Edward Connery Latham, Henry Holt and Co., New York, 1949.

Gaarder, Kenneth R., *Eye Movements, Vision and Behavior,* John Wiley & Sons, New York, 1975.

Gardner, Herb, *I'm Not Rappaport,* Grove Press, New York, 1986.

Gärling, Tommy, "Studies in visual perception of architectural spaces and rooms I: judgment scales of open and closed space," *Scandinavian Journal of Psychology,* Vol. 10, 1969, pp. 250–256.

Gärling, Tommy, "Studies in visual perception of architectural spaces and rooms II: judgments of open and closed space by category rating and magnitude estimation," *Scandinavian Journal of Psychology,* Vol. 10, 1969, pp. 257–268.

Gärling, Tommy, "Studies in visual perception of architectural spaces and rooms III: a relation between judged depth and size of space," *Scandinavian Journal of Psychology,* Vol. 11, 1970, pp. 124–131.

Gärling, Tommy, "Studies in visual perception of architectural spaces and rooms IV: the relation of judged size of space under different viewing conditions," *Scandinavian Journal of Psychology,* Vol. 11, 1970, pp. 133–145.

Gerritsen, Frans, *Theory and Practice of Color,* revised, 2nd ed., Van Nostrand Reinhold, New York, 1983.

Gerstner, Karl, "Structure and movement," in *The Nature and Art of Motion,* edited by Gyorgy Kepes, George Braziller, New York, 1965.

Ghiselin, Brewster, Ed., *The Creative Process,* University of California Press, Berkeley, 1952, pp. 44–45.

Gibson, Eleanor, J. J. Gibson *et al.,* "Motion parallax as a determinant of perceived depth," *Journal of Experimental Psychology,* Vol. 58, 1959, pp. 40–51.

Gibson, James J., *The Senses Considered as Perceptual Systems,* Houghton Mifflin, Boston, 1966.

Gibson, James J., *The Perception of the Visual World,* originally published by Houghton Mifflin, Boston, 1950, Greenwood Press, Westport, Connecticut, 1974.

Gibson, James J., *The Ecological Approach to Visual Perception,* Houghton Mifflin, Boston, 1979.

Gibson, J. J., J. Purdy, and L. Lawrence, "A method of controlling stimulation for the study of space perception: the optical tunnel," *Journal of Experimental Psychology,* Vol. 50, No. 1, July 1955, pp. 1–14.

Gilchrist, A. L., "Perceived lightness depends on perceived spatial arrangement," *Science,* Vol. 195, No. 4274, January 1977, 185–187.

Gilchrist, Alan L., "The perception of surface blacks and whites," *Scientific American,* Vol. 240, No. 3, March 1979, pp. 112–124.

Gilchrist, Alan, and Alan Jacobsen, "Perception of lightness and illumination in a world of one reflectance," *Perception,* Vol. 13, No. 1, 1984, pp. 5–19.

Giovannini, Joseph, "Beyond convention," *Architecture,* May 1993, pp. 52–63.

Gordon, Gary, and James L. Nuckolls, *Interior Lighting for Designers,* 3rd edition, John Wiley & Sons, New York, 1995.

Graham, Clarence H., Ed., *Vision and Visual Perception,* John Wiley & Sons, New York, 1965.

Greer, Nora Richter, "Lighting design: state of the art," *Architecture,* October 1984, pp. 64–67.

Gregory, R. L., *Eye and Brain, The Psychology of Seeing,* World University Library, McGraw-Hill, New York, 1974.

Gropius, Walter, *Scope of Total Architecture,* Collier Books, New York, 1970 (1943).

Gropius, Walter, "The human scale," in *The Heart of City: Towards the Humanisation of Urban Life,* edited by J. Tyrwhitt, Lund Humphries, London, 1952.

Gruber, H. E., and W. C. Clark, "Perception of slanted surfaces," *Perceptual and Motor Skills,* Vol. 6, 1956, pp. 97–106.

Guilford, J. P., "The affective value of color as a function of hue, tint and chroma," *Journal of Experimental Psychology,* Vol. 17, 1934, pp. 342–370.

Guilford, J. P., and P. C. Smith, "A system of color preferences," *American Journal of Psychology,* Vol. 72, 1959, pp. 487–502.

Gump, P., "Milieu, environment and behavior," *Design and Environment,* Vol. 2, No. 4, 1971, pp. 48–52.

Gundlach, E., and C. Macoubrey, "The effect of color on apparent size," *American Journal of Psychology,* Vol. 43, 1931, pp. 109–111.

Gutheim, Frederick, "Urban space and urban design," in *Cities and Space,* edited by Lowdon Wingo, Jr., The Johns Hopkins Press, Baltimore, 1963.

Haber, Ralph N., and Maurice Hershenson, *The Psychology of Visual Perception,* Holt, Rinehart and Winston, New York, 1973.

Hall, Edward T., *The Hidden Dimension,* Doubleday & Co., Garden City, 1966.

Hall, Victoria K., "The aesthetics of color: A review of fifty years of experimentation," *Journal of Aesthetics and Art Criticism,* Vol. 23, No. 4, 1965, pp. 441–452.

Hamlin, Talbot, *Forms and Functions of Twentieth-Century Architecture, Vol. II: The Principles of Composition,* Columbia University Press, New York, 1952.

Hanes, R. M., "The long and short of color distance," *Architectural Record,* Vol. 127, No. 4, 1960, pp. 254–256.

Harold, Rita M., "Lighting for effective merchandising, *Lighting Design & Application,* Vol. 7, No. 5, 1977, pp. 15–17.

Hayward, S. C., and S. S. Franklin, "Perceived openness-enclosure of architectural space," *Environment and Behavior,* Vol. 6, No. 1, March 1974, pp. 37–52.

Heimstra, Norman W., and Leslie H. McFarling, *Environmental Psychology,* 2nd ed. Brooks/ Cole, Monterey, 1978.

Helms, Ronald N., and M. Clay Belcher, *Lighting for Energy-Efficient Luminous Environments,* Prentice Hall, Englewood Cliffs, N.J. 1991.

Helson, H., *Adaptation Level Theory,* Harper and Row, New York, 1964.

Helson, H., and T. Lansford, "The role of spectral energy source and background color in the pleasantness of object colors," *Applied Optics,* Vol. 9, 1970, pp. 1513–1562.

Hesselgren, Sven, *The Language of Architecure,* Studentlitteratur, Lund, Sweden, 1967.

Hesselgren, Sven, *Man's Perception of Man-Made Environment,* Dowden, Hutchinson & Ross, Stroudsburg, 1975.

Hochberg, J., "In the mind's eye," in *Contemporary Theory and Research in Visual Perception,* edited by R. N. Haber, Holt, Rinehart and Winston, New York, 1968, pp. 309–331.

Hochberg, J., "Perception: I. color and shape," in *Woodworth and Schlosberg's Experimental Psychology,* 3rd ed., edited by J. W. Kling and L. A. Riggs, Holt, Rinehart and Winston, New York, 1971, pp. 395–474.

Hochberg, J., "Perception: II. space and movement," in *Woodworth and Schlosberg's Experimental Psychology,* 3rd ed., edited by J. W. Kling and L. W. Riggs, Holt, Rinehart and Winston, New York, 1971, pp. 475–550.

Hochberg, J., and E. McAlister, "A quantitative approach to figural 'goodness,'" *Journal of Experimental Psychology,* Vol. 46, 1953, pp. 361–364.

Hochberg, J. E., and J. Beck, "Apparent spatial arrangement and perceived brightness," *Journal of Experimental Psychology,* Vol. 47, No. 4, 1954, pp. 263–266.

Hochberg, Julian, "Visual perception in architecture," *Via 6,* The Graduate School of Fine Arts, University of Pennsylvania, 1983, pp. 27–45.

Holahan, Charles J., *Environmental Psychology,* Random House, New York, 1982.

Holmberg, L., "Stability of individual and group data in the perception of volume content of rectangular rooms as measured by a production and an estimation method," *Psychological Research Bulletin,* Lund University, Sweden, Vol. 7, 1966.

Holmberg, L., R. Kuller, and I. Tidblom, "The perception of volume content of rectangular rooms as a function of the ratio between depth and width," *Psychological Research Bulletin,* Lund University, Sweden, Vol. 1, 1966.

Holmberg, L., *et al.,* "The perception of volume content of rectangular rooms—comparison between model and full-scale experiments," *Psychological Research Bulletin,* Lund University, Sweden, Vol. 2, 1969.

Hooper, Kristina, "The use of computer-controlled videodisks in the study of spatial learning," *Behavioral Research Methods and Instrumentation,* Vol. 13, 1981, pp. 77–84.

Hopkinson, R. G., *Architectural Physics: Lighting,* Her Majesty's Stationery Office, London, 1963.

Hopkinson, R. G., and J. B. Collins, *The Ergonomics of Lighting,* Macdonald Technical and Scientific, London, 1970.

Hopkinson, R. G., and J. D. Kay, *The Lighting of Buildings,* Frederick A. Praeger, New York, 1969.

Hoyt, Charles K., Ed., *More Places for People,* Architectural Record, McGraw-Hill, New York, 1983.

Humphreys, Glyn W., and Vicki Bruce, *Visual Cognition: Computational, Experimental, and Neuropsychological Perspectives,* Lawrence Erlbaum Associates, Hove and London, 1989.

Hurvich, Leo M., and Dorothea Jameson, *The Perception of Brightness and Darkness,* Allyn and Bacon, Boston, 1966.

IES Color Committee, *Color and Illumination,* Illuminating Engineering Society of North America, New York, 1990.

Illuminating Engineering Society of North America, *Lighting Handbook, Reference & Application,* edited by Mark S. Rea, Illuminating Engineering Society of North America, New York, 1993.

Inui, M., and T. Miyata, "Spaciousness in interiors," *Lighting Research & Technology,* Vol. 5, 1973, pp. 103–111.

Ittelson, William H., *Visual Space Perception,* Springer-Verlag, New York, 1960.

Ittleson, William H., "Perception of the large-scale environment," *Transactions of the New York Academy of Sciences,* Vol. 32, 1970, pp. 807–815.

Ittelson, William H., Ed., *Environment and Cognition,* Seminar Press, New York, 1973.

Ittelson, William H., *et al., An Introduction to Environmental Psychology,* Holt, Rinehart and Winston, Inc., New York, 1974.

Ittelson, W. H., K. A. Franck, and T. J. O'Hanlon, "The nature of environmental experience," in *Experiencing the Environment,* edited by S. Wapner, S. B. Cohen, and B. Kaplan, Plenum, New York, 1976.

Itten, Johannes, *The Art of Color,* Van Nostrand Reinhold, New York, 1973.

Itten, Johannes, *Design and Form, The Basic Course at the Bauhaus and Later,* revised ed., Van Nostrand Reinhold, New York, 1975.

Jackman, Dianne R., and Mary K. Dixon, *The Guide to Textiles for Interior Designers,* 2nd ed., Peguin Publishers Limited, Winnipeg, 1990.

Jay, P. A., "Lighting and the search for meaning," *Developments in Lighting—1,* edited by J. A. Lynes, Applied Science Publishers, London, 1978.

Jerome, C. W., "Flattery vs. color rendition," *Journal of the Illumination Engineering Society,* Vol. 1, No. 3, April, 1972, p. 208.

Jerome, C. W., "The flattery index," *Journal of the Illuminating Engineering Society,* Vol. 2, No. 4, 1973, pp. 351–354.

Johns, E. H., and F. C. Sumner, "Relation of the brightness differences of colors to their apparent distances," *Journal of Psychology,* Vol. 26, 1948, pp. 25–30.

Judd, D. B., "A flattery index for artificial illuminants," *Illuminating Engineering,* Vol. 62, October, 1967, p. 593.

Juola, James F., "Pattern recognition," in *Cognitive Psychology and Information Processing,* edited by Roy Lachman, Janet L. Lachman, and Earl C. Butterfield, Lawrence Erlbaum Associates, Hillsdale, 1979, pp. 489–523.

Kafka, Franz, *Amerika,* Doubleday, Garden City, New York, 1946.

Kaniza, Gaetano, *Organization in Vision, Essays on Gestalt Perception,* Praeger, New York, 1979.

Kaplan, Stephen, and Rachel Kaplan, Eds., *Humanscape: Environments for People,* Ulrich's Books, Ann Arbor, 1982.

Kaplan, Stephen, and Rachel Kaplan, *Cognition and Environment: Functioning in an Uncertain World,* Praeger, New York, 1982.

Katz, David, *The World of Colour,* translated by R. B. MacLeod and C. W. Fox, Kegan Paul, Trench, Trubner & Co., London, 1935.

Katz, D., *Gestalt Psychology: Its Nature and Significance,* New York, Ronald Press Co., 1950.

Kaufman, Lloyd, *Sight and Mind,* Oxford University Press, New York, 1974.

Kaufman, Lloyd, *Perception, the World Transformed,* Oxford University Press, New York, 1979.

Keighley, E. C., "Visual requirements and reduced fenestration in office buildings in a study of window shape," *Building Science,* Vol. 8, 1973, pp. 311–320.

Keighley, E. C., "Visual requirements and reduced fenestration in offices in a study of multiple aperture and window area," *Building Science,* Vol. 8, 1973, pp. 321–331.

Kelly, K. L., "The universal color language," *Color Engineering* 3(2), 1965, pp. 16–21.

Kelly, K. L., and D. B. Judd, *The ISCC-NBS Centroid Color Charts, SRM #2106,* The Office of Standard Reference Materials, National Bureau of Standards, Washington, DC, 1965.

Kepes, Gyorgy, Ed., *Structure in Art and in Science,* George Braziller, New York, 1965.

Kepes, Gyorgy, "Light as a creative medium," *Arts and Architecture,* October 1966, pp. 12–29.

Kepes, Gyorgy, "Light and design," *Design Quarterly,* No. 68, Walker Art Center, Minneapolis, 1968.

Kepes, Gyorgy, *Language of Vision,* Paul Theobald and Company, Chicago, 1969.

Kilmer, Rosemary, and W. Otie Kilmer, *Designing Interiors,* Harcourt Brace Jovanovich, New York, 1992.

Koffka, Kurt, *Principles of Gestalt Psychology,* Harcourt Brace, New York, 1935.

Köhler, Wolfgang, *Dynamics in Psychology,* Liveright, New York, 1940.

Kouwenhoven, John, Ed., *Leaves of Grass and Selected Prose by Walt Whitman,* Random House, New York, 1950.

Krampen, Martin, "The correlation of 'objective' facade measurements with subjective facade ratings," in *Meaning and Behaviour in the Built Environment,* edited by Geoffrey Broadbent, Richard Bunt, and Tomas Llorens, John Wiley & Sons, Chichester, 1980, pp. 61–78.

Kreitler, Hans, and Shulamith Kreitler, *Psychology of the Arts,* Duke University Press, Durham, N.C., 1972.

Küller, Rikard, "A semantic model for describing the perceived environment," *National Swedish Building Research,* Vol. D12, 1972.

Küller, Rikard, ed., *Architectural Psychology, Proceedings of the Lund Conference,* Hutchinson & Ross, Inc., Stroudsburg, 1973

Kunishima, Michiko, and Takuko Yanase, "Visual·effects of wall colours in living rooms," *Ergonomics,* Vol. 28, No. 6, 1985, pp. 869–882.

Künnapas, Teodor, "Distance perception as a function of available visual cues," *Journal of Experimental Psychology,* Vol. 77, No. 4, 1968, pp. 523–529.

Küppers, Harald, *Color,* Van Nostrand Reinhold, New York, 1972.

LaGuisa, F., and L. R. Perney, "Further studies on the effects of brightness variations in attention span in a learning environment," *Lighting Design & Application,* May 1973, pp. 26–30.

Lam, William M. C., "Lighting for architecture," *Architectural Record,* Vol. 128, October 1960, pp. 225–227.

Lam, William M. C., *Perception and Lighting as Formgivers for Architecture,* edited by Christopher Hugh Ripman, McGraw-Hill, New York, 1977.

Lam, William M. C., *Sunlighting as Formgiver for Architecture,* Van Nostrand Reinhold, New York, 1986.

Land, Edwin, H. "The retinex theory of color vision," *Scientific American,* Vol. 237, No. 6, December 1977, pp. 108–128.

Lang, Jon, "Theories of perception and 'formal' design," in *Designing for Human Behavior: Architecture and the Behavioral Sciences,* edited by Jon Lang, Dowden, Hutchinson & Ross, Inc., Stroudsburg, 1974.

Langer, Susanne K., *Feeling and Form,* Charles Scribner's Sons, New York, 1953.

Langer, Susanne K., *Problems of Art,* Charles Scribner's Sons, New York, 1957.

Larson, Leslie, *Lighting and Its Design,* Whitney Library of Design, New York, 1964

Le Corbusier, *Towards a New Architecture,* John Rodker, London, 1931.

Le Corbusier, *New World of Space,* Reynal & Hitchcock, New York, 1948.

Le Corbusier, *Le Corbusier Talks with Students,* Translated by Pierre Chase, The Orion Press, New York, 1961.

Le Corbusier, *The Radiant City,* The Orion Press, New York, 1967.

Leibowitz, H., Nancy A. Myers, and P. Chinetti, "The role of simultaneous contrast in brightness constancy," *Journal of Experimental Psychology,* Vol. 50, No. 1, 1955.

Libby, William Charles, *Color and the Structural Sense,* Prentice Hall, Englewood Cliffs, N.J., 1974.

Linton, Harold, *Color Model Environments, Color and Light in Three-Dimensional Design,* Van Nostrand Reinhold, New York, 1985.

Livingstone, Margaret S., "Art, illusion and the visual system," *Scientific American,* Vol. 258, No. 1, 1988, pp. 78–83.

Longmore, J., "The engineering of daylight," in *Developments in Lighting—1,* edited by J. A. Lynes, Applied Science Publishers, London, 1978.

Lowenthal, David, and Marquita Riel, "The nature of perceived and imagined environments," in *Meaning and Behaviour in the Built Environment,* edited by G. Broadbent, T. Bunt, and R. Llorens, John Wiley & Sons, New York, 1980.

Lowry, Bates, *The Visual Experience,* Prentice-Hall, Englewood Cliffs, N.J., 1961.

Luckiesh, M., and S. K. Guth, "Brightness in visual field at borderline between comfort and discomfort (BCD)," *Illuminating Engineering,* Vol. 44, No. 11, November 1949, pp. 650–670.

Lutyens, Edwin, "Persian brickwork," *London Country Life,* February 1933, p. 118.

Lynch, Kevin, *The Image of the City,* The MIT Press & Harvard University Press, Cambridge, 1960.

Lynes, J. A., *Principles of Natural Lighting,* Applied Science Publishers Ltd., London, 1968.

Lynes, J. A., Ed., *Developments in Lighting—1,* Applied Science Publishers Ltd., London, 1978.

Mackworth, Norman H., and Anthony J. Morandi, "The gaze selects informative details within pictures," *Perception and Psychophysics,* Vol. 2, No. 11, 1967, pp. 547–552.

Mahnke, Frank H., "Color in Medical Facilities," *Interior Design,* April 1981, pp. 256–263.

Mahnke, Frank H., and Rudolf H. Mahnke, *Color and Light in Man-Made Environments,* Van Nostrand Reinhold, New York, 1987.

Marr, David, *Vision,* W. H. Freeman and Company, New York, 1982.

Maslow, A. H., and N. L. Mintz, "The effects of esthetic surroundings I: Initial effects of three esthetic conditions upon perceiving 'energy' and 'well-being' in faces," *Journal of Psychology,* Vol. 41, 1956, pp. 247–254.

Meyers, Marshall, "Masters of light: Louis Kahn" *American Institute of Architects Journal,* September 1979, p. 60ff.

Miller, George A., "The magic number seven plus or minus two," *Psychological Review,* Vol. 63, 1956, pp. 81–97.

Mintz, N. L., "Effects of esthetic surroundings II: prolonged and repeated experience in a 'beautiful' and 'ugly' room, *Journal of Psychology,* Vol. 41, 1956, pp. 459–466.

Moholy-Magy, László, *Vision in Motion,* Paul Theobold and Co., Chicago, 1969.

Moore, Charles, and Gerald Allen, *Dimensions, Space, Shape & Scale in Architecture,* Architectural Record, New York, 1976.

Moore, Fuller, "Daylighting: six Aalto libraries," *American Institute of Architects Journal,* June 1983, pp. 58–69.

Moore, Fuller, *Concepts and Practice of Architectural Daylighting,* Van Nostrand Reinhold, New York, 1985.

Moore, Gary T., and Reginald G. Golledge, *Environmental Knowing, Theories, Research, and Methods,* Dowden, Hutchinson & Ross, Stroudsburg, 1976.

Moos, Rudolf H., *The Human Context: Environmental Determinants of Behavior,* John Wiley & Sons, New York, 1976.

Muir, John, *Wilderness Essays*, Peregrine Smith, New York, 1980 (1895).

Mumford, Lewis, "The social functions of open spaces," *Landscape*, Vol. 10, No. 2, Winter 1960–61, pp. 1–6.

Murch, Gerald M., *Visual and Auditory Perception*, Bobbs-Merrill Co., Indianapolis, 1973.

Natsoulas, Thomas, "On homogeneous retinal stimulation and the perception of depth," *Psychological Bulletin*, Vol. 60, No. 4, 1963, pp. 385–390.

Ne'eman, E., and R. G. Hopkinson, "Critical minimum acceptable window size: a study of window design and provision of view," *Lighting Research Technology*, Vol. 2, 1970, pp. 17–27.

Nelson, Thomas M., and Paul C. Vasold, "Dependence of object identification upon edge and surface," *Perceptual and Motor Skills*, Vol. 20, 1965, pp. 537–546.

Nervi, Pier Luigi, *Structures*, translated by Giuseppina and Mario Salvadori, F. W. Dodge Corporation, New York, 1956.

Neutra, Richard, *Survival Through Design*, New York: Oxford University Press, 1954.

Nishihara, Kiyoyuki, *Japanese Houses: Patterns for Living*, Japan Publications, San Francisco, 1967.

Norberg-Schulz, Christian, *Intentions in Architecture*, The MIT Press, Cambridge, 1965.

Norberg-Schulz, Christian, *Existence, Space & Architecture*, Praeger, New York, 1971.

Nuckolls, James L., *Interior Lighting for Environmental Designers*, 2nd ed. John Wiley & Sons, New York, 1983.

Oetting, R. L., "Can walls be too bright?" *Lighting Design & Application*, December 1971, pp. 30–33.

Ortega y Gasset, José, *The Dehumanization of Art and Other Writings on Art and Culture*, Doubleday & Company, Garden City, N.J. 1956.

Osborne, Roy, *Lights & Pigments, Color Principles for Artists*, Harper & Row, New York, 1980.

Ott, John N., *Light, Radiation & You*, The Devin-Adair Co., Old Greenwich, 1982.

Padgham, C. A., and J. E. Sanders, *The Perception of Light and Color*, Academic Press, New York, 1975.

Parr, A. E., "Environmental design and psychology," *Landscape*, Vol. 14, No. 2, Winter 1964, p. 65.

Payne, Ifan, "Pupillary responses to architectural stimuli," *Man-Environment Systems*, S-11, July 1969.

Pérez-Gómez, Alberto, *Architecture and the Crisis of Modern Science*, The MIT Press, Cambridge, 1984.

Piaget, Jean, *The Child's Construction of Reality*, translated by Margaret Cook, Basic Books, New York, 1954.

Piaget, Jean, *The Mechanisms of Perception*, translated by G. Seagrim, Routledge and Kegan Paul, London, 1969.

Pierce, James Smith, "Visual and auditory space in Baroque Rome," *Journal of Aesthetics and Art Criticism*, Vol. XVIII, No. 1, September 1959, pp. 55–67.

Plummer, Henry, *Poetics of Light*, a+u Publishing Co., Ltd., Tokyo, 1987.

Plummer, Henry, "The strange rejuvenating beauty of radiant things," *Architecture*, October 1987, pp. 68–75.

Ponti, Gio, *In Praise of Architecture*, translated by Giuseppina and Mario Salvadori, F. W. Dodge Corporation, New York, 1960.

Pope, Arthur Upham, *Persian Architecture, The Triumph of Form and Color*, George Braziller, New York, 1965.

Porter, Tom, *Architectural Color, A Design Guide to Using Color on Buildings*, Whitney Library of Design, New York, 1982.

Porter, Tom, and Byron Mikellides, *Color for Architecture*, Van Nostrand Reinhold, New York, 1976.

Prak, Niels L., *The Visual Perception of the Built Environment*, Delft University Press, 1977.

Rapoport, A., and R. E. Kantor, "Complexity and ambiguity in environmental design," *Journal of American Institute of Planners*, Vol. 33, No. 4, July, 1967, pp. 210–221.

Raskin, Eugene, *Architecturally Speaking*, 2nd ed., Bloch Publishing Co., New York, 1966.

Rasmussen, Steen Eiler, *Experiencing Architecture*, The MIT Press, Cambridge, 1959.

Rea, Mark S., Ed., *Lighting Handbook, Reference and Application*, Illuminating Engineering Society of North America, New York, 1993.

Rosar, William H., "Visual space as physical geometry," *Perception*, Vol. 14, No. 4, 1985, pp. 403–425.

Ross, Donald K., "Task lighting—yet another view," *Lighting Design & Application*, May 1978, pp. 37–43.

Ross, Helen E., *Behaviour and Perception in Strange Environments*, Basic Books, New York, 1975.

Salvadori, Mario, and Robert Heller, *Structure in Architecture*, Prentice-Hall, Englewood Cliffs, N.J., 1963.

Samonà, Joseph, "Man, matter and space, on the architecture of Frank Lloyd Wright," translated by Edgar Kaufmann Jr., *Architects' Year Book 5*, Elek Books Limited, London, 1953.

Sanders, M., J. Gustanski, and M. Lawton, "Effect of ambient illumination on noise level of groups," *Journal of Applied Psychology*, Vol. 59, No. 4, August 1974, pp. 527–528.

Sanoff, Henry, "Visual attributes of the physical environment," in *Response to Environment*, Student Publications of the School of Design, North Carolina State University, Raleigh, Vol. 18, 1969.

Schiffman, Harvey Richard, *Sensation and Perception*, 3rd ed., John Wiley & Sons, New York, 1990.

Schiler, Mark, *Simplified Design of Building Lighting*, John Wiley & Sons, New York, 1992.

Scott, Robert Gillam, *Design Fundamentals*, McGraw-Hill, New York, 1951.

Scutt, Der, "Esthetics in ceiling systems lighting," *Lighting Design & Application*, December 1972, pp. 35–42.

Segall, Marshall, *et al.*, *The Influence of Culture on Visual Perception*, Bobbs-Merrill, Indianapolis, 1966.

Shahn, Ben, *The Shape of Content*, Random House, New York, 1975.

Shemitz, Sylvan R., "Lighting: tools that suit architectural objectives," *Architectural Record*, March 1968, pp. 165–172.

Simonds, John Ormsbee, *Landscape Architecture, A Manual of Site Planning and Design*, McGraw-Hill, New York, 1983.

Smith, Fran Kellogg, and Fred J. Bertolone, *Bringing Interiors to Light, The Principles and Practices of Lighting Design*, Whitney Library of Design, New York, 1986.

Smithsonian Annual II, *The Fitness of Man's Environment*, Smithsonian Institution Press, Washington, 1968.

Sommer, Robert, *Personal Space, The Behavioral Basis of Design,* Prentice-Hall, Englewood Cliffs, N.J., 1969.

Sommer, Robert, *Design Awareness,* Rinehart Press, San Francisco, 1972.

Sommer, Robert, *Tight Spaces, Hard Architecture and How to Humanize It,* Prentice-Hall, Englewood Cliffs, N.J., 1974.

Spreiregen, Paul D., *Urban Design: The Architecture of Towns and Cities,* McGraw-Hill, New York, 1965.

Stea, David, "Space territory and human movements, *Landscape,* Vol. 15, Autumn 1965, pp. 13–16.

Stea, David, "Architecture in the head: cognitive mapping," in *Designing for Human Behavior,* edited by Jon Lang et al., Dowden, Hutchinson & Ross, Stroudsburg, 1974.

Stea, David, "Program notes on a spatial fugue," in *Environmental Knowing,* edited by Gary T. Moore and Reginald G. Golledge, Dowden, Hutchinson & Ross, Stroudsburg, 1976.

Stechow, Wolfgang, "Problems of structure in some relations between the visual arts and music." *The Journal of Aesthetics and Art Criticism,* June 1953, pp. 324–333.

Steffy, Gary R., *Architectural Lighting Design,* Van Nostrand Reinhold, New York, 1990.

Stevens, S. S., "To honor Fechner and repeal his law," *Science* 133, pp. 80–86.

Swirnoff, Lois, *Dimensional Color,* Birkhäuser, Boston, 1988.

Tanizaki, Jun'ichiro, *In Praise of Shadows,* Leete's Island Books, New Haven, 1977.

Tate, Allen, and C. Ray Smith, *Interior Design in the 20th Century,* Harper & Row, New York, 1986.

Taylor, F. A., *Color Technology for Artists, Craftsmen, and Industrial Designers,* Oxford University Press, London, 1962.

Taylor, L. H., and E. W. Sucov, "The movement of people towards lights," *Journal of Illuminating Engineering Society,* Vol. 3, 1974, pp. 237–241.

Thiel, Philip, "A sequence-experience notation for architectural and urban spaces," *Town Planning Review,* Vol. 32, April 1961, pp. 33–52.

Thiel, Philip, "Experiment in space notation," *Architectural Review,* Vol. 131, May 1962, p. 327.

Thiel, Philip, Ean Duane Harrison, and Richard S. Alden, "The perception of spatial enclosure as a function of the position of architectural surfaces," *Environment and Behavior,* Vol. 18, No. 2, March 1986, pp. 227–245.

Thomas, Lewis, *Late Night Thoughts on Listening to Mahler's Ninth Symphony,* Bantam Books, New York, 1983.

Thompson, D'Arcy, *On Growth and Form,* edited by J. T. Bonner. Cambridge University Press, Cambridge, 1961.

Thoreau, Henry David, *The Natural History Essays,* Peregrine Smith Inc., Salt Lake City, 1980.

Tinker, M. A., "Desired illumination specifications," *Journal of Applied Psychology,* Vol. 35, 1951, pp. 377–382.

Traister, John E., *Principles of Illumination,* Howard W. Sams & Co., Bobbs-Merrill Co, Indianapolis, 1974.

Tuan, Yi-Fu, *Topophilia. A Study of Environmental Perception, Attitudes, and Values,* Prentice-Hall, Englewood Cliffs, N.J., 1974.

Tuan, Yi-Fu, *Space and Place,* University of Minnesota Press, Minneapolis, 1977.

Twain, Mark, *The Innocents Aborad,* from *The Complete Travel Books of Mark Twain,* edited by Charles Neider, Doubleday & Co., Garden City, New York, 1966.

Van Dyke, John C., *The Desert,* Peregrine Smith, Inc., Salt Lake City, 1980 (1901).

Vernon, M. C., *Perception Through Experience,* Methuen, London, 1970.

Wald, G. "Eye and camera," *Scientific American,* Vol. 183, 1950, pp. 32–41.

Waldram, J. M., "Studies in interior lighting," *Transcripts of the Illumination Engineering Society,* Vol. 19, 1954, pp. 95–133.

Waldram, J. M., "Designed appearance lighting," in *Developments in Lighting—1,* edited by J. A. Lynes, Applied Science Publishers, London, 1978.

Wall, Harriet M., Catherine Karl, and Joseph Smigiel, "Use of contextual information in the formation of cognitive maps," *American Journal of Psychology,* Vol. 99, No. 4, 1986, pp. 547–558.

Wallace, Robert, and the editors of Time-Life Books, *The World of Van Gogh 1853–1890,* Time-Life Books, New York, 1969.

Wallach, H., "Brightness constancy and the nature of achromatic colors," *Journal of Experimental Psychology,* No. 38, 1948, pp. 310–324.

Wasserman, Gerald S., *Color Vision: An Historical Introduction,* John Wiley & Sons, New York, 1978.

Wexner, L. B., "The degree to which colors (hues) are associated with mood tones," *Journal of Applied Psychology,* Vol. 38, 1954, pp. 432–435.

White, Michael, "The effect of the nature of the surround on the perceived lightness of grey bars within square-wave test gratings," *Perception,* Vol. 10, No. 2, 1981, pp. 215–230.

White, Minor, *Zone System Manual,* new revised ed., Morgan & Morgan, Inc., Hastings-on-Hudson, N.Y., 1968.

White, Minor, Richard Zakia, and Peter Lorenz, *The New Zone System Manual,* Morgan Press Inc., Dobbs Ferry, N.Y., 1976.

Wilson, G. D., "Arousal properites of red versus green," *Perceptual and Motor Skills,* Vol. 23, 1966, pp. 947–949.

Wohlwill, J. F., "The physical environment: a problem for a psychology of stimulation," *Journal of Social Issues,* Vol. 22, No. 4, 1966, pp. 29–38.

Woodford, G. P., "Open spaces, blind alleys," in *Developments in Lighting—1,* edited by J. A. Lynes, Applied Science Publishers, London, 1978.

Wools, R., and D. Canter, "The effect of the meaning of rooms on behaviour," *Applied Ergonomics* Vol. 1, No. 3, 1970, pp. 144–150.

Wright, Frank Lloyd, *An Autobiography,* Duell, Sloan and Pearce, New York, 1943.

Wright, L., "How many bits," *The Architectural Review,* April 1973, pp. 251–252.

Wurtman, R. J., "The effects of light on the human body," *Scientific American,* Vol. 233, No. 1, 1975, pp. 68–77.

Yarbus, A. L., *Eye Movements and Vision,* Plenum Press, New York, 1967.

Yonemura, G. T., "Light and vision," *Developments in Lighting—1,* edited by J. A Lynes, Applied Science Publishers, Ltd., London, 1978.

Zekowski, G., "The art of lighting is a science/The science of lighting is an art," *Lighting Design & Application,* January 1981, pp. 10–15, and March 1981, pp. 39–45.

Zevi, Bruno, *Architecture As Space,* translated by Milton Gendel, edited by Joseph A. Barry, Horizon Press, New York, 1957.

Zucker, Paul, "The space-volume relation in the history of town planning," *The Journal of Aesthetics and Art Criticism,* June 1956, pp. 439–444.

Zucker, Paul, *Town and Square,* Columbia University Press, New York, 1959.

Zucker, Wolfgang M., "Inside and outside in architecture," *The Journal of Aesthetics and Art Criticism,* Vol. 25, No. 1, 1966, pp. 7–13.

Name Index

(Note: Numbers preceded by C- indicate color plates.)

Peckham Guyton Albers Viets Architects, 232
Pei Cobb Freed & Partners, 147, C-2
Pei, I. M., and Partners, C-1, C-63
Perney, L. R., 164
Perry Dean Rogers and Partners, C-24, C-71
Philips Lighting Co., C-15
Piacentini, Marcello, 146, 148
Piaget, Jean, 106, 164
Picasso, 54
Pope, Arthur Upham, 145

Q

Quantum Design Group, C-40, C-43, C-75

R

Raskin, Eugene, 245
Ravel, Maurice Joseph, 210
Repin, I. E., 60, 63
Rosenthal, Steve, 250
Rubin, Edgar, 53
Ryan, James P., C-38

S

Saarinen, Eero, 141, 142, 143, 144, 215, 216
Saarinen, Eliel, C-41
Salvadori, Mario, 148, 157
Sanders, M., 230
Sasaki Associates, Inc., 18
Scutt, Der, 182
Shahn, Ben, 230
Socov, E. W., 164
SOM (Skidmore, Owings, and Merrill), 46, 48, 58, 105,
    233, C-25, C-28
Spencer, Terry J., 189
Stea, David, 59
Steffy, Gary, C-47
Sumner, F. C., 98
SWA Group, 162
Swirnoff, Lois, 98
Sylvan R. Shemitz Associates, C-42

T

Tanizaki, Junchiro, 39
Taylor, L. H., 164
Tchaikovsky, Pyotr Ilich, 210
Thiel, Philip, 118
Thompson, Ben, & Associates, 36, C-6
Thompson, D'Arcy, 50
Thoreau, Henry David, 4
Tidblom, I., 119
Tiepolo, Giovanni Battista, 138
Twain, Mark, 31, 109, 110

V

van der Rohe, Mies, 111, 112
Van Dyke, John C., 88, 97
van Gogh, Vincent, 4

W

Wagner, Richard, 4, 227
Wald, G., 9
Waldram, J. M., 208
Weber, E. H., 75
Weese, Harry, & Associates, 191
Wensley Webster Fry Architects, C-42
Wertheimer, Max, 19
Whaley, James, C-74
White, Minor, 70
Whitman, Walt, 1
Wright, Frank Lloyd, 4, 117, 123, 138, 139, 146, 147, 149,
    150, 156, 163, 230
Wright, L., 51, 52

Y

Yamasaki, Minoru, 214
Yarbus, A. L., 60, 61, 63, 234

Z

Zevi, Bruno, 111
Zimmerman, Eric, C-68, C-69, C-70

Subject Index

(Note: Numbers preceded by C- indicate color plates.)

L

Pattern
  and brightness, 76
  as design, 15, 148, 234, 238, C-28, C-29, C-77
  as focal accent, 65, 123–125
  illuminated, 183
  in lighting design, 184–189
  linear, 133, 233
  on spatial envelope, 123–127
  as stimulus for movement, 159, 160
  and structural design, 145–149
  See also Spatial banding
People, as focal accent, 62
Periodicity, and pattern recognition, 65
Persian brickwork, 145
Paseo Pergola, Kansas City, Missouri, 16
Pergola, Seattle, 123, 124
Photography vs. human vision, 248–250
Phototropism, 163, 165, 198
Piazza della Santissima Annunziata, Florence, Italy, 129, 130
Place des Vosges, Paris, 129, 130
Place Plumereau, Tours, France, 111
Planetary clock, 2
Pluralistic culture
  and fashions, 69
  and manufactured goods, 69
Port of Seattle proposal, C-66
Previsualizing, in design, 69, 238
Primary hues. *See* Color
Psalette, The, Tours, France, 129
Pursuit, saccadic, 59

Q

Queen Hatshepsut's Temple, Deir el-Bahari, Egypt, 135, 136

R

Radiolaria, 50–52
Reciprocity, photographic, 168, 249
Reflectance
  absorption, 35
  and color, 96, 237, C-18
  diffuse, 37, 82
  IESNA recommendations, 73, 235
  specular, 37, 178
  spread, 37, 178
  transmission, 35
  and urban blight, 48
  and vision through grilles, 223
  and water landscaping, 47–48
Reflections, 1, 2, 35–38, 237, C-2, C-68, C-69, C-76
Reims Cathedral, France, 118
Residenz, Wurzburg, Germany, 138
Retina
  adaptation to light, 5
  and human culture, 5
  receptor cells, 9
  See also Light adaptation; Dark adaptation

Retinal simultaneous contrast, 91
Rhythm
  of brightness sequencing, 166
  human response, 5
  visual movement, 131, 132, 233, 234
Robie House, Chicago, 156, 230
Romanticism, 4, 229
Rowes Wharf, Boston, C-28

S

75 State Street, Boston, 233, 234, C-25
7400 Lighton Plaza, Overland Park, Kansas, 166
S. Andrea al Quirinale, Rome, 131
Saccadic movement of the eye
  electronic traces, 60–61
  process defined, 59
S. C. Johnson Wax Administration Building, Racine, Wisconsin, 149, 150
Saks Fifth Avenue, Palm Beach Mall, C-38
Sant' Andrea, Mantua, Italy, 127
Scala Regia, Vatican, Rome, 210–212
Scanning, visual, 59, 63, 120, 232, 234
Schematic mapping, perceptual, 59
Screened space
  and daylight, 173, 225, 226
  and light, 220–227, C-35, C-62
  in nature, 56
  staircase design, 140, C-33
  by structural design, 155
  transparent plane, 220
  See also Grilles
Seattle Science Center, 213, 214, 220
Secondary hues. *See* Color
Selection, perceptual, 60–62, 120, 232
Sequential space design, 166, 167, 239–243, C-72, C-73
Shadow
  attached, 38–39
  and beauty, 39
  cast, 39
  and color, 88, 97, C-19
  for design, 166
  and gradient, 11, 39
  and spatial depth, 26, 39
  and the spatial envelope, 238
Shape
  defined, 49
Shoji, Japanese, 31
Shore Country Day School, 99, C-24
Simplicity comprehension limit, 23–24, 111
Simplicity, perceptual, 52, 122, 123, 234. *See also* Clarity
Simplification/amplification theory, 51–53
Simultaneous contrast, 13–14, 33, 91, 149, 224, 226
Slant
  and brightness, 81, 84
  spatial envelope, 107
  and surface detailing, 83
  and texture, 81
  visual angle, 68

U. S. Federal Building, Topeka, Kansas, 16
UTILICORP, Kansas City, Missouri, C-7

V

Valley Bank, Des Moines, Iowa, C-3
(VCP) Visual comfort probability, 133
Venice, Italy, 120
Visual comfort probability (VCP), 133
Visual field, perceptual, 28–30, 240, 249
Visual objective
    connecting frame, 211, 213, 214
    contrasting frame, 211, 213, 214
    curiosity, expectation, and exploration, 210
    defined, 210
    form dominant, 212, 213, C-55, C-56
    framing, 211, 228, 234, C-54
    historical examples, 210, 217
    planning, 216–220, 240
    and quality design, 215
Visual overload, 5, 19, 67, 103, 114, 115, 121, 132, 159, 182
Visual world, perceptual, 28-30, 240

W

Washington Metropolitan Area Transit Authority Stations, 191
Water Garden, Fort Worth, Texas, 125
Wayne Towne Center Mall, Wayne, New Jersey, 95
Weber-Fechner Law, 75
Westridge Mall, Topeka, Kansas, 151
Wilcox Electric, Inc., Kansas City, Missouri, C-5
Williams College Museum of Art, Williamstown, Massachusetts, C-50
Williams Square, Irving, Texas, 47–48, 57, 104, 105, 106
Windows and spatial influence, 128
Wood Index, 78

Z

Zone of transition, 165, 166, 167, 227, 228, C-1, C-36, C-38, C-67
Zone system
    LBR System, 72
    numerical boundaries of LBR Scale, 76
    photographic, 70–71

Figure C-74. **Spatial activity with Gestalt simplicity.**
[Katella Deli, Los Alamitos, California. Architect: James Whaley. Interior Design: Hatch Bros. Photograph: Courtesy of Pittsburgh Corning Corporation]

Figure C-75. **Lighting the directions of space.** *[Troy Place, Troy, Michigan. Architects: Quantum Design Group, Inc. Photograph: © Glen Calvin Moon]*

Figure C-76. **Reflections for tranquility.** *[Private residence. Photograph: © Balthazar Korab]*

Figure C-77. **Spatial composition of harmonic patterns.** *[Propylaeum, The Dayton Art Institute, Dayton, Ohio. Architect: Levin Porter Architects. Photograph: © Glen Calvin Moon]*